BILINGUAL GRAMMAR OF ENGLISH-SPANISH SYNTAX

A Manual with Exercises and Key

Revised Edition

Sam Hill
California State University, Sacramento

William Bradford
University of Puerto Rico, Rio Piedras

University Press of America, ® Inc.
Lanham • New York • Oxford

Copyright © 2000 by
University Press of America, ® Inc.
4720 Boston Way
Lanham, Maryland 20706

12 Hid's Copse Rd.
Cumnor Hill, Oxford OX2 9JJ

ISBN 0-7618-1719-0 (pbk: alk. ppr.)

About
the Authors

SAM HILL, an Arizona native and descendant of early pioneers there, received his B.A. in secondary education from Arizona State University with a major is Spanish and minors in English and Russian. A Woodrow Wilson fellowship for graduate study at Stanford University led to a Ph.D. in Hispanic Linguistics with a minor concentration in Portuguese. He has taught at California State University, Sacramento since 1968, during which time he spent an academic year as an exchange professor at the University of Hawaii, Manoa. There he completed the predecessor to the current text titled *Contrastive English-Spanish Grammatical Structures*.

Professor Hill has been awarded two sabbatical leaves, one in Brazil (1980) and the other in Puerto Rico (1991). He has been active in his department's "3–Summer M.A. Program," having taught summer sessions in Spain, Mexico, and Peru. His teaching assignments in Sacramento routinely include lower-division Spanish courses, upper-division courses in phonetics and advanced grammar, and graduate seminars in historical and comparative Spanish linguistics. He is well-known on campus as an exceptional teacher and advisor.

Dr. Hill was among a small group of faculty and students fortunate enough to be able to tour Cuba in 1999. Now, after a 30-year career in teaching, he is looking forward to retirement within a few years and anticipates a renewed interest in physical activities such as swimming and bicycling.

WILLIAM BRADFORD, although born near Chicago, Illinois, was schooled in Puerto Rico, which he considers home. He received a B.A. in English/Spanish Linguistics and an M.A. in TESOL from the Inter American University in San Juan, graduating *summa cum laude*. His doctoral degree was awarded at the University of the West Indies, Mona, Jamaica, for studies in Linguistics, specializing in dialects of the Caribbean. He is an English-Spanish bilingual who also speaks French, Italian, and Portuguese.

William initiated his career in academia as a teacher of French at his alma mater. From there he transferred to the University of Puerto Rico, where over the space of twenty-five years he taught in the Departments of Linguistics, Translation, and English. During a part of his tenure he served as director of the English for Foreigners Program in the Extension Division. A proud recipient of the *Diploma Superior de Español del Ministro de Educación y Ciencia del Reino de España*, he has lectured far and frequently. Recently relocated in the southwestern United States, he continues championing his cause for recognition of the merits of bilingualism and for the continuance of bilingual education.

This thorough revision of *Bilingual Grammar of English-Spanish Syntax* is only the most recent publication among Dr. Bradford's many language, linguistics, and bilingual writings. Other noteworthy bilingual publications are *Readings in Spanish-English Contrastive Linguistics, Vol. II* (1980), *El tapiz por revés* (1986), *Using Bilingual Grammar of English-Spanish Syntax* (1992), and latest *Write It Right! ↔ ¡Escríbalo Bien!* (2000). Much more is expected from him in the future.

CONTENTS   ÍNDICE

Key to Exercises

Appendices

Clave para los Ejercicios

Apéndices

Introduction

The ability to "speak one's native language and another with approximately equal facility" is a fitting description of a bilingual person.[1] Ultimately somewhere in the career of a person intent on attaining bilingual proficiency or of an inquisitive bilingual speaker, the individual must at some point look carefully at the grammatical structures of the two languages involved. In this process of conscious introspection of a bilingual's language competence, areas of differences must inevitably come to light. Upon further examination it should be apparent which structures of one language are most similar to or most divergent from those of the other. This is simply one fundamental type of language analysis which has served as a tool for the foreign language instructor, the ESL instructor, the translator, and the language textbook writer.

Two assumptions serve as the foundation for this comparative approach: (1) that we are all native speakers of one language and potentially successful learners of another, and (2) that we tend in our acquisition of a foreign or second language to carry over into it many of the linguistic features of our first language. Linguists contend that where the features of the target language are similar to those of the speaker's native language, few significant teaching or learning problems will be anticipated. But, in cases where the grammars of the two languages are at some variance, the instructor can predict serious learning problems on the part of the student.

In recent years there has been much interest in language acquisition through a concern with actual communicatory skill development. The errors learners make have been discovered to be interferential primarily in the earliest phases of instruction. Developmental errors—errors logically occurring as the learners attempt to expand their active skills patterned upon those which they already dominate in the new language—soon became the focus of scholarly attention. The discipline of error analysis has tended to assume an ever-important role in language teaching.

One of the most sought-after goals in the professional training of the foreign language or ESL/EFL instructor is total competency in both English and the target language. To achieve this, instructors require a framework within which they can organize and categorize the host of seemingly disparate linguistic errors their students commonly make in the classroom. Training in recognizing the areas of differences between the native language and the target language will help potential instructors comprehend and evaluate the linguistic behaviors of their students. This is an essential component of the professional preparation of the foreign language or ESL/EFL instructor.

A comparative analysis, then, to the extent to which it fosters analytical skills on the part of instructors is clearly a necessary facet of any future language instructor's professional training. This manual focuses upon the development of such analytical abilities by presenting the inter-lingual differences between English and Spanish as simply and directly as possible and by providing numerous exercises through which the nature of such differences can be readily perceived and acted upon.

---

1 *Webster's Encyclopedic Unabridged Dictionary.*

For Whom the Manual Is Intended

This manual was prepared for advanced upper-division or graduate students whose career plans include the teaching of Spanish to English speakers, the teaching of English to Spanish speakers, and work in the field of translation in these two languages—English and Spanish. Bilingual speakers whose professional goals do not include education or translation will find the manual useful, especially as a reference work or as a tool for self-improvement in their linguistic performance. Whether the student's native language is Spanish or English matters little provided skills in both languages are essentially equal and well-developed. Ideally students using the text will have taken previous course work in advanced grammar and composition in both Spanish and English. A general knowledge of phonetics would be useful but not a requisite. However, a solid knowledge of grammar terminology will be essential.

Before the era of proliferation of bilingual teaching programs, students bilingual in English and Spanish directed their professional preparation in the area of education toward the teaching of Spanish to English speakers. In recent times, however, professionals with competencies in two languages and with a desire to teach have been called upon increasingly to demonstrate their capabilities in the areas of ESL/EFL. Witnessed was a profusion of bilingual/cross-cultural programs at virtually every educational level throughout the United States, and interest in such projects seems to persist despite recent attempts by some Governmental Agencies to curtail certain programs. Adult education programs in English as a second language continue to grow as more immigrants who are native Spanish speakers prepare themselves for life and work in an English-speaking world. The other side of the bilingual coin is the reality that there is a large demand in Spanish-speaking nations for teachers of English, a need which continues to increase. Clearly, then, career opportunities for people who are bilingual in English and Spanish continue to expand at an astonishing tempo.

A more recent development in the domain of bilingual activities is that of the creation and implementation of the North American Free Trade Agreement (NAFTA) in 1993–94. The nations of Canada, Mexico, and the United States of America are the three original signers to this agreement. These constitute the whole of North America. It is expected that Chile may soon become a member, followed by other countries of Central and South America, and the Caribbean. These timely advancements in New World inter-American cooperation for commerce can only further bolster the need and substantially expand opportunities for proficient bilingual speakers of Spanish and English.

This manual, in its newly revised edition, will prove helpful to instructors and students alike in various ways. We see four areas where a manual such as this should be indispensable to its users.

(1) This latest text represents a further contribution to the body of material useful to those preparing to teach or to those teaching Spanish to speakers of English.

(2) The text provides the ESL/EFL instructor with a long needed and complete inventory of the major grammatical contrasts between the English and Spanish of modern-day usage.

(3) The text provides the professional translator with a ready and extensive frame of reference on contemporary English and Spanish grammar systems.

(4) The text will serve as an authoritative guide for bilinguals when so many doubts arise as to how correctly to say or write an intended thought or utterance and will facilitate their continued development of and control over their own bilingual skills.

Any one of these four areas amply validates the current usefulness of this manual.

Using the Revised Edition

All of the thirty-six units of the manual have been revised, some substantially and others by necessary cosmetic changes. The Index is greatly expanded for better access to the extensive repository of materials. Totally new to this edition is the "Key to the Exercises," which was requested by so many users of the former text.

The study units in the manual are organized into four integrated parts: "Basic Syntax and Verbal Forms," "The Complex Noun Phrase," "Verb Phrase Complementation," and "Syntactic and Lexical Variances,"—Sintaxis Fundamental y Formas Verbales, La Frase Nominal Compleja, Complementos del Área Verbal, Variantes Sintácticas y Léxicas—all of similar length. The units seek to represent an extensive inventory of the major grammatical differences between English and Spanish, but by no means has every possible contrast been covered. Except for its presentation of the few essential phonetic items, of gender/number inflections, and verb conjugations, the text deals exclusively with syntactic structures.

As was done in the former text, a continued attempt has been made to cover a broad scope of standard dialects of the Spanish-speaking world by including opinions on matters of acceptable grammar usage of scholars from Spain, South America, the Caribbean, and Eastern United States alongside those from Mexico, Central America, and Southwestern United States. Incorporated in the revised text are the findings and most recent rulings by the Grammar Commission of the Real Academia Española on Spanish language usage. American English usage is the norm for the grammar; however, many common examples of British English are included also. If you find any conflicting lexical items or uses in this text or in the "Key to the Exercises" not common to your locale, it is suggested that these be substituted by what would be more acceptable in your particular dialectal area.

The Exercises

A most salient feature of the original text was its exercises. This feature has been retained and further refined in the new revision. Students seem to profit most from the comparative analytical method when, after studying the nature of any given contrast, they perform exercises to consolidate their understandings and to discern clearly the linguistic rule which applies. The exercises are generally of two types, (1) translation from one language into the other as a means of determining one's ability to perceive or apply inter-lingually a certain grammatical rule, and (2) restatement in the same language of a particular grammatical construction. These types of exercises prove particularly useful when either language has an alternate structure for conveying the same idea.

Many of the exercise units have been framed bilingually, that is, alternating between English and Spanish on consecutive lines. We feel that this may possibly be a unique approach to dual language learning. Some few reservations about the format have been voiced; however, the authors find that this practice aids in developing complete bilingual competence in students. There occurs a switching between the two languages often even without awareness on behalf of the students.

The manual offers three categories of exercises. There are exercises which are to be done in their entirety by all students who use the manual; they have no particular marking to identify them beyond their regular numbering: **Exercise 1, Exercise 2,** etc. There are exercises which are divided into two equal parts, often with a difference in level of difficulty. The first half of these is to be completed by undergraduate students of a one-semester course. Students of a full year course and all graduate students should do both parts of these exercises. Exercises of this type are designated by parentheses: **(Exercise 1), (Exercise 2),** etc. Optional exercises are included for use at the most advanced level of study or for courses planned to take a full year. These are designated **(Optional)** and may be selectively assigned or done.

Note for Instructors/Users

As a guideline to instructors and users of the manual for different courses or diverse purposes, the following recommendations are made. Depending upon the contents of a particular course and the different career goals students and professionals may have in mind, certain units and parts are more pertinent to specific requirements and individual needs. These recommendations are as follows:

(1) Persons pursuing a career in teaching Spanish or English as a foreign or second language should cover all four parts.
> Basic Syntax and Verbal Forms
> The Complex Noun Phrase
> Verb Phrase Complementation
> Syntactic and Lexical Variances

(2) Students of linguistics should concentrate on Parts 1, 2, and 3.
> Basic Syntax and Verbal Forms
> The Complex Noun Phrase
> Verb Phrase Complementation

(3) Persons training for a career in translation should cover Units 1, 5, and 8 of Part 1 and all of Parts 2, 3, and 4.
> "Basic Word Order in English and Spanish"
> "The Spanish Imperfect-Preterite Contrast"
> "Modal Auxiliaries and their Equivalents"
>
> The Complex Noun Phrase
> Verb Phrase Complementation
> Syntactic and Lexical Variances

Experience in using the first edition of this text has shown that some additional units can be eliminated for the expedience of time limitations if need be. According to the users' language proficiency, any one or combination of the following Units may be suppressed or be covered very superficially:

Fluent English:
> Unit 2 "The Verb Forms of English"
> Unit 6 "Basic Sentence Structure in English and Spanish"
> Unit 7 "English Phrasal Verbs"
> Unit 17 "English and Spanish Contractions"
> Unit 32 "Elliptical Verbal Usages and Verification Tags"

Fluent Spanish:
Unit 3 "The Forms of Regular Verbs in Spanish" (except §3.7–8)
Unit 5 "The Spanish Imperfect-Preterite Contrast"
Unit 6 "Basic Sentence Structure in English and Spanish"
Unit 19 "The Spanish Personal Accusative"
Unit 33 "**Por** versus **Para**"
Unit 35 "Spanish Constructions with **Gustar, Faltar,** and Similar Verbs"

Revised Edition Acknowledgements

To the many enthusiastic instructors who have used our former text and have communicated to us their constructive comments and suggestions, we give our special thanks. And foremost, to all learners who benefitted from our manual and subsequently informed us, we are greatly indebted.

Mention must be made of three exceptionally valued friends who assiduously read the revised text and contributed much valuable input: Nicolás García Montoya (Mexico), Prof. Ana Castro de Drake (Colombia), and Prof. Víctor M. Nazario (Puerto Rico). Gracias, amigos.

William Bradford, Ph.D.
Department of Linguistics
University of New Mexico, Albuquerque

Sam Hill, Ph.D.
Department of Foreign Languages (Spanish Area)
California State University — Sacramento

January, 2000

Part One

BASIC SYNTAX AND VERBAL FORMS

SINTAXIS FUNDAMENTAL Y FORMAS VERBALES

"Parte de la gramática, que enseña a coordinar y unir las palabras para formar las oraciones y expresar conceptos."

Diccionario de la Real Academia Española

"Palabras con que se expresan las acciones y estados de los seres, y los sucesos."

María Moliner

1

Basic Word Order in English and Spanish

INTRODUCTION
1.1

In our study of syntactic structures we will be comparing the grammars of two major world languages—English and Spanish. English, it has been said, is the world's most widely used and, perhaps, most important language, and Spanish is either the first or second language of many peoples throughout the Western Hemisphere. Spanish is spoken in parts of Europe, Africa, and areas of the Pacific. The importance of both English and Spanish is well established.

The linguistic origins of the two languages under study are quite different, both coming from essentially diverse backgrounds, but with some convergence in certain areas. The Latinized elements of English and its heavy Romance borrowings illustrate some of these converging areas. English belongs to the Germanic family of languages, and in its evolution it has experienced a reduction and in many cases a complete loss of the grammatical inflections which characterize other members of the family. A more rigidly structured word order has been the compensatory result of this morphological reduction. Spanish is a Romance language which evolved from Latin, a highly inflected language with an extremely flexible word order. Modern Spanish retains many of those categories of inflection and variable word order in its grammar.

ELEMENTS OF PREDICATION
1.2

Traditionally, both English and Spanish sentences consist of predications, that is, something is said (predicated) about the subject. With this fact in mind, we may then state that the main grammatical divisions of a sentence in these languages are the subject and the predicate, although in Spanish the subject may not always be so overtly discernible as it is in English. Alternatively, these two major divisions of a sentence may be seen to comprise units called elements of sentence structure, each element named for the function it performs in the overall predication. An element may consist of a single- or a multi-word unit which is further divided into parts-of-speech categories.

Because Spanish is directly derived from Latin and because its verbal forms are so clearly marked for person, number, tense, aspect, and mood, Spanish allows considerable flexibility in the ordering of elements in its sentences. English, however, exhibits less variation with respect to word order. This general observation is particularly important when we consider the positioning of the subject and its verb.

BASIC WORD ORDER IN ENGLISH
1.3
English generally organizes its sentence structure elements with the subject (S) first and then follows it with the verb (V). The verb, which forms part of the predicate, may be followed by other elements of the predicate, either singularly or in combinations. According to the grammar being followed, these are variously called complement (C), direct object (DO), indirect object (IO), adverb (A), prepositional phrase (PP), in addition to others. In the examples given, the subject of the sentence is underlined once while the predicate has a double underline. Structural elements are shown in parenthesis.

> Several men came. (S+V)
>
> The lion killed a person. (S+V+DO)
>
> I sent my friend a copy. (S+V+IO+DO)
>
> Few students came into the classroom today. (S+V+PP+A)

English does deviate much more often that is commonly thought from its usual subject + verb word order, as can be seen in these examples:

> There are three of them. (existential **there**)
>
> Am I ever bored! (emphatic statement)
>
> "Ha, ha," said the clown. (direct quotation)

BASIC WORD ORDER IN SPANISH
1.4
Spanish, as will be seen, positions the subject after the verb as often as before it. Spanish may not even use an overt subject at all since the idea of the subject can be expressed in the endings of the verb. About this point, the Real Academia Española in its *Gramática* states (§202) that the inflected verb "contains in itself the subject, be it definite or indefinite, and is equivalent [the inflected verb] on its own to a complete sentence." Examine the following pairs of sentences in Spanish, both renditions meaning the same thing, but with a somewhat different emphasis, as will be explained in §1.6.

> La maestra vino. (S+V)
>
> Vino la maestra. (V+S)
>
> El hombre nos dijo la verdad. (S+IO+V+DO)
>
> Nos dijo la verdad el hombre. (IO+V+DO+S)
>
> Tus amigos te esperaban ayer. (S+DO+V+A)
>
> Te esperaban ayer tus amigos. (DO+V+A+S)

Subject not overtly expressed:

> <u>Llegó en 1970</u>. (V+PP)
>
> <u>En 1970 llegó</u>. (PP+V)

COMPARISON
1.5

English speakers are often baffled by the word order V+S of Spanish since this occurs only under restricted conditions in English. Early in their studies of Spanish, English speakers should be made aware of the frequency of the V+S word order of Spanish and should understand that this word order, somewhat restricted in English, is very normal and of very high frequency in Spanish.

Similar attention should be drawn to Spanish speakers, and they should be alerted to the restrictions in English placed on the usage of the V+S word order. The most common instance where the V+S word order is found in English is in certain interrogative sentences where this is the normal structure. All or part of the predicate is fronted also in assertive and in some common or folk expressions.

> <u>Who is</u> that? (interrogative)
>
> <u>There standing before me was</u> my accuser. (assertive)
>
> <u>Gone are</u> the good old days. (common expression)

A point of comparison for the Spanish speaker is the fact that the very common Spanish structure not overtly expressing a subject as such is paralleled in the English imperative sentence but not, however, in normal declarative sentences.

> <u>Stand in front of them</u>! (V+PP)

Exercise 1

Write original English and Spanish sentences patterned after the structural types illustrated in each of the examples given in the paragraphs above. Underline their subjects and predicates.

LANGUAGE	STRUCTURAL TYPE	LANGUAGE	STRUCTURAL TYPE
1. Eng.	(S+V)	10. Span.	(IO+V+DO+S)
2. Eng.	(S+V+DO)	11. Span.	(S+V+DO)
3. Eng.	(S+V+DO+IO)	12. Span.	(V+DO+S)
4. Eng.	(S+V+PP+A)	13. Span.	(V+PP)
5. Eng.	(existential **there**)	14. Span.	(PP+V)
6. Eng.	(direct quotation)	15. Eng.	(interrogative)
7. Span.	(V+S)	16. Eng.	(assertive)
8. Span.	(S+V)	17. Eng.	(common expression)
9. Span.	(S+IO+V+DO)	18. Eng.	(imperative) (V+PP)

(Exercise 2)

Translate the following sentences into Spanish, placing the subject after the predicate in all cases. Then rewrite each translation, using the S+V+Complement word order, the one which is the most usual for the English speaker.

1. Juan will do the job.
2. Four of my friends left the bus.
3. The guests didn't arrive until after ten (o'clock).
4. Freddy has my book and his parents know it.

5. Your papers are on the desk. (familiar)[1]
6. A salesman with a loud voice showed me the house.
7. Joseph didn't see anyone at the station this morning.
8. The birds were singing, but the deaf girl couldn't hear them.

WORD ORDER AND EMPHATIC USAGE IN ENGLISH AND SPANISH
1.6

When an English speaker wishes to place particular emphasis on a certain element of a sentence, vocal stress (phonic intensification) is used. In the written language, the stressed element is often italicized or underlined.

> *The woman* bought an orange. (ie not the man)
> The woman *bought* an orange. (ie she didn't just take one)
> The woman bought *an orange*. (ie not an apple)

The use of vocal stress for the purpose of placing special emphasis on a particular element of a sentence is found in Spanish also, and it is usually combined with strategically placed pauses. Pauses may occur between the subject and predicate or between the S+V element and a complement.

> La mujer | compró la naranja.
> La mujer compró | la naranja.

In the first example vocal stress accompanies the first element of the sentence *la mujer*, and in the second example it accompanies the last element *la naranja*.

In addition to vocal stress, and perhaps more frequently employed than vocal stress, is a syntactic device used for emphasis in Spanish. In order to achieve the effect of emphatic stressing, since Spanish word order is quite flexible, it will place the desired element to be emphasized at the beginning of the sentence whenever grammatically possible.

> *La niña* compró una naranja. (S+V+DO) = *The girl* bought an orange.
> *Compró* la niña una naranja. (V+S+DO) = The girl *bought* an orange.

---

[1] This is an indication of the level of formality to be used in the Spanish pronominal form. In many of the exercises throughout the manual, when asked to translate "you/your" into Spanish, we will specify in parenthesis what form you should use.

(familiar) = **tú, tu**; (familiar, plural) = **vosotros(as), vuestro(a)**; (formal) = **usted, su**; (formal, plural) = **ustedes, su**.

Compró una naranja la niña. (V+DO+S) = The girl *bought an orange.*
Una naranja compró la niña. (DO+V+S) = The girl bought *an orange.*

Note: Attention should be called to the fact that the verb is not found in final position in any of these examples of conversational or normal usage. Final positioning of the verb is ordinarily reserved for classical poetry or archaic literary styles.

These same formulas are permitted when the predicate contains a complement of circumstance (ie A or PP) and where the subject is not overtly expressed and the predicate contains both direct and indirect object complements.

La mujer vendrá *inmediatamente/dentro de poco.* (S+V+C)

Vendrá la mujer *inmediatamente/dentro de poco.* (V+S+C)

Vendrá *inmediatamente/dentro de poco* la mujer. (V+C+S)

Inmediatamente/Dentro de poco vendrá la mujer. (C+V+S)

Spanish concurs with English in permitting the interchanging of direct object with indirect object complements in the predicate. However, when the direct object is a simple pronoun and not a pronominal phrase, certain restrictions apply in both languages (See Unit 14, §14.12–13).

Trajo un libro para mí. (V+DO+IO)
Trajo para mí un libro. (V+IO+DO)
Para mí trajo un libro. (IO+V+DO)
Un libro trajo para mí. (DO+V+IO)

(Exercise 3)
Translate the following sentences into Spanish, noting carefully the underlined elements of each sentence which are stressed. Within the permissible bounds of good grammar, order the elements of the Spanish translation so as to place the stressed element of the English sentence as near as possible to the front of the Spanish sentence. Four of the sentences are practice in interchanging the direct and indirect objects.

1. <u>Many people</u> rent houses.
2. Many people <u>rent</u> houses.
3. Our daughter left <u>last night</u>.
4. My father isn't in <u>his office</u>.
5. I brought <u>a letter</u> for you. (familiar)
6. I bring this gift <u>for all of you</u>.
7. Your sister gave the box to my friends. (familiar)
8. Your sister gave my friends the box. (formal)
9. <u>Many people</u> bought that book.
10. Many people <u>bought</u> that book.
11. Classes end <u>next week</u>.
12. The boys are <u>at home</u>.
13. They showed <u>the examples</u> to the teacher.
14. They showed the examples <u>to the teacher</u>.
15. Two men sold a watch to the girl.
16. Two men sold the girl a watch.

2

The
Verb Forms
of English

2.1

The most characteristic aspect of the English verbal system is its very limited number of verb forms and its heavy reliance upon auxiliary verbs. In classifying verbs according to their function, we distinguish lexical verbs (LV) from the closed system of auxiliary verbs (AUX). The English verbal system is normally represented as having five forms: the base, the -s form, the preterite, the present participle, and the past participle. Variations occur within this system where some verbs have less than five forms and others have more. Examples are the eight-form verb **be**, which is over-differentiated, and the modal verb **must**, which is classified as defective since it has but one form.

One form:	must
Two forms:	shall, should
Three forms:	let, lets, letting
Four forms:	call, calls, calling, called
Five forms:	show, shows, showed, showing, shown
Eight forms:	be, am, is, are, was, were, being, been

There are many irregular verbs found in the English verb inventory, and these are often difficult to classify. Some irregular verbs will follow consistent phonological patterns, and others must simply be memorized since there often is no way to predict their pattern. The correct spelling of many forms is also problematic, not only for non-native but for native speakers of English as well. We shall begin by giving examples of the standard verbal forms as they are found used in the verb phrase (VP). A later section follows where examples are given of a regular verb and various irregular verbs used in sentences; the irregularities include both morphologic and orthographic variations.

LEXICAL VERB FORMS

FORM	EXAMPLE	USE
(1) BASE	**call** **drink** **put**	(a) All persons, except 3rd person singular, in the present tense. (b) With all auxiliaries except **have** and **be** to form verb compounds. (c) Infinitive, either alone or in combination with the prepositional verbal particle **to**. (d) Imperative. (e) Subjunctive.
(2) **-s** FORM	**calls** **drinks** **puts**	3rd person singular present tense.
(3) PRETERITE	**called** **drank** **put**	Past tense.
(4) PRESENT PARTICIPLE	**calling** **drinking** **putting**	(a) Progressive aspect (**be** + base **-ing**). (b) Non-finite **-ing** clauses.
(5) PAST PARTICIPLE	**called** **drunk** **put**	(a) Perfective aspect (**have** + past participle). (b) Passive voice (**be** + past participle). (c) Non-finite **-ed** clauses.

THE REGULAR VERB
2.2
An English verb is considered to be regular if its past tense and past participle forms are identical and end in **-ed**. A regular verb has only four distinct forms.

Taking the regular verb **walk** as an example, we find its forms to be as follows:

BASE	**walk**	(a) I/You/We/They walk to school. (present tense) (b) You can walk now. (with auxiliary) (c) I made them walk/I want to walk. (infinitive) (d) Walk straight ahead. (imperative) (e) They require that he walk a lot. (subjunctive)
-s FORM	**walks**	She walks beautifully.
PRETERITE	**walked**	It walked past us.

PRESENT PARTICIPLE	**walking**	(a) We are walking too fast. (progressive aspect) (b) Walking is good for you. (non-finite clause)
PAST PARTICIPLE	**walked**	(a) They have walked a lot. (perfective aspect) (b) The dog is walked each day for exercise. (passive voice) (c) Walked to exhaustion, she went home. (non-finite **-ed** clause)

THE MORPHOLOGICALLY IRREGULAR VERB

2.3

An English verb is viewed as morphologically irregular if:
   (a) its preterite and past participle forms are different,
   (b) its preterite and past participle forms are the same but do not end in **-ed**,
   (c) its present tense form does not use **-s** in the 3rd person singular.

An irregular verb will usually demonstrate all five different forms (with some very common exceptions).
   Taking the irregular verb **go**, for example, the forms are as follows:

BASE	**go**	(a) I/You/We/They go to school. (present tense) (b) You may go. (with auxiliary) (c) I saw them go/I want to go. (infinitive) (d) Go straight home! (imperative) (e) The law requires that he go to school. (subjunctive)
-s FORM	**goes**	He goes to work early.
PRETERITE	**went**	She went past us.
PRESENT PARTICIPLE	**going**	(a) We are going too fast. (progressive aspect) (b) Going by way of downtown, you save time. (non-finite clause)
PAST PARTICIPLE	**gone**	(a) They have gone two blocks. (perfective aspect) (b) It was gone when we came. (passive voice) (c) Funds gone, we declared bankruptcy. (non-finite clause)

2.4

The verb **be** is particularly irregular since it has three forms in the present tense and two in the preterite tense. Furthermore, its preterite forms are different from its past participle form. The verb **be** as an LV or an AUX, then, has a total of eight distinct forms, the most differentiated verb in English. Our five-form system of classification must per force be slightly altered to accommodate **be**.

BASE	**be**	(a) You may be late to school. (with auxiliary)
		(b) I let them be here/I want to be a lawyer. (infinitive)
		(c) Be on time! (imperative)
		(d) They asked that we be on time. (subjunctive)
PRESENT	**am** **is** **are**	I am a student. He/She/It is at work. You/We/They are at school.
PRETERITE	**was** **were**	I/He/She/It was on time. You/We/They were late.
PRESENT PARTICIPLE	**being**	(a) You are being difficult again. (progressive aspect) (b) Being well prepared, we knew all of the answers. (non-finite clause)
PAST PARTICIPLE	**been**	They have been here twice. (Note: **be** is not used in the passive voice nor in an **-ed** clause.)

You will find a fairly complete listing of English irregular verbs in Appendix I.

THE ENGLISH AUXILIARY VERBS
2.5
The English auxiliary verbs are divided into two classes—primary and modal. The primary English auxiliary verbs do not carry a lexical or dictionary meaning of their own and are inflected for person, number, and tense. They are **do, have,** and **be**. Do not be confused; they can be used as lexical verbs also where they have meaning. Thus we have **do, have, be** LV and **do, have, be** primary AUX.

Do (primary AUX) is used to form negative statements or in any type of question structure in the English present or past tenses. It combines with the base form of an LV as follows:

PRESENT: **do/does**	PAST: **did**
I don't go often.	I didn't go often.
Do they go every day?	Did they go every day?
Doesn't he go every day?	Didn't he go every day?
When does she go?	When did she go?

Have (primary AUX) is used with the past participle of an LV in the formation of the perfect tenses, which express anteriority to other actions or completion (perfection) of an action.

PRESENT PERFECT: **has/have**	PAST PERFECT: **had**
I have left.	I had gone earlier.
She hasn't left yet.	She hadn't left yet.
Have you done everything?	Had you done everything last week?
Haven't they arrived?	Hadn't they arrived already?
Where has he gone?	Where had he gone when you called?

Be (AUX), which was described above as both a lexical and a primary auxiliary verb, is used with the present participle of an LV ending in **-ing** in the formation of the progressive tenses, which express actions as being in progress, and with the past participle to form the passive voice. As illustrated in the various examples above, the progressive tense formula is **be + LV -ing,** and the passive voice formula is **be +** past participle of an LV. (See Unit 29 for more details.)

PROGRESSIVE TENSE	PASSIVE VOICE
I am working.	I am worked too much.
We aren't working.	We aren't mentioned often.
Are you working?	Are you worked enough?
Isn't he/she/it working?	Isn't he/she/it mentioned?
Where are they working?	Where are they mentioned?
I was eating.	I was seen by them.
They weren't eating.	They weren't seen in the library.
Were you eating?	Were you seen by anyone?
Wasn't he/she/it eating?	Wasn't he/she/it seen there?
When were we eating?	When were we seen?

The modal auxiliary verbs carry a dictionary or true lexical meaning of their own. Listed below are the most commonly cited ones. They are not inflected for person or number and regularly combine with the base form infinitive; the last two examples usually require **to +** base form. Modal auxiliaries are taken up in detail in Unit 8.

NON-NEGATIVE	NEGATIVE
can	cannot/can not/can't
could	could not/couldn't
may	may not
might	might not/mightn't
shall	shall not/shan't
should	should not/shouldn't
will/ 'll	will not/ 'll not/won't
would/ 'd	would not/ 'd not/wouldn't
must	must not/mustn't
need	need not/needn't
dare	dare not/daren't
ought (to)	ought not/oughtn't
used to	used not to/didn't used to

THE VERBS WITH ORTHOGRAPHIC IRREGULARITIES
2.6

There are verbs whose only irregularity is that their spelling varies slightly in the present and past participles. They are classified in five major categories.

(1) Verbs ending in a single consonant preceded by a single accented vowel, before adding the **-ing** or **-ed**, you double the consonant.

BASE FORM	PRESENT PARTICIPLE	PAST PARTICIPLE
commit	committing	committed
control	controlling	controlled
prefer	preferring	preferred
wed	wedding	wedded

(2) Verbs ending in **-l, -m**, and some few in **-p**, even though the preceding vowel is not stressed, you double the consonant in the present participle and in the past participle in British English but not in American English except in computer and technological English.

cancel	(Br) cancelling	(Br) cancelled
	(Am) canceling	(Am) canceled
program	(Br) programming	(Br) programmed
	(Am) programing	(Am) programed
worship	(Br) worshipping	(Br) worshipped
	(Am) worshiping	(Am) worshiped

Note: This same differentiation also applies to the nouns formed from such verbs: (Br) traveller, (Am) traveler.

(3) Verbs ending in the letter **-c** change this to **-ck** before adding the **-ing/-ed** endings.

traffic	trafficking	trafficked
picnic	picnicking	picnicked

(4) If a verb ends in silent **-e**, this is dropped before adding the **-ing/-ed** inflections.

accuse	accusing	accused
compare	comparing	compared
excite	exciting	excited
prove	proving	proved
smile	smiling	smiled

You retain the silent **-e** before **-ing**, however, in a few verbs like **dye** and **singe** and the few that end in **-oe:** dyeing, singeing, hoeing.

(5) If a verb ends in a consonant + **y**, change the **-y** to **-ied** in the preterite and past participle forms.

BASE FORM	PRETERITE	PAST PARTICIPLE
apply	applied	applied
carry	carried	carried

The past of **lay, pay,** and **say,** which end in a vowel + **y**, drops the **-y** after the vowel and adds **-id**. The base in the **-ing** form, however, is unaltered.

BASE FORM	PAST PARTICIPLE	PRESENT PARTICIPLE
lay	laid	laying
pay	paid	paying
say	said	saying

On the other hand, in monosyllabic verbs such as **die** and **lie**, you change the **-ie** to **-y** before adding the **-ing** ending: **dying, lying.**

Exercise 1

Select ten regular verbs other than those already mentioned and give all of their forms.

Exercise 2

Give the present participle and past participle forms of the following verbs:

1. prove	6. travel	11. traffic
2. control	7. worry	12. lay
3. dye	8. prefer	13. program
4. commit	9. lie	14. say
5. try	10. compare	15. worship

RULES OF PRONUNCIATION FOR CERTAIN ENGLISH VERBS
2.7

The 3rd person singular verb form consistently ends in **-s** for most verbs, but this **s** may have three different pronunciations, depending on the end sound of the lexical verb before adding the inflection.

The rule is as follows:

(a) If the lexical verb ends in a voiceless consonant sound other than [s], [ʃ], or [tʃ], **-s** is added with the value of [s]: **hit/hits** [hɪts], **kick/kicks** [kɪks] **rap/raps** [ræps], **laugh/laughs** [læfs].[1] The voiceless consonant sounds that this applies to are [p, t, k, f, θ].

(b) If the lexical verb ends in a vowel sound or a voiced consonant sound other than [z, ʒ, dʒ], **-s** is added with the value of [z]: **know/knows** [noz], **see/sees** [siz], **rain/rains** [renz], **give/gives** [gɪvz]. The voiced consonant sounds that this applies to are [b, d, g, m, n, ŋ, v, ð, l, r].

(c) If the lexical verb ends in the sibilants [s, z, ʃ, tʃ, ʒ, dʒ], the 3rd person singular marker **-s** has the value of [-ɪz] pronounced as an extra syllable and written in many instances as **-es**: **race/races** [resɪz], **lose/loses** [luzɪz],

---

[1] All phonetic transcriptions of English vocabulary items are based on *A Pronouncing Dictionary of American English* by John S. Kenyon and Thomas A. Knott.

wish/wishes [wɪʃɪz], **enrich/enriches** [ɪnrɪtʃɪz], **pledge/pledges** [plɛdʒɪz].

Note: It should be mentioned here that exactly the same rules as above apply to the English plural formation of nouns as will be seen in Unit 9.

Pronunciation of the regularly formed preterite and past participial forms (those ending in **-ed**) is a follows:

(a) If the lexical verb ends in a voiceless consonant sound other than [t], **-ed** is added with the value of [t]: **leap/leaped** [lipt], **kick/kicked** [kɪkt], **pass/passed** [pæst], **laugh/laughed** [læft]. The voiceless consonants that can occur in final position in verbs are [p, t, k, f, θ, s, ʃ, tʃ].

(b) If the lexical verb ends in a vowel sound or in a voiced consonant sound other than [d], **-ed** is added with the value of [d]: **sew/sewed** [sod], **tease/teased** [tizd], **blame/blamed** [blemd], **stab/stabbed** [stæbd], **tag/tagged** [tægd]. The voiced consonants that can occur in final position in verbs are [b, g, v, ð, z, ʒ, dʒ, m, n, ŋ, l, r].

(c) If the lexical verb ends in either the sound of [t] or [d], then **-ed** is added with the value of [ɪd] pronounced as an extra syllable: **seat/seated** [sitɪd] **wade/waded** [wedɪd].

Exercise 3

Give the 3rd person singular present tense form of the verbs in group A and the preterite form of the verbs in group B. For all the verbs, state what the pronunciation of each form would be and cite the applicable rules.

A. 1. sneeze   6. strive   11. judge
    2. swim   7. search   12. pass
    3. cook   8. slap   13. cough
    4. prefer   9. go   14. sing
    5. cry   10. skate   15. sew

B. 1. test   6. seem   11. pay
    2. live   7. precede   12. guarantee
    3. sob   8. raise   13. try
    4. learn   9. convey   14. drag
    5. cash   10. crack   15. breathe

Exercise 4 (Optional)

After examining the list of English Irregular Verbs to be found in Appendix I, make a listing of all the verbs which demonstrate the same types of irregularities; for example, **drink-drank-drunk** is like **sink-sank-sunk**. Group the verbs under the following classifications:

(1) The verb has only two forms and has a consonant change only (eg, **have-had-had**).

(2) The verb has only two forms, and the forms differ with respect to a vowel only (eg, **run-ran-run**).

(3) The verb has two forms and has both a vowel and a consonant change (eg, **say-said-said**).

(4) The verb has three forms, and the forms differ with respect to the vowel only (eg, **swim-swam-swum**).

(5) The verb has three forms and they all differ with respect to both vowels and consonants. The past participle form of such verbs often ends in **-n** or in **-en** (eg, **see-saw-seen**).

(6) Place in a special category any verbs you find which do not fit patterns (1) through (5) above. The verb **put**, whose forms are identical in all three tenses, would go in this class.

The Forms of Regular Verbs in Spanish

3.1
An impressive characteristic of the Spanish verbal system is its numerous forms of a same verb, each form normally being marked morphologically for person, number, tense, aspect, and mood. By person and number we are referring to the three grammatical persons in the singular and the three grammatical persons in the plural that are reflected in the normal conjugations of Spanish verbs.

PERSON	SINGULAR	PLURAL
1st	yo	nosotros, nosotras
2nd	tú, usted, (vos)	vosotros, vosotras, ustedes
3rd	él, ella	ellos, ellas

To person and number agreement, an additional dimension is added to the regular tripartite paradigm, that is one of formality. The pronouns **usted (Ud./Vd.)** 'you' singular (**vos** in some dialectal areas) and **ustedes (Uds./Vds.)** 'you' plural are in complementary distribution with **tú** and **vosotros/vosotras** when a degree of formality is desired, and this is reflected in the verb marking. Since the forms, **usted** and **ustedes**, were originally derived from **vuestra merced**, the verb form which corresponds to the third person, not the second, is used in conjugation. (In our illustrative paradigms under §3.3, we use the **usted/ustedes** pronoun forms only in the imperative mood section.)

By tense we mean the three general time frames in which verbs are cast: present, past, and future. These time frames may be represented by a simple verb form or by a compound verb form utilizing an auxiliary. Aspect tells us how the verbal action is realized, whether it is punctual, progressive, durative, repetitive, completed, or incomplete. The base verb form is morphologically inflected to show the different tenses and aspects.

Mood in the verb form is a broader classification which describes the speaker's attitude towards the verbal process. Spanish has three moods: indicative, subjunctive, and imperative. The indicative mood expresses the fact that an act, state, or occurrence is actual, real, and perceivable. The subjunctive mood denotes an unreal condition, the *idea* of a verbal process and not the actual process. A subjunctive form verb is always subordinate to another verb or expression which conveys a wish, or a degree of conjecture or urgency. The imperative mood is used for commands, requests, and advice.

MORPHEMES OF THE SPANISH VERB
3.2

The Spanish verb traditionally is described in morphological terms as consisting of four elements: a stem morpheme (morfema lexemático), a thematic morpheme (vocal temática), a tense/aspect morpheme (morfema auxiliar), and a person/number morpheme (morfema concordante). We describe the verb in a slightly different manner following what appears to be of sounder pedagogical implications. William E. Bull was the first to propose this change.[1] Elements two and three (thematic morpheme and tense/aspect morpheme) are combined into one (mood/tense/aspect) and thereby lessens the learner's memorization burden. In certain conjugations, some of the suffix elements will be found to carry Ø morphemes. Taking the verbs **amar, temer,** and **vivir** as our examples, they would illustrate these three morphemic elements as follows:

VERB FORM	STEM	MOOD/ TENSE/ ASPECT	PERSON/ NUMBER
(tú) **amabas**	**am-**	**-a ba-**	**- s**
(nosotros) **temeremos**	**tem-**	**-e re-**	**-mos**
(ellas) **vivieron**	**viv-**	**-ie ro-**	**-n**

According to the vowel found in the infinitive form ending, regular Spanish verbs are classified in three groups. The 1st conjugation has an **-ar** ending in the infinitive, the 2nd conjugation has an **-er** ending, and the 3rd conjugation an **-ir** ending. The **-r** in each case is the infinitive marker. In turn, each conjugation is traditionally presented in the three moods described above—indicative, subjunctive, and imperative—these being reflected in the second morphemic element.

Falling outside of the above classifications is another group of verbal forms which are distinguished by their non-finite, non-personal character. These are the so-called verbids of which the infinitive is one—gerunds and participles complete the group. Traditional Spanish grammars show a regular Spanish verb paradigm to have a total of 62 simple verb forms and 56 compound verb forms, making the grand total of 118 conjugated forms in a complete regular verb paradigm.

SIMPLE TENSES OF THREE MODEL REGULAR VERBS
3.3

	FIRST CONJUGATION	SECOND CONJUGATION	THIRD CONJUGATION
INFINITIVE (*INFINITIVO*)	**am a r**	**tem e r**	**viv i r**
PRESENT PARTICIPLE (*GERUNDIO*)	**am a ndo**	**tem ie ndo**	**viv ie ndo**
PAST PARTICIPLE (*PARTICIPIO*)	**am a do**	**tem i do**	**viv i do**

---

[1] In *Spanish for Teachers: Applied Linguistics,* (1965).

INDICATIVE MOOD *(INDICATIVO)*

PRESENT	(yo)	am o	tem o		viv o	
(PRESENTE)	(tú)	am a s	tem e s		viv e s	
	(él)	am a	tem e		viv e	
	(nosotros)	am a mos	tem e mos		viv i mos	
	(vosotros)	am á is	tem é is		viv í s	
	(ellos)	am a n	tem e n		viv e n	

IMPERFECT[2]	(yo)	am aba†	tem ía†		viv ía†	
(PRETÉRITO	(tú)	am aba s	tem ía s		viv ía s	
IMPERFECTO)	(él)	am aba†	tem ía†		viv ía†	
	(nosotros)	am ába mos	tem ía mos		viv ía mos	
	(vosotros)	am aba is	tem ía is		viv ía is	
	(ellos)	am aba n	tem ía n		viv ía n	

PRETERITE	(yo)	am é	tem í		viv í	
(PRETÉRITO	(tú)	am aste Ø [3]	tem iste Ø [3]		viv iste Ø [3]	
INDEFINIDO)	(él)	am ó	tem ió		viv ió	
	(nosotros)	am a mos	tem i mos		viv i mos	
	(vosotros)	am aste is	tem iste is		viv iste is	
	(ellos)	am aro n	tem iero n		viv iero n	

FUTURE	(yo)	am aré	tem eré		viv iré	
(FUTURO	(tú)	am ará s	tem erá s		viv irá s	
IMPERFECTO)	(él)	am ará	tem erá		viv irá	
	(nosotros)	am are mos	tem ere mos		viv ire mos	
	(vosotros)	am aré is	tem eré is		viv iré is	
	(ellos)	am ará n	tem erá n		viv irá n	

CONDITIONAL	(yo)	am aría†	tem ería†		viv iría†	
(POTENCIAL	(tú)	am aría s	tem ería s		viv iría s	
SIMPLE)	(él)	am aría†	tem ería†		viv iría†	
	(nosotros)	am aría mos	tem ería mos		viv iría mos	
	(vosotros)	am aría is	tem ería is		viv iría is	
	(ellos)	am aría n	tem ería n		viv iría n	

---

[2] Note should be taken that the 1st and 3rd persons singular in all three conjugations of this tense have identical forms. If the context does not clearly state the person referred to, then the optionality in the use of subject pronouns must not be followed and a pronoun (**yo/él/ella/usted**) must accompany the verb to avoid misunderstanding. This phenomenon affects twelve different tenses; all of these forms are followed by a (†) symbol in the paradigms.

[3] The 2nd person singular preterite form is exceptional in that it does not use the **-s** person/number morpheme. More details on this exception are given in § 3.6, footnote (8).

SUBJUNCTIVE MOOD *(SUBJUNTIVO)*

PRESENT	(yo)	am	e†	tem	a†	viv	a†
(PRESENTE)	(tú)	am	e s	tem	a s	viv	a s
	(él)	am	e†	tem	a†	viv	a†
	(nosotros)	am	e mos	tem	a mos	viv	a mos
	(vosotros)	am	é is	tem	á is	viv	á is
	(ellos)	am	e n	tem	a n	viv	a n

IMPERFECT I [4]	(yo)	am	ara†	tem	iera†	viv	iera†
(PRETÉRITO IM-	(tú)	am	ara s	tem	iera s	viv	iera s
PERFECTO en -ra)	(él)	am	ara†	tem	iera†	viv	iera†
	(nosotros)	am	ára mos	tem	iéra mos	viv	iéra mos
	(vosotros)	am	ara is	tem	iera is	viv	iera is
	(ellos)	am	ara n	tem	iera n	viv	iera n

IMPERFECT II [4]	(yo)	am	ase†	tem	iese†	viv	iese†
(PRETÉRITO IM-	(tú)	am	ase s	tem	iese s	viv	iese s
PERFECTO en -se)	(él)	am	ase†	tem	iese†	viv	iese†
	(nosotros)	am	áse mos	tem	iése mos	viv	iése mos
	(vosotros)	am	ase is	tem	iese is	viv	iese is
	(ellos)	am	ase n	tem	iese n	viv	iese n

FUTURE[5]	(yo)	am	are†	tem	iere†	viv	iere†
(FUTURO	(tú)	am	are s	tem	iere s	viv	iere s
IMPERFECTO)	(él)	am	are†	tem	iere†	viv	iere†
	(nosotros)	am	áre mos	tem	iére mos	viv	iére mos
	(vosotros)	am	are is	tem	iere is	viv	iere is
	(ellos)	am	are n	tem	iere n	viv	iere n

IMPERATIVE MOOD *(IMPERATIVO)*

am	a	(tú)[6]	tem	e		viv	e	
am	e	(usted)	tem	a		viv	a	
am	e mos	(nosotros/-as)	tem	a mos		viv	a mos	
am	a d	(vosotros/-as)	tem	e d		viv	i d	
am	e n	(ustedes)	tem	a n		viv	a n	

---

[4] As a general rule, the Imperfect I forms (**-ra**) are preferred in Latin America, while the Imperfect II forms (**-se**) are more frequently found in Spain.

[5] The future subjunctive tense is used principally in legal and administrative texts and in sayings. We give it here only for reference as it is seldom encountered in everyday use.

[6] When used, the personal pronouns are postpositioned and lend emphasis to the imperative nature of the command.

THE PERFECT TENSES
3.4

The perfect tenses are formed in Spanish as in English by conjugating an auxiliary before the past participle form of the lexical verb. The Spanish auxiliary is **haber.**

		AUXILIARY			1ST CONJ.	2ND CONJ.	3RD CONJ.
INFINITIVE *(INFINITIVO PERFECTO)*		**hab**	**e**	**r**	**amado**	**temido**	**vivido**
PRESENT PARTICIPLE *(GERUNDIO PERFECTO)*		**hab**	**ie**	**ndo**	**amado**	**temido**	**vivido**

INDICATIVE MOOD *(INDICATIVO)*

PRETERITE	(yo)	h	e		amado	temido	vivido
PERFECT	(tú)	ha	Ø	s	amado	temido	vivido
(PRETÉRITO	(él)	ha	Ø		amado	temido	vivido
PERFECTO)	(nosotros)	h	e	mos	amado	temido	vivido
	(vosotros)	hab	é	is	amado	temido	vivido
	(ellos)	ha	Ø	n	amado	temido	vivido

> Note: The preterite perfect tense is also called *pretérito perfecto compuesto* (compound preterite perfect), and it corresponds to the present perfect tense in English (see §3.9). Unlike its English counterpart, it is not so widely used and would seem reserved for certain types of educated or literary speech; it is not frequently found in daily conversational use. The preterite perfect tense is probably heard more in Spain than in Latin America.

PLUPERFECT	(yo)	hab	ía†		amado	temido	vivido
(PRETÉRITO	(tú)	hab	ía	s	amado	temido	vivido
PLUSCUAM-	(él)	hab	ía†		amado	temido	vivido
PERFECTO)	(nosotros)	hab	ía	mos	amado	temido	vivido
	(vosotros)	hab	ía	is	amado	temido	vivido
	(ellos)	hab	ía	n	amado	temido	vivido

ANTERIOR	(yo)	hub	e		amado	temido	vivido
PRETERITE	(tú)	hub	iste	Ø	amado	temido	vivido
(PRETÉRITO	(él)	hub	o		amado	temido	vivido
ANTERIOR)	(nosotros)	hub	i	mos	amado	temido	vivido
	(vosotros)	hub	iste	is	amado	temido	vivido
	(ellos)	hub	iero	n	amado	temido	vivido

FUTURE	(yo)	hab	ré		amado	temido	vivido
PERFECT	(tú)	hab	rá	s	amado	temido	vivido
(FUTURO	(él)	hab	rá		amado	temido	vivido
PERFECTO)	(nosotros)	hab	re	mos	amado	temido	vivido
	(vosotros)	hab	ré	is	amado	temido	vivido
	(ellos)	hab	rá	n	amado	temido	vivido

					amado	temido	vivido
CONDITIONAL	(yo)	hab	ría†		amado	temido	vivido
PERFECT	(tú)	hab	ría	s	amado	temido	vivido
(POTENCIAL	(él)	hab	ría†		amado	temido	vivido
COMPUESTO)	(nosotros)	hab	ría	mos	amado	temido	vivido
	(vosotros)	hab	ría	is	amado	temido	vivido
	(ellos)	hab	ría	n	amado	temido	vivido

SUBJUNCTIVE MOOD *(SUBJUNTIVO)*

					amado	temido	vivido
PRETERITE	(yo)	ha	ya†		amado	temido	vivido
PERFECT[7]	(tú)	ha	ya	s	amado	temido	vivido
(PRETÉRITO	(él)	ha	ya†		amado	temido	vivido
PERFECTO)	(nosotros)	ha	ya	mos	amado	temido	vivido
	(vosotros)	ha	yá	is	amado	temido	vivido
	(ellos)	ha	ya	n	amado	temido	vivido

					amado	temido	vivido
PLUPERFECT I	(yo)	hub	iera†		amado	temido	vivido
(PRETÉRITO PLUS-	(tú)	hub	iera	s	amado	temido	vivido
CUAMPERFECTO	(él)	hub	iera†		amado	temido	vivido
en -ra)	(nosotros)	hub	iéra	mos	amado	temido	vivido
	(vosotros)	hub	iera	is	amado	temido	vivido
	(ellos)	hub	iera	n	amado	temido	vivido

					amado	temido	vivido
PLUPERFECT II	(yo)	hub	iese†		amado	temido	vivido
(PRETÉRITO PLUS-	(tú)	hub	iese	s	amado	temido	vivido
CUAMPERFECTO	(él)	hub	iese†		amado	temido	vivido
en -se)	(nosotros)	hub	iése	mos	amado	temido	vivido
	(vosotros)	hub	iese	is	amado	temido	vivido
	(ellos)	hub	iese	n	amado	temido	vivido

					amado	temido	vivido
FUTURE	(yo)	hub	iere†		amado	temido	vivido
PERFECT	(tú)	hub	iere	s	amado	temido	vivido
(FUTURO	(él)	hub	iere†		amado	temido	vivido
PERFECTO)	(nosotros)	hub	iére	mos	amado	temido	vivido
	(vosotros)	hub	iere	is	amado	temido	vivido
	(ellos)	hub	iere	n	amado	temido	vivido

Note: The future perfect subjunctive form, like its companion the future subjunctive, is used principally in legal and administrative texts and in aphorisms. We list it only for reference.

THE PROGRESSIVE TENSES
3.5
Contrary to the custom in English grammar of including the progressive tenses as part of the verbal paradigms, Spanish treats the **-ndo** gerundial forms as *verbal phrases* or bi-predicates (bipredicación) and does not include them in the conjuga-

---

[7] As stated before, the preterite perfect tense corresponds to the present perfect tense of English grammar.

tion paradigms. This is a more feasible treatment than would be to follow the English grammar custom because the progressive aspect in Spanish is not restricted to the use of one auxiliar only as in English, the **be** auxiliary. Spanish expresses the progressive aspect according to the following formula:

> PROG AUX + V-stem + thematic morpheme + **-ndo**
>
> PROG AUX → **estar, ir, venir, andar, seguir,** and **llegar**

Here we can appreciate one area where the progressive aspect covers different parameters in Spanish, that of employing other verbs in addition to **estar** as progressive auxiliaries.

Another difference between the English and Spanish progressive aspect is the fact of its far less frequent usage in educated Spanish. Much to the dismay of Spanish grammarians and under the influence of certain business correspondence manuals translated from the English, the progressive aspect is gradually creeping into more frequent usage in some regions. Gili Gaya (1980) gives an example where *Estamos enviando esta carta para comunicarle ...* was written instead of *Le enviamos esta carta ... ,* which is the grammatically correct form (§98). The verb **enviar** 'send' describes an action of brief duration and its usage in the progressive aspect is inconceivable.

The Spanish progressive aspect, when used, is formed in the three conjugations on the models that follow:

		estar		GERUNDIO		
PRESENT	(yo)	est	oy	amando	temiendo	viviendo
INDICATIVE	(tú)	est	á s	amando	temiendo	viviendo
(PRESENTE DE	(él)	est	á	amando	temiendo	viviendo
INDICA-	(nosotros)	est	a mos	amando	temiendo	viviendo
TIVO)	(vosotros)	est	á is	amando	temiendo	viviendo
	(ellos)	est	á n	amando	temiendo	viviendo

		haber	PARTICIPIO	GERUNDIO		
PRETERITE PERF.	(yo)	he	estado	amando	temiendo	viviendo
INDICATIVE	(tú)	has	estado	amando	temiendo	viviendo
(PRETÉRITO	(él)	ha	estado	amando	temiendo	viviendo
PERFECTO)	(nosotros)	hemos	estado	amando	temiendo	viviendo
	(vosotros)	habéis	estado	amando	temiendo	viviendo
	(ellos)	han	estado	amando	temiendo	viviendo

As stated above, any of the several verbs could have been chosen as a progressive auxiliary (PROG AUX) to illustrate these aspects. Of the five shown, **estar** was selected since it corresponds to the English auxiliary **be**.

COMPARISON OF THE ENGLISH AND SPANISH VERBAL SYSTEMS
3.6

Spanish person and number morphemes are four, with a Ø morpheme for the 1st and 3rd person singular forms. An **-s** morpheme marks the 2nd person singular form whereas **-is/-s** marks the plural.[8] The plural markers for 1st and 3rd persons are **-mos** and **-n** respectively. These person and number markers found on the verb forms preclude the need to use personal pronouns in most verb phrases, their usage would only result in redundancy in many cases. Thus, **amas, amáis, amamos,** and **aman** are normally preferred to **tú amas, vosotros/vosotras amáis, nosotros/nosotras amamos,** and **ellos/ellas aman.** Since the English verb has retained but one morphemic representation of person and number (the **-s** form) and this is absent in the subjunctive mood, the use of personal pronouns in the verb phrase is indispensable.

It is worth noting that in Spanish the perfect, the progressive, and the perfect progressive tenses are virtually identical to those of English in their formulas. In most cases the meanings of the corresponding forms concur in the two languages also. A comparison of the Spanish and English perfect, progressive, and perfect progressive tense/aspect formations is shown:

COMPOUND VERB FORMULAS

PERFECT:	AUX-**haber** + PAST PART	**He amado.**
	AUX-**have** + PAST PART	**I have loved.**
PROGRESSIVE:	PROG AUX + GERUND	**Estoy amando.**
	AUX-**be** + BASE **-ing**	**I am loving.**
PERFECT PROGRESSIVE:	AUX-**haber** + PROG AUX PAST PART + GERUND	
		He estado amando.
	AUX-**have** + **been** + BASE **-ing**	**I have been loving.**

Although the perfect and progressive tenses generally concur in formation and meaning in Spanish and English, this is not the case in their respective uses. There are considerable differences between the two languages in their employment of these tenses. Some of these differences have already been pointed out in this unit, and others are cited in Unit 27.

Exercise 1

Find three regular Spanish **-ar**, three **-er**, and three **-ir** verbs, other than **amar, temer,** and **vivir.** For each example give the following forms:

1. Preterite indicative, 1st person plural.
2. Present indicative, 2nd person plural (vosotros/-as).
3. Imperfect indicative, 1st person singular.
4. Conditional indicative, 3rd person singular.

---

[8] There is one exception to this observation and that is the 2nd person singular form of the preterite tense, which has a Ø marker as does the 1st and 3rd person singular forms. However, according to the *Real Academia Española*, the use of **amastes** instead of **amaste** is found rather frequently throughout the Spanish-speaking world and is even quite prevalent in some areas (*Esbozo*, §2.10.2).

5. Future indicative, 2nd person singular.
6. Imperative, formal plural (3rd person) (ustedes).
7. Present subjunctive, 3rd person singular.
8. Imperfect subjunctive I, 1st person plural.
9. Future subjunctive, 2nd person plural.
10. Imperfect subjunctive II, 3rd person plural.
11. Preterite perfect indicative, 1st person singular.
12. Pluperfect indicative, 2nd person singular.
13. Anterior preterite indicative, 3rd person singular (usted)
14. Future perfect indicative, 3rd person plural (ustedes)
15. Preterite perfect subjunctive, 2nd person plural.
16. Future perfect subjunctive, 1st person plural.
17. Pluperfect subjunctive I, 1st person singular.
18. Imperative, 1st person plural.
19. Pluperfect subjunctive II, 1st person singular.
20. Imperative, 2nd person singular familiar.

VERBS WITH ORTHOGRAPHIC CHANGES
3.7
Spanish has a fairly large number of verbs which, although generally regular, exhibit changes in the spelling of their consonants at the end of their stems when various vowel endings are added to those stems. Such verbs are referred to as orthographically changing verbs. Some such verbs are also stem (radical) changing verbs which are irregular, for example **empezar** and **seguir.** However, radical changes (vowel or consonant changes in the stem of the verb, treated in the next unit) and orthographic changes (consonant spelling changes at the end of the stem) are completely unrelated and independent phenomena.

The following bracketed phonetic symbols, which appear again in Figure 1, represent consonant sounds of Spanish which have more than one spelling. Each symbol is presented with various Spanish words whose bold type portions represent the symbol's sound when the words are pronounced.

(1) [k] as in **c**ama, **c**oma, **c**una, **qu**eso, **qu**iso

(2) [g] as in **g**ata, **g**ota, **g**usta, **g**uerra, **g**uía

(3) [x] or [h] as in **j**ala, **j**ota, **j**ura, **j**efe, **j**irafa, **g**ema, **g**ima
(The sound [x] is a voiceless fricative used in some Spanish dialectal areas whereas [h] is the related sound used in other areas.)

(4) [ş] as in **z**anca, **z**ona, **z**umo, **c**edro, **c**ifra
(This sound [ş] in the Americas is pronounced as [s]. In the Spanish Castilian dialect, the sound is pronounced [θ].)

(5) [gw] as in **Gu**atemala, anti**gu**o, a**gü**ero, lin**gü**ista

In the following chart, the Spanish consonant sounds from the above paragraph are listed top to bottom at the left. The Spanish vowels are listed across the top of the chart. In the squares are found the correct spellings for each consonant sound when it occurs before each Spanish vowel.

CONSONANT SOUND	a	o	u	e	i
[k]	ca	co	cu	que	qui
[g]	ga	go	gu	gue	gui
[x] or [h]	ja	jo	ju	je/ge	ji/gi
[ş]	za	zo	zu	ce	ci
[gw]	gua	guo	—	güe	güi

Figure 1

You will see the application of the spelling chart to various Spanish verb forms below. We give four forms for each infinitive listed under each consonant sound symbol. The forms are (1) the 1st person singular, present indicative; (2) the 2nd person singular, present indicative; (3) the 1st person singular, present subjunctive; and (4) the 1st person singular, preterite. Observe how the consonant spelling changes manifested in the verb forms operate in accordance with the spelling chart. They are highlighted in bold type.

PHONETIC SYMBOL	VERBAL INFINITIVE	1ST SGL. PRES. IND.	2ND SGL. PRES. IND.	1ST SGL. PRES. SUBJ.[9]	1ST SGL PRETERITE
[k]	sacar	saco	sacas	saque	saqué
	delinquir	delinco	delinques	delinca	delinquí
[g]	llegar	llego	llegas	llegue	llegué
	seguir	sigo	sigues	siga	seguí
[x, h]	recoger	recojo	recoges	recoja	recogí

(Verbs whose infinitive roots end in **-ger** or **-gir** must be spelled with **g** whenever that spelling is possible. Where **g** is not permissible to represent the [x, h] sounds before any Spanish vowel, the spelling must be changed to **j**.)

	dejar	dejo	dejas	deje	dejé

(Verbs whose infinitive roots end in **j** use that spelling in all forms since, as can be seen in the chart, **j** can represent the [x, h] sounds before any Spanish vowel.)

[ş]	rezar	rezo	rezas	rece	recé
	vencer	venzo	vences	venza	vencí
[gw]	averiguar	averiguo	averiguas	averigüe	averigüé

(Very few spelling changes of this type occur in the Spanish verb system.)

---

[9] Throughout the Manual SUBJ is the abbreviation used for **subjunctive** not **subject**. **Subject** in linguistic formulas is always represented as S.

Certain consonant sounds occurring in the stems of the following Spanish verb forms are indicated phonetically in brackets. Show how the given verb form would be normally spelled. Also, write the infinitive from which the form is derived.

1. conse[g]imos
2. se[k]an
3. esco[x]a
4. apa[ş]i[gw]emos
5. ar[gw]í
6. lle[g]a
7. [ş]ur[ş]iste
8. enco[x]en

9. apa[g]ó
10. reco[x]í
11. traba[x]o
12. men[gw]a
13. averi[gw]es
14. sa[k]o
15. conven[ş]es
16. prose[g]í

17. se[k]emos
18. ven[ş]a
19. co[x]es
20. to[k]é
21. si[g]e
22. amorti[gw]o
23. [ş]an[x]e
24. re[ş]o

3.8
In addition to the five orthographic changes listed above, there are several additional changes that reflect Spanish phonological processes operating in the verbal system.

(a) **d → Ø**   **levantad + os → levantaos**

(b) **s → Ø**   **volvamos + nos → volvámonos**

(c) **i → y**   in certain verbs, the endings **ió, ieron, iera, iese,** etc. become **oyó, oyeron, oyera, oyese, oyendo** since Spanish spelling conventions do not permit an unstressed **i** between vowels.

(d) **i → Ø**   when the verb stem ends in **-i** or a palatal sound, the **i** of **-iendo** is either lost or assimilated: **reir** becomes **ri + iendo → riendo, bullir** becomes **bull + iendo → bullendo, tañer** becomes **tañ + iendo → tañendo.**

Write the indicated forms of the following Spanish verbs, paying special attention to spelling.

1. arrancar: 1st person singular, preterite indicative.
2. distinguir: 3rd person singular, present subjunctive.
3. colgar: 1st person plural, present subjunctive.
4. escoger: 1st person plural, present subjunctive.
5. esparcir: 3rd person singular, present subjunctive.
6. averiguar: 1st person plural, present subjunctive.
7. freír: 1st person singular, preterite indicative.
8. pagar: 1st person singular, present subjunctive.
9. remolcar: 3rd person plural, preterite indicative.
10. bruñir: gerund.
11. conseguir: 1st person plural, present subjunctive.

12. sentarse: 2nd person plural, imperative (**vosotros, -as**).
13. oír: 3rd person plural, preterite indicative.
14. volverse: 1st person plural, imperative.
15. refreír: gerund.

3.9

A final note on differences in verb nomenclature in Spanish and English is necessary. Spanish grammarians are not always in agreement with the *Real Academia* in all its dictates. As refers to grammatical terminology, many renowned authorities in Spanish grammar have devised and used through the years their own nomenclature. This is much like what has happened among the modern linguists in contrast with conventional grammarians in describing English. Moreover, not always does the Spanish and English terminology have a one-to-one correspondence. English *present perfect* in contrast with Spanish *pretérito perfecto* is a prime example which never fails to be commented on by Spanish speakers knowledgeable in grammar. This lack of correspondence between the English and Spanish grammatical terms referring to a same time frame has prompted the authors to use *preterite perfect* in lieu of *present perfect* in an attempt to mitigate somewhat this disparity. Throughout the text we have attempted to adopt the *Real Academia* terminology wherever feasible.

A table showing the most common verb tense terminology with frequently encountered variations is supplied in Appendix II.

4

The Forms
of Irregular Verbs
in Spanish

4.1
Spanish grammar traditionally describes irregular verbs as those verbs which demonstrate forms that depart from the conjugations established for the three regular verb patterns. The vast majority of these departures take the forms of allomorphic variations of the stem (radical) morpheme or of the mood-tense-aspect morpheme and are the result of phonological laws which have affected the whole system of the Spanish language. The person/number morpheme is constant with but one exception, the 2nd person singular form of the preterite tense explained in the previous unit (§3.6. footnote 8). Some few verbs have suppletive stems (q.v. §4.6).

For the sake of better organization, we will divide the irregular verbal examples in two major groups: verbs with vowel irregularities and verbs with consonant irregularities. Since many verbs exhibit a combination of vowel and consonant irregularities and, strictly speaking, fall outside the two systematic categories designated, an exhaustive analysis of these latter would be overly complicated and perhaps even counterproductive. With this in mind, the most important of the multivariable verbs will be listed in the Appendix III without benefit of a detailed discussion.

Larousse de la conjugación, a well-known publication frequently consulted as a reference of over 10,000 verbs, lists just under seventy different types of irregular verb conjugations in Spanish and an additional twenty different types of verbs which undergo orthographic and prosodic modifications. Several of these were mentioned in Unit 3 (§3.7–8).

VOWEL CHANGES IN THE RADICAL
4.2
Irregular verbs of the radical-changing type are characterized by predictable changes in the vowel of the verb stem. Since the root vowel nearest the infinitive **-r** ending is that vowel which receives syllable stress in many of the forms, stressing is the determining factor of these changes. The changes are commonly described as taking the form of vowel diphthongization or of vowel raising by substitution of a semi-close vowel with a close vowel. When the vowel **e** occurs in the infinitive, it is subject to change in the verb forms to **ie** or to **i**: **sentir** becomes **si*e*nto** and **s*i*ntió.** The vowel **o** of the infinitive changes to **ue** and in exceptional cases to **u**: **dormir** becomes **du*e*rmo** and **d*u*rmió.** Such changes in the radical are totally

29

predictable since they obey specific rules involving whether the vowel of the root is stressed or not, or whether certain phonetic factors are present in the endings of the conjugated verb forms.

By examining only a verb's infinitive, one cannot tell whether it is irregular or not. For example, **comer** is not a radical-changing verb, whereas **mover** is. A better indication of whether a verb belongs to the radical-changing category is to look at its 1st person singular, present or preterite indicative form. If the root vowel is diphthongized or is raised in this form, then the verb is clearly a radical-changing verb.

By way of illustration:

DIPHTHONGIZATION			RAISING		
sentir:	**e** → **ie**	*si**e**nto*	pedir:	**e** → **i**	**p*i*do**
dormir:	**o** → **ue**	*d**ue**rmo*	poder:	**o** → **u**	**p*u*do**

It should be noted that if a verb is radical-changing, the radical vowel of the root will always be the one nearest the infinitive ending. In the verb **preferir**, for example, the second **e** is the affected vowel. In verbs such as **resolver**, it is the **o** that is affected. All radical-changing verbs can be categorized under three groupings, and the verbs in each of these categories obey rules applicable to their specific group.

Radical verbs of the first and second conjugations (ie those whose infinitives end in **-ar** like **pensar** and **volar** and those ending in **-er** like **perder** and **volver**) are less complex in their changes than are those of the third conjugation (**-ir** verbs like **sentir, dormir,** and **pedir**).

RADICAL-CHANGING VERB GROUPS AND GOVERNING RULES
4.3
Group A verbs
To Group A belong radical verbs drawn from the first two conjugations only, the **-ar** and **-er** verbs. Such verbs will have two possible roots, a diphthongized root which is stressed and an atonic root in which the unstressed vowel is unaltered. Representative members of Group A are as follows:

- **pensar** with the roots **pens-** (containing an atonic or unstressed vowel) and **piens-** (containing a tonic or stressed vowel). Other examples like **pensar** are **acertar, cerrar, comenzar, despertar, empezar, sentar,** etc.

- **volar** with the roots **vol-** (atonic) and **vuel-** (tonic). Like **volar** are **acordar, acostar, almorzar, apostar, colgar, contar, costar, encontrar, mostrar, probar, recordar, rogar, sonar,** etc.

- **perder** with the roots **perd-** (atonic) and **pierd-** (tonic). Like **perder** are **ascender, condescender, entender, defender,** etc.

- **volver** with the roots **volv-** (atonic) and **vuelv-** (tonic). Like **volver** are **doler, mover, soler,** etc.

Group A verbs are governed by this rule:

WHEN THE VERBAL ROOT IS STRESSED, ITS VOWEL IS DIPHTHONGIZED; OTHERWISE, NO CHANGE OCCURS IN THE ROOT VOWEL.

A survey of all tenses reveals that the diphthongized root of Group A radical-changing verbs occurs only in the following tenses and persons:

(1) present indicative; 1st, 2nd, and 3rd persons singular and 3rd person plural.

> pienso, piensas, piensa, piensan
> vuelo, vuelas, vuela, vuelan
> pierdo, pierdes, pierde, pierden
> vuelvo, vuelves, vuelve, vuelven

(2) present subjunctive; 1st, 2nd, and 3rd persons singular and 3rd person plural.

> piense, pienses, piense, piensen
> vuele, vueles, vuele, vuelen
> pierda, pierdas, pierda, pierdan
> vuelva, vuelvas, vuelva, vuelvan

(3) imperative; 2nd and 3rd persons singular and 3rd person plural.

> piensa (tú), piense (usted), piensen (ustedes)
> vuela, vuele, vuelen
> pierde, pierda, pierdan
> vuelve, vuelva, vuelvan

(4) the root vowel is atonic in all the other tenses, so the non-diphthongized form of the radical occurs.

> pensé, volaba, perdía, volví, etc.

4.4
Group B

To the second group of radical-changing verbs, Group B, belong assorted verbs of the 3rd conjugation only, verbs with **-ir** endings in the infinitive. Verbs in this group will have three possible roots: the unaltered root, a root with a diphthongized tonic vowel, and a root showing vowel raising. Shown here are examples of Group B radical-changing verbs:

- **sentir** with the roots **sent-** (atonic, unstressed vowel), **sient-** (tonic, stressed vowel), and **sint-** (raised vowel). Like **sentir** are **mentir, preferir, sugerir,** etc.

- **dormir** with the roots **dorm-** (atonic), **duerm-** (tonic), and **durm-** (raised vowel). Like **dormir** are **adormir** and **morir;** this latter also has the irregular participle **muerto.**

Three rules govern Group B verbs:

RULE 1. A DIPHTHONGIZED ROOT OCCURS WHEN THE ROOT IS STRESSED. THIS IS OBSERVED IN THE 1ST, 2ND, 3RD PERSONS SINGULAR AND 3RD PERSON PLURAL, PRESENT INDICATIVE AND PRESENT SUBJUNCTIVE FORMS.

> Indicative: siento, sientes, siente, sienten
>   duermo, duermes, duerme, duermen
>
> Subjunctive: sienta, sientas, sienta, sientan
>   duerma, duermas, duerma, duerman

RULE 2: WHEN THE VERBAL ROOT IS FOLLOWED BY STRESSED -IE-, -IO-, OR -A-, ITS VOWELS O AND E ARE RAISED TO U AND I RESPECTIVELY. AFFECTED FORMS ARE:

(A) 3RD PERSON SINGULAR AND PLURAL PRETERITE AND ALL FORMS OF IMPERFECT SUBJUNCTIVE I AND II.

| Preterite: | sintió, sintieron |
| | durmió, durmieron |

Imperfect	sintiera, sintieras, sintiera, sintiéramos, sintierais, sintieran
Subjunctive:	sintiese, sintieses, sintiese, sintiésemos, sintieseis, sintiesen
	durmiera, durmieras, durmiera, durmiéramos, durmierais, durmieran
	durmiese, durmieses, durmiese, durmiésemos, durmieseis, durmiesen

(B) 1ST AND 2ND PERSONS PLURAL, PRESENT SUBJUNCTIVE.

| Present | sintamos, sintáis |
| Subjunctive: | durmamos, durmáis |

(C) GERUND.

sintiendo; durmiendo

RULE 3. ALL OTHER FORMS NOT COVERED BY RULES (1) AND (2) CARRY THE UNALTERED RADICAL VOWEL OF THE INFINITIVE.

4.5
Group C

Only verbs of the third conjugation belong to Group C. These verbs with an **-ir** ending in their infinitive have only two roots—one root with the atonic vowel unaltered and the other with the radical tonic vowel raised.

An example of a Group C verb is **pedir**, which has **ped-** and **pid-**. Like **pedir** are **ceñir, elegir, reír, repetir, seguir, servir, vestir,** etc. There are three rules which condition the phonetic variations of Group C verbs:

RULE 1: IF ROOT VOWEL -E- IS STRESSED, IT IS RAISED TO -I-. THIS OCCURS IN THE 1ST, 2ND, AND 3RD PERSONS SINGULAR, AND THE 3RD PERSON PLURAL OF THE PRESENT INDICATIVE AND THE PRESENT SUBJUNCTIVE.

| Indicative: | pido, pides, pide, piden |

| Subjunctive: | pida, pidas, pida, pidan |

RULE 2: WHEN STRESSED -IE-, -IO-, OR -A- IS IN THE SYLLABLE FOLLOWING THE ROOT, PHONOLOGICAL CONDITIONING ALSO RAISES THE ROOT VOWEL TO -I-. IT AFFECTS THE 3RD PERSON SINGULAR AND PLURAL PRETERITE AND ALL FORMS OF THE IMPERFECT SUBJUNCTIVE I AND II, THE 1ST AND 2ND PERSONS PLURAL OF THE PRESENT SUBJUNCTIVE, AND THE GERUND.

| Preterite: | pidió, pidieron |

| Imperfect | pidiera, pidieras, pidiera, pidiéramos, pidierais, pidieran |
| Subjunctive: | pidiese, pidieses, pidiese, pidiésemos, pidieseis, pidiesen |

| Present subj.: | pidamos, pidáis |

Gerund: pidiendo

RULE 3: IF THE ROOT -E- IS EITHER UNSTRESSED OR IF IT IS NOT FOLLOWED BY STRESSED -IE-, -IO-, or -A-, IT REMAINS AS E IN ALL THE FORMS.

You must be especially careful not to include by analogy verbs which do not belong to the separate categories described above. By way of example, **defender** does belong to the **perder** group but **ofender** does not; **renovar** belongs to the **volar** group, and **innovar** does not. When in doubt, consult Appendix III or some other reference source to ascertain what type of modification, if any, a verb requires.

4.6

There are two additional vowel changes which affect the tonic vowel of the radical of certain verbs. Since these variations apply to a very limited number of verbs (one having but a single example), a detailed exposition will be reserved for inclusion in Appendix III. Consult it for particulars of each affected form.

    u → ue   **jugar** (only)   **i → ie**   **adquirir, inquirir,** etc.

Exercise 1

Find the indicated forms for the following stem-changing verbs. Be able to state why a stem vowel change does or does not occur.

    (1) cerrar, (2) acostar, (3) perder, (4) hervir, (5) seguir, (6) volver

        1. 1st person singular, present indicative.
        2. 3rd person singular, present indicative.
        3. 1st person plural, present indicative.
        4. 3rd person plural, present indicative.
        5. 2nd person singular, present subjunctive.
        6. 3rd person singular, present subjunctive.
        7. imperative, **ustedes** form.

Exercise 2

Give the indicated forms for these stem-changing verbs. Be able to state why a vowel change does or does not occur: (1) sugerir, (2) morir, (3) mentir, (4) dormir.

        1. 2nd person singular, present indicative.
        2. 3rd person singular, preterite indicative.
        3. imperative, **tú** form.
        4. 1st person plural, present subjunctive.
        5. 3rd person plural, imperfect subjunctive I.
        6. 1st person plural, imperfect subjunctive II.
        7. 2nd person plural, future subjunctive.

Exercise 3 (optional)

After carefully examining the following list of forms derived from radical-changing Spanish verbs, for each example determine (1) the tense, person, and number represented, (2) to which radical-changing group the verb belongs, and (3) the conditions which govern the form. At the same time be able to state if no conditions apply in any given case.

1. defienden	6. mueren	11. repitas
2. durmiendo	7. comencemos	12. prefiriéramos
3. suelen	8. sirvió	13. muestre
4. pidiendo	9. costó	14. cerré
5. sugiramos	10. sintieron	15. empezarán

CONSONANT CHANGES IN THE RADICAL
4.7
Like vowel changes in the radical of the irregular verb, consonant changes also occur. These changes are predictable in many of the registered instances; however, they are often accompanied by other variations which complicate classification. Three types of irregularities are observed: (1) the substitution of one stem consonant for another, (2) the addition of a second consonant to the stem when this ends in a consonant, or (3) the addition of a consonant or of a second vowel plus a consonant to a final vowel in the radical. These irregularities apply only to verbs of the 2nd and 3rd conjugations.

4.8
Consonant Substitution
There is only one productive consonant substitution process—the replacing of [ş], written **c + e/i**, or **z**, with [g]. This affects the 1st person singular present indicative form and all persons of the present subjunctive. The imperative suffers apocope of the **tú** form and consonant substitution in the **nosotros** and **Ud/Uds** forms.

z/c → g

hacer	Pres. Indicative:	hago, haces, hace, hacemos, hacéis, hacen
	Pres. Subj.:	haga, hagas, haga, hagamos, hagáis, hagan
	Imperative:	haz, haga, hagamos, haced, hagan

Also belonging to the **hacer** group are **deshacer, rehacer, satisfacer,** etc.

4.9
Velar Extension
The phenomenon of velar extension is manifested in four different environments, each conditioned by a postpositioned back vowel **a/o.**

(1) A stem ending in **z/c** [ş] and preceded by a vowel becomes [-şk].

    nacer   V[ş] → V[şk] /___ + a/o   **nazco**

(2) The nasal of the stem of a verb ending in **-oner, -ener,** or **-enir** is extended to **-ng**.

    poner   o/e + n → ong/eng /___ + a/o **pongo**

(3) The **l** of a stem when its infinitive is **-aler** or **-alir** is extended to **-lg**.

    salir   a + l → alg /___ + a/o   **salgo**

(4) The **a** of the radical of verbs whose infinitives are **-aer** is extended to **-aig**.

    traer   a → aig /___ + a/o   **traigo**

Affected are the 1st person singular present indicative form and all of the present subjunctive forms. To the first category of velar extension (**c + e/i**, or **z**, becomes **zc**) belong over two hundred Spanish verbs, which makes this the most productive of all irregular verb processes.

(1) **c → zc**

parecer	Pres. Ind.:	parezco, pareces, parece, parecemos, parecéis, parecen
	Pres. Subj.:	parezca, parezcas, parezca, parezcamos, parezcáis, parezcan
deducir	Pres. Ind.:	deduzco, deduces, deduce, deducimos, deducís, deducen
	Pres. Subj.:	deduzca, deduzcas, deduzca, deduzcamos, deduzcáis, deduzcan

(2) **n → ng**

poner	Pres. Ind.:	pongo, pones, pone, ponemos, ponéis, ponen
	Pres. Subj.:	ponga, pongas, ponga, pongamos, pongáis, pongan
tener	Pres. Ind.:	tengo, tienes, tiene, tenemos, tenéis, tienen
	Pres. Subj.:	tenga, tengas, tenga, tengamos, tengáis, tengan
venir	Pres. Ind.:	vengo, vienes, viene, venimos, venís, vienen
	Pres. Subj.:	venga, vengas, venga, vengamos, vengáis, vengan

(3) **l → lg**

valer	Pres. Ind.:	valgo, vales, vale, valemos, valéis, valen
	Pres. Subj.:	valga, valgas, valga, valgamos, valgáis, valgan
salir	Pres. Ind.:	salgo, sales, sale, salimos, salís, salen
	Pres. Subj.:	salga, salgas, salga, salgamos, salgáis, salgan

(4) **a → aig**

| caer | Pres. Ind.: | caigo, caes, cae, caemos, caéis, caen |
| | Pres. Subj.: | caiga, caigas, caiga, caigamos, caigáis, caigan |

Included in the above categories are other verb examples showing like patterns, although some have other irregularities also.

Like **parecer** are **conocer, nacer,** and countless other verbs.

Like **deducir** are **lucir** and its derived forms.

Like **poner** are **componer, disponer, imponer, oponer, posponer, reponer**, and many other derived forms.

Like **tener** are **atenerse, contener, obtener, sostener**, etc.

Venir has various derived verbs patterned in the same manner (eg **convenir**, etc.).

Like **valer** are **equivaler** and **prevaler.**

Like **salir** are **resalir** and **sobresalir.**

Like **caer** are **traer** and derived forms.

4.10

Verbs with y-extention

Y-extension, which is also called yod-extension, is employed in all verbs whose infinitives end in **-uir.** This sizeable group of verbs adds a **-y** to the final **-u** of the stem in most persons of the present indicative, present subjunctive, and imperative forms.

u → uy

huir	Pres. Ind.:	huyo, huyes, huye, huimos, huís, huyen
	Pres. Subj.:	huya, huyas, huya, huyamos, huyáis, huyan
	Imperative:	huye, huya, huyamos, huid, huyan

Some other very common verbs that are inflected like **huir** are **atribuir, concluir, construir, excluir, incluir, instruir, obstruir, sustituir,** etc.

4.11

Three additional consonant changes are found among the irregular verbs. As was the case with additional vowel changes, these variations apply to such a limited number of verbs that they can best be served by including them in the list of irregular verbs in Appendix III.

b → y	**haber** only (**hay**)
s → sg	**asir (asgo), desasir**
ab → ep	**caber (quepo), saber, resaber**

Exercise 4

Give the 3rd person singular and the 1st and 2nd person plural forms for the present subjunctive; also give the imperative forms corresponding to **tú** and **ustedes** for the following verbs:

(1) satisfacer, (2) nacer, (3) relucir, (4) oponer, (5) atenerse,
(6) convenir, (7) prevaler, (8) sobresalir, (9) caer, (10) incluir.

4.12
Strong Past Tense Forms

A legacy from Latin is found in various present-day Spanish verbs, the majority with a high frequency of occurrence. This legacy concerns the verbs with strong past tense forms. Similar to the so-called strong verbs of English which have variable past forms (**teach-taught, sing-sang, get-got,** etc), the Spanish strong verbs show irregularities in the preterite indicative and the imperfect subjunctive I and II forms.[1] These may appear in a variety of guises. Verb roots may show vowel substitution and/or consonant substitution and vowel extension and/or consonant extension. The strong past tense forms are all classified under three categories.

STRONG FORM IN **-a-**

traer:	traje	trajera/trajese

---

[1] The future subjunctive is also affected, but, as stated earlier, this tense is rarely used.

STRONG FORM IN -**i**-

decir:	dije	dijera/dijese
hacer:	hice	hiciera/hiciese
querer:	quise	quisiera/quisiese
venir:	vine	viniera/viniese

STRONG FORM IN -**u**-

andar:	anduve	anduviera/anduviese
caber:	cupe	cupiera/cupiese
conducir:	conduje	condujera/condujese
estar:	estuve	estuviera/estuviese
haber:	hube	hubiera/hubiese
poder:	pude	pudiera/pudiese
poner:	puse	pusiera/pusiese
saber:	supe	supiera/supiese
tener:	tuve	tuviera/tuviese

Note: All these verbs have other irregularities in addition to the strong past tense forms.

4.13
Suppletive Verb Forms

There are two very important verbs in Spanish which transcend even the many irregularities already documented; these verbs are **ser** and **ir**. Due to the fact that both have multiple verb stems, which have neither vowel nor consonant changes exclusively but show suppletion of the whole stem, they are classified in a separate category from other irregular verbs as **suppletive verb forms**. Both verbs have a great deal in common with the over-differentiated **be** of English.

Ser has four stems: **s-**, **er-**, **fu-**, and Ø while **ir** has three: **v-** in the present, **fu-** in the preterite, imperfect subjunctive I and II, and future subjunctive, and Ø in the imperfect. One example, **ser**, is given here; **ir** will be found in the supplemental list of irregular verbs (Appendix III).

ser

PRESENT	soy, eres, es, somos, sois, son
IMPERFECT	era, eras, era, éramos, erais, eran
PRETERITE	fui, fuiste, fue, fuimos, fuisteis, fueron
PRES. SUBJ.	sea, seas, sea, seamos, seáis, sean
IMPERF. SUBJ. I	fuera, fueras, fuera, fuéramos, fuerais, fueran
IMPERF. SUBJ. II	fuese, fueses, fuese, fuésemos, fueseis, fuesen
IMPERATIVE	sé, sea, seamos, sed, sean

Exercise 5

Give the 2nd person singular preterite, the 1st person plural imperfect subjunctive I, and the 3rd person plural imperfect subjunctive II for these verbs.

(1) traer, (2) decir, (3) hacer, (4) querer, (5) venir, (6) conducir, (7) saber, (8) haber, (9) poder, (10) poner, (11) estar, (12) tener.

LEXICALLY CONDITIONED IRREGULARITIES
4.14
Irregular Participles

Another inheritance from Latin like strong past tense forms, although on a more limited scale, is a series of verbs with two grammatically acceptable past participles. One participle is usually regular and the other irregular, this latter coming more directly from the Latin. This irregularity applies to only certain verbs of all three conjugations.

The regular form is usually reserved for use in compound perfective verb tenses while the irregular form more often functions as an adjectival. **Atender** has **atendido, atento; bendecir** has **bendecido, bendito; corregir** has **corregido, correcto,** etc.

A fairly complete list of verbs with two past participles will be found in Appendix IV.

4.15
Defective (Incomplete) Verbs

Due to their inherent semantic properties, certain verbs cannot be conjugated in all three persons nor in all tenses. These verbs, which are semantically incompatible with certain given conditions and consequentially have incomplete conjugations, belong to a special group called **defective verbs.** Some thirty-odd verbs belong to the group of defective verbs.

Many syntactic structures will admit only non-personal subjects. Such structures exclude all but the 3rd person forms of a verb. **Acontecer** is one such verb —people are not usually *happening.* Other verbs with similar idiosyncrasies are **atañer** and **concernir.** Another defective verb is **soler,** which has limited use in both the indicative and subjunctive moods. There are other verbs that are defective due to their phonological nature; certain forms produce disagreeable cacophony.

In addition to the type of verb limited by syntactic or phonetic structures, there is another considerable list of verbs which are classified as **unipersonal verbs.** These verbs all deal with phenomena of nature and are restricted to the 3rd person form of the conjugation paradigm. *Larousse de la conjugación* lists forty-five such verbs like **llover** 'rain', **tronar** 'thunder', **atardecer** 'get dark'.

IN SUMMARY
4.16

Like many world languages, Spanish is no exception in having an abundance of verb forms which resist systematic classification. Some changes may be predictable, and others seem randomly applied. There are morphophonemic features which operate to the exclusion of others (in complementary distribution) and others which are applied only in conjunction with other features; some are applied only as a consequence of other features. Take the very common verb **tener** as an example and compare it to the regular paradigm for **-er** verbs. It can be seen clearly by the large number of irregular forms shown in bold type in Figure 2 that to establish a comprehensible systematic classification of this verb would incur more exceptions than concurrences with the regular conjugation pattern.

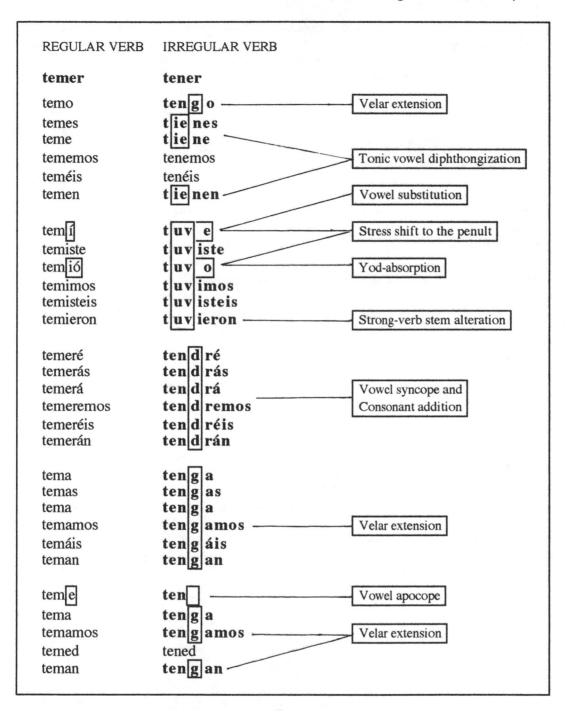

FIGURE 2

It would be unduly complicated to systematize verbs such as **tener**, which show mixed variations, since they run the whole gamut of possible irregularities. Even if a classification were accomplished, it is doubtful that the effort involved in surveying such a complex description would prove equally compensatory in its pedagogical usefulness.

The most common verbs demonstrating uniqueness in their morphology and those belonging to a specific class with a very reduced number of members have been grouped together in Appendix III. The listing represents a fairly complete inventory of many commonly used Spanish irregular verbs.

Exercise 6

Choose three irregular verbs, one each from the 1st, 2nd, and 3rd conjugations and give their 1st persons singular and plural present subjunctive forms. Derive the forms from the stem of the 3rd person singular present indicative and change the theme vowel of the mood-tense-aspect morpheme to the so-called *opposite vowel*. Example: the 3rd person singular present indicative forms of **amar, temer,** and **vivir** are am*a*, tem*e*, and vi*ve*. The 3rd person singular present subjunctive forms are am*e*, tem*a*, and vi*va*. If you observe closely, the mood-tense-aspect vowel changes are **a** → **e** for **amar** and **e** → **a** for **temer** and **vivir**. This is often referred to as a change in the subjunctive to the *opposite vowel*.

Exercise 7 (Optional)

For all future and conditional forms found in the list of irregular verbs in Appendix III, make a three-part classification based upon: (a) forms which show only the loss of the infinitive vowel (syncope), (b) forms in which the infinitive vowel is replaced by **d**, and (c) forms where the **c** and **e** have been lost from the original infinitive root.

Exercise 8 (Optional)

For all the irregular strong form preterites listed in Appendix III, classify them under three headings: (a) those with a stem vowel of **u**, (b) those with a stem vowel of **i**, and (c) those with a stem vowel of **a**.

Exercise 9 (Optional)

Select all the 1st person singular present indicative forms from the list of irregular verbs in Appendix III and list them under headings which show identical irregularities. Example: **u** → **uy** in **construir, incluir.**

The Spanish
Imperfect-Preterite Contrast

5.1

Simple past time is expressed in Spanish through two different past tenses, the imperfect and the preterite. These two tenses record past events, states, or conditions from distinct points of view, that is, from two different aspects. Aspectual differences come from the speakers' ways of conceptualizing events that they are describing. Certain pertinent questions must be asked before one can ascertain which of the two tenses is applicable. Is the event which is being described specific to one point in time and thus instantaneous, or is it recurrent or lasting over an extended period of time? What part of the event is referred to in the description—the beginning, the end, the middle, or the overall aspect including beginning and end?

English does not distinguish very clearly between these different points of view concerning past events, but when pressed to do so, it can render past time from two distinct viewpoints as Spanish does. English, however, has to use verbal periphrasis (ie constructions involving more than one verbal form) to accomplish what Spanish does with a single verb form.[1]

DESCRIPTION OF IMPERFECT TENSE
5.2

The Spanish imperfect verb form describes an event, state, or condition in terms of a recalled point at the middle of a single event in the past or of a series of repeated events. The description is reasonably free of boundaries or references to a beginning or end. The imperfect is useful in describing scenes in the past or the reliving of experiences. Unlike the preterite described below, imperfect action is ongoing in relation to the point of recollection. Its use is less frequent than the preterite tense.

The Spanish imperfect is rendered in English in a variety of ways since the tense may express either past description or past repetition. The aspectual concept held by the speaker is instrumental in choosing the mode of expression in English.

Past Description
The Spanish imperfect expresses past description. English uses the past progressive tense to express past description: AUX-**be**[PAST] + LV-**ing.**

---

[1] For a different but thorough and clear presentation of the Spanish imperfect and preterite contrast see William E. Bull's *Spanish for Teachers: Applied Linguistics.*

Caía la lluvia y el viento soplaba.
The rain was falling and the wind was blowing.

Aprendían sus tablas de multiplicación.
They were learning their multiplication tables.

Estudiábamos en México en la Universidad Autónoma.
We were studying in Mexico at the Autonomous University.

Repeated Actions
The Spanish imperfect expresses the repetition of actions in the past. English uses any of the following three structures to show repetition of actions in the past.

(1) MODAL AUX-**used to** + LV

Juan buscaba toda clase de excusas antes, pero ya no.
John used to look for all kinds of excuses before, but not now.

Yo comía de vez en cuando en ese lugar.
I used to eat occasionally in that place.

Demitrio trabajaba con el gobierno.
Demitrius used to work for the government.

(2) MODAL AUX-**would** + LV[2]

Ella jugaba con sus compañeras todas las tardes.
She would play with her playmates every afternoon.

Yo de niño comía demasiado, y me enfermaba.
As a child I would eat too much, and I would get sick.

Él asistía a las actividades solo para impresionarnos.
He would attend the activities only to impress us.

(3) PRETERITE + ADV[indefinite time] placed initially, medially, or final; eg, **sometimes, once in a while, occasionally, always, now and then, never**, etc.

Yo nunca llegaba a tiempo.
I never arrived on time.

A veces yo traía una hora de retraso.
Sometimes I was an hour late.

Ella salía temprano de vez en cuando.
She left early once in a while.

---

[2] This usage of AUX-**would** must not be confused with its use as the conditional tense of English. When **used to** + LV can be substituted for **would** + LV, **would** functions to show repetition of past actions, not conditionality. For example, **Before, I would exercise more** means **I used to exercise more.** AUX-**would** with conditional force functions in conditional clause sentences such as **I would go if I had the time** (cf Unit 22), or as a future to past time like in **Yesterday, he said he would go with me tomorrow.**

DESCRIPTION OF PRETERITE TENSE
5.3

The Spanish preterite verb form expresses a completed past event, state, or condition viewed at the moment of speaking as over and done with in its entirety. It covers all aspects but the middle part of the description, that is, either the beginning or the end. The preterite indicates that an event was initiated or culminated at a specific, recalled point, or that an event simply happened at a point in the past, or that an event continued during a certain past time period but that now it has ended. The meaning of the preterite covers a broader expanse than that of the imperfect; consequently, it is used more frequently.

The Spanish preterite is generally rendered in English by the simple past tense.

Ella pensó que no venías [imperfect].
She thought that you weren't coming.

Era temprano cuando entré a la tienda.
It was early when I entered the store.

Salieron de la función a las seis.
They came out of the performance at six (o'clock).

Exercise 1

Translate the following sentences into the other language, always being mindful of the contexts in which the sentences might occur. In your choice of tenses, follow the general guidelines just presented. Use either preterite or imperfect for the Spanish and their equivalents for the English.

1. I was waiting for you until they closed the building.
2. Según su costumbre, apenas ella salía de casa.
3. We weren't watching the road when a truck crossed in front of us.
4. Unos comían mientras otros esperaban para comer.
5. It never snowed, but it was always very cold.
6. Ángela cantaba antes en ese club nocturno.
7. When we were younger, my brother would tease me a lot.
8. No hacían nada cuando los vi.
9. More people used to travel by train than by airplane before.
10. Llegué a clase a las ocho; ya estaban allí los otros.

TWO PERSPECTIVES OF SIMPLE PAST TENSE USAGES IN SPANISH
5.4

The two simple past tenses of Spanish are contrasted here according to their most common usages. We give an extended explanation of the contrasting conditions under which each of the tenses are to be used, followed by illustrative sentences. Close examination of these examples will be beneficial to the non-Spanish speaker in deciding which tense most appropriately describes the aspectual situation being expressed.

Contrast 1

IMPERFECT	PRETERITE
The imperfect expresses a repeated or continued past activity upon which no limitation of time is imposed.	The preterite, in contrast, expresses a repeated or ongoing past activity which came to a end at a specific point prior to the moment of speaking.
Íbamos a la playa a menudo.	Fuimos a la playa a menudo el año pasado.
We used to go to the beach frequently.	We went to the beach frequently last year.
Visitábamos de vez en cuando ese lugar.	Visitamos de vez en cuando ese lugar hasta que encontramos otro mejor.
We would occasionally visit that place.	We visited that place once in a while until we found a better one.

Contrast 2

The imperfect describes an action, state, or situation in the past as a continuum in time without reference either to the beginning or the end. Neither is there any reference made to the outcome or the resolution of that action, state, or condition.	The preterite expresses the resolution, outcome, end, or result of an action, state, or situation in the past. It may express also the beginning of a state of mind or a state of affairs of the individual involved—both transpiring prior to the moment of speaking.
Teníamos que llegar a tiempo.	Tuvimos que llegar a tiempo.
We had to (felt obliged to) arrive on time.	We had to arrive on time. (not only had to but did)
Había un concurso de belleza.	Hubo un concurso de belleza.
There was (scheduled to be) a beauty contest.	There was a beauty contest. (It was scheduled and took place.)

Contrast 3

The imperfect tense is used in describing a scene in the past.	The preterite, on the other hand, is used to narrate actions that occurred in the past.
Llovía a cántaros y yo andaba sin paraguas.	Llovió, salió el sol y me fui a andar.
It was raining cats and dogs, and I was without an umbrella.	It rained, the sun came out, and I went for a walk.
Mientras ellos dormían yo leía.	Colón descubrió América en 1492 y regresó en 1493, en 1498 y en 1502.
While they were sleeping, I was reading.	Columbus discovered America in 1492 and returned in 1493, 1498, and 1502.

Contrast 4

The imperfect implies that mentally the speaker is back in the past reliving the experiences for the benefit of the listener.

The preterite refers to the past simply from a more detached viewpoint as this relates to the moment of speaking. When speakers use the preterite they avoid going into descriptive detail. There is no attempt to relive the past.

Estaba en El Salvador el mes pasado, y ...
I was in El Salvador last month, and ... (prepare yourself for a reliving of what happened)

Estuve en El Salvador el mes pasado ...

I was in El Salvador last month ... (and that is probably all you are going to hear about it. You asked where I was, and I told you.)

5.5
Imperfect Progressive versus Preterite Progressive

The Spanish imperfect progressive tense describes a continuing, progressing past activity on which no time limit has been imposed. It is a substitute for the simple imperfect indicative tense. It is used simply to intensify the notion of durative action or action in progress in past time since an imperfect verbal form already conveys the durative aspect. To express the same ongoing event in the past, English uses the past progressive tense.

> Estábamos tomando (tomábamos) café en aquel restaurante.
> We were having coffee in that restaurant over there.
> No más que estaba viajando yo (viajaba yo) por México.
> I was only traveling through Mexico.

When we wish to express a continuing, progressing past action which ended at a specific point in the past, the preterite progressive is used. The English preterite progressive does not imply, in contrast to the Spanish, the termination of an action. Since Spanish preterite progressive denotes perfectivity and English denotes only progression, the two tenses cannot be used as equivalents in structures. Spanish preterite progressive must be expressed in English as the past perfect progressive or the simple preterite.

Both the preterite progressive and the imperfect progressive tenses of Spanish depend strongly on the inherent semantic qualities of the verb that is being considered for use. Gili Gaya gives this example of an ungrammatical usage: ***El soldado estuvo disparando un tiro** (§97).

> Estuvimos tomando café hasta que cerraron el restaurante.
> We had been drinking coffee until they closed the restaurant.
> We drank coffee until they closed the restaurant.
> We were drinking coffee until they closed the restaurant.

> Estuve viajando por Argentina hasta que tuve el accidente.
> I had been traveling through Argentina until I had the accident.
> I traveled through Argentina until I had the accident.
> I was traveling through Argentina until I had the accident.

IMPLIED SEMANTIC DIFFERENCES BETWEEN THE TENSES
5.6

There are a limited number of verbs, which, because of their particular semantic qualities vis-à-vis differences in Spanish-oriented and English-oriented cultures, cannot be translated literally from one language to the other by following the equivalencies outlined in the previous sections. Reality, as interpreted through different logic and different frames of reference in Spanish and English, is seen to vary considerably when these particular verbs are placed in a durative imperfect time frame or an initiative or terminal preterite time frame. Often—in order to express equivalent conditions of knowledge, perception, and being—a different verb from the Spanish lexical verb must be used in English.

The classic example of this semantic difference is found in the verb **saber: Supe la respuesta ayer** 'I *learned* the answer yesterday,' and **Sabía la respuesta todo el tiempo** 'I *knew* the answer all along.'

IMPERFECT	PRETERITE
Imperfect tense describes the middle of a continuing physical state, a state of affairs, or a state of mind that has already begun and is in effect.	The preterite tense emphasizes the beginning of a state of being or the end, outcome, or resolution of that state. It tells more about the past than does the imperfect.
conocía = I knew or was acquainted with someone.	conocí = I met, got to know, or became acquainted with someone.
costaba = It was priced at …	costó = It was bought for …
creía = I thought, was under the impression.	creí = I believed, got the impression.
me gustaba = I liked it.	me gustó = It pleased me (right then).
quería = I wanted to, was willing to.	quise = I tried to. no quise = I refused.
podía = I was able (latent ability and potentiality, unculminated).	pude = I could (ability put to test and fulfilled). no pude = I tried but failed.
sabía = I knew, had the knowledge.	supe = I learned, found out.
tenía la noticia = I had the news (already).	tuve la noticia = I received the news.

Exercise 2

The following sentences are to be translated into the other language. Keep ever in mind the possible contexts in which each sentence might occur as you use the imperfect and preterite tenses in Spanish or their equivalents in English.

1. Last night we went to the theater.
2. Había muchas personas inocentes que no sabían el peligro que corrían.
3. She studied for the exam until at least ten o'clock.
4. Se me acercaron, me saludaron y se fueron sin decir nada más.
5. I never knew (found out) her name.

6. La joven quería comprar la cadena, pero no lo hizo, pues costaba mucho.
7. It was raining and no one was walking along the streets.
8. Tuve que trabajar todo el día para obtener beneficios.
9. My brother knew them well; he met them in Bogotá.
10. Isabel tuvo mucho miedo al ver los veinticinco animales sueltos.
11. I wasn't wearing a shirt, and later it got cold.
12. Guillermo tenía náuseas y no quiso comer nada.
13. I couldn't hear you because there was lots of noise.
14. Hubo una huelga en la compañía porque el administrador no quiso pagarle a nadie lo suficiente.

Exercise 3 (Optional)

From your readings or experiences, cite other verbal examples like those listed above where Spanish and English semantic ranges differ.

(Exercise 4)

Rewrite the following paragraphs changing the present tense verbs, when appropriate, to either the imperfect or the preterite, whichever would be applicable according to the context.

A. Por la mañana, a mediodía y al ocaso, resuenan leves pisadas en las estancias del piso bajo. Hablan un hidalgo y un mozuelo. El hidalgo se halla sentado en un pozo del patio; el mozuelo, frente a él, va comiendo unos mendrugos de pan que ha sacado del seno. Tanta es la avidez con que el rapaz yanta, que el hidalgo sonríe y le pregunta si tan sabroso, tan exquisito es el pan que come. Asegura el muchacho que de veras tales mendrugos son excelentes, y entonces el hidalgo, sonriendo como por broma—mientras hay una inenarrable amargura allá en lo más íntimo de su ser—le toma un mendrugo al muchachito y comienza a comer. (Excerpt from "Lo Fatal" in *Castilla* by Azorín [José Martínez Ruíz]).

B. Cuando Colón llega al nuevo mundo, cambia el nombre que tienen los indígenas y les da otro nombre. Colón cree que va a llegar a la India, pero no es así. Cuando llega, Colón observa que los indios viven en pequeños pueblos y que son muy pobres. La tierra, sin embargo, es muy hermosa, pero no tiene las riquezas que los españoles quieren encontrar. Colón no está nada satisfecho, pero como tiene que escribir a sus benefactores, los Reyes Católicos, decide exagerar bastante, pues sabe que los reyes nunca van a ver esas tierras. Aunque está cansado después de su viaje por el Atlántico, sale de las islas para continuar sus expediciones en busca de oro.

Exercise 5

Translate the following narrative excerpt into Spanish, attempting to interpret the verbal forms correctly in the imperfect or the preterite tenses. Be prepared to explain in any particular case why you chose either tense.

The room in which I found myself was very large. The windows were long and narrow, and at so vast a distance from the floor as to be altogether inaccessible from within. Feeble gleams of light made their way through the panes, and served to render sufficiently distinct the more prominent objects around; the eye struggled in vain to reach the remoter angles of the chamber, or the recesses of the vaulted ceiling. Dark draperies hung upon the walls. The general furniture was profuse, antique, and tattered. Many books and musical instruments lay scattered about, but failed to give any vitality to the scene. I felt that I breathed an atmosphere of sorrow. An air of deep and irredeemable gloom hung over all.

Upon my entrance, Usher arose from a sofa on which he had been lying, and greeted me with warmth which had much in it, I thought at first, of an overdone cordiality. A glance, however, at his countenance, convinced me of his sincerity. We sat down; and for some moments, while he spoke not, I gazed upon him with a feeling half of pity, half of awe. It was with difficulty that I could bring myself to admit the identity of the being before me with the companion of my early boyhood. (Adapted from *The Fall of the House of Usher* by Edgar Allan Poe.)

6

Basic Sentence Structure in English and Spanish

6.1
English and Spanish predications each have three families of tenses—the present tense, the past tense, and the future/conditional tense. Four basic tenses are found in each of these three time families. These four tenses are illustrated as follows:

	PRESENT	PAST
SIMPLE	He teaches here. Él enseña aquí.	He taught here. Él enseñaba aquí. Él enseñó aquí.
PROGRESSIVE	He is teaching here. Él está enseñando aquí.	He was teaching here. Él estaba enseñando aquí. Él estuvo enseñando aquí.
PERFECT	He has taught here. Él ha enseñado aquí.	He had taught here … Él había enseñado aquí …
PERFECT PROGRESSIVE	He has been teaching here. Él ha estado enseñando aquí.	He had been teaching here … Él había estado enseñando aquí…

	FUTURE/CONDITIONAL
SIMPLE	He will/would teach here … Él enseñará/enseñaría aquí …
PROGRESSIVE	He will/would be teaching here … Él estará/estaría enseñando aquí …
PERFECT	He will/would have taught here for twenty years in May. En mayo, él habrá/habría enseñado aquí por veinte años.
PERFECT PROGRESSIVE	In May, he will/would have been teaching here for twenty years. En mayo, él habrá/habría estado enseñando aquí por veinte años.

6.2
Each of the English and Spanish tenses listed above occur in basic sentences which may be of five different structural types. We list these five possible structural types below. Only the simple present tense of both languages is used in the examples.

AFFIRMATIVE STATEMENT	John wants an interview. Juan desea una entrevista.
NEGATIVE STATEMENT	John doesn't want an interview. Juan no desea una entrevista.
AFFIRM. YES/NO QUESTION	Does John want an interview? ¿Desea Juan una entrevista?
NEGATIVE YES/NO QUESTION	Doesn't John want an interview? ¿No desea Juan una entrevista?
CONTENT QUESTION	What does John want? ¿Qué desea Juan?

6.3
The verbal constituents of the three English and Spanish tense families are outlined below. For each tense both English and Spanish sentence examples are given for affirmative and negative statements, affirmative and negative Yes/No questions, and content questions. A brief discussion then follows each set. Different main verbs are used in each set of examples.

The Present Tense Family

SIMPLE PRESENT

He appeals to honor.	Él acude al honor.
He doesn't appeal to honor.	Él no acude al honor.
Does he appeal to honor?	¿Acude él al honor?
Doesn't he appeal to honor?	¿No acude él al honor?
What does he appeal to?	¿A qué acude él?

ENGLISH: The lexical verb (LV) is inflected (two forms) in the affirmative structure only. In all the other structures, the AUX-**do** [inflected] must be introduced, followed by the base form of the LV. The interrogative structures have subject/AUX inversion.

SPANISH: The lexical verb (LV) is consistently inflected in all six forms (1st, 2nd, 3rd pers., sgl. and pl.). The interrogative structures have subject/verb inversion where there is an expressed subject. No auxiliaries occur.

PRESENT PROGRESSIVE

Sarah is writing a book.	Sara está escribiendo un libro.
Sarah isn't writing a book.	Sara no está escribiendo un libro.
Is Sarah writing a book?	¿Está escribiendo Sara un libro?
Isn't Sarah writing a book?	¿No está escribiendo Sara un libro?
What is Sarah writing?	¿Qué está escribiendo Sara?

ENGLISH: The LV is in **-ing** form. The inflected AUX-**be** must be used. The interrogative structures have subject/AUX-**be** inversion.

SPANISH: The LV is in **-ndo** form. Inflected AUX-**estar** is used. The interrogative structures have subject/VP inversion where there is an expressed subject. VP is interpreted here as meaning "verb phrase, consisting of the main verbal unit conjugated in any of its simple or compound tenses."

PRESENT (PRETERITE) PERFECT[1]

Robert has expressed his doubts.	Roberto ha expresado sus dudas.
Robert hasn't expressed his doubts.	Roberto no ha expresado sus dudas.
Has Robert expressed his doubts?	¿Ha expresado Roberto sus dudas?
Hasn't Robert expressed his doubts?	¿No ha expresado Roberto sus dudas?
What has Robert expressed?	¿Qué ha expresado Roberto?

ENGLISH: The LV is in the past participle form. The inflected AUX is **have**. The interrogative structures have subject/AUX-**have** inversion.

SPANISH: The LV is in the participle form. The AUX is **haber** [inflected]. The interrogative structures have subject/VP inversion where there is an expressed subject.

PRESENT (PRETERITE) PERFECT PROGRESSIVE[2]

She has been spending a lot.	Ella ha estado gastando mucho.
She hasn't been spending a lot.	Ella no ha estado gastando mucho.
Has she been spending a lot?	¿Ha estado gastando ella mucho?
Hasn't she been spending a lot?	¿No ha estado gastando ella mucho?
How much has she been spending?	¿Cuánto ha estado gastando ella?

ENGLISH: The lexical verb is in **-ing** form. Two auxiliaries occur; the first, **have**, is inflected, and the second, **be**, is in the past participle form. The interrogative structures have subject/AUX-**have** inversion.

SPANISH: Two auxiliaries occur; the first, **haber**, is inflected, and the second, **estar**, is in the participle form. The LV is in the **-ndo** form. The interrogative structures have subject/VP inversion where there is an expressed subject.

6.4
The Past Tense Family

SIMPLE PAST

Frank justified his actions.	Paco justificaba/justificó sus acciones.

---

[1] The Spanish examples are termed "preterite perfect." (See Unit 4.)

[2] The Spanish examples are termed "preterite perfect progressive." (See Unit 4.)

Frank didn't justify his actions.	Paco no justificaba/justificó sus acciones.
Did Frank justify his actions?	¿Justificaba/Justificó Paco sus acciones?
Didn't Frank justify his actions?	¿No justificaba/justificó Paco sus acciones?
What did Frank justify?	¿Qué justificaba/justificó Paco?

ENGLISH: The verb (LV) is in the preterite in the affirmative structure only. In all other structures, AUX-**do** [preterite] is used with the LV in base form. The interrogative structures have subject/AUX-**do** inversion.

SPANISH: Since in Spanish the simple past may be expressed by either the *pretérito imperfecto* or the *pretérito indefinido*, the verb may be in either tense. No auxiliaries occur. The interrogative structures have subject/VP inversion where there is an expressed subject.

PAST PROGRESSIVE

Anna was visiting her sister.	Ana estaba/estuvo visitando a su hermana.
Anna wasn't visiting her sister.	Ana no estaba/estuvo visitando a su hermana.
Was Anna visiting her sister?	¿Estaba/Estuvo visitando Ana a su hermana?
Wasn't Anna visiting her sister?	¿No estaba/estuvo visitando Ana a su hermana?
Who(m) was Anna visiting?	¿A quién estaba/estuvo visitando Ana?

ENGLISH: The main verb (LV) is in **-ing** form. The AUX is **be** [inflected]. The interrogative structures have subject/AUX-**be** inversion.

SPANISH: The main verb is in **-ndo** form. The AUX-**estar** is either in the *pretérito imperfecto* or the *pretérito indefinido* form. The interrogative structures have subject/VP inversion where there is an expressed subject.

PAST PERFECT

He had finished in May.	Él había terminado en mayo.
He hadn't finished in May.	Él no había terminado en mayo.
Had he finished in May?	¿Había terminado él en mayo?
Hadn't he finished in May?	¿No había terminado él en mayo?
When had he finished?	¿Cuándo había terminado él?

ENGLISH: The main verb (LV) is in past participle form. The AUX is **have** [preterite]. The interrogative structures have subject/AUX-**have** inversion.

SPANISH: The main verb (LV) is in participle form. The AUX is **haber** [imperfect]. The interrogative structures have subject VP inversion where there is an expressed subject.

PAST PERFECT PROGRESSIVE

Helen had been showing her works.	Elena había estado exhibiendo sus obras.
Helen hadn't been showing her works.	Elena no había estado exhibiendo sus obras.
Had Helen been showing her works?	¿Había estado exhibiendo Elena sus obras?
Hadn't Helen been showing her works?	¿No había estado exhibiendo Elena sus obras?
What had Helen been showing?	¿Qué había estado exhibiendo Elena?

ENGLISH: The main verb (LV) is in **-ing** form. Two auxiliaries occur: the first, **have** [preterite], and the second, **be** [past participle]. The interrogative structures have subject/AUX-**have** inversion.

SPANISH: The main verb is in **-ndo** form. Two auxiliaries occur: the first, **haber** [imperfect], and the second, **estar** [participle]. The interrogative structures have subject/VP inversion where there is an expressed subject.

6.5
The Future/Conditional Family

SIMPLE FUTURE/CONDITIONAL

He will/would render an opinion.	Él rendirá/rendiría una opinión.
He won't/wouldn't render an opinion.	Él no rendirá/rendiría una opinión.
Will/Would he render an opinion?	¿Rendirá/Rendiría él una opinión?
Won't/Wouldn't he render an opinion?	¿No rendirá/rendiría él una opinión?
What will/would he render?	¿Qué rendirá/rendiría él?

ENGLISH: The main verb (LV) is in the base form. The AUX-**will** or **would** must be used. The interrogative structures have inversion of the subject/AUX-**will/would**.

SPANISH: The lexical verb is in either the future or conditional tense. No auxiliaries occur. The interrogative structures have subject/verb inversion where there is an expressed subject.

PROGRESSIVE FUTURE/CONDITIONAL

She will/would be distributing presents.	Ella estará/estaría repartiendo regalos.
She won't/wouldn't be distributing presents.	Ella no estará/estaría repartiendo regalos.
Will/Would she be distributing presents?	¿Estará/Estaría repartiendo ella regalos?
Won't/Wouldn't she be distributing presents?	¿No estará/estaría repartiendo ella regalos?
What will/would she be distributing?	¿Qué estará/estaría repartiendo ella?

ENGLISH: The main verb is in **-ing** form. Two auxiliaries are used: the first, **will/would**, and the second, **be** [base form]. The interrogative structures have subject/AUX-**will/would** inversion.

SPANISH: The main verb is in **-ndo** form. **Estar** [future or conditional] is the only auxiliary used. The interrogative structures have subject/VP inversion where there is an expressed subject.

PERFECT FUTURE/CONDITIONAL

Alice will/would have finished on time.	Alicia habrá/habría terminado a tiempo.
Alice won't/wouldn't have finished on time.	Alicia no habrá/habría terminado a tiempo.
Will/Would Alice have finished on time?	¿Habrá/Habría terminado Alicia a tiempo?
Won't/Wouldn't Alice have finished on time?	¿No habrá/habría terminado Alicia a tiempo?
When will/would Alice have finished?	¿Cuándo habrá/habría terminado Alicia?

ENGLISH: The main verb is in past participle form. Two auxiliaries occur; the first is **will/would** and the second is **have** [base form]. The interrogative structures have subject/AUX-**will/would** inversion.

SPANISH: The main verb is in participle form. **Haber** [future or conditional] is the only auxiliary used. The interrogative structures have subject/VP inversion where there is an expressed subject.

PERFECT PROGRESSIVE FUTURE/CONDITIONAL

He will/would have been washing the car.	Él habrá/habría estado lavando el auto.
He won't/wouldn't have been washing the car.	Él no habrá/habría estado lavando el auto.
Will/Would he have been washing the car?	¿Habrá/Habría estado él lavando el auto?
Won't/Wouldn't he have been washing the car?	¿No habrá/habría estado él lavando el auto?
What will/would he have been washing?	¿Qué habrá/habría estado él lavando?

Note: This type of structure is not frequently used in everyday speech.

ENGLISH: The main verb is in **-ing** form. Three auxiliaries occur: the first, **will/would**, the second, **have** [base form], and the third, **be** [past participle]. The interrogative structures have subject/AUX-**will/would** inversion.

SPANISH: The main verb is in **-ndo** form. Two auxiliaries are used, the first being **haber** [future or conditional] and the second, **estar** [participle]. The interrogative structures have subject/VP inversion where there is an expressed subject.

Exercise 1

Examine the following English and Spanish sentences. For each, determine the structural type (affirmative or negative statement, affirmative or negative question, or content question) and the tense of the verb units. Then translate each sentence into the other language and determine the nature of all the verbal constituents.

1. Mis padres no vieron esa película.
2. When did he ask you for the money?
3. ¿No habías estado recorriendo la biblioteca?
4. Don't they need help with their work?
5. Almorzaremos hoy en un lugar cercano.
6. What are they doing right now?
7. ¿Estarán aprendiendo Uds. algún idioma extranjero?
8. We hadn't used very much gasoline.
9. ¿No lo estuvieron ayudando ellos ayer hasta muy tarde?
10. Have you been waiting for the bus? (familiar)

Exercise 2

Write original English (EN) or Spanish (SP) sentences of the structural types and in the tenses called for. Be able to account for the nature of every lexical and auxiliary verb in all the sentences.

1. EN affirmative statement, present progressive.
2. SP negative statement, preterite.
3. EN affirmative yes-no question, present perfect progressive.
4. SP content question, past progressive.
5. EN content question, present.
6. SP affirmative statement, future perfect.
7. EN negative yes-no question, present perfect.
8. SP negative yes-no question, future perfect progressive.
9. EN negative statement, past progressive.
10. SP affirmative yes-no question, past perfect progressive.

BASIC SENTENCE TYPES AND THEIR STRUCTURAL FORMULAS
6.6

Below is a listing of the structural formulas for the five basic sentence types of English and Spanish. A detailed description, several examples, and a contrastive analysis of each formula and sentence type then follows. Each formula accounts only for the subject, question elements (whether as words or as intonation), negative elements, auxiliaries, and lexical verbs.

The structural symbols used are these:

LEGEND

AUX = auxiliary verb.
INTERROG = interrogative word or phrase.
LV = lexical verb (main verb in base form).
(S) = exclusively optional subject.

VP = verb phrase, consisting of the main verbal unit conjugated in any of its simple or compound tenses.

VR = verbal remainder, that is, the portion of the verbal unit remaining intact after auxiliary has been separated from it by some non-verbal element. The VR is italicized in the following examples: **What has he *been doing*? Where will she *be going*? They don't *know* him.**

↑ = rising terminal intonation when spoken.

↓ = falling terminal intonation when spoken.

* = indicates that a contraction between AUX and **not** is optional.

** = indicates that a contraction between AUX and **not** is mandatory.

SENTENCE TYPE	ENGLISH STRUCTURE	SPANISH STRUCTURE
Affirmative Statement	S + VP ↓	(S) + VP + (S) ↓
Negative Statement	S + AUX* + **not** + VR ↓	(S) + **no** + VP + (S) ↓
Affirmative Yes-No Question	AUX + S + VR ↑	(S) + VP + (S) ↑
Negative Yes-No Question	AUX** + **not** + S + VR ↑	(S) + **no** + VP + (S) ↑
Content Question	INTERROG+AUX+S+VR ↓	INTERROG+VP+(S) ↓

6.7
The Affirmative Statement

ENGLISH: S + VP ↓
   a. The subject must be expressed either as a noun, a pronoun, or an equivalent form.
   b. The entire verb phrase unit follows the subject.
   c. Examples:
      She lives here.
      My boss likes his new car.
      They would have done anything for you.
      We have been working very hard.

SPANISH: (S) + VP + (S) ↓
   a. The subject may be optionally expressed depending on circumstances.
   b. If stated, the subject may either precede or follow the entire verb phrase, never in both positions.
   c. As in English, the verb phrase is kept intact.
   d. Examples:
      Mi padre trabaja. (Subject expressed and stated first.)
      Han estado corriendo. (No subject expressed.)
      Había llegado una señora. (Subject expressed last.)

CONTRASTIVE ANALYSIS:
   a. The affirmative structures of English and Spanish are virtually the same, except that,
   b. In English the subject must be expressed and precedes the verb phrase.
   c. In Spanish the subject is frequently optional, but if stated, it may either precede or follow the verb phrase.

6.8
The Negative Structure

ENGLISH: S + AUX* + **not** + VR ↓
    a. The subject in English must be expressed.
    b. An auxiliary follows the subject. It may be **do, have, be, will, would,** or a modal auxiliary plus **not.**
    c. An optional contraction occurs between the auxiliary (AUX*) and **not.**
    d. The verbal remainder (VR) is stated last. It is composed of whatever is left of the verbal unit after the AUX has been separated from it.
    e. Examples:
        You have not read the newspaper as yet.
        My brother isn't going to Colombia next summer.
        They didn't understand your questions.
        My students would not be studying this late.

Note: The indication that a contraction between AUX and **not** may or may not occur is a bit misleading. Usually there is a choice, as in **will not = won't, does not = doesn't, are not = aren't,** etc. There are cases, however, in which contractions are not possible. These cases generally involve the modal auxiliaries. For example, usually no contraction will occur between **may** or **might** and **not. Shall + not** can be rendered as **shan't**, but the form may seem somewhat archaic.

SPANISH: (S) + **no** + VP + (S) ↓
    a. As always in Spanish, the subject is frequently optional and may precede or follow the verb phrase.
    b. Negation is accomplished by placing **no** before the entire VP.
    c. The verb phrase (VP) is kept intact, regardless of the number of elements of which it is composed.
    d. Examples:
        El autor no ha escrito nada esta semana.
        No ha estado resultando fácil la tarea.
        Los jóvenes no están aquí en este momento.

CONTRASTIVE ANALYSIS
    a. The English and Spanish negative structures are at great variance one with the other.
    b. The English subject is mandatory and occurs first, while the Spanish subject frequently may be optional and, when expressed, can either precede or follow the verb phrase.
    c. English breaks up its verbal unit, removing from it the first auxiliary. A contraction may or may not be made between this auxiliary and **not** (See **Legend** and **Note** above).
    d. Spanish, as always, keeps the verb phrase intact, allowing nothing to intervene between or among its elements.

6.9
The Affirmative Yes-No Question Structure

ENGLISH: AUX + S + VR ↑
    a. An auxiliary is stated first, followed by the mandatory subject and then the verbal remainder.
    b. Characteristic of this type of sentence when rendered orally is a terminal-

ly rising intonation (↑). In the written idiom, a question mark (?) must be used.

    c. Examples:

        Have you been eating too much?
        Did your parents see the movie?
        Are the Russians planning a new system?
        May I have a little more wine, please?

SPANISH: (S) + VP + (S) ↑

    a. The Spanish affirmative yes-no structure is virtually identical to the Spanish affirmative statement structure.

    b. There is, however, a terminally rising oral intonation, and in writing, the double question marks (¿?) must be used.

    c. Almost always the subject, if stated at all, occurs after the verb phrase in Spanish yes-no questions, but it may occur before as well.

    d. Examples:

        ¿Ha estado manteniendo él a sus padres?
        ¿Estás peinándote?
        ¿Su hijo tiene novia?

CONTRASTIVE ANALYSIS

    a. The Spanish and English structures are quite different.

    b. English states the first auxiliary in initial position, follows it with the mandatory subject and then states the verbal remainder.

    c. Spanish uses the same structure it employs for affirmative statements, but the subject tends to be stated after the verb phrase.

    d. English and Spanish affirmative yes-no question structures, however, are similar in that terminal rising oral intonation accompanies them both.

6.10
The Negative Yes-No Question Structure

ENGLISH: AUX** + **not** + S + VR ↑

    a. A mandatory contraction occurs between the first auxiliary AUX** (always prepositioned) and **not**.[3]

    b. Following this contraction appears the mandatory subject, which, in turn, is followed by the verbal remainder (VR).

    c. Rising terminal intonation characterizes this type of question when it is rendered orally. In written English, a question mark (?) must be used.

---

[3] In modern spoken English there are some dialectal variations upon the negative yes-no question structure. The English of the British Commonwealth nations tends to prefer the structure: AUX + S + **not** + VR. Examples: **Are you not seeing him regularly? Have your friends not seen the Queen? Will you not try a little harder?** It should be noted, furthermore, that modern American English has a peculiar way of rendering the negative yes-no structure when the subject is the 1st person singular pronoun "I" in conjunction with the verb **be.** In the affirmative structure, ***I are** is clearly ungrammatical, but in the negative yes-no structure **Aren't I?** is absolutely acceptable. British English, following its own negative yes-no structural formula, prefers **Am I not?**

d. Examples:
>Didn't you visit your friends in Peru?
>Can't your friend find his car?
>Won't he have been complaining excessively by then?
>Weren't your problems causing you trouble?

SPANISH: (S) + **no** + VP + (S) ↑
a. The Spanish negative yes-no question structure is almost identical to the Spanish negative statement structure.
b. The subject, if stated, usually occurs after the verb phrase as is the general case with Spanish questions, but the option of its occurring before the verb phrase still remains; **no** precedes the verb phrase for negation purposes.
c. When stated orally, rising terminal intonation occurs. In writing, (¿?) must be used.
d. Examples:
>¿No se está preocupando mucho tu abuela?
>¿No vienes mañana?
>¿Su hija no ha llegado esta mañana?

CONTRASTIVE ANALYSIS
a. The English and Spanish negative yes-no question structures differ considerably.
b. In English, the 1st AUX is stated first, and a contraction is required between it and **not.** The mandatory subject and the verbal remainder (VR) then follow.
c. In Spanish, the verb phrase is kept intact, **no** precedes it for the purposes of negation, and the subject, if stated at all, usually occurs after the VP. However, the speaker may opt to state the subject before the VP as well.
d. The structures are similar, nevertheless, in their requirement of a terminally rising oral intonation.

6.11
The Content Question Structure

ENGLISH: INTERROG + AUX + S + VR ↓
a. The INTERROG (interrogative element) is stated first.
b. Then appears the 1st auxiliary in the sentence.
c. Third in the structure is the mandatory subject, expressed either as a noun, a pronoun, or an equivalent form.
d. Finally comes the verbal remainder.
e. Although the content question, when written, requires a question mark in English, the terminal oral intonation for such questions is falling rather than rising.
f. Examples:
>Where have you been studying?
>What time will your friends arrive?
>How much did they spend?
>What can you see?

SPANISH: INTERROG + VP + (S) ↓
   a. As in English, the interrogative element is stated first.
   b. Then comes the entire VP, nothing appearing between or among its elements.
   c. The subject is optional; if stated, it must occur after the VP.
   d. The written language requires (¿?), but in oral renditions, as in English, falling rather than rising intonation is heard.
   e. Examples:
        ¿Adónde van tus amigos?
        ¿A qué hora vienes?
        ¿Con quién has estado comentando el asunto?
        ¿Qué han resuelto los senadores?

CONTRASTIVE ANALYSIS
   a. The English and Spanish content question structures show numerous differences.
   b. Both languages state the interrogative element first, but in Spanish, the following verb phrase is integrated, while in English, an auxiliary must be separated from it by the intervening subject.
   c. The English subject is mandatory; in Spanish it is optional and stated after the VP.
   d. Content questions have falling oral intonation in both languages.

Exercise 3

For each of the following English and Spanish sentences, (a) name the tense used, (b) cite the basic sentence type represented (affirmative or negative statement, affirmative or negative yes-no question, or content question), and (c) write the structural formula for each sentence, accounting for only the S, AUX, negative element, interrogative element, verbal unit, and terminal intonation.

   1. ¿A qué has estado aspirando en tus esfuerzos?
   2. They didn't tell their story to anyone.
   3. ¿No tiene esa ley un propósito muy importante?
   4. Will your parents be giving a lot of parties?
   5. Los jóvenes de esta generación no están haciendo nada de importancia.
   6. This summer hasn't been as hot as the one before.
   7. Muchos viajeros visitan las ruinas antiguas.
   8. When would you have told them the truth?
   9 ¿Saben tus amistades tu número de teléfono?
   10. Didn't you do all the assigned exercises?

Exercise 4

Examine the following list of structural formulas, each marked EN for English and SP for Spanish. Determine the basic sentence type represented—affirmative or negative statement, affirmative or negative yes-no question, or content question. **(Optional)** Write an original sentence in the language indicated which fits the specifications of the structural formula. Use any subject and any tense.

1. EN: INTERROG + AUX + S + VR ↓
2. SP: (S) + VP + (S) ↑
3. EN: S + AUX* + **not** + VR ↓
4. SP: (S) + VP + (S) ↓
5. EN: AUX** + **not** + S + VR ↑
6. SP: INTERROG + VP + (S) ↓
7. EN: AUX + S + VR ↑
8. SP: (S) + **no** + VP + (S) ↓
9. EN: S + VP ↓
10. SP: (S) + **no** + VP + (S)↑

Exercise 5

All of the following sentences are ungrammatical in the strictest sense of the word even though some of the examples can be heard in everyday speech. (An asterisk preceding a word, a phrase, or a clause denotes that it is an unacceptable form.) Each sentence has been formulated by speakers of the opposite language who have carried over into the new language structures from their native language. State the nature of the error based upon the structure of the speaker's language and correct the error in each case.

1. *Mis padres han no estado pagando impuestos.
2. *I not will work here anymore.
3. *¿Están los alumnos estudiando francés?
4. *Have worked you here before?
5. *¿Había no usted conocido antes a esa chamaca?
6. *Your brother no will be helping us.
7. *¿Con quién estaba el profesor hablando?
8. *What would have done Poland about that?

(Exercise 6)

Examine the following English and Spanish sentences. For each determine the tense and the structural type and write the structural formula. In writing the formulas, you need account only for S, negative element, INTERROG, AUX, VP or VR, and terminal intonation.

1. John was here yesterday.
2. ¿No habían calculado los daños por causa de la marea alta?
3. Had your father seen a doctor?
4. ¿Estás leyendo (tú) algo de interés?
5. Won't you have been living there by then?
6. La criatura habrá cumplido un año para el verano.
7. Would you give him that much money?
8. El gobierno no había estado realizando cabalmente sus obligaciones.
9. Where have you been living during the past few months?
10. ¿Cuánto dinero habían gastado tus amigos en Chile?

11. Has your mother met my friends?
12. ¿Iba tu abogado a corte con frecuencia?
13. What language had they been speaking in the restaurant?
14. Un señor estaba dándole instrucciones a mi mujer.
15. The secretary didn't know my name.

16. ¿A dónde han ido todos los guardias?
17. Hadn't your brother seen any of them before?
18. ¿Qué novela estabas leyendo (tú) en días pasados?
19. She hadn't been doing any work at all at school.
20. ¿No vendieron nada las muchachas en la feria?

Exercise 7 (Optional)

Determine the tense and structural type of each of the following English and Spanish sentences. Write the structural formula for each. Then translate each sentence into the other language and again write the structural formula. In the formulas you need account only for S, AUX, negative element, interrogative element, VP, or VR, and terminal intonation. Finally, compare and contrast the original sentence with its translated version and be able to state in general terms the nature of the structural contrasts you encounter.

1. They saw a movie this afternoon.
2. ¿A dónde trasladan los policías a esos ladrones?
3. Aren't you working in the library?
4. Los sabios no habían discutido el fenómeno.
5. Do the students bring their books every day?
6. Los turistas no han visto la catedral.
7. He will have gone home between nine or ten o'clock.
8. ¿No considerarías algo así para mí?
9. At what time were you watching TV last night?
10. ¿Estuvieron saliendo trenes de la estación continuamente?
11. My boss hadn't seen his secretary that day.
12. ¿Con quién jugarás la próxima temporada?

ALTERNATE STRUCTURES
6.12
As noted earlier, the AUX-**do** [present/preterite] is mandatory in all structures except the affirmative in rendering simple present and past tenses in English. English has an emphatic structure, however, in which this auxiliary is employed also in the affirmative structure.

Alternate Emphatic English Structures
In both the simple present and simple past affirmative tenses, English can employ the AUX-**do** in alternate structures to denote emphasis. Compare, for example, the sentences on the left, which are non-emphatic and do not use AUX-**do**, with those on the right, which are emphatic and do use AUX-**do**.

NON-EMPHATIC AFFIRMATIVE	EMPHATIC AFFIRMATIVE
He wants a car.	He *does* want a car.
They needed some money.	They *did* need some money.
She likes your house.	She *does* like your house.
We came here last night.	We *did* come here last night.

English can make its negative statement structures in the simple present and past emphatic too. This is done simply by avoiding the contraction which may occur between AUX-**do** and NEG-**not**. Heavy vocal emphasis is placed upon the **not**.

NON-EMPHATIC NEGATIVE

I don't want that car.
She didn't see anyone.
We didn't need any money.
They don't know me.
He doesn't like ice cream.

EMPHATIC NEGATIVE

I *do not* want that car.
She *did not* see anyone.
We *did not* need any money.
They *do not* know me.
He *does not* like ice cream.

6.13
Spanish Emphatic Structures

Although Spanish has no way to make emphatic negative structures, it can generate emphatic affirmative statement structures in any tense. This is done by adding **sí** (**que**) to the sentence, generally between the subject and the verb. Compare the non-emphatic examples on the left with emphatic examples on the right.

NON-EMPHATIC AFFIRMATIVE

Rubén vino a mi casa.
Ella salió con su tía.
Ustedes saben eso.

EMPHATIC AFFIRMATIVE

Rubén sí (que) vino a mi casa.
Ella sí (que) salió con su tía.
Ustedes sí (que) saben eso.

Exercise 8

Rewrite the following sentences making the non-emphatic examples emphatic and the emphatic examples non-emphatic.

1. He went to Ecuador last year.
2. They do not want to see you now.
3. They did see the accident.
4. My mother doesn't speak Spanish.
5. She sings in the choir every Sunday.
6. We don't know the answer.
7. Our priest worked in Uruguay for some time.
8. The men did not come on time.

9. La comida estaba sabrosa.
10. A pesar de la mucha niebla, el avión sí que pudo aterrizar.
11. La suerte favoreció a nuestro equipo.
12. Desde la montaña se divisa la llanura.
13. Esta sugerencia sí que cuenta con el beneplácito del grupo.
14. Esa rosa tiene un bello color.
15. A esta muchacha le crece mucho el pelo.
16. Sí que me apeno de su pronta partida de ella.

6.14
The English Verb *have* in the Expression of Possession
As seen previously, the English verb **have** functions as an auxiliary in the formation of the perfect tenses. In this capacity, it occurs with the past participle. **Have** can also function as a main verb in the expression of possession. In such usage, it most commonly occurs with AUX-**do**. It can, however, appear without the auxiliary when possession is expressed.

Generally speaking, **have,** expressing possession with AUX-**do**, is representative of American English while its use without AUX-**do**, in conveying the idea of possession, is British English. As far as the affirmative statement structure alone is concerned, **have** used with AUX-**do** is viewed as an emphatic usage, while its occurrence without the auxiliary is non-emphatic. This observation applies to both American and British English.

HAVE WITH AUX-**DO**; AMERICAN USAGE

He does have a car.	He did have a car.
(Emphatic in both American and British dialects)	
He doesn't have a car.	He didn't have a car.
Does he have a car?	Didn't he have a car?
Doesn't he have a car?	Didn't he have a car?
What does he have?	What did he have?

HAVE WITHOUT AUX-**DO**; BRITISH USAGE

He has a car.	He had a car.
(Non-emphatic in both American and British dialects)	
He has no car.	He had no car.
Has he a car?	Had he a car?
Hasn't he a car?	Hadn't he a car?
What has he?	What had he?

Exercise 9
Rewrite the following English sentences which contain the verb **have** in its function as an expression of possession. Rewrite those which use AUX-**do** in a form which does not employ the AUX and vice versa. In each case name the tense (present or past) and the structural type (affirmative or negative statement, affirmative or negative question, or content question).

1. They have a house in the country.
2. Do you have friends in town?
3. My parents had no money at the time.
4. Why have you a problem with my suggestion?
5. Don't you have a large dog?
6. Did we have some food left over?
7. When do I have the time to do it?
8. She doesn't have any choice in the matter.
9. You did have class today, didn't you?
10. Hadn't you a book or two when I saw you?

English
Phrasal Verbs

7.1
Just as modern Spanish has its rich inheritance from Latin, English shares an inheritance with other Germanic languages of a rich store of special verb forms. The product of this inherited semantic-syntactic process is called by various names. Perhaps the simplest name is the descriptive "two-word verbs"; also heard are "multi-word verbs," "two-part verbs," and "composite verbs." We use the term **phrasal verbs** in the sense of "two or more words conveying a single thought and functioning as a grammatical unit." A clear distinction should be drawn between verb phrase (VP) and phrasal verb.

7.2
Phrasal verbs are formed by adding a particle to a standard lexical verb. The particle is usually a preposition or an adverb. The verb + particle often has a meaning identical to or at least similar to the base form lexical verb. Here are some examples: **eat** in contrast with **eat up, start** with **start up, burn** with **burn down.** In each of these examples the particle serves simply as an intensifier or an augmentative. In other cases—and these are the most prevalent—the phrasal verb differs considerably in meaning from the base form or even from the sum meaning of the base form plus the preposition/adverb. Observe these examples: **get**, meaning **obtain** in contrast with **get up**, meaning **rise; turn**, meaning **rotate**, with **turn off** meaning **stop; give**, in the sense of **bestow**, with **give in**, meaning **yield**, or **give up** meaning **surrender.**

Since Spanish has nothing comparable in extended use to this English verbal system, these English verbs composed of base verb + particle will be difficult for the majority of Spanish-speaking learners. The problem is further complicated by the fact that many of these multi-word verbs have various meanings. Compare, for example, **pass out** (intransitive) meaning **faint** with **pass out** (transitive) meaning **distribute.** The particles are often used in apparently inexplicable pairings. For example, you can **slow up** or **slow down** and **speed up**, but you cannot **speed down.** The system is highly productive in English, and new verbs are continually being created in the language on the basis of verb + particle, ie, **count down, blast off, gross out,** and so on.

Many of the phrasal verb combinations have been converted into adjectives and even into nouns, for example:

The engineers will *count down* beginning tonight.   (verb)
The *count down* crew arrived early.   (adjective)
The astronauts were waiting for the *countdown*.   (noun)

7.3
When analyzing the syntactical behavior of the phrasal verb, certain peculiarities must be considered.

- When a phrasal verb takes a direct object and the direct object is expressed as a noun, the noun may follow the entire verb + particle unit, or it may intervene between the lexical verb and its adjunct particle.

    He filled out the forms.
    He filled the forms out.

- When a phrasal verb takes a direct object, and the direct object is a pronoun, the pronoun must be placed between the verb and the adjunct particle.

    She filled them out.
    *She filled out them. (This usage is accepted, however, in British English.)

7.4.
Pedagogical Implications
One way of introducing the Spanish speaker to the difficulties of the English phrasal verb system is to demonstrate that these verbs can often be expressed in an alternate way. Frequently the Spanish speaker who has studied English for any time at all and who has acquired some basic English vocabulary knows one-word verbal equivalents for the newly presented verb + particle units. For example, the speaker of Spanish may not know the meaning of the phrasal verb **pass out** 'desmayarse' but may be familiar with the meaning of the one-word English equivalent **faint.** Often the one-word equivalent for a phrasal verb may be cognate from Latin in both English and Spanish, a possibility which facilitates the learning and manipulation of these structures. As an illustration, **put off** means **postpone**, which in Spanish is **posponer**, both words being Latin cognates. Taking this approach to learning phrasal verbs should greatly expedite the learning process.

The Spanish speaker studying English should become aware early on that neat, one-word equivalencies are not always to be found for every English phrasal verb. In probably two-thirds or more of the total number of cases, the Spanish speaker simply must learn the meaning of the verb + particle unit, with no aid whatsoever from another one-word verb having the same meaning.

Exercise 1
Examine the following English sentences, all of which contain phrasal verbs shown in italics. From the list at the right, find the one word equivalent which best matches each verb + particle construction used in the sentences. Which of the one word verbs are cognates with Spanish verbs? Give the Spanish cognate when possible.

1. We'd better *cut down* on what we spend.   appear
2. Please *think* it *over* before tomorrow.   cancel
3. They *put up* that house in less than a week.   consider
4. They plan to *tear down* the old theatre.   continue

5. You can't believe how she *takes after* her mother.   delay
6. I have to *look over* some papers right now.   delete
7. I'm here, so please don't *cross out* my name.   demolish
8. It will *take up* too much time to do it now.   discuss
9. It rained, so we *called off* the picnic.   display
10. This project *calls for* a lot of planning.   encounter
11. You should *take back* what you said.   erect
12. She *made up* a story to entertain them.   examine
13. Try not to *leave out* any of the details.   execute
14. I have to *turn in* my report before Christmas.   invent
15. He *showed off* his muscles, which impressed us all.   occupy
16. As usual they *showed up* late and unprepared.   omit
17. Let's *talk* it *over* after a good night's sleep.   reduce
18. The captain refused to *carry out* those orders.   represent
19. The teacher *went over* the exam carefully.   require
20. I *came across* several mistakes in her paper.   resemble
21. The bad weather is *holding up* our project.   retract
22. She *went on* talking and talking like a parrot.   review
23. *Cut* that *out!* You're not supposed to do that.   stop
24. The lone star *stands for* the State of Texas.   submit
25. I won't *stand for* arguing in my presence.   tolerate

Exercise 2 (Optional)

Below and to the right is a list of English prepositions; to the left is a list of English lexical verbs. Match each verb with each preposition and determine if a verbal with meaning (phrasal verb) results in English. Then do the following:

- If no meaning results from combining a base verb with a particle, make a note of it. Example: *break on

- If a meaning results, check to see if you can get more than one meaning. Example: **run off** can be used transitively to mean 'prepare copies,' but it can also be used intransitively with the meaning of 'disappear suddenly.'

- If a meaning results, write an English sentence for each meaning you get and the best Spanish translation you can for each meaning.

- In those cases in which meaning results and English has a one word verb which matches the meaning of the phrasal verb combination, give the one-word verbal cognate in Spanish when possible. For example, **give back** has the meaning of **return (devolver)**, but **devolver** is not cognate with **return.** However, **give in**, another phrasal combination, is equivalent to **assent,** and this verb is cognate with **asentir** in Spanish.

VERB LIST		PREPOSITION LIST	
break	run	away	on
keep	take	down	out
pull	throw	in	up
put		off	

7.5

Other Structures with Phrasal Verbs

Some phrasal verbs as the main predicators of a sentence may be used both intransitively or transitively. Thus, we find in English "I stood up" and "I stood it up." In these two examples we are describing essentially a similar action. The same phrasal transitive verb **stand up** can have also a different meaning when used in "I stood her up." Here the action described is that of failing to keep an engagement, which entails a totally different semantic reading.

A phrasal verb itself may be followed by a preposition which links the verb + particle to the rest of a sentence as in "I stood up before the audience." Used in this way, a phrasal verb maintains the same meaning as in the intransitive verbal structure. However, the phenomenon becomes further complicated since a phrasal verb may be followed by a second particle in which case the combined meaning is totally altered: **I stood up for my rights.** Here, the verbal unit **stood up for**, called a phrasal-prepositional verb, has the meaning of **defend**, which is very different from all of the other semantic readings.

(Exercise 3)

Try to find a Spanish translation for the following English sentences which contain a phrasal verb followed by a linking preposition or a phrasal-prepositional verb. In which cases might the verb + particle(s) unit be expressed with only one English word which is cognate with a Spanish verb?

1. Then I *caught on to* the funny aspect of the story.
2. May I please *look on with* you since I forgot my book? (familiar)
3. I don't *go in for* wild parties at all.
4. I should *check up on* my mother since she has been ill.
5. My wife won't *put up with* my smoking.
6. We *dropped in on* them last Friday night.
7. You simply can't *run away from* your obligations. (familiar)
8. My friends *get along with* my husband very well.
9. He tried to *get away from* the shark.
10. If you ran a little faster, you would *catch up with* me. (familiar)

11. I *look back on* my childhood with fondness.
12. The President wants to *do away with* many regulatory agencies.
13. When will you ever *get through with* your homework? (familiar)
14. Despite the problems, we *went ahead with* our plans.
15. The professor plans to *get together with* us tomorrow.
16. How will we ever *make up for* the lost time?
17. I don't *feel up to* going out today.
18. He won't pass the course unless he *keeps up with* his classmates.
19. One must *watch out for* cars when crossing the highway.
20. How can I *get out of* going to Monterrey?

7.6

Contrastive Analysis

Since Spanish has no verbal construction exactly the same as the English phrasal verbs, any contrastive analysis must be based on a comparison of equivalent manner of expressing in Spanish the same or similar actions of the English original.

The syntactic examples given above are contrasted here.

ENGLISH PHRASAL VERB	SPANISH EQUIVALENT
I *stood up.*	Me puse de pie.
I *stood* it *up.*	Lo enderecé.
I *stood* her *up.*	La dejé plantada.
I *stood up before* the audience.	Me paré frente al público.
I *stood up for* my rights.	Defendí mis derechos.

In the first example, the English phrasal verb is intransitive, whereas the Spanish verb is reflexive. Both the second examples correspond favorably. The third example in English is classified as familiar usage as is the Spanish equivalent; a more formal translation might be **Falté a una cita con ella.** The fourth example, a phrasal verb plus a preposition, again places an intransitive English verb in contrast with a reflexive Spanish verb. The last example, that of a phrasal-prepositional verb in English, is expressed in Spanish by the Latin cognate **defender** 'defend.'

7.7
English Adjectives Based Upon Phrasal Verbs

Some of the many phrasal verbs that are found in English have been converted into adjectives, following the lead of standard verbids. In many instances, a hyphen is used in written English between the verb and the particle when the compound form functions as an adjective.

Many of the adjectives formed by verb + particle are quite new in the language and represent terms taken recently from technical fields or modern advertising.

(Exercise 4)

The following list gives many examples of phrasal verbs derived from adjectives. Examine each and try to find an acceptable Spanish translation.

1. trade-in allowance
2. pickup truck
3. cleanup campaign
4. tryout schedule
5. lookout post
6. close-out sale
7. play-off game
8. run-off election
9. take-off time
10. slow-down strike
11. giveaway show
12. throwaway bottle
13. getaway car
14. take-out counter
15. make-up examination
16. layaway (lay-away) plan
17. run-on sentence
18. write-in vote
19. checkout time
20. touch-up work
21. drop-out rate
22. warm-up exercise
23. touchdown play
24. drive-in restaurant

7.8
English Nouns Based Upon Phrasal Verbs

Just as adjectives have been derived from the English verb + particle system, likewise many nouns have come into being by the same process. Again, these nouns are often rather new elements in the English lexicon, many coming from computer technology, politics, advertising, and so on.

The written language seems somewhat ambivalent in deciding how to represent these compound nouns orthographically—whether to write them as two separate elements, two hyphenated elements, or two combined elements. (This same vacillation exists among the adjectival forms also.) Generally speaking, the older lexemes do not employ the hyphen and are written as one unit, while the more recent additions to the lexicon do use the hyphen since they are still in the formative stage.[1]

The government of Bolivia had another big *shake-up*.
There is great danger from atomic *fallout*.
Some stores offer plans to buy on *lay-away (layaway)*.

(Exercise 5)

Attempt to translate into Spanish the following sentences, all of which host a noun formed from a phrasal verb.

1. William bought a brand new Ford pickup.
2. He did several push-ups and then began his weight lifting.
3. There was a tremendous pile-up on the freeway last night.
4. The professor always gives us helpful handouts.
5. The beggar was asking for a handout.
6. They gave her a big send-off before she left for Venezuela.
7. Paul is a real show-off, but he is still a fine person.
8. The government suffered a severe economic setback.

9. I need to have feedback from everyone before I continue.
10. She suffered a nervous breakdown and had to be hospitalized.
11. The movie was a terrible letdown for us all.
12. He was fired because he had a run-in with his boss.
13. That bank has had three holdups in the past month.
14. People like them have entirely too many hangups.
15. Most movie actors use stand-ins for dangerous scenes.
16. They anticipate a substantial buildup of funds.

---

[1] The same linguistic incertitude exists among other nominal compounds as well: **Delta *Air Lines* and American *Airlines* serve many of the same routes.**

Modal Auxiliaries
and Their Equivalents

8.1

Nothing so characterizes the English verbal system as its dependence upon auxiliary verbs. The least complicated of the English auxiliaries are the non-modals, which carry no true lexical meaning of their own but which serve the purely grammatical functions of expressing progression (**be**), present and past tense (**do**), or perfectiveness (**have**). The position these non-modals assume in the five basic sentence types of English is highly predictable. The modal auxiliaries, in spite of their other intricacies, assume the same positions as the non-modals in basic English syntax.

Some grammarians are far from agreement upon even such fundamental matters as the exact number of modal auxiliaries in English (see §2.5). Any discussion of the English modal auxiliary system is complicated to organize, particularly since most such verbs have more than one meaning and often do not function in all structures, tenses, and/or persons.

The exact meaning any modal may have in any given case is often a function of context, as can be seen when "He *must* work very hard to always look so tired" expressing probability or conjecture is contrasted with "He *must* work very hard to accomplish his goal" conveying obligation. The degree of the social connection between the speakers often determines the exact nature of modal usages, and the affective domain of linguistic performance comes into play, introducing such factors as human emotions into the exact selection of one modal over another with only slight changes of meaning or overtone. Thus, any modal usage has ultimately to be examined on an individual case basis, and differences between speakers, to say nothing of dialectal variation, must be taken into consideration.

Unlike English, Spanish makes much less use of modal auxiliary verbs; three frequently cited ones will be treated in this unit. In order to translate English modal usages accurately, Spanish must often rely on intonation, special verbal tenses, or verbal periphrases. Often an exact translation into Spanish of an English modal sentence is problematic; occasionally such translation borders upon the impossible. Nevertheless, an attempt has been made throughout this unit to present the most common meanings of the various English modals.

8.2.

Modal Function and Classification

Listed below is the order of presentation of the English modal auxiliary system. You will note that the English modals have been grouped under assorted semantic categories. In every case the modals listed will be discussed along with the most feasible Spanish counterparts for them. Many modals cross over from category to category since they can convey various different meanings depending on context, speaker, and dialect used.

- •Modals expressing PHYSICAL and/or MENTAL ABILITY:
     can, could, be able to.

- •Modals expressing PERMISSION and MAKING OF REQUESTS:
     can, could, may, will, would.

- •Modals expressing CONJECTURE/PROBABILITY, POSSIBILITY, and
     SUPPOSITION: **can, could, may, might, must, should.**

- •Modal expressing WISHES: **may.**

- •Modal expressing VOLITION: **will.**

- •Modal expressing INEVITABILITY: **must.**

- •Modals expressing the SOLICITATION OF OPINIONS: **shall, should.**

- •Modals of OBLIGATION:
     (weak) **should, ought to.**
     (medium) **had better, be supposed to.**
     (strong) **must, have to, have got to.**

- •Spanish Modals of OBLIGATION:
     (personal obligation) **haber de, tener que.**
     (impersonal obligation) **haber que.**

8.3
Modal Positioning in English
As previously noted, the syntax of English sentences containing modal auxiliaries is identical to that of those with non-modal auxiliaries. Compare, for example, the positions occupied by the non-modal and the modal auxiliaries in the following sets of sentences. Note that the modal auxiliaries **must** and **can** take the same syntactical ordering as do the non-modal auxiliaries **do** and **have.**

POSITION OF MODALS

SENTENCE TYPE	NON-MODAL AUX-**do** [past]	MODAL AUX-**must**
Affirmative	They *did* go. (emphatic)	They must go.
Negative	They didn't go.	They must not go.
Yes-No Quest.	Did they go?	Must they go?
Neg. Quest.	Didn't they go?	Mustn't they go?
Content Quest.	Where did they go?	Where must they go?

	NON-MODAL AUX-**have**	MODAL AUX-**can**
Affirmative	They have eaten.	They can eat.
Negative	They haven't eaten.	They can't eat.
Yes-No Quest.	Have they eaten?	Can they eat?
Neg. Quest.	Haven't they eaten?	Can't they eat?
Content Quest.	What have they eaten?	What can they eat?

8.4
Physical and/or Mental Ability
The modals which express physical and/or mental ability, as we have seen above, are **can, could,** and **be able to.** The principal auxiliaries **can** and **could** have a modal equivalent in the phrasal **be able to.**

Whenever the English modals **can** and **could** are found to express either physical or mental abilities, the phrasal modal **be able to** can replace them.

PRESENT	They can solve the problem.	They are able to solve the problem.
FUTURE	They can work tomorrow.	They will be able to work tomorrow.
PAST	They could do it yesterday.	They were able to do it yesterday.

CONDI-
    TIONAL
	They could accomplish it if
	    they tried.
		They would be able to accomplish it if
		    they tried.

However, when physical or mental ability is expressed in a tense other than the four listed above, **can** and **could** do not occur. The only possibility is phrasal **be able to.** This restriction applies to all the perfect tenses.

PRESENT PERFECT	They haven't been able to work every day. (**can/could** not possible)
PAST PERFECT	They hadn't been able to go. (**can/could** not possible)
FUTURE PERFECT	They will have been able to go, I'm sure. (**can/could** not possible)

Unlike the English modals which do not readily differentiate between physical and mental abilities, Spanish makes a distinction, expressing them with different verbs.

8.5
Modal *Can*
Can functions in all persons and structures for present time in the expression of physical or mental ability. The Spanish equivalent is **poder** when physical ability is intended and **saber** when mental ability is expressed. Spanish **ser capaz de** would translate English **can** for either type of ability. It should be noted, however, that Spanish often seems to follow the English model of distinguishing poorly between physical and mental ability, using **poder** for both.

PHYSICAL ABILITY	They can do it.	Pueden hacerlo.
MENTAL ABILITY	They can do it.	Saben hacerlo.
EITHER TYPE	They can do it.	Son capaces de hacerlo.

8.6
Modal *Could*
Could renders ability, either physical or mental, for past time in all persons and structures. Spanish again uses **poder** for physical ability in the imperfect indicative if mere possession of the ability is stressed, and in the preterite if a demonstration of that ability is emphasized. **Saber,** imperfect tense only, shows mental ability in the past. **Ser capaz de,** again, conveys either type of ability in past time.

PHYSICAL ABILITY: They could do it.	Podían hacerlo. (possession)
	Pudieron hacerlo. (demonstration)

MENTAL ABILITY	: They could do it.	Sabían hacerlo. (possession)*
EITHER TYPE	: I could do it.	Eran capaces de hacerlo. (possession)
		Fueron capaces de hacerlo. (demonstration)

*What would normally complete this paradigm *Supe hacerlo* (demonstration) has a different meaning than "I could do it" (an accomplished deed). *Supe hacerlo* means "I found out/learned how to do it." (See Unit 5, §5.6.)

Exercise 1

Whenever change is possible, rewrite these English sentences which express ability. Substitute **can/could** for **be able to** and vice versa. In each case, state why a second version of each is or is not possible.

1. I am able to help you.
2. She can't see you now.
3. They haven't been able to find the professor.
4. When will you be able to bring it?
5. Could you see the mountain from there?
6. The students can be here by nine o'clock.
7. We weren't able to read the message.
8. I could explain it to you before, but I can't now.

Exercise 2

Give a Spanish translation which best fits the following English expressions of ability. The type of ability implied is given in parenthesis.

1. I can't see you. (familiar) (physical)
2. Could they read German at that time? (mental)
3. They couldn't bring it. (demonstrated physical ability)
4. What could we do? (possession of physical ability)
5. Are you able to write well? (familiar) (mental)
6. I could go with you. (familiar) (physical)
7. They were able to leave early. (demonstrated physical ability)
8. Wasn't he able to accomplish anything? (possession of physical ability)
9. He can't help us. (either type)
10. Who could do it? (either type)

8.7

A total of five modals are used in the requesting or granting of permission and in the making of requests. These are **can, could, may, will,** and **would.**

Permission Granting

In formal English **may** and in colloquial usage **can** are employed in affirmative and negative statements to indicate that permission to perform some act has or has not been granted. Only **can** functions in all three question structures, whereas **may** is defective, not occurring in the negative yes-no question.

All persons, singular or plural, may be involved in these structures. Spanish uses **poder** or **permitir** to render **can** or **may** when either expresses the requesting or granting of permission.

AFFIRMATIVE:	You may/can leave.	Puedes/Te permito salir.
NEGATIVE:	You may not/can't leave.	No puedes/No te permito salir.
YES-NO QUEST:	May/Can I leave?	¿Puedo/Me permites salir?
NEG. QUEST.:	Can't I leave?	¿No puedo/No me permites salir?
	(**May** is not used in the negative question.)	
CONTENT Q.:	When may/can I leave?	¿Cuándo puedo/me permites salir?

Granting permission in past time is accomplished by English **could. Might** as the past of **may** is not generally used in this context. Spanish uses **poder** [imperfect] or **permitir** [preterite].

| I could go home. | Yo podía ir a casa./Me permitieron ir a casa. |
| I couldn't go home. | Yo no podía/No me permitieron ir a casa. |

Exercise 3

Render the following English sentences expressing permission with **may, can**, and **could** into Spanish. Use a variety of translations and the familiar form for **you.**

1. May/Can I visit her tomorrow?
2. You can't/may not go to Santiago this weekend.
3. Your brother can/may bring a friend if he wants to.
4. The children couldn't play outside.
5. When may/can we see your new car?
6. Can't I have a little more time to study?
7. The children may not/can't play in the street.
8. When may/can I paint the house?

8.8
Making of Requests
Can, could, will, and **would** are used interchangeably in English in making requests of a 2nd person listener. Although one might maintain that **can** and **could** emphasize the physical abilities of the speaker while **will** and **would** stress one's intentions, most native speakers make no real distinction. It is true, nevertheless, that **can** and **will** render the request in a fairly direct fashion, while **could** and **would** soften it or make it to some degree more polite. Since requests are usually phrased as commands or questions, these four modals function only in the question structures when expressing requests.

As will be seen below, Spanish has a variety of ways of translating these four English modals of request.

•Use the verb **querer** in one of four possible tenses, (a) the present indicative, (b) the imperfect indicative, (c) the conditional, or (d) the imperfect subjunctive usually in **-ra** form, all plus the infinitive, to make requests. The request becomes increasingly more polite or attenuated as we proceed from tense (a) through tense (d).

Can/Could/Will/Would you (please) leave?	a. ¿Quiere(s) salir?
	b. ¿Quería(s) salir?
	c. ¿Querría (s) salir?
	d. ¿Quisiera(s) salir?

•Use the verb **poder** in the same tenses and with the same degrees of softening as illustrated with **querer**.

Can/Could/Will/Would you (please)   a. ¿Me puede(s) ayudar?
     help me?   b. ¿Me podía(s) ayudar?
                                       c. ¿Me podría(s) ayudar?
                                       d. ¿Me pudiera(s) ayudar?

•Use the simple present indicative of the LV in questions when the action is for the benefit of the petitioner(s).

Can/Could/Will/Would you (please) bring it to me?   a. ¿Me lo trae(s)?
Can/Could/Will/Would you (please) read it for us?   b. ¿Nos lo lee(s)?

•Several periphrastic expressions may be used in Spanish to make requests of listeners; each are delivered orally with a falling final intonation contour. The particular mode of expression may vary from dialect to dialect and even from individual to individual.

Can/Could/Will/Would you (please)   a. Haz/Haga el favor de no fumar.
     not smoke?   b. Ten/Tenga la bondad de no fumar.
                                     c. Sé/Sea tan amable como para no fumar.

Although most of our illustrations show requests of a single 2nd person listener, requests can be made of more than one person listeners in each of the above structures. The verb forms and possessives would reflect plurality (ie **ustedes, vosotros, vosotras, su, sus, vuestros, vuestras**).

Exercise 4

Give various Spanish versions of the following English sentences which express requests made of a listener (sentences 1–4) or listeners (sentences 5–8).

     1. Would you please open the door?
     2. Will you please give me some money for the car?
     3. Could you explain the assignment to me?
     4. Would you please bring me a box of sodas?
     5. Can you close your eyes for a few seconds?
     6. Can you all please say a few words at the meeting?
     7. Will you close your books now?
     8. Can you (all) please sit down?

8.9

Semantic readings of verb forms in English which express conjecture or probability, or possibility and supposition include the auxiliaries **can, could, may, might, must,** and **should.** Spanish uses **deber** and **deber de** along with a variety of specific verbal tense forms.

Much disagreement exists among native Spanish speakers on both sides of the Atlantic on the usage of **deber de** + INF and **deber** + INF as modals of supposition, conjecture, and probability, as well as belief and obligation. The lack of agreement seems to stem from many sources—dialectal, idiolectal, societal, educational, etc. In the light of so many varying opinions, it is probably more prudent to follow the current dictates of the *Real Academia Española* :

> En la lengua clásica se encuentran ya ejemplos de confusión entre *deber de* y *deber* seguido del infinitivo sin preposición; en la actualidad la confusión es muy frecuente en el habla corriente oral y escrita. En la lengua literaria se mantiene más clara la diferencia entre *deber de* (suposición) y *deber* (estar obligado): *Deben de volver* significa *supongo, creo que vuelven,* en tanto que *Deben volver* equivale a *tienen obligación de volver.* La diferencia es muy expresiva y la Academia recomienda mantenerla (*Esbozo,* §3.12.4. h).

8.10
Conjecture/Probability
The expression of conjecture and probability in English is confined to affirmative and negative statements. All persons can be involved, and the times referred to are either present or past.

The modal used in the expression of conjecture/probability is **must.** It functions as follows:

PRESENT AFFIRMATIVE:	**must** + LV
PRESENT NEGATIVE:	**must*** + **not** + LV (*optional contraction)
PAST AFFIRMATIVE:	**must** + **have** + PAST PARTICIPLE
PAST NEGATIVE:	**must*** + **not have** + PAST PARTICIPLE (*optional contraction)

Note: See Unit 6 for more information about optional contractions (§6.6–10).

The test for a sentence expressing conjecture or probability in English is the substitution of the word **probably** for the modal in the sentence. Observe the following sentence equivalencies.

He must be a doctor.	He probably is a doctor.
He must not be a doctor.	He probably isn't a doctor.
She must have been sick.	She probably was sick.
She must not have been sick.	She probably wasn't sick.

8.11
Spanish Equivalents of *Must*
The English modal **must** as an expression of conjecture or probability has several Spanish equivalents. Perhaps the most controversial among these are **deber de** + INF and **deber** + INF.

•With verbs expressing states or action, the present indicative of **deber de** + INF is used. This is the usage recommended by the Academy. As stated above, you will also find **deber** alone.

He must be sick.	Él debe de (debe) estar enfermo.
Mary must have a problem.	María debe de (debe) tener un problema.
Victor must live here.	Víctor debe de (debe) vivir aquí.
She must read a lot to be so smart.	Ella debe de (debe) leer mucho para ser tan inteligente.

•With stative verbs (verbs expressing only states and not actions: **ser, estar, tener, haber,** etc.), the so-called future of probability is used. **Deber de** can be used also with stative verbs.

It must be eight o'clock.	Serán las ocho. Deben de (Deben) ser las ocho.
She must be far from here.	Ella estará lejos de aquí. Ella debe de (debe) estar lejos de aquí.
He must have many children.	Él tendrá muchos hijos. Él debe de (debe) tener muchos hijos.
There must be a serious problem.	Habrá un problema grave. Debe de (Debe) haber un problema grave.

•With verbs expressing states or actions in the past, you use **deber de** + PERFECT INFINITIVE. Here again some speakers use **deber** + PERFECT INF.

He must have been ill.	Él debe de (debe) haber estado enfermo
He must have had a problem.	Él debe de (debe) haber tenido un problema.

Victor must have worked here
   before.
	Víctor debe de (debe) haber trabajado
	   aquí antes.

She must have left early.	Ella debe de (debe) haber salido tem- prano.

•With stative verbs in the past, the so-called conditional of probability is used, although **deber de** can be used also in these cases.

She must have had many children.	Ella tendría muchos hijos. Ella debe de (debe) haber tenido muchos hijos.
There must have been a problem.	Habría un problema. Debe de (Debe) haber habido un problema.

Exercise 5

Rewrite the following Spanish sentences, which use some form of **deber de** + non-action (stative) verbs to express conjecture/probability, using the future or conditional of probability.

1. Ese señor debe de ser un arquitecto famoso.
2. Los indígenas de este valle deben de haber sido bajos de estatura.
3. Esa anciana debe de tener mucho dinero.
4. El asesino debe de haber estado en este mismo sitio.
5. Debe de haber un teléfono por aquí.
6. Mi padre no debe de estar en su oficina después del día doce.
7. No deben de haber tenido suficiente gasolina para llegar.

Translate the following sentences involving conjecture/probability into the other language. Give assorted renditions.

1. You must be very tired. (familiar)
2. Tendrían algún problema con el coche.
3. They must have brought very little money.
4. Juanita debe de pronunciar muy bien el ruso porque tiene buen oído.
5. He must not have many friends here.
6. Anoche habría un incendio muy grande en el centro.
7. That boy must not know the answer.
8. ¡Qué contento estará ese señor!
9. The tribe must have been very small.
10. Debe de haber sido la señora Méndez quien llamó.

8.12
Possibility
It is often difficult to distinguish clearly between the semantic concepts of probability and possibility in English. Spanish would seem to distinguish even less sharply than does English between the two ideas, as evidenced by the fact that the so-called future and conditional of probability may be used, as we shall see, to render certain English sentences which express possibility, especially in the question structures.

For the purpose of our discussion here, let it be said that when English uses the word "possibly" with a verb as a substitute for a true modal, we can prove thereby that possibility rather than probability is intended.

English sentences expressing possibility may refer to the past, the present, or the future and occur in all five basic structures and in all persons. Sentences which refer to the future are indistinguishable from those whose reference is to the present. The auxiliary **have** is introduced into English sentences of possibility to convey that concept in past time.

The following English sentences on the left containing modals are equivalent to those on the right which do not use modals, but instead, the word **possibly.** All examples refer to the present.

AFFIRMATIVE	He could/may/might work here.	He possibly works here.
NEGATIVE	He may not/might not work here. (**could** restricted)	He possibly doesn't work here.
YES-NO QUEST.	Could he/Might he work here? (**may** restricted)	Does he possibly work here?
NEG. QUEST.	Couldn't he work here? (**may, might** restricted)	Doesn't he possibly work here?
CONTENT QUEST.	Where can/could/might he work?	Where does he possibly work?

Note: In the above examples of affirmative and negative structures, the adverbs **maybe** and **perhaps** followed by the simple present tense could be used also.
Maybe/Perhaps he works here.   Maybe/Perhaps he doesn't work here.

8.13

To translate the English modals of possibility, Spanish uses a wide variety of expressions. **Poder** works well in all structures. Since a measure of doubt is involved in the expression of possibility, the following paraphrastic phrases also occur: **poder ser que, ser posible que, tal vez,** and **quizá(s).** All of these phrases are routinely followed by the main verb in the subjunctive mood. **Acaso** and **a lo mejor** are used also, but they take the indicative mood more often than they do the subjunctive.

In the content question structure, the future tense of the main verb with conjectural force or the verb **poder** as an auxiliary seem to be the main means of expressing possibility.

AFFIRMATIVE
He could/may/might work here. =   Puede ser que él trabaje aquí.
Es posible que él trabaje aquí.
Tal vez él trabaje aquí.
Quizá(s) él trabaje aquí.

Acaso él trabaja aquí.
A lo mejor él trabaja aquí.

NEGATIVE
He may/might not work here. =   Puede ser que él no trabaje aquí.
Es posible que él no trabaje aquí.
Tal vez él no trabaje aquí.
Quizá(s) él no trabaje aquí.

Acaso él no trabaja aquí.
A lo mejor él no trabaja aquí.

YES-NO QUESTION
Could he/Might he work here? =   ¿Puede ser que él trabaje aquí?
¿Es posible que él trabaje aquí?

NEGATIVE QUESTION
Couldn't he work here?   =   ¿No puede ser que él trabaje aquí?
¿No es posible que él trabaje aquí?

CONTENT QUESTION
Where can/could/might he work? = ¿Dónde podrá trabajar él?
¿Dónde podría trabajar él?

Exercise 7

Translate the following sentences, all of which express possibility, into the other language. Give varied answers.

1. Tal vez la mujer sepa hablar chino.
2. Where could he be at this late hour?
3. Puede ser que no tenga ella bastante dinero.
4. Could he be the new Spanish professor?
5. ¿No es posible que surja una crisis?

6. My nephew may leave tomorrow night.
7. Es posible que no te conozcan.
8. He might not be as intelligent as you are? (familiar)

8.14
Supposition
Should is the English modal auxiliary most frequently used to express supposi-
tions concerning some state or action. All persons occur in sentences expressing
supposition, but apparently only the affirmative statement, negative statement, and
content question structures are involved. Spanish most appropriately translates the
should of supposition with **deber de** + INF. (See quotation above under §8.9.)
Spanish uses the conditional and imperfect subjunctive **-ra** forms interchangeably
with no apparent difference in meaning.

I should finish soon.	Yo debería de/debiera de terminar pronto.
She shouldn't be late.	Ella no debería de/no debiera de tardar.
When should he have arrived?	¿Cuándo debería de/debiera de haber llegado él?
We should have fun.	Deberíamos de/Debiéramos de divertirnos.
They shouldn't have problems.	No deberían de/debieran de tener problemas.
How much should I earn?	¿Cuánto debería de/debiera de ganar?

Exercise 8

Translate the following sentences, all of them expressing supposition, into the other
language.

1. A estas horas mi prima debería de estar ya en casa.
2. He shouldn't need any help.
3. No debiéramos de encontrar a nadie esta noche.
4. When should the train leave?
5. Deberían de llegar muy cansados.
6. You should know all of your students within a few days. (indefinite
subject)

8.15
Wishes
English **may** is the modal used in the expression of a wish that something may or
may not take place at some future time. This usage of **may**, often referred to as the
optative mood in grammar, is confined to affirmative and negative statements.
    Spanish renders the optative with **que** + PRES. SUBJUNCTIVE of the LV.

May you live forever!	¡Que vivas para siempre!
May you never have problems!	¡Que nunca tengas problemas!
May they know the truth!	¡Que sepan la verdad!

Also heard is the expression **I hope that ...** which does not use a modal.

8.16
Volition
In addition to its use as a future auxiliary, the modal **will** is used to express volition or determination. It is accompanied by vocal stress and is restricted to the first person singular and plural in the non-past affirmative.

Spanish generally will use a periphrastic expression to communicate strong determination towards action. (See §6.13.)

I *will* win!	¡Yo *sí que* ganaré! ¡Voy a ganar.
We *will* overcome!	¡*Sí que* venceremos! ¡Vamos a vencer!

Will in the negative present (**will not/won't**) and past (**would not/ wouldn't**) denotes refusal to act. It is used in the 1st and 3rd persons.

I will not/won't do it.	No quiero hacerlo.
He would not/wouldn't do it.	No quiso hacerlo.

Exercise 9

Translate the following into the other language. In all cases, the sentences express optative ideas or wishes and/or volition.

1. Que nunca oigas lo que me han dicho.
2. May you always have enough money. (familiar)
3. Ojalá no estén aquí cuando llegue yo.
4. May you live in peace. (formal)
5. ¡Que te cases con una bruja!
6. May we not ever see them again.
7. Yo sí que lograré lo imposible.
8. We *will* reach our goal!
9. El señor no quiso cooperar.
10. I won't stand for insults!

8.17
Inevitability
In addition to expressing probability, **must** conveys the idea of inevitability. This is an example of the multifaceted nature of so many of the English modals.

Spanish uses **tener que** + INF to express inevitability.

All things must die.	Toda cosa tiene que morir.
The sun must rise.	El sol tiene que salir.
The months must pass.	Los meses tienen que pasar.
Birds must leave the nest.	Los pájaros tienen que dejar el nido.

8.18
Modals Expressing the Solicitation of Opinions
1st Person Forms
Shall and **should** are used interchangeably with 1st person subjects, singular and plural, in order to obtain the listener's opinion of or reaction to an intended action. Only the affirmative yes-no and content question structures are involved. Spanish expresses the solicitation of opinions with the interrogative **querer que** + PRES-

ENT SUBJUNCTIVE, or with a simple present indicative in the 1st person singular or plural spoken as a question.

Shall/Should I help you?	¿Quieres que te ayude?
	¿Te ayudo?
When shall/should we leave?	¿Cuándo quieres que salgamos?
	¿Cuándo salimos?

It should be noted that **should** (not **shall**) is used in the negative yes-no question structure to solicit opinions concerning 1st persons, singular and plural. Spanish commonly uses **deber** in the translation of this usage of **should**.

Shouldn't I/we help?	¿No debo/No debemos ayudar?

Note: **Shall** is not possible in negative yes-no questions with 1st person subjects.

2nd and 3rd Persons

Should, however, is the only allowable modal for soliciting opinions concerning second or third persons. Again, it is confined to the question structures—yes-no and content.

Should you be here?	¿Debes estar aquí?
Shouldn't they work?	¿No deben ellos/-as trabajar?
When should he go?	¿Cuándo debe ir él?

Exercise 10

Translate the following sentences into the other language. All express the solicitation of opinions. Give a variety of translations.

1. Shall I bring my relatives?
2. ¿No debemos regresar antes de que llegue ella?
3. Should he tell us the truth?
4. ¿Bailamos?
5. Shall we write him a letter?
6. ¿No debo negarle a él un permiso?
7. Should they be playing in the street?
8. ¿Trasnochémonos?
9. When should we arrive?
10. ¿Compramos un modelo nuevo?

8.19
Modals of Obligation

We have divided the modals of obligation into three separate groupings: those that express weak obligation, those that express obligation of medium force, and those that express strong obligation. (See the quotation under §8.9 for recommended uses in Spanish by the Real Academia.)

Weak Obligation: *should, ought (to)*

These modals, **should** and **ought** (**to**), express a weak type of obligation which some grammarians refer to as "moral obligation." Speakers or listeners under this type of obligation probably feel no immediate, strong compulsion to act. These modals do, however, convey a sense of some pressure, often internally generated, to do or not to do something.

Should functions in all persons and in all structures. It is best rendered in Spanish by **deber** + INF, **deber** conjugated in one of the so-called "tenses of attenuation." These are the (a) imperfect indicative, (b) the conditional, or (c) the imperfect subjunctive in **-ra** form. In most dialects of Spanish, **deber** in the present indicative is simply too strong to render the ideas of **should** and **ought (to)**. The present tense of **deber** would have the meaning of **must**.

I should leave now.	Yo debía/debería/debiera salir ahora.
You shouldn't go.	No debías/deberías/debieras irte.
What should she do?	¿Qué debía/debería/debiera hacer ella?

Ought (to) expresses a type of weak obligation roughly equivalent to **should**. However, it is a defective modal since it does not appear in all structures.

Ought (to) functions:
•In the affirmative statement structure in conjunction with the English lexical verb.

> I ought to go.
> She ought to work more.

•In the negative statement structure; **not** in non-contracted form appears between **ought** and the LV as a bare infinitive.

> They ought not go.
> We ought not mention it.

•**Ought (to)** rarely appears in question structures, where it is replaced by **should.**

> Should they go?   Ought they go? (rare in Am.Eng.)
> Shouldn't they go?
> Where should they go?

Note: When **should** substitutes for **ought (to)** in the question structures, the usage might be construed either as an expression of obligation or as a solicitation of opinion as illustrated in §8.18. Care must be taken to avoid misinterpretation.

Ought (to), like **should,** is translated into Spanish with **deber** in the attenuated forms previously mentioned.

You ought to leave.	Debías/Deberías/Debieras irte.
I ought to remain here.	Yo debía/debería/debiera permanecer aquí.
You ought not go.	No debía/debería/debiera irse usted.
They ought not stop.	No debían/deberían/debieran parar.

Exercise 11

Translate the following expressions of weak obligation into the other language. Give a variety of versions.

1. You ought to see that film. (familiar)
2. Usted debía ir a verlo a su despacho.
3. We shouldn't drink so much beer.
4. ¿A qué hora deberían llegar?

5. He ought not spend so much money.
6. No deberías prestarles tanta importancia.
7. I should buy a new car this year.
8. ¿No debiéramos invitarlos a la fiesta?

8.20
Medium Obligation: *had better, be supposed to*
Had better and **be supposed to** express a type of obligation which is intermediary between **should** or **ought (to)** and **must/have to/have got to**, these latter three showing strong obligation. The type of obligation conveyed by **had better** and **be supposed (to)** seems often to be imposed from the outside or to be the product of the speakers' inner rationalizations. Whichever the case may be, it is clear that the speaker senses a more urgent need to act when using these auxiliaries than when employing **should** or **ought (to)**.

Had better functions for all persons and occurs primarily in the affirmative and negative statement structures. It takes the LV in base form and is restricted to use in a present time frame. Spanish translates **had better** with **deber** in the appropriately attenuated tenses.

We had better leave.	Debíamos/Deberíamos/Debiéramos irnos.
You had better eat.	Usted debía/debería/debiera comer.
I had better not drink that.	Yo no debía/debería/debiera beber eso.
He had better not run.	Él no debía/debería/debiera correr.

Be supposed to carries roughly the same obligatory force as **had better.** Again, you render it in Spanish by **deber.** Aside from **have to**, which is discussed later as a modal of strong obligation, **be supposed to** is the only modal of obligation which can express a time frame other than the present. Since it can function in all persons, tenses, and structures, it is considerably less defective than its semantic equivalent **had better.**

I was supposed to do it.	Yo debía hacerlo.
You're not supposed to go.	Ud. no debía/debería/debiera irse.
Isn't he supposed to work?	¿No debía/debería/debiera trabajar él?
Are you supposed to speak?	¿Debías/Deberías/Debieras hablar?
When were we supposed to go?	¿Cuándo debíamos/deberíamos/debiéramos irnos?

Exercise 12
Translate the following sentences of medium obligation into the other language. Use a variety of versions.

1. You had better see a doctor. (formal)
2. Debiéramos complacerles a nuestros padres.
3. Are they supposed to help you with the project? (familiar)
4. ¿Dónde deberían vivir durante el invierno?
5. I'm not supposed to say anything about it.
6. Debieras ir pensando en lo que vas a contestar.
7. Aren't we supposed to be working now?
8. Debías vender ese cuadro viejo.

8.21

Strong Obligation: *must, have to, have got to*

These three modals **must, have to,** and **have got to** express strong, compulsory obligation with which the speaker feels there can be no compromise. When using these modals, the speaker implies that unless the obligation is met and brought to fruition, painful consequences or even sanctions may result.

Must operates in all persons and in all structures, with the exception of negative yes-no questions. In Spanish it is best translated by **tener que** + INF, except in the negative structure in which Spanish must use negative **deber** in the present indicative.

I must leave now.	Tengo que salir ahora.
Must we stay here?	¿Tenemos que permanecer aquí?
When must you arrive?	¿Cuándo tienes que llegar?

But,

They must not leave.	No *deben* salir.

Have to functions in all persons and structures and, unlike a great majority of obligation modals, in all tenses. In all structures except the affirmative statement, it uses one of the non-modal auxiliaries **do, have, will,** and a limited number of modals, such as **may, might, should,** etc. When occurring in the negative structure, **have to** expresses the "absence" of obligation (**I don't have to**) rather than the obligation "not to do" a certain thing. **Must** is mandatory for expressing the latter idea (**I must not/mustn't**). Spanish translates **have to** with **tener que** + INF.

He has to work.	Él tiene que trabajar.
I don't have to work.	No tengo que trabajar.
(expresses "absence" of obligation)	

You mustn't work.	No debes trabajar.
(expresses "obligation not to")	

Will you have to leave?	¿Tendrás que salir?
Haven't they had to agree?	¿No han tenido que consentir ellos?
When do we have to arrive?	¿Cuándo tenemos que llegar?

Have got to belongs more to the colloquial idiom than do either **must** or **have to** and is most common in British English. It functions well in all persons and in all structures to express strong obligation, with one exception. In the negative statement structure, as was the case with **have to**, it expresses the absence of obligation. Unlike **have to**, however, **have got to** (like **must**) refers to present or future time only and uses no other auxiliaries in the five basic structures.

You use **tener que** + INF to depict the idea of strong, compulsory obligation in Spanish in all structures except negative statements. In negative statements **no deber** + INF must be used.

He has got to work.	Él tiene que trabajar.
He hasn't got to work. (absence of obligation)	Él no tiene que trabajar.
He mustn't work. (obligation not to)	Él no *debe* trabajar.
Has he got to work? (BrEng)	¿Tiene que trabajar él?
Hasn't he got to work? (BrEng)	¿No tiene que trabajar él?
When has he got to work? (BrEng)	¿Cuándo tiene que trabajar él?

Translate the following expressions of strong obligation into the other language. Give various renditions and make certain that you distinguish between the absence of obligation and the obligation not to do something.

1. No debes fumar.
2. My father mustn't work so hard.
3. Mi madre no tiene que trabajar mucho.
4. You don't have to smoke.
5. ¿Cuándo tenemos que salir del hotel?
6. Haven't you got to speak French with her? (Br.Eng.) (formal)
7. Tienes que visitar a tus compañeros.
8. We must go there more often.
9. No debemos contemplar más eso.
10. When have we got to be there? (Br.Eng.)

THREE SPANISH MODALS OF OBLIGATION AND THEIR ENGLISH EQUIVALENTS
8.22

Three Spanish modals of obligation are found in current use. These are **haber de, haber que,** and **tener que**, all followed by the infinitive. **Haber de** is the oldest recorded modal form and seems more literary; **tener que** has been substituted for it and is the preferred expression in all Spanish-speaking regions.

Haber de/Tener que + INF

These are the so-called personal modals of obligation which assign obligation to particular individuals such as the speaker, the addressee, third persons, etc. They can be used to convey obligation in essentially any time.

Haber de is best translated into English as **to be** + INF. This is a less intimidating obligation, one that we ourselves have imposed.

Tener que is best translated as **have to** + LV. The obligation here seems stronger, more intense, an obligation put upon us by factors outside our sphere of influence.

Había de hablar con mi padre.	I was to speak to my father.
Tenía que hablar con mi padre.	I had to speak to my father.
Hemos de llegar esta noche.	We are to arrive tonight.
Tenemos que llegar esta noche.	We have to arrive tonight.
Han de comprar unas cosas.	They are to buy some things.
Tienen que comprar unas cosas.	They have to buy some things.

Haber que + INF

Haber que is an impersonal modal of obligation which means that the obligation is assigned to all listeners in general, not just to particular individuals such as the addressee, third persons, and the like. Because it is impersonal, the verb always assumes 3rd person singular form.

English best translates the expression in one of three ways when obligation in present time is intended. These versions are (a) **it is necessary to** + LV, (b) **one must** + LV, and (c) **you should** + LV. Usage of **haber que** in past and future tenses is best expressed only by **it was/will be necessary ....**

Hay que estudiar más.	It is necessary to study more.
	One must study more.
	You should study more.
Hubo que matarlo.	It was necessary to kill it.
Habrá que venderlo.	It will be necessary to sell it.

Exercise 14

Translate the following sentences expressing both personal and impersonal obligation into the other language. Give all versions.

1. Hemos de llamarlos cuando lleguemos.
2. One must see it to believe it.
3. Hay que darle cuerda para que funcione bien.
4. They are to bring several samples.
5. Este verano tengo que enseñar una clase sobre la filosofía clásica.
6. It's a horrible job because you have to get up so early.
7. Supongo que habrá que cuidarla, como siempre.
8. It was necessary to buy a house.
9. Tenías que confesármelo todo, pero no me dijiste nada.
10. It will be necessary to use force.

Part Two

THE COMPLEX NOUN PHRASE

LA FRASE NOMINAL COMPLEJA

Conjunto de palabras "constituido por un nombre, un adjetivo o un sintagma o preposición en función nominal ..."
Diccionario de la Real Academia Española

Nouns
and Articles

NOUN GENDER
9.1
A major difference between Spanish and English nouns is that all Spanish nouns have the characteristic of gender (masculine versus feminine). English nouns do not have gender except, of course, in the case of nouns which represent masculine or feminine animate beings—**man/woman, bull/cow, buck/doe, ram/ewe, boy/girl,** etc. The problem for English speakers learning Spanish with regards to the nominal system is that they must learn to which gender class each noun belongs. Following are some useful clues to the gender of the Spanish noun.

9.2.
Masculine Gender of Spanish Nouns
The classes of Spanish nouns which belong to the masculiine gender are numerous. The principal classes are outlined here.

i. Most nouns ending in **-o: el brazo, el beso, el banco, el fuego, ...** There are exceptions, however: **la mano, la radio, la foto, la moto** (the latter two being shortened forms of **la fotografía** and **la motocicleta**).

ii. Nouns referring to masculine persons: **el rey, el cura, el hombre, el sacerdote, ...**

iii. Days of the week, months of the year, and the cardinal numbers: **el domingo, junio, octubre, tres, once, ...**

iv. Names of rivers, oceans, seas, and the four cardinal points: **el Amazonas, el Mediterráneo, el Pacífico, el sur, el norte, ...**

v. Names of languages: **el griego, el francés, el español, el árabe, ...**

vi. Infinitives used as nouns: **el mover, el volar, el ser humano, ...**

vii. Certain nouns of Greek origin, most of them ending in **-ma, -pa,** or **-ta,** and all cognate with English nouns of the same Greek origin: **el problema, el sistema, el clima, el tema, el idioma, el mapa, el programa ...**

viii. Nouns ending in **-or** or **-ón** (but not **-ión,** except **camión, guión**): **el pintor, el pastor, el patrón, el rincón, ...**

ix. Nouns representing colors: **el azul, el verde, el rojo, el negro, el blanco, ...**

9.3.
Feminine Gender of Spanish Nouns

There are fewer classes of Spanish nouns belonging to the feminine gender than those which are masculine. We list here the principal classes.

i. Most nouns ending in **-a: la palabra, la carta, la sala, la escuela ...** (exceptions are those in the class listed under [vii] above).

ii. Nouns referring to feminine persons: **la doctora, la profesora, la dama, la reina, la condesa, ...**

iii. Most nouns ending in **-ión, -dad, -tad, -tud, -umbre, -ie,** and **-dez: la estación, la verdad, la libertad, la virtud, la muchedumbre, la serie, la honradez, ...**

iv. The letters of the alphabet: **la a, la be, la hache, la elle, la zeta, ... (a, b, h, ll, z).**

9.4.
Masculine/Feminine Forms of Spanish Animate Nouns

The masculine and feminine forms of certain Spanish nouns which refer to animate beings (persons or animals) are determined morphologically.

i. The **-o** ending of masculine nouns changes to **-a** in the feminine: **el hijo/la hija, el santo/la santa, el abuelo/la abuela, el perro/la perra, ...**

ii. Masculine nouns ending in **-or** or in **-ón** add **-a** to form the feminine: **el pastor/la pastora, el director/la directora, el patrón/la patrona, ...**

iii. Many nouns exhibit the same form in both genders. Only the article is interchanged to designate the exact gender intended: **el/la amante, el/la mártir, el/la estudiante, el/la testigo.** To this category belong all animate nouns ending in **-ista: el/la dentista, el/la socialista, el/la artista, ...**

iv. In a number of cases, the Spanish masculine and feminine forms of nouns are different words altogether: **el hombre/la mujer, el padre/la madre, el toro/la vaca, el caballo/la yegua, ...**

9.5

Meaning and Gender Changes

There is a group of nouns which undergo a change of meaning when they are employed in one instance with the masculine article or in another with the feminine article.

MASCULINE	FEMININE
el capital 'the capital' (money)	la capital 'the capital' (city)
el cólera 'the cholera'	la cólera 'the anger'
el coma 'the coma' (illness)	la coma 'the comma' (punctuation)
el corte 'the cut'	la corte 'the court'
el frente 'the front'	la frente 'the forehead'
el guía 'the guide" (person)	la guía 'the guide' (book)

Exercise 1

Determine, according to the gender classifications just presented, the gender of the following Spanish nouns. Which would belong to both genders? Indicate those nouns whose gender cannot be determined from the above rules.

1. género	11. solicitud
2. página	12. comunista
3. x	13. especie
4. ocho	14. redacción
5. calle	15. portugués (language)
6. caracol	16. martes
7. avestruz	17. calidad
8. Orinoco	18. costumbre
9. oeste	19. vestirse
10. tema	20. actor

9.6

Number

Both Spanish and English nouns have the characteristic of number, that is, they are either singular (representing one) or plural (representing two or more). Although in reality the English system of pluralization is more complicated than that of Spanish, the two systems are at least partially similar in that both pluralize with **-s** or **-es** in the majority of cases.

Pluralization of Spanish Nouns

Spanish nouns form their plural according to specific rules which are here listed and oulined.

i. Nouns ending in an unaccented vowel or in an accented **-é** add **-s**: **caja/cajas, acto/actos, café/cafés, ...**

ii. Nouns ending in a consonant, in **-y**, or in any accented vowel except **-é** add **-es**: **farol/faroles, león/leones, rey/reyes, rubí/rubíes, ...**

iii. Nouns ending in **-z** change the **-z** to **c** and then add **-es**: **voz/voces, luz/luces, lápiz/lápices, ...**

iv. If a Spanish singular noun ends in **-s** and the vowel before that **s** is the stressed vowel of the word, the plural is formed by adding **-es**: **mes/meses, revés/reveses, inglés/ingleses, ...**

v. However, if the Spanish singular noun ends in **-s** and the vowel before that **s** is unstressed, the singular and the plural forms are identical and only the article indicates whether singular or plural meaning is intended: **el lunes/los lunes, el viernes/los viernes, el cumpleaños/los cumpleaños, ...**

vi. Surnames are pluralized in Spanish by placing the plural form of the article before them. English adds an apostrophe + **s** (**'s**) to names and surnames: **los Rivera, los Negrón, ...** There are occasions when you will need to pluralize a first name (nombre de pila) in Spanish. Follow rules (a) and (b) above: **las Marías, los Juanes.**

vii. In their masculine plural form, many Spanish animate nouns may refer either to more than one masculine being or to two or more beings of both sexes: **los reyes 'the kings'** or **'the king and queen', los hermanos 'the brothers'** or **'the brothers and sisters', los padres 'the fathers'** or **'the parents.'**

viii. Occasionally Spanish presents a plural concept of a thing while English will view it as singular and vice versa: **muebles** (pl.) = **furniture** (sgl.), **noticias** (pl.) = **news** (sgl.), **consejos** (pl.) = **advice** (sgl.), **vacaciones** (pl.) = **vacation** (sgl.); **ropa** (sgl.) = **clothes** (pl.), **bosque** (sgl.) = **woods** (pl.), **pantalón** (sgl.) = **pants** (pl.), **ganado** (sgl.) = **cattle** (pl.), ...

Exercise 2

Give the plural form of the following singular nouns and be able to state the rule upon which the pluralization is based.

1. columna	7. alelí
2. buey	8. pie
3. andaluz	9. pez
4. consejo	10. alemán
5. miércoles	11. clase
6. cordobés	12. carácter

9.7
Pluralization of the English Noun

In the vast majority of cases, English plural formation of nouns, like Spanish, is accomplished by the adding of the suffix **-s** or **-es** to the singular word form. There are some few orthographical adjustments to this process which are stated below.

By far the most difficult aspect of the English pluralization system is its oral rendering. This can be somewhat confusing and rather tedious for non-native speakers. The phonological rules governing these changes are outlined below. You will note that these are the same rules that applied to the 3rd person singular present tense form of the verb (Unit 2, §2.7).

i. A noun ending in one of the sibilant sounds [s, z, ʃ, tʃ, ʒ, dʒ] adds the plural inflection **-s/-es** to the singular form with the pronunciation of [ɪz], an extra syllable: **lass/lasses** [læsɪz], **nose/noses** [nozɪz], **wish/wishes** [wɪʃɪz], **rouge/rouges** [ruʒɪz], **beach/beaches** [bitʃɪz], **badge/badges** [bædʒɪz]. (See footnote 1 on page 14.)

ii. A noun ending in a voiceless consonant sound other than the sibilants listed above adds **-s** with the pronunciation of [s]: **pick/picks** [pɪks], **bit/bits** [bɪts], **rope/ropes** [rops], **fife/fifes** [faɪfs], bath/baths [bæθs]. Those voiceless consonants that occur in final position in nouns are [p, t, k, f, θ].

iii. A noun ending in a voiced consonant sound other than the sibilants listed above or in a vowel sound other than **-o** also adds **-s**, but with the sound of

[z]. Nouns ending in -**o** preceded by a consonant usually add -**es** and preceded by another vowel add just -**s** (two common exceptions are **potatoes** and **tomatoes**). Both -**s** and -**es** endings having the sound of [z]. Since Spanish does not have the [z] sound as a phoneme separate from /s/, the pronunciation of this type of English plural may need special attention for the Spanish speaker: **bead/beads** [bidz], **bag/bags** [bægz], **can/cans** [kænz], **name/names** [nemz], **tool/tools** [tulz], **car/cars** [karz], **ray/rays** [rez], **sea/seas** [siz], **snow/snows** [snoz]. Apart from the sibilants mentioned above, the other voiced consonants that are found in final position in nouns are [b, d, g, v, ð, m, n, ŋ, l, r].

iv. A noun ending in -**y** preceded by a vowel adds -**s** to form the plural: **boy/boys, key/keys, day/days.** If, however, the final -**y** is preceded by a consonant, the **y** is changed to **i** and -**es** is added to form the plural: **spy/spies, fly/flies, century/centuries.** Whichever inflection is added, its pronunciation is still [z].

v. Finally, English has a host of irregularly formed plurals which must simply be memorized by the Spanish speaker, as they are especially complicated to classify in any simple way: **leaf/leaves, child/children, woman/women, mouse/mice, foot/feet, sheep/sheep,** etc.

Exercise 3

Give the plural form of the following English singular nouns and be able to state a rule for each pluralization. Designate the phonetic symbol which represents the proper pronunciation of the plural ending, and identify which plurals defy convenient classification.

1. singer	6. church	11. class	16. knife
2. rack	7. thrush	12. clash	17. breeze
3. cylinder	8. fool	13. station	18. man
4. snap	9. toy	14. grudge	19. potato
5. hat	10. fly	15. goose	20. thread

THE DEFINITE ARTICLES OF SPANISH AND ENGLISH
9.8
The Spanish Definite Article

There are five definite articles in Spanish: **el, la, los, las,** and **lo.** The articles **el, la, los,** and **las** must agree in gender and number with their nouns: **el hombre, la tía, los hombres, las tías.** **Lo** is a neuter definite article which does not show agreement. It may be used with both masculine and feminine gender words, usually adjectives, to produce a nominalization with abstract meaning: **Lo bueno que eres/Lo buena que eres** (see §10.12).

Spanish feminine singular nouns beginning with a stressed **a-** or **ha-** use what would appear to be the masculine singular article **el.** This **el** is really an old allomorph of the feminine singular article **la** and in Old Spanish was required before any feminine noun beginning with a vowel: **el espada.** Feminine singular nouns with **el** as their article in the singular use **las** in the plural: **el agua/las aguas, el hacha/las hachas, el águila/las águilas.**

The English Definite Article
English has only one written form of the definite article, **the**, but this single form has two pronunciations, [ðə] and [ðɪ]. Unstressed [ðə] is the pronunciation of **the** before words beginning with a consonant sound. Unstressed [ðɪ] is used before words beginning with a vowel sound: **the man** [ðə mæn], **the army** [ðɪ armɪ]. The same form is used also before a plural noun, with the same pronunciation distinctions.

9.9
Spanish and English Definite Article Usage
Both Spanish and English use the definite article in the same way in many cases. Various examples of these usages in both languages are illustrated.

i. When the speaker and the listener are aware both of the existence and the identity of the person or thing under discussion:

La ciudad está triste.	The city is sad.
La bandera tricolor es vuestra.	The tricolor flag is yours.

ii. With elements of nature:

El cielo es azul.	The sky is blue.
El sol nunca brilla aquí.	The sun never shines here.

iii. With animals, plants, or individuals spoken of in the singular as representatives of their species, sex, race, religion, or nationality:

La zorra es muy astuta.	The fox is very cunning.
La rosa es una flor.	The rose is a flower.
El bautista es protestante.	The Baptist is a protestant.
El argentino no lo haría.	The Argentinian would not do it.
El indígena tiene derechos.	The native has rights.

iv. With the organs of the body:

El corazón es pequeño.	The heart is small.
El ojo es de menor tamaño.	The eye is smaller in size.

v. With nouns restricted by modifying or defining words:

la flor de papel	the paper flower
la señorita de Cuba	the young lady from Cuba
el número más pequeño	the smallest number

vi. With epithets (words used to characterize famous people) and nicknames:

Pedro el Grande	Peter the Great
Bolívar el Libertador	Bolivar the Liberator
Pepe el toro	Pete the bull

vii. With names of rivers, seas, and oceans:

El Río Grande es largo.	The Rio Grande is long.
La isla se encuentra en el Atlántico.	The island is located in the Atlantic.

viii. With the expression of exact dates, provided that English uses the construction **the** + date + **of** + month:

Él vino el 20 de abril.	He came the 20th of April.
Voy el dos de julio.	I'm going the 2nd of July.

Note: Spanish uses the cardinal number whereas English uses the ordinal. There is one exception to this practice. Spanish uses the ordinal number like English for the first day of the month (cf §36.8).

Comienzan el primero de mayo.	**They begin the 1st of May.**

9.10
Divergent Uses of Definite Articles
Spanish uses the definite article while English does not in some instances, or English will use another word in place of the article.

i. With nouns spoken of in a general sense, whether concrete or abstract in meaning:

El griego es difícil.	Greek is difficult.
No mencionan los sacrificios.	They don't mention sacrifices.
El hombre no es divino.	Man is not divine.
La drogas causan daño.	Drugs cause harm.
La ciencia define la naturaleza.	Science defines nature.

ii. With days of the week and in the expression of exact dates, provided that English uses the construction **on** + month + date:

Ella llegó el lunes.	She arrived on Monday.
La vemos los martes.	We see her on Tuesdays.
Él vino el diez de mayo.	He came on May 10th.
Salieron el 24 de agosto.	They left on August 24th.

iii. With expressions of the time of day:

Son las doce en punto.	It's twelve o'clock.
Eran las cuatro y treinta/media.	It was four-thirty.
Él nos encontró a las siete.	He met us at seven.

iv. With Spanish **en** (English **at**) and Spanish **a** (English **to**) + a commonly frequented or often referred to place or event. Note that in this regard Spanish uses the article much more than does English, albeit in several instances both languages do use the definite article.

•Spanish uses the definite article; English does not:

Van al cielo.	They're going to heaven.
Estoy en la escuela.	I'm in/at school.
Vas a la cárcel.	You're going to jail.
Están en la iglesia.	They're in/at church.
Vas al infierno.	You're going to hell.
Voy al pueblo.	I'm going to town.
¿Vas al mercado?	Are you going to (the) market?

•Neither language uses the definite article:

Están en clase.	They are in class.
Estoy en casa.	I'm at home.
Vamos a misa.	Let's go to Mass.

v. Before the name of a country or continent if it is in any way modified:

La América Latina	Latin America
El Asia central	Central Asia
La Europa clásica	Classical Europe

vi. With classified nouns in indirect address. A classified noun is one which bears a title or which is in some way modified. Indirect address means that the noun is being spoken about rather than being directly spoken to:

¿Dónde está el Sr. Gómez?	Where is Mr. Gomez?
Es la clase del Dr. Smith.	It's Dr. Smith's class.
Vivo en la calle Ocho.	I live on Eighth Street.
Corresponde con la página 25.	It matches page 25.

vii. With nouns used in apposition to a personal pronoun. A noun used in apposition is one which clarifies a personal pronoun.

Ustedes los rebeldes ...	You rebels ...
Nosotros los técnicos ...	We technicians ...
Vosotros los romanos ...	You Romans ...

viii. With parts of the body or articles of clothing. English in these cases uses the possessive adjective rather than the definite article. This lack of correspondence between Spanish and English is one of the most frequent causes of production errors.

Me puse el vestido.	I put on my suit (dress).
Él bajó la cabeza.	He bowed his head.
Me quemé el dedo.	I burned my finger.
Ud. se cortó la cara.	You cut your face.
Ella se quitó los zapatos.	She took off her shoes.

9.11

English and Spanish, it must be observed, have different ways of viewing reality when parts of the body or articles of clothing are being discussed. When the reference is to bodily parts or articles of clothing found singularly among a group of individuals, Spanish uses the singular form of the noun meaning that each individual has one item. English uses the plural form of the noun in these references since more than one item is involved in the whole group.

Nos quitamos *el sombrero.*	We took off *our hats.*
(Each person has one hat.)	(There is more than one hat involved.)

Similarly:

Mantuvieron *la boca* cerrada.	They kept *their mouths* closed.
Levantaron *la mano.*	They raised *their hands.*
Bajaron *la cabeza.*	They bowed *their heads.*

But:

> Levantaron las manos. (This implies that each person raised both his/her hands.)
>
> *Bajaron las cabezas. (The implication is that each person has two heads; therefore, the sentence is ungrammatical.)

Exercise 4

Translate the following sentences into the other language and be able to state in each case why you did or did not use the definite article.

1. The oak is a very important tree in Portugal.
2. Es obvio que no sabes nada de la cocina francesa.
3. We are going to travel through western France.
4. Me quité los zapatos y me puse las sandalias.
5. He wants to visit us on July 4th.
6. ¿No conoce Ud. a la profesora Serrano?
7. The lungs are very near the heart.
8. No quiero caminar contigo a la cárcel.
9. It's nine o'clock and I have to go home.
10. Los lunes no voy al centro hasta tarde.
11. The earth was once considered flat.
12. Leímos la triste historia de Diana la Cazadora.
13. John cut his arm in the accident.
14. No quiero comprar ninguna casa en la calle Riviera.
15. They live in ignorance and poverty because they lack money.
16. Algunos van al cielo y otros van al infierno.
17. Dr. Brown spoke to Dr. Smith at the meeting.
18. Ustedes los alumnos creen que lo saben todo.
19. They left on Saturday, but they plan to return on Sunday.
20. Abrí los ojos cuando la profesora Roscoe se sentó a mi lado.

THE INDEFINITE ARTICLES OF SPANISH AND ENGLISH
9.12

Spanish has four forms of the indefinite article: **un, una, unos, unas.** There is no neuter indefinite article form. Again, the indefinite articles must agree in gender and number with their nouns.

English has two forms or allomorphs of its singular indefinite article: **a** and **an.** You use **a** before words beginning with a consonant sound: **a dog, a man, a house, a book, a tiger, a lady.** You use **an** before words beginning with a vowel sound: **an apple, an onion, an honor, an eye.**

The English plural indefinite article in no way resembles the singular forms **a** and **an.** The plural form is **some**, and it is often omitted.

SINGULAR	PLURAL
I have a book.	I have (some) books.
She has an answer.	She has (some) answers.
He needs a lesson.	He needs (some) lessons.

Spanish and English generally use the indefinite article in the same way, although some exceptions are to be noted.

With an unmodified singular predicate noun indicating profession or with a singular predicate adjective of nationality, Spanish does not normally use the indefinite article while English does.

Mi padre es capitán.	My father is a captain.
Susana es actriz.	Susan is an actress.
Rafael es mexicano.	Ralph is a Mexican.
Ella es inglesa.	She's an Englishwoman.

However, when the predicate noun of profession or adjective of nationality is in any way modified, both English and Spanish use the indefinite article.

Mi padre es un capitán de reserva.	My father is a reserve captain.
Susana es una buena actriz.	Susan is a good actress.
Rafael es un mexicano romántico.	Ralph is a romantic Mexican.
Es una inglesa curiosa.	She is a curious Englishwoman.

Finally, if the predicate noun of profession or adjective of nationality assumes plural form, neither language uses the indefinite article, unless, and this applies to Spanish only, the noun or adjective is modified is some way.

Ellos son dominicanos.	They are Dominicans.
Mis padres son científicos.	My parents are scientists.
Son médicos.	They are doctors.

But:

Son unos dominicanos ricos.	They are rich Dominicans.

Exercise 5

Translate the following sentences into the other language. Determine whether or not the indefinite article is to be used and be able to explain why or why not.

1. Quiero buscar unos documentos de historia en la biblioteca.
2. His father is a businessman.
3. Estos señores son brasileños.
4. Her uncle is a very good doctor.
5. Osvaldo es ingeniero.
6. All your friends are students. (familiar)
7. ¿Es guatemalteco tu tío?
8. She is an Italian.
9. El perro se comió un hueso y unos trozos de carne.
10. Cantinflas was a very famous Mexican comedian.
11. Ellos son unos actores bien conocidos.
12. My parents are French.

Descriptive and Limiting Adjectives

10.1
The Spanish adjective always has at least two forms and often has four or even five. It is consistently inflected for number (singular vs plural) and is often inflected for gender (masculine vs feminine). The English adjective has only one form, unless used in comparison, and is never marked either for gender or for number. Many English adjectives are marked, however, to show comparative and superlative degrees. (See Unit 23.)

CLASSIFICATION OF THE SPANISH ADJECTIVE
10.2
Class I
Class I adjectives have a dictionary masculine singular form ending in -o. They always have at least four forms which are marked for gender and for number.

	SINGULAR		PLURAL
MASCULINE	FEMININE	MASCULINE	FEMININE
cómodo	cómoda	cómodos	cómodas
delicioso	deliciosa	deliciosos	deliciosas
sano	sana	sanos	sanas
simpático	simpática	simpáticos	simpáticas

Some adjectives of this class drop their final -o and assume apocopated (shortened) forms when they precede a masculine singular noun. These adjectives, then, exhibit five forms—the apocopated form and the other four forms; all are limiting adjectives (See §10.6). The following are the main Spanish adjectives in Class I which are subject to apocopation.

	SINGULAR		PLURAL
MASCULINE	FEMININE	MASCULINE	FEMININE
un(o)	una	unos	unas
algún/alguno	alguna	algunos	algunas
ningún/ninguno	ninguna	ningunos	ningunas
primer(o)	primera	primeros	primeras
tercer(o)	tercera	terceros	terceras
mal(o)	mala	malos	malas
buen(o)	buena	buenos	buenas

10.3
Class II
Class II adjectives have a dictionary masculine singular form ending in a letter other than **-o**, with the exclusion of the endings mentioned under Class III below. Class II adjectives have two forms and are marked for number but not for gender.

MASCULINE AND FEMININE

SINGULAR	PLURAL
gris	grises
inteligente	inteligentes
conforme	conformes
genial	geniales
liberal	liberales
feliz	felices
inferior	inferiores

In this class **reciente** has an apocopated form **recién**, like others in Class I.

10.4
Class III
Class III are the adjectives ending in **-án, -ón, -ín** (except **ruin**), and **-or**, except the comparatives **mejor, peor, superior,** etc. All adjectives of nationality or origin whose masculine singular form ends in other than **-o** are also included. Class III adjectives always have four forms and are marked for both gender and number.

SINGULAR		PLURAL	
MASCULINE	FEMININE	MASCULINE	FEMININE
español	española	españoles	españolas
inglés	inglesa	ingleses	inglesas
alemán	alemana	alemanes	alemanas
dulzón	dulzona	dulzones	dulzonas
pequeñín	pequeñina	pequeñines	pequeñinas
labrador	labradora	labradores	labradoras

Exercise 1

Give all possible forms of the following Spanish adjectives and determine whether they belong to Class I, II, or III.

1. portugués	10. infantil
2. poco	11. permanente
3. holgazán	12. profesional
4. tercero	13. chiquitín
5. chino	14. hablador
6. remolón	15. capaz
7. superior	16. común
8. malo	17. santo
9. activista	18. patán

Exercise 2

Give all possible forms in Spanish for the following English adjectives. Again, determine whether they belong to Class I, II, or III adjectives.

1. poor
2. modern
3. French
4. intelligent
5. first

6. German
7. small
8. racial
9. Spanish
10. useful

10.5

In English the adjective precedes the noun it modifies almost without exception.

> The *first* man arrived in a *black* car.
> The *poor* nations of the *Third* World have many *political* problems.
> We live in a *small* house next to the *American* River.

Some exceptions to this rule are **court *martial*, attorney *general*, heir *apparent*, notary *public*,** etc, where the adjective follows the noun it modifies. These are all borrowings from French.

Spanish adjectives, however, can either precede or follow the noun they modify according to the classification they have. Spanish adjectives may be classified as either limiting or descriptive, among other classes. Many adjectives can function under both categories, limiting and descriptive. Limiting adjectives usually precede nouns while descriptive adjectives generally follow them.

10.6
Limiting Adjectives in Spanish

Limiting adjectives relate the noun to its environment, describe its order in a succession, or state its relative amount or quantity. Unlike descriptive adjectives, limiting adjectives say virtually nothing about the true nature of the noun itself. In Spanish they include the articles (definite and indefinite), the possessive adjectives (the short unstressed forms), the demonstrative adjectives, numerical adjectives, adjectives of quantity, indefinites, and so on. These, however, are not called limiting adjectives in English; they are considered **determiners.**

> No me gusta *el* gobierno.
> Tienen *unos* camaradas que son de Venezuela.
> ¿Dónde vas a colocar *tu* capa?
> Tienen que hablar con *ese* maestro.
> Vamos a añadir *dos* ejemplos.
> Van a comer *más/menos* frijoles.
> Procedió con *toda* tranquilidad.
> No podemos revelar *tantos* secretos.
> Usa *mucha/poca* corriente eléctrica.
> *Otro* caballero murió después de la conquista.
> No vamos a leer *ningún* periódico *esta* semana.
> Llevas el *mismo* vestido que ayer.
> Han tirado la *última* edición.
> Vivimos en el *cuarto* piso del edificio.
> Quiero reunir a los *demás* empleados.

10.7
Descriptive Adjectives in Spanish
Descriptive adjectives generally follow the nouns they modify, although several exceptions to this rule of thumb will be cited later. Descriptive adjectives say something about the nature of their nouns; that is, they differentiate them from other possible nouns. This function of differentiation may range from classification to contrast.

Classification categories involve nationality, social affiliations, technical descriptions, and the like.

> Es un escritor *alemán.*
> Fue un presidente *católico.*
> Es un suelo *ácido.*

In expressing contrasts, the descriptive adjectives imply that the noun belongs to "x category" rather than to a supposed "y category."

> Es un príncipe *pobre* (y no rico).
> Fue un proceso *complicado* (y no sencillo).
> Es una raza *noble* (y no inferior).

Whether they express classification or contrast, true descriptive adjectives follow the noun even when they themselves are modified.

> Es un país *tan lejano.*
> Parece una persona *medio falsa.*
> Quiero un vino *bien seco.*

10.8
Prepositioned Spanish Adjectives
Although descriptive adjectives generally follow the noun, they may precede it. Whether the descriptive adjective precedes or follows is a function of what might be described as "relative informativeness," that is, the amount or degree of relevant information provided by the adjective.

In the sentence **Sebastián iba acompañado de su feroz perro,** where the descriptive adjective precedes, relatively little new, significant, or unexpected information is provided about the noun **perro.** What is stressed, in fact, is the "viciousness of the dog."

In **Sebastián iba acompañado de su perro feroz,** however, where the descriptive adjective follows, the implication is that Sebastián perhaps has more than one dog, some of which are relatively tame. On this occasion, however, he is in the company of the "more vicious one."

The matter of relative informativeness and descriptive adjective positioning can be further extended. When the descriptive adjective precedes the noun, it enhances the noun or offers a personal estimation or value judgment (good vs bad) concerning it. It is for this reason that the adjectives **bueno** and **malo**, which express such judgmental ideas, routinely precede their nouns, even when they themselves are modified.

> El guiso adquirió un buen gusto. (Speaker voices pleasure with the taste.)
> Tuve una mala experiencia. (Speaker suffered a really bad experience.)
> Fue una verdadera sorpresa. (Speaker expresses his true surprise.)
> No vuelvo a ese miserable salón. (Speaker really detests the room.)

Ambos sostuvieron una tremenda lucha.   (Speaker is impressed by the intensity of both's fight.)

When following the noun, the descriptive adjective serves its normal function of differentiation rather than expressing personal estimations such as enhancement or denigration.

Recibí un sueldo bueno.   (There are good and bad salaries; this one was good.)

Fue un triunfo verdadero.   (Accomplishment was authentic and not a deception.)

Tuvieron una lucha tremenda.   (Some spats are insignificant, others relatively more serious; this one was serious.)

10.9

Some adjectives may be regarded as either limiting or descriptive. When functioning with a limiting meaning, they precede the noun, but in expressing description and carrying literal or concrete meaning, they follow the noun.

English must often use two different adjectives to convey this duality of meaning found in Spanish. The following contrastive examples are illustrative of the two variations in meaning.

Eso contiene diferentes elementos.	That contains various elements.
Eso contiene un elemento diferente.	That contains a different element.
Él tiene un nuevo automóvil.	He has a different automobile.
Él tiene un automóvil nuevo.	He has a new automobile.
Ella es una pobre víctima.	She's an unfortunate victim.
Ella es una víctima pobre.	She's an impoverished victim.
Tengo mi propio plan.	I have my own plan.
Es un plan propio.	It is a suitable (proper) plan.
Decían puras tonterías.	They spoke sheer nonsense.
Exigían conducta pura.	They demanded chaste conduct.
Es un simple soldado.	He's just a plain soldier.
Es un soldado simple.	He's a dull-minded soldier.
Discuten varios casos.	They are discussing various cases.
Discuten temas varios.	They discuss miscellaneous topics.
Es mi vieja amiga.	She's my long-time friend.
Es mi amiga vieja.	She's my old (aged) friend.

10.10
The Problematic Adjective *grande*

When following a noun, **grande** and its plural **grandes** carry the descriptive meaning of **large/big,** stressing physical size.

Es una estancia grande.	It is a large estate.
Son una niñas grandes.	They are big girls.

When preceding a singular noun of either gender, **grande** assumes the apocopated form **gran** and must then be translated as **great, grand,** or **famous.**

| Pasamos un gran rato. | We had a great/grand/fabulous time. |
| Fue una gran marquesa. | She was a famous marquise. |

Grandes expresses the English idea of **famous/great** when it occurs before a plural noun.

Fernando e Isabel fueron unos grandes reyes.
Ferdinand and Isabel were great monarchs.

La producción en el teatro prescinde de grandes actores.
The production in the theatre does without famous actors.

(Exercise 3)

Translate the following English sentences into Spanish, placing all limiting adjectives before the noun and all descriptive adjectives after the noun.

1. I am reading the same book.
2. They arrived in a large airplane.
3. He needs another glass.
4. You missed an important meeting. (familiar)
5. She came to my house three times.
6. I want a cup of hot tea.

7. They sell fortified rice in that store.
8. There was a general strike in the second factory.
9. Some friends live on the fifth floor.
10. I bought the first book with my Spanish pesetas.
11. The same man solved three difficult problems.
12. This complicated machine didn't cost so much money.

(Exercise 4)

Write original Spanish sentences in which the following adjectives will be used before nouns, thereby providing little information about the noun but expressing value judgments (goodness or badness) about it.

bueno	gran
malo	bendito
mejor	loco
peor	estúpido
verdadero	tremendo
alto	pequeño

Exercise 5

Translate the following pairs of English sentences into Spanish. Use the same adjective in your translation, accomplishing the shift in meaning through correct placement of the adjective with respect to the noun it modifies.

1. He is an old employee. (aged)
   He is an old employee. (long-time employee)

2. He arrived in a different car.
   He arrived in a new car.
3. It is a poor country. (It has many wars and other difficulties.)
   It is a poor country. (economically)
4. I am looking for a certain answer.
   I am looking for an accurate answer.
5. It contains pure milk
   He opened it with pure (sheer) force.
6. Among my own clothes, I have clothes suitable for work.
7. She has big hands.
   She is a great teacher.

NOMINALIZATION OF THE ADJECTIVE IN SPANISH AND ENGLISH
10.11

Nominalization is the use of a word from some other part of speech category as a noun in a nominal function. Adjectives are frequently involved in this process and used as nouns.

Spanish has a rather simple system for producing nominalization involving the adjective. It simply omits the noun in a construction of an **article + noun + adjective,** leaving behind both the article and the adjective. By this process, the adjective becomes nominalized or, in other words, acts as a noun.

Me atrevo a apoyar una ~~causa~~ diferente.
No me convienen los ~~cursos~~ nocturnos.
Vamos a necesitar unos ~~recursos~~ privados.
Tenemos que conservar los ~~logros~~ grandes.

The English system for nominalizing adjectives is more complex. English occasionally follows the Spanish system of omitting the noun and leaving the **article + adjective** combination. This occurs in only a few cases involving singular nouns.

A blonde ~~lady~~ just arrived.
I must speak to the brunette ~~girl~~.

If English follows the Spanish system of merely omitting a noun and leaving an **article + adjective** combination, the resulting nominalization normally refers to plural entities only, usually human.

I refuse to have any more to do with the poor ~~souls~~.
He feels we should tax the rich ~~persons~~.
What will be done with the sick ~~people~~ and the aged ~~people~~?
There are no more institutions for the insane ~~individuals~~.

English most often produces nominalizations from adjectives by omitting the noun, replacing it with the indefinite pronoun **one** if the noun is singular, or **ones** if the noun is plural, and leaving behind any article or other type of noun marker.

Compare the Spanish examples below with the usual English method of nominalization.

los ~~hombres~~ ricos	the rich ~~men~~ *ones*
la ~~mujer~~ mayor	the older ~~lady~~ *one*
esa ~~chica~~ de los ojos verdes	that ~~girl~~ *one* with the green eyes
este ~~libro~~ está roto	this ~~book~~ *one* is torn
unos ~~libros~~ más grandes	some larger ~~books~~ *ones*
diez ~~mujeres~~ casadas	ten married ~~women~~ *ones*
otro ~~perro~~ mejor	another better ~~dog~~ *one*
una ~~casa~~ más pequeña	a smaller ~~house~~ *one*
la ~~muchacha~~ que viste ayer	the ~~girl~~ *one* you saw yesterday

Exercise 6

Rewrite the following English and Spanish sentences. The italicized phrases should be nominalized in the new sentences.

1. If I can't buy a new car, then I'll buy a *used car*.
2. La línea verde está cerca de *la línea amarilla*.
3. I don't have any *good pencils* left.
4. Voy a comprar unas frutas dulces, porque no me gustan *las frutas agrias*.
5. The book on the table is a *very valuable book*.
6. Los conocidos nuevos siempre son más interesantes que *los conocidos viejos*.
7. Poor people are often forced to beg for money from *the rich people*.
8. Busco un clima más templado porque *el clima de aquí* es muy fresco.

10.12

Spanish has a system by which it uses the neuter article **lo** with adjectives, adverbs, and even prepositions to produce a form of nominalization with an abstract meaning.

English has a very limited and restricted system for producing this type of nominalization which may partially resemble Spanish. Often English must rely upon various constructions of its own to convey the abstract meaning of the relatively simple Spanish structure. The most commonly used English equivalents for Spanish abstract nominalizations using **lo** are listed here.

a. **how + ADJ/ADV**

No sabes *lo claro* que es el cielo.   You don't know *how clear* the sky is.

Veo *lo rápido* que él conduce.   I see *how fast* he drives.

b. **the + ADJ + aspect/thing/part**

Eso es *lo bonito* de mi vida.   That's *the pretty aspect* of my life.
Es *lo más complicado* de mi asignatura.   It's *the most complicated part* of my course (in school).

c. **the (that) business (stuff) about**

Lo de Josué no me importa.   I don't care about *that stuff about* Joshua.

Lo de tu marido me preocupa.	*The business about* your husband worries me.

d. **the** + NOUN[**-ness**] + **of**

Me impresionó *lo conciso* de tu ensayo.	I was impressed by *the conciseness of* your essay.
Vas a comprender *lo inútil* de este método.	You will understand *the uselessness of* this method.

e. **what** (non-interrogative)

Él me dijo *lo que* necesitaba.	He told me *what* he needed.
Él no te puede decir *lo que* dijo ella.	He can't tell you *what* she said.

(Exercise 7)

Translate the English sentences into Spanish using a **lo** type abstract nominalization. Translate the Spanish sentences into English, giving as good an English equivalent as you can from the various possibilities listed.

1. I haven't words to tell you how funny that movie is.
2. Lo interesante es que ya habían recibido la comunicación.
3. The bad part is that I have to get up so early.
4. Algún día te voy a contar lo mucho que he sufrido en esta vida.
5. You can't imagine how badly he reads. (familiar)
6. Haz lo que quieras con lo que tienes.

7. That business about Susan is not as serious as that stuff about her mother.
8. No me gusta ese novelista por lo revolucionario que es su estilo.
9. I scolded him for the ridiculousness of his actions.
10. Lo de tu padre es triste, pero peor es lo que tú hiciste.
11. What I do with my time is my own business.
12. Nadie se ha enterado de lo mala que es ella.

11

Possessive and Demonstrative Adjectives and Pronouns

POSSESSIVE ADJECTIVES
11.1
Whereas English has only one set of possessive adjectives, Spanish has two. These are the unstressed set, which always precede nouns, and the stressed possessives, which always follow nouns. The possessive adjectives of the stressed set are regularly nominalized.

	SINGULAR			PLURAL	
	UNSTRESSED	STRESSED		UNSTRESSED	STRESSED
my	mi, mis	mío, mía míos, mías	our	nuestro, -a nuestros, -as	nuestro, -a nuestros, -as
your	[FAMILIAR] tu, tus	[FAMILIAR] tuyo, tuya tuyos, tuyas	your	[FAMILIAR] vuestro, -a vuestros, -as	[FAMILIAR] vuestro, -a vuestros, -as
your	[FORMAL] su, sus	[FORMAL] suyo, suya suyos, suyas de usted, -es	your	[FORMAL] su, sus	[FORMAL] suyo, suya suyos, -as de usted, -es
his/her	su, sus	suyo, suya suyos, suyas	their	su, sus	suyo, suya suyos, suyas de ellos, de ellas
his	su, sus	de él			
her	su, sus	de ella			
its	su, sus	de él, de ella, de ello			

PEDAGOGICAL IMPLICATIONS
11.2
The Spanish unstressed possessive adjective always precedes the noun and consistently shows at least a singular and plural form. In the 1st and 2nd persons plural, it shows gender also. The Spanish stressed possessive adjective always follows its noun and is always marked for both gender and number.

As we have mentioned in other units of the book, a Spanish speaker's mode of expression frequently reflects a different way of viewing reality than that of the English speaker. *The Spanish possessive adjective, whether stressed or unstressed, agrees with the noun possessed rather than with the possessor. Just the opposite is the case of English possessives since they agree with the possessor, whose gender and number are reflected in the 3rd person forms.* The complete lack of correspondence in this area contributes much to the confusion and uncertainty experienced by both Spanish and English speakers when they attempt to carry over their linguistic intuitions to the respective target languages.

The unstressed Spanish possessive adjective **su(s)** is highly ambiguous in its meaning for the English speaker since, as can be seem from the preceding chart, it has at least six possible translations in English. Depending upon the antecedent, **su lado** can mean **his side, her side, its side, your** (singular) **side, their side,** or **your** (plural) **side.** By the same token, the Spanish speaker will confuse **su cama** (de él), which means **his bed** (often rendered mistakenly as **her bed** because of the feminine gender of **cama**), with **su cama** (de ella), which means **her bed.** Likewise, **su lado** (de ella) is frequently translated as **his side** since **lado** is a masculine noun. This confusion is due to the differing focus on concordances in the two languages. Again, the Spanish speaker aligns the possessive adjective's gender and number concordance with the gender and number of the object possessed, whereas the English speaker aligns gender and number with that of the possessor.

In modern Spanish usage, the stressed possessive adjectives **suyo, suya, suyos,** and **suyas** generally refer to the addressee (the person being spoken to), that is **you** (singular) or **you** (plural). **La cama suya** usually means **your** (singular or plural) **bed.** **Suyo** and **suya,** can however, refer to third person possessors, depending upon context. Should ambiguity result, an alternate prepositional construction may be used. Note the following examples.

La cama suya usually means **your** (sgl. and pl.) **bed.** However, **la cama suya** can also mean:

> **his bed,** more often expressed as **la cama de él**
> **her bed (la cama de ella)**
> **their bed (la cama de ellos, de ellas)**

The unstressed possessive adjective of Spanish must precede the noun, and no article is used in the construction: **mi comida, tu lado, sus dientes.**

However, the stressed possessive adjective of Spanish follows the noun, and the noun must be accompanied by an article or by some other type of determiner or noun marker: **la comida mía, este lado tuyo, diez dientes suyos.**

Exercise 1

Give both Spanish unstressed and stressed versions of the following English possessive adjective constructions. Example: **his cousin** (feminine) = **su prima** or **la prima de él.**

1. her cousin (masc.)
2. my adventure
3. our aunt
4. your (familiar sgl.) cigarettes
5. their brothers
6. your (formal sgl.) dog
7. his grandmother
8. your (formal pl.) uncle
9. its paws
10. your (familiar pl.) ballpoint pen

POSSESSIVE PRONOUNS
11.3
The English possessive pronoun is generally a different form from the possessive adjective, as can be seen by comparing this chart with the chart in §11.1.

The Spanish possessive pronoun is merely a nominalized form of the stressed possessive adjective. The noun of the stressed possessive adjective construction has been omitted, but the article retained, thereby producing a nominalization.

	SINGULAR		PLURAL
mine	el mío, la mía los míos, las mías	ours	el nuestro, la nuestra los nuestros, las nuestras
	[FAMILIAR]		[FAMILIAR]
yours	el tuyo, la tuya los tuyos, las tuyas	yours	el vuestro, la vuestra los vuestros, las vuestras
	[FORMAL]		[FORMAL]
	el suyo, la suya los suyos, las suyas el/la/los/las de usted		el suyo, la suya los suyos, las suyas el/la/los/las de ustedes
his	el suyo, la suya los suyos, las suyas el de él, la de él los de él, las de él	theirs	el suyo, la suya los suyos, las suyas el de ellos, el de ellas la de ellos, la de ellas los de ellos, los de ellas las de ellos, las de ellas
hers	el suyo, la suya los suyos, las suyas el de ella, la de ella los de ella, las de ella		

Exercise 2
Render in the other language these short sentences using possessive pronoun constructions Example: **It's ours** (the car) = **Es nuestro; Vi la de ellos** (casa) = **I saw theirs.**

1. It's mine. (= house)
2. Vi el de él. (= libro)
3. I met yours. (= friends)
4. Hirieron a los suyos. (= enemigos de Ud.)
5. We enjoyed ours. (= party)
6. Detén la tuya. (= aventura)
7. They smoked theirs. (= cigars)
8. Defendió a las de ellas. (= amigas de ellas)
9. He has finished his. (= work)
10. Cultivamos las nuestras. (= flores)

Exercise 3

Rewrite the following English and Spanish sentences by replacing the second possessive *adjective* construction in each with possessive *pronoun* constructions. Example: **Their cards are here with our cards. = Their cards are here with *ours*.**

1. Mi secretaria está hablando con tu secretaria.
2. Their cousins want to meet our cousins.
3. Su esposa está con tu esposa.
4. Our money was all spent along with his money.
5. Su copia (de ella) llegó junto con nuestra copia.
6. Your nephew is fighting with my nephew.
7. Nuestros ciudadanos son mejores que sus ciudadanos. (de ellos)
8. Their parents don't know your parents.
9. Su papá (de Uds.) quiere ver al papá de ella.
10. His books seem to be locked up with my books.

DEMONSTRATIVE ADJECTIVES

11.4.

Demonstrative adjectives always precede their nouns in both English and Spanish. They are used to indicate relative proximity of persons or things from the speaker, either in spacial relation or in time.

	SINGULAR			PLURAL	
this	este	esta	these	estos	estas
that	ese	esa	those	esos	esas
	aquel	aquella		aquellos	aquellas

The English demonstrative adjectives distinguish in their forms only between a singular and a plural. Spanish demonstrative adjectives are marked for both gender and number as can be seen in the above chart.

Spanish also distinguishes between **that (ese, esa)** and **those (esos, esas)**, which are relatively nearer to the speaker in either space or time, and **that (aquel, aquella)** and **those (aquellos, aquellas)**, which are relatively farther from the speaker, again, either in space or time. No such distinctions may be made in Modern English unless you use extra words in addition to the demonstrative adjective. For example, **ese barco** would be translated as **that boat**, but **aquel barco** would best be render as **that boat over there** or as **that boat over yonder. Yonder**, it should be noted, is a more dialectal term.

Exercise 4
Translate the following sentences, all of which contain demonstrative adjectives, into the other language.

1. I don't want to buy those bananas. (near)
2. El director no va a utilizar a aquellos actores en la comedia.
3. My parents say that they are going to sell that house. (far)
4. No me dejaron cruzar ese campo, por eso, subo por este camino.
5. They gave me five dollars for this old watch.
6. En aquel gobierno estos diputados formaron una junta independiente.
7. During that (near) time, we swam in this river every day.
8. Este fraile quiere hablar con aquella doña.
9. These books are old, but those books (near) are very new.
10. Si quieres comprar esta empresa, debes comunicarte con ese dueño.

11.5. Demonstrative Pronouns

As we have seen, both Spanish and English have possessive adjectives and pronouns; likewise both languages have demonstrative adjectives and demonstrative pronouns. The demonstrative pronouns in the two languages are merely nominalized versions of the demonstrative adjectives. They are pronouns since they substitute for persons or things rather than modify them.

SINGULAR			PLURAL			NEUTER	
this one	éste	ésta	these	éstos	éstas	this	esto
that one	ése	ésa	those	ésos	ésas	that	eso
	aquél	aquélla		aquéllos, aquéllas			aquello

Nominalization is accomplished in Spanish by omitting the noun of the demonstrative adjective construction and by adding a written accent mark to the demonstrative word. In English the singular nominalization is produced by omitting the noun and replacing it with the indefinite pronoun **one.** In the plural, the noun is simply omitted, and no word is needed to replace it, although **ones** is sometimes used.

As seen above, both Spanish and English have neuter demonstrative pronouns. These refer to items whose gender cannot be determined or to entire ideas or abstract concepts. In English the neuter demonstrative pronouns are simply the singular demonstrative pronoun forms not accompanied by the pronoun **one.** The Spanish neuter forms end in **-o** and bear no written accent mark. Neither English nor Spanish has a plural neuter demonstrative pronoun.

Exercise 5
Rewrite the following English and Spanish sentences using a demonstrative pronoun construction in place of the demonstrative adjective constructions. For some of the sentences no rewrite will be possible.

1. I don't like these grapes; let's buy those grapes.
2. Este alcalde es muy buen amigo de ese otro alcalde.
3. I don't know anything about this.
4. Este capítulo del libro llegó ayer, pero aquel capítulo llegó anteayer.
5. Are you going to speak to your boss about that?
6. Aquellos ministros convencen al pueblo, pero estos ministros, no.
7. Before buying this apartment, you should see those apartments.
8. Aquello constituye un grave problema.
9. He brought me these letters, but I can answer only that letter today.
10. Insistió en que aceptáramos estos artículos, pero no esos artículos.

12

Expressions of Possession

12.1

The Spanish and English systems used for expressing possession are quite different. Considerable practice is required for both the English speaker and the Spanish speaker to master the system of the other language. The Spanish speaker, however, will have more difficulties with the English system than the English speaker will have with the Spanish one.

The Spanish System

The Spanish system consistently uses the preposition **de** in periphrastic possession expressions. The formula to show possession is as follows:

POSSESSED THING + **de** + POSSESSOR

la sonrisa	de	la Virgen
los hijos	de	mis vecinos
el gesto	de	ese héroe
las emociones	de	una madre

When asking a question concerning who possesses what in Spanish, one or the other of the following patterns is employed when referring to human possessors.

i. ¿De quién(es) es + NOUN [singular]?
>>> Example: ¿De quién(es) es esta llave?
¿De quién(es) son + NOUN [plural]?
>>> Example: ¿De quién(es) son estos dibujos?

ii. ¿A quién(es) + pertenece + NOUN [singular]?
>>> Example: ¿A quién(es) pertenece esta llave?
¿A quién(es) + pertenecen + NOUN [plural]?
>>> Example: ¿A quién(es) pertenecen los dibujos?

In the patterns illustrated above, the possessor whose identity is sought may be referred to in the singular **¿quién?** or in the plural **¿quiénes?**, both forms accented. English makes no such distinction, using either **whose?** or **of whom?**, each with both singular or plural meaning.

116

12.2
The English System
The English system for the expression of possession is essentially the reverse of the Spanish system with some added features.

•The possessor, expressed in a special form, is stated first, followed by the possessed thing.

•No preposition intervenes between the elements of the construction.

•If the possessor (expressed first) is singular, or if it is plural but does not end in **-s**, then **-'s** is added to the word: **John/John's, my niece/my niece's, the men/the men's, the women/the women's.**

•If the possessor (expressed first) is plural and the plural form ends in **-s** as most English plurals do, or is singular and ends in **-s**, then just an apostrophe (**'**) is added to form the possessive: **the girls/the girls', the boys/the boys', the dogs/the dogs', Agnes/Agnes', Jonas/Jonas'.**

The English formula for the expression of possession is:

POSSESSOR [possessive form] + POSSESSED THING

Mary's	friend
my brother's	books
Robert's	uncle
his parents'	car
the professors'	salaries
the children's	toys

12.3
English has an alternate possessive construction which resembles the Spanish formula to a considerable degree. However, the construction is found more frequently in dialectal speech than in the standard variety.

POSSESSED THING + **of** + POSSESSOR[possessive form]
Note: The possessor (stated last in Spanish) must assume possessive form in English.

the new house	of	my uncle's
that friend	of	Robert's
those boys	of	your sister's
some dogs	of	our neighbors'
this bad feeling	of	mine (possessive pronoun)

When asking a question concerning who possesses what in English, you may use one of the four following patterns. The first and third patterns represent the less formal mode of expression, whereas the second and fourth are of a more formal nature.

i. **whose** + NOUN [sgl./pl.] + **be** + DEMONSTRATIVE PRONOUN
    Whose book is this?
    Whose children are these?

ii. **whose** + **be** + DEMONSTRATIVE ADJECTIVE + NOUN [sgl./pl.]
Whose is this book?
Whose are these children?

iii. **who(m)** + AUX-**do** + DEMONS. ADJ + NOUN [sgl./pl.] + **belong to**
Who/Whom (formal) does this book belong to?
Who/Whom (formal) do these children belong to?

iv. **to whom** + AUX-**do** + DEMONS. ADJ + NOUN [sgl./pl.] + **belong**
To whom does this book belong?
To whom do these children belong?

Exercise 1

Give the possessive construction in the other language for the following possessive phrases.

1. my father's brother	9. the secretary's office
2. la bondad de nuestros amigos	10. las faldas de las chicas
3. his brother's son	11. Chris' new home
4. los peligros de mi profesión	12. las niñas de las mujeres
5. the children's shoes	13. her parents' factory
6. la cocina de mi madre	14. la ópera de Verdi
7. the girls' dresses	15. the cat's paws
8. los concejos de tus padres	16. los enemigos de los judíos

Exercise 2

A. Give six versions in Spanish asking who possesses a certain magazine or magazines or who all possess a certain magazine or magazines: patterns i. and ii. of §12.1.

B. Give eight versions in English asking the same questions about a book or books: patterns i–iv. under §12.3.

12.4

In Spanish and English there are certain structures which resemble possessive structures but are not possessive. Certain lexical items in English are composed along the lines of that language's possessive system, but these are other parts of speech.

i. A base word, usually a noun, is preceded by an attributive noun to form a new word, for example: **dog food, garbage can, alarm clock, bookstore.**

ii. The Spanish equivalent for such terms may be one word (eg, **alarm clock = despertador**), or the Spanish equivalent may be formed by a construction using **de**, the first element of English being expressed last in Spanish and the reverse (eg **housewife = ama de casa, dog food = comida de perros,**).

Here are some examples of both types of constructions.

•English construction composed of two elements in a compound word; one word equivalent in Spanish.

mailman	cartero
doorman	portero
bookstore	librería
highway	carretera

•English construction composed of more than one word: Spanish uses a construction with **de**, the elements placed in reverse order with respect to English.

silver chain	cadena de plata
bathing suit	traje de baño
silk cape	capa de seda
dining room table	mesa de comedor

Exercise 3

Find at least ten examples on your own of English constructions rendered in Spanish by one word as illustrated above and ten examples of English constructions rendered in Spanish with a construction using **de**.

13

Partitive
Constructions

13.1

In both English and Spanish there are count nouns (nouns that can be counted), eg, **books/libros, houses/casas, friends/amigos, dogs/perros,** and non-count nouns (nouns that cannot be counted but which can be broken down only according to quantity), eg, **water/agua, milk/leche, meat/carne, sugar/azúcar.** Although both languages employ the count/non-count classificatory system, all nouns are not classified the same in each language, and caution must be exercised. One such example is **furniture/muebles.** **Furniture** is a non-count noun in English, whereas **muebles** is a count noun in Spanish. (See §9.6.viii.)

> The furniture is new. (non-count)
> Two *pieces* of furniture are broken. (count conversion)
>
> El mobiliario es nuevo. (a non-count equivalent of **furniture**)
> El mueble está roto. (count noun, one item only)
> Dos muebles están rotos. (count noun)

ENGLISH AND SPANISH PARTITIVE SYSTEMS
13.2
Count Nouns

With count nouns, English and Spanish use the quantifiers in their partitive systems which are here outlined.

SMALL DEGREE	a few, few	pocos/-as, unos pocos/unas pocas
MEDIUM DEGREE	some	unos/-as, algunos/-as, unos cuantos/unas cuantas
LARGE DEGREE	a lot of, many, lots of	muchos/-as

EXAMPLES:

I have (a few, few) friends.	Tengo (pocos/unos pocos) amigos.
I have some friends.	Tengo (unos/algunos/unos cuantos) amigos.
I have (many/a lot of/lots of) friends.	Tengo muchos amigos.

13.3.
Non-Count Nouns
The partitive system for Spanish and English non-count nouns is as follows.

SMALL DEGREE	a little	un poco de
MEDIUM DEGREE	some	algo de/ Ø
LARGE DEGREE	a lot of, lots of, much	mucho/-a

EXAMPLES:

I carry a little water.   Cargo un poco de agua.
I carry some water.   Cargo (algo de) agua.
I carry (a lot of/lots of/much) water.   Cargo mucha agua.

Note: Some nouns may belong to both categories, count and non-count. Good examples are **wine/wines** and **vino/vinos.**

Count: There are various wines in the cellar.
          Hay varios vinos en la bodega.
Non-count: I like to drink a little wine with dinner.
          Me gusta beber un poco de vino con la cena.

Exercise 1
Translate the following English partitive constructions into Spanish. State in each case whether the italicized item is a count noun or a non-count noun in the target language.

1. We don't want to read many *books*.
2. Put a little *sugar* on the fruit.
3. He thinks he can depend on a few *friends* in Brazil.
4. Please buy me some *cigarettes*. (familiar)
5. She poured lots of *water* into the glass.
6. Why didn't they bring some *beers?*
7. Few *Europeans* live in Paraguay.
8. Do you want some *orange juice?*
9. Please buy me a little *cheese*. (formal)
10. Does your car use much *gasoline?*
11. Do they have a lot of *relatives* in Ecuador?
12. We are going to visit some *friends* in Mendoza.

Exercise 2
Translate the following Spanish partitive constructions into English. State in each case whether the italicized item is a count noun or a non-count noun in the target language.

1. Tengo algunos *tíos* en Colombia.
2. ¿Tiene muchos *hijos* el profesor de la academia?
3. Algunas mujeres usan mucho *perfume* fino.
4. Esta noche mi señora va a servir un poco de *sopa*.

5. ¿Dónde podemos comprar *trigo?*
6. Hay pocos *católicos* en nuestra patria.
7. ¿No me dijiste que trajera *aceite de oliva?*
8. Se le llenó el pecho de mucha *sangre*.
9. ¿Cuándo vas a prestarme unas *revistas de arte?*
10. Tengo unos cuantos *dólares* en el bolsillo.
11. Una buena dieta consiste en algo de *fruta* entre otros alimentos.
12. Durante esta primavera el profesor asignó mucha *lectura*.

English and Spanish Personal Pronouns

GENERAL CLASSIFICATION

14.1

The Spanish personal pronouns are divided into two classes, the **disjunctives** and **conjunctives**. The **disjunctive** pronouns, so called because they may be separated from the verb in the sentence by other grammatical items, these include the subject pronouns and the prepositional object pronouns. The **conjunctive** pronouns are so called because they must accompany the verb in the sentence, either directly preceding it or following and being attached to it. These include the direct object pronouns, the indirect object pronouns, and the reflexive object pronouns. Spanish subject pronouns and object pronouns are treated in their entirety in this Unit. The reflexive object pronouns used with reflexive pronominal verbs are discussed in Unit 15, §15.2.

English personal pronouns are divided into three classes. These are the subject pronouns, the object pronouns, and the reflexive pronouns. The object pronouns may function as direct objects, indirect objects, or prepositional objects, in whichever case their forms are identical for each of the various uses. The reflexive pronouns refer to the subject in the sentence and are formed by adding the English suffix **-self/-selves** to the pronoun base.

SPANISH DISJUNCTIVE PRONOUNS AND THE ENGLISH EQUIVALENTS

14.2

The following discussion is organized around the Spanish classificational system.

The Subject Pronouns

The subject pronouns are the pronouns which identify the actors in any given Spanish or English sentence.

	SINGULAR		PLURAL	
1st pers.	yo	I	nosotros, nosotras	we
2nd pers.	tú	you	vosotros, vosotras	you
	usted	you	ustedes	you
3rd pers.	él	he	ellos	they
	ella	she	ellas	they
	ello	it		

The usage of these pronouns in Spanish is frequently optional (see Unit 1, §1.4). In general, personal pronouns used redundantly occur only to provide emphasis or contrast: **Yo hablo inglés, pero ella no.** In English, however, some expressed subject, either in noun phrase or in pronoun form, must accompany the verb. For this reason, the English subject pronouns will occur with far greater frequency than will the corresponding forms of Spanish.

One of the most difficult contrasting problems for the English speaker learning Spanish is that the English subject pronoun **you** has five different Spanish equivalents commonly: **tú, usted, ustedes, vosotros, vosotras.** All but the last two of these have their own distinct verbal forms. The Spanish speakers learning English have a simple task—they simply learn to use **you** with any addressee, singular or plural, familiar or formal. The English speaker, on the other hand, must come to understand Spanish formal usage versus Spanish familiar usage, as well as the concept of singular versus plural equivalents for English **you.** Another perspective of this dilemma was mentioned in Unit 3 (§3.1, 6).

Spanish has no subject pronoun equivalent for English **it** when this refers to a specific thing. This causes the Spanish speaker to tend to render English **It's on the table** as *Is on the table.** The Spanish neuter, subject pronoun **ello** has limited use, and when it is used, it refers to abstract concepts or to whole ideas, never to concrete things.

Spanish shows gender distinctions in all its plural subject pronouns, except **ustedes.** In English, **we, you** (plural), and **they** do not show gender.

Exercise 1

Give all possible Spanish subjects in personal pronoun form for these Spanish verbal forms.

1. adelanté	4. calláis	7. fue
2. ascenderán	5. había crecido	8. asistimos
3. celebrabas	6. tuviera	9. habré

Exercise 2

Give all possible English subjects in personal pronoun form for these English indicative verbal forms.

1. goes	4. will go	7. is working
2. saw	5. would be	8. were
3. have done	6. am	9. are gone

THE PREPOSITIONAL OBJECT PRONOUNS
14.3
The prepositional object pronouns are the pronouns used as objects of prepositions in Spanish and English.

Those forms which precede the slash in the following chart are non-reflexive, whereas those which follow the slash are reflexive. If no slash is used, then both forms of the pronoun are identical.

SINGULAR		PLURAL	
mí	me/myself	nosotros, -as	us/ourselves
ti	you/yourself	vosotros, -as	you/yourselves
usted/sí	you/yourself	ustedes/sí	you/yourselves
él/sí	him/himself	ellos, ellas, sí	them/themselves
ella/sí	her/herself		
él/sí	it/itself		
ella/sí	it/itself		
ello/sí	it/itself		

In either language, the non-reflexive forms occur as objects of a preposition when the subject of the sentence and the object of the preposition are different entities. The reflexive forms are found when the subject and the object of the preposition are the same entities. In the Spanish reflexive usage of the prepositional object pronouns, the words **mismo, misma, mismos, mismas** generally accompany the reflexive prepositional pronouns.

NON-REFLEXIVE EXAMPLES:

Esto es para mí.	This is for me.
Ese libro está cerca de él.	That book is near him.
Ella salió sin nosotras.	She left without us.
Yo sé de ello.	I know about it. (a concept)

REFLEXIVE EXAMPLES:

Lo hice para mí misma.	I did it for myself.
Él habló de sí mismo.	He spoke about himself.
Te mentiste a ti misma.	You lied to yourself.
Apuntó la pistola contra sí mismo.	He turned the gun against himself.

In Spanish if the preposition **con** governs **mí, ti,** or **sí,** then new words are formed: **conmigo, contigo, consigo,** respectively. **Fueron al pueblo conmigo; They went to town with me.**

The subject pronouns and the prepositional object pronouns (non-reflexive) are identical in Spanish, except in the 1st and 2nd persons singular. The non-reflexive English prepositional object pronouns are the same as the English direct and indirect object pronouns.

Spanish, as usual, distinguishes between formal and familiar address in both the singular and the plural prepositional object pronouns, while English makes no morphological distinction. Gender distinctions are the norm in Spanish plural non-reflexive prepositional object pronoun usage, while in English no such distictions are made.

The three Spanish prepositional object pronouns **ello, él,** and **ella** may be translated as **it** in English with the following stipulations:

•When the **it** of English refers to an idea in its entirety or to some abstract concept, then **ello** is used: **No sé nada de ello = I don't know anything about it.** Here, the **it** might refer to what happened at the party last night or to some other event or occurrence.

•In **No sé nada de él (de ella) = I don't know anything about it,** the **it** of the English translation refers to a specific thing, for example **the book (él)** or **the note (ella).**

Finally, it should be noted that not every Spanish preposition governs the Spanish prepositional object pronouns. Some prepositions take the subject pronouns as their complements.

Entre tú y *yo,* no debe haber más discusión de este tipo.
Todos quieren ir, *menos yo.*
Nadie lo puede hacer, *excepto tú.*

(Exercise 3)

Translate the following English sentences into Spanish, taking care to use the correct prepositional object pronoun and to distinguish between reflexive and non-reflexive usage.

1. There is a letter for you on the table. (singular **you**)
2. I think you received a letter for me. (familiar)
3. They don't know anything about us.
4. He wants to go with me.
5. Does your mother want to live with you? (familiar)
6. She doesn't know how to do anything for herself.
7. They weren't able to tell us anything about themselves.

8. The train was passing below them.
9. He showed me this poem. Do you know anything about it? (formal)
10. He died in Puerto Rico. I don't know anything else about it.
11. The box was under the chair when I sat on it. (the chair)
12. My parents live near you. (singular)
13. He seemed very pleased with himself.
14. I would like to study with you. (familiar)

(Exercise 4)

Translate the following Spanish sentences into English, taking care to use the correct prepositional object pronoun and to distinguish between reflexive and non-reflexive usages.

1. ¿No sabes nada de ella? (la cámara que guardó el oficial)
2. Nadie quiere compartir conmigo.
3. ¿Alguien quiere pintar con nosotros?
4. ¿Vive el matrimonio cerca o lejos de ti?
5. El árbol cayó encima de él. (el arco)
6. Ese gobernador siempre habla de sí mismo.
7. Juana no va a decirme nada de ello.

8. Anunciaron que el premio era para mí.
9. Cecilia lo hace todo por sí misma.
10. El desconocido podría depender más de nosotros.
11. No puedo celebrar contigo esta ocasión.
12. No lo complazco por ella; lo hago por mí misma.

13. No van a dejar que salgamos sin ellos.
14. ¿Qué confianza le van a tener si lo oyen hablando consigo mismo?

14.4
Emphatic Usage of the Spanish Prepositional Object Pronouns

In either Spanish or English, speakers often wish to clarify or to emphasize certain elements of a sentence, especially if that element is a pronoun. Spanish usually does this by adding a prepositional object pronoun construction to a sentence which already contains a direct or an indirect object noun or pronoun. English does it by placing particularly heavy vocal emphasis on the direct or indirect object pronoun. Compare the following Spanish and English sentences.

SENTENCE WITH A DIRECT OBJECT PRONOUN IN SPANISH:
A ella la conozco.   I know *her*.
A él no lo veo.   I don't see *him*.
A ti te amo, pero a ella, no.   I love *you*, but not *her*.

SENTENCE WITH AN INDIRECT OBJECT PRONOUN IN SPANISH:
A mí me gusta la estatua.   *I* like the statue.
No te escribí a ti.   I didn't write *you*.
A ellos no les hablo.   I don't speak to *them*.

Exercise 5

Express the following English sentences in Spanish, using a prepositional object pronoun construction to emphasize the items in italics as emphatic in English. State in each case whether the prepositional pronoun construction is used in conjunction with a Spanish direct or indirect object.

1. *We* like him. (use **gustar**)
2. You didn't meet *him;* you met *her*. (familiar)
3. You never saw *me* before. (formal)
4. I wrote to *them*, but not to *him*.
5. *She* doesn't care. (use **importar**)
6. He sent the flowers to *you*. (familiar)
7. She never told *us* the truth.
8. The dog bit *him*, but it only barked at *me*.
9. He's going to sell *me* everything.
10. We're about to visit *her* right now.

SPANISH CONJUNCTIVE PRONOUNS AND ENGLISH EQUIVALENTS
14.5

Spanish has three sets of conjunctive pronouns. They are the direct object pronouns, the indirect object pronouns, and the object pronouns used with reflexive pronominal verbs. The object pronouns used with reflexive verbs are treated in Unit 15. Our discussion of the Spanish conjunctive pronouns and their English equivalents will be organized under the following headings:

•Position(s) assumed by Spanish conjunctive pronouns with respect to the verb, and the positioning of such pronouns in English.

•Spanish direct object pronouns.

•Spanish indirect object pronouns.

•Spanish direct and indirect object pronouns occurring in the same sentence, and English equivalents for such Spanish constructions.

Conjunctive pronouns are so called because they invariably appear in direct association with a verb form, either directly before or after (and attached to) a verb. Nothing intervenes between these pronouns and the verb in a sentence.

The nature of the verb form itself conditions the positioning of the conjunctive pronouns. Some verb forms require that the pronoun come before the verb, others that it come after, and still others allow both positions. Here are the syntactical rules for conjunctive pronoun positioning with respect to the verb in Spanish. We include examples of the reflexive pronominal verbs, discussed in a later unit, merely to illustrate the consistency in positioning compared with the other pronouns.

- The conjunctive pronouns must precede the verb form if it is a conjugated verb showing person, number, tense, and mood, or if it is a negative command (imperative).

Conjugated Verb Form:

DIRECT OBJECT	INDIRECT OBJECT	REFLEXIVE
Juan lo ve.	Juan nos habla .	Juan se viste.
Juan me verá.	Juan me escribe.	Ella se levantó.
Juan nos ha visto.	Él nos vendió comida.	Me acosté.

Negative Command (Imperative):

DIRECT OBJECT	INDIRECT OBJECT	REFLEXIVE
¡No lo mate!	¡No me escribas!	¡No se vista Ud.!
¡No me intimides!	¡No le digas eso!	¡No te levantes!
¡No los pongáis aquí!	¡No nos hable!	¡No os acostéis!

- The conjunctive pronouns must follow and be attached to an affirmative command (imperative).

DIRECT OBJECT	INDIRECT OBJECT	REFLEXIVE
¡Mátalo!	¡Excríbeme!	¡Vístete!
¡Véame mañana!	¡Díganme la verdad!	¡Levántese!
¡Ponedlos aquí!	¡Tráeme tu libro!	¡Sentaos!

Note: In **sentaos**, the **-d** of the **vosotros** imperative form is dropped when the reflexive pronoun is added. Theoretically, this allows a distinction to be made between the command form and the plural past participle **sentados.** In actual spoken Peninsular Spansih, however, ***sentaros** is heard.

- The conjunctive pronouns may either precede the entire verbal unit or follow and be attached to the last element of the verbal unit if the last element of this unit is either a dependent infinitive (ie, an infinitive preceded by a conjugated verb) or a dependent **-ndo** form (ie, an **-ndo** form preceded by a conjugated verb).

A dependent infinitve:

DIRECT OBJECT	INDIRECT OBJECT	REFLEXIVE
Me quiere matar.	Le voy a escribir.	Se tiene que vestir.
Quiere matarme.	Voy a escribirle.	Tiene que vestirse.

Note: There are a few exceptions to this rule. In the expression **haber** + INF, the pronoun must always follow and be attached to the infinitive: **Hay que hacerlo mañana.** To express **We are going to see her,** either position is possible: **Vamos a verla** or **La vamos a ver.** But to say **let's see her,** only **Vamos a verla** is possible.

A dependent *-ndo* form:

DIRECT OBJECT	INDIRECT OBJECT	REFLEXIVE
Me está matando.	Le estaba escribiendo.	Se está vistiendo.
Está matándome.	Estaba escribiéndole.	Está vistiéndose.

• The conjunctive pronouns must follow and be attached to non-dependent infinitives and to non-dependent **-ndo** forms.

A non-dependent infinitive:

DIRECT OBJECT	INDIRECT OBJECT	REFLEXIVE
Al verlo así, me puse muy triste.	Después de escribirle, voy a vistar a su madre.	Tuvo que ir a trabajar sin afeitarse.

A non-dependent *-ndo* form:

DIRECT OBJECT	INDIRECT OBJECT	REFLEXIVE
Viéndola así, no sabía qué hacer.	Diciéndole la verdad, la convencerás.	Se cortó afeitándose.

Exercise 6

Examine the following sentences which contain various Spanish conjunctive pronouns, all italicized. Do not concern yourself at this time with whether any given pronoun is a direct, an indirect, or a reflexive object pronoun. Simply state why the pronoun must assume the position it does. Base your answers on the rules just presented for conjunctive pronoun positioning according to the type of verbal form involved. Also, be able to say if another positioning of the pronoun is allowable in any given case.

1. Sé que no *me* van a decir nada.
2. *Lo* tienes que hacer cuando puedas.
3. No *te* acuestes tan tarde mañana.
4. Acosta*os* temprano, niños, pues tenemos mucho que aprovechar.
5. Levánte*se*, don Rafael.
6. Su esposo no *le* ha dicho nada.
7. No voy a permitir que *te* vayas en seguida.
8. Jorge no *me* está facilitando mucha ayuda con este proyecto.

9. ¿Quién estaba acompañándote cuando te vi esta mañana?
10. Estudié alemán durante cinco años, pero no lo hablo muy bien.
11. Mi amada no se había peinado durante muchos días.
12. Vete, hijo. No te puedo hablar en este momento.
13. No te alejes. No te he dicho todavía todo lo que te quiero decir.
14. Quería que me lo acordaras, pero no tenías mente para hacerlo.
15. Viéndola así, cualquiera hubiera creído que se había enfermado.

14.6

The position assumed by the English equivalents for the Spanish conjunctive pronouns is always a postverbal one. Examine these examples.

> She sees *me* every day.
> She writes *to him* every month.
> She needs to see *us* tomorrow.
> She is dressing *herself* in the bedroom.
> Help *her!*
> Don't help *her!*

SPANISH DIRECT OBJECT PRONOUNS AND ENGLISH EQUIVALENTS
14.7

The Spanish direct object pronouns and their English equivalents function as the objects of transitive verbs.

SINGULAR		PLURAL	
me	me	nos	us
te [FAMILIAR]	you	os [FAMILIAR]	you
lo/le [FORMAL]	you	los/les [FORMAL]	you
la [FORMAL]	you	las [FORMAL]	you
lo/le	him	los/les [MASCULINE]	them
la	her	las [FEMININE]	them
lo/la	it	los [INANIMATE]	them

There are virtually no important contrastive problems in the 1st person singular or plural, or in the 2nd persons familiar since there are one-to-one correspondences here.

In the 3rd persons singular and plural, however, numerous important contrasts occur, and even standard Spanish usage varies, depending upon the dialect. Of these dialectal variations, the most important is the distinction between **loísmo** and **leísmo.**

14.8
Loísmo
Spanish speakers from Latin America are generally **loísta** in their direct object pronoun usage. The **loísta** will use **le/les** for the indirect object but not generally

for the direct object. Hence, for direct object pronoun usages, in the strictest sense, generally no distinction is made between masculine animate and inanimate beings but **lo** is assigned to refer to both.

The **loísta** direct object pronoun system follows.

> **lo = you** (masculine, formal)/**him/it** (masculine)
> **la = you** (feminine, formal)/**her/it** (feminine)
> **los = you** (plural, formal, if some males included)
>   **them** (people or things, one or more males included)
> **las = you** (plural, feminine, formal)/**them** (feminine, people or things)

14.9
Leísmo

The **leísta** speakers of Spanish are generally from Spain and will always use **le** or **les** for the indirect object. However, they also use **le(s)** for the direct object representing masculine animate beings in the following manner.

> **le = you** (masculine, singular, formal)/**him**
> **les = you** (plural, formal, if some males included)/**them** (animate beings,
>   some males included)
> **lo = it** (masculine)
> **los = them** (things only)
> **la = you** (feminine, formal)/**her/it** (feminine)
> **las = you** (feminine plural, formal)/**them** (feminine, people or things)

Both **loísmo** and **leísmo** are considered by all authorities to be fully standard usages in modern Spanish. However, in teaching Hispano-American Spanish to the English speaker, it is wise to present the **loísta** usage. In that way, the beginner will not become confused since **le/les** will be reserved for indirect object use only. **Lo, la, los,** and **las** then are being reserved as the 3rd person direct object pronouns. The Real Academia Española recommends this practice which it categorizes as etymologically sound, but it also includes the alternate use of **le** for the masculine direct object when this is a person, a practice predominantly found in Spain.

Exercise 7

Translate the following English sentences into Spanish, giving both the **loísta** and **leísta** version whenever they differ.

1. I see them. (the men)
2. I know her.
3. He sees them. (the books)
4. I don't know you. (fem. sgl., formal)
5. He knows you. (masc. sgl., formal)
6. He saw them. (the girls)
7. They know you. (masc. pl., formal)
8. We saw you. (fem. pl., formal)
9. I want it. (the letter)
10. She saw it. (the glass)
11. We don't know him.
12. They don't see her.

(Exercise 8)

Translate the following English sentences, all of which contain a direct object pronoun, into Spanish. Be consistently either **loísta** or **leísta**. Give a variety of acceptable positions for the direct object pronoun where more than one position is possible.

1. I don't need to see you tomorrow. (singular, formal)
2. He is studying it right now. (lección)
3. Where did you put it? (arma) (familiar, singular)
4. Bring it tomorrow! (dinero) (familiar, singular)
5. Don't put them there! (dulces) (familiar, singular)
6. When do we have to see him?
7. He is trying to call them. (Marta y Ofelia)
8. Don't eat it! (pan) (formal, plural)
9. Don't smoke them! (puros) (familiar, plural)
10. I know her well.

11. Where did he meet her?
12. Do they want to visit me in Spain?
13. Don't you want to use them? (datos) (formal, singular)
14. He is attacking us.
15. Drink it! (vino) (familiar, singular)
16. I haven't seen her today.
17. Do we have to lead them? (ciegos)
18. Are they reading them? (revistas)
19. He doesn't want to write it. (párrafo)
20. Don't bother me! (familiar, singular)

14.10
Redundant Direct Object Pronoun Usage

The English speaker learning Spanish often has trouble deciding whether or not to use a redundant direct object pronoun in a Spanish sentence which already contains a direct object expressed as a noun. Usage varies among native speakers, but generally a direct object pronoun is used in conjunction with a direct object noun only when the noun precedes the verb in the sentence.

Veo a Julia. (No direct object pronoun needed, since D.O. noun follows verb.)
A Julia la veo. (Direct object noun precedes verb, so direct object pronoun is added redundantly.)

No conozco a tus padres.
A tus padres, no los/les conozco. (**Les** is leísmo usage.)

No voy a traer al duque.
Al duque, no lo/le voy a traer. (**Le** is leísmo usage.)

Exercise 9

Translate the following sentences into Spanish, giving two versions, (a) one in which the direct object expressed as a noun follows the verb, and, (b) one in which the direct object expressed as a noun precedes the verb and is then accompanied by a redundant direct object pronoun.

1. We don't see Alexander.
2. They don't know our mayor.
3. Aren't you going to bring your mother? (familiar)
4. Don't they know your father?

5. I don't see Norma.
6. Haven't we met your wife? (formal)

SPANISH INDIRECT OBJECT PRONOUNS AND ENGLISH EQUIVALENTS
14.11
The indirect objects in both Spanish and English expresses "to whom" or "for whom" something is done.   Their forms are outlined below.

SINGULAR		PLURAL	
me	(to/for) me	nos	(to/for) us
te, le	(to/for) you	os, les	(to/for) you
le	(to/for) him	les	(to/for) them
le	(to/for) her		
le	(to/for) it		

The English direct and indirect object pronouns are identical in form. English often, but by no means not always, indicates an indirect object usage by preceding it with **to** or **for.**

If not already knowledgable in their usage, English speakers must learn to distinguish between direct and indirect objects. They must learn to make such distinctions in English in order to master the relatively more complex Spanish system. The direct object (D.O.) receives the direct action of the verb. The indirect object (I.O.) receives the benefit of that action, that is, the action is done **to** or **for** the indirect object. The objects, direct or indirect, may be pronouns or nouns, or any other type of noun phrase. Example: **They gave it** (D.O.) **to me** (I.O.), **Carlos bought the flowers** (D.O.) **for his sweetheart** (I.O.), **They sold her** (I.O.) **a new chevrolet** (D.O.). Notice that in the last example, the indirect object is not introduced by **to/for**.

In Spanish the 1st and 2nd persons singular and plural use the same pronouns for both the direct and the indirect object. In the 3rd persons singular and plural, the following should be noted with regard to similarities and differences between direct and indirect object forms.

(a) The **leísta** speaker uses **le(s)** for masculine animate beings which occur as direct objects and **le(s)** also for any third person indirect object. All other 3rd person direct and indirect objects are distinct forms.

(b) For the **loísta** speaker, which is the more common in Spanish America, the 3rd person singular or plural direct and indirect object pronouns are always different in form. This is because **le(s)** is used by such speakers as an indirect object only.

Note that, rather uncharacteristically for Spanish, no gender distinctions occur in the 3rd person singular or plural indirect object pronouns.

Exercise 10

Determine in the following English examples which element is the direct and which is the indirect object.

1. He gave me the book.
2. They told everything to us.
3. She offered him some cigarettes.
4. We proposed some new plans to them.
5. They brought my mother some candy.
6. I think I owe you a couple of dollars.
7. The professor plans to teach her Portuguese.
8. The manager suggested a new approach to the employees.
9. She wrote them a very long letter.
10. Please introduce your friend to me.

(Exercise 11)

Translate the following English sentences, all of which contain indirect object pronouns, into Spanish. Give all possible word orders.

1. Bring me the cup! (familiar)
2. He is going to give us the money.
3. Don't lend them your car! (formal)
4. He is going to offer us a bribe.
5. You owe me a lot of money. (familiar)
6. He paid them five dollars for the coat.
7. Read us the story. (familiar)
8. He is selling all of his books to them little by little.
9. Don't show her those papers. (formal)
10. He has to teach us English.

11. I wrote them a long letter.
12. Explain the lesson to him. (familiar)
13. He was mentioning his mother to me.
14. Don't return that copy to us. (familiar)
15. We prefer to show them these articles.
16. When is he going to tell me where he lives?
17. The professor is teaching them Swahili now.
18. Don't send us pesos; send us dollars! (formal)
19. Lend me the money or don't ever speak to me again! (familiar)
20. I am going to suggest something interesting to them.

14.12

Redundant Indirect Object Pronoun Usage

The English speaker often wonders when to use in Spanish an indirect object pronoun in conjunction with an indirect object expressed as a noun. Again, usage varies, but standard Spanish prefers that an indirect object pronoun accompany any noun used as an indirect object. This so-called redundant pronoun usage was discussed earlier in §14.10 as it applies to direct object pronoun usage. The following are some examples of redundant indirect object pronoun usages in Spanish.

¿No le vas a entregar la regla a Miguel?
Ella le está enseñando griego a Julia.
A mi mamá, mi papá nunca le dice una mentira.
¿Cuándo les vas a escribir a tus tíos?
A Elena, Antonio no le quiere dar un beso.

Exercise 12

Translate the following English sentences, all of which have indirect object nouns, into Spanish. In each case use a redundant indirect object pronoun with the indirect object noun.

1. I think he is writing his girlfriend a letter.
2. He always offers tequila to his friends.
3. Don't give Henry that much money! (familiar)
4. He is going to explain the incident to Bertha.
5. They showed this book to their colleagues.
6. I have to teach foreign languages to my students.

Spanish sentences containing indirect object pronouns are often ambiguous to the English speaker already accustomed to a different word order, particularly when the context is unclear or lacking. The Spanish indirect object is therefore best viewed as a so-called *involved entity,* that is, the individual affected in some way by the action expressed in the sentence.

Depending on context, **Me robó el dinero** can mean **He robbed the money** *from me,* or **He robbed the money** *for me.* Again, depending on the context, **Le vendieron la casa** can have three interpretations: **They sold the house** *to him,* **They sold the house** *for him,* or **They sold the house** *on him* (the selling of the house occurring unexpectedly and catching him unaware). See §16.3 for further discussion of this type of sentence.

14.13
Both Direct and Indirect Object Pronouns in a Same Sentence
When both direct and indirect object pronouns occur in the same sentence, Spanish and English show variances in their respective treatments.

In Spanish, without exception, the indirect object pronoun precedes the direct object pronoun. As a unit, these two pronouns assume the same position with respect to any given verbal form that they would have assumed if only one pronoun had been used. However, if a 3rd person indirect object pronoun (**le/les**) precedes a 3rd person direct object pronoun beginning with **l-** (**lo, le, la, los, les, las**), the indirect objects **le/les** must become **se.** Since this **se** substitute for indirect object **le/les** can be ambiguous in its reference, it is often clarified by a prepositional pronoun construction (**a él, a ella, a usted, a ellos, a ellas, a ustedes**).

The syntax of conjunctive pronouns was presented in §14.5, and is here reviewed as it affects sentences with both indirect and direct object pronouns. With conjugated verbal forms or negative commands, the pronoun unit (I.O./D.O.) precedes the entire verbal form.

Eugenio *me lo* entrega.
Eugenio ~~le~~ *se lo* entregó (a él).
Eugenio, no *me lo* entregues.
Eugenio, no ~~le~~ *se lo* entregues (a ella).

With affirmative commands, the pronoun unit (I.O./D.O.) follows and attaches to the verbal form.

Entréga*melo*.
Explíque~~le~~*selo* (a ella).

Explíca*noslo*.
Explíca~~le~~*selo* (a él).

With dependent infinitives or dependent **-ndo** forms, the pronoun unit (I.O./ D.O.) may precede the entire verbal unit or follow and be attached to the last element of the verbal unit.

Alberto *te lo* va a entregar, *or* Alberto va a entregár*telo*.

Alberto ~~le~~ *se lo* tiene que entregar (a ella), *or,*
Alberto tiene que entregár~~le~~*selo* (a ella).

Berta *me lo* está explicando, *or,* Berta está explicándo*melo*.

Berta ~~les~~ *se lo* está mostrando (a ellos), *or,*
Berta está mostrando~~les~~*selo* (a ellos).

Exercise 13

Translate the following English sentences, all of which contain both indirect object and direct object pronouns, into Spanish. Give all possible word orders.

1. He didn't tell it to me. (the joke)
2. She wants to bring them (the books) to me.
3. He is explaining them (the lessons) to her.
4. Don't bring it to her! (the glass)
5. Give them (the bottles) to him! (familiar)
6. He didn't offer it (the wine) to me.
7. She is going to read it (the story) to them.
8. They taught it (Spanish) to her.
9. Who sold them (the oranges) to you? (familiar)
10. Don't lend it (the pencil) to him!
11. Send it (the package) to her. (formal)
12. They returned them (the letters) to me.

14.14
The English System
English generally allows two structures (both with the same meaning) when an indirect object and a direct object pronoun occur in the same sentence, although cerain word-stress factors will restrict the use of some pronouns. Structure (a) below most closely resembles the Spanish system, since the indirect object precedes the direct object.

(a) V + IO + DO

Give me some.
Don't give them any.
He wants to give you that.
He is giving her one.
She gave us these.

(b) V + DO + **to/for** + IO

Give some to me.
Don't give any to them
He wants to give that to you.
He is giving one to her.
She gave these to us.

English clearly prefers structure (a) above when the direct object is expressed as a noun, as in **He gave me the book,** and structure (b) above is preferred when both the indirect and the direct object are expresseed as pronouns. **He gave it to me.**   Moreover, in American English two personal pronouns do not generally occur together in an indirect-direct object combination making (?)**He gave me it** of questionable acceptance, notwithstanding the fact that it is admissible in British English. **He gave us these** and **He gave us some** are wholly acceptable. The sentence stress pattern would seem to be an important factor in this determination.

English verbs which permit either structure (a) or (b) include, among others, **bring, give, lend, mail, offer, owe, pay, read, sell, send, show, teach, tell, throw, write.**

English verbs which allow only structure (b) include, among others, **apply, describe, explain, introduce, mention, present, prove, report, return, suggest.**

Exercise 14

Translate the following Spanish sentences, all of which have both an indirect and a direct object, into English. If the verb permits it, give both structures (a) and (b) in the English translation.

1. Ella nos está leyendo un cuento ahora.
2. ¿No quieres devolverme el libro?
3. Susana se lo dará cuando lo vea (a Ud.).
4. Yo se lo presté el año pasado.
5. Efraín nunca nos la presentó.
6. No te voy a sugerir ningún plan nuevo.
7. ¿Cuándo puedo enseñarte francés?
8. No se lo puedo explicar a ellos.
9. Marianne me mostró su casa recién pintada.
10. Nunca te lo mandaron.
11. Díganos el resto del cuento.
12. No me arrojes esa bola.
13. Julio todavía no se lo ha apuntado.
14. ¿Quién te envió ese brillante tan lindo?

15

Reflexive and Reciprocal Actions

OVERVIEW
15.1
In the transitive usage of a verb, the subject acts on an object, the object being a different person or thing from the subject.

ENGLISH TRANSITIVE	SPANISH TRANSITIVE
He accuses me.	Él me acusa.
They appreciate him.	Ellas lo aprecian.
You need more advice.	Tú necesitas más consejos.

In the reflexive pronominal usage of the verb, the subject is both the actor and the receiver of the action.

She weighs herself.	Ella se pesa.
I improved myself.	Yo me mejoré.

A major problem in the comparison of English and Spanish reflexive pronominal usages is that the two languages often fail to use parallel constructions, or they may select different vocabulary items to express ideas which are clearly reflexive actions in both languages. For example, **He goes to bed** cannot be rendered in English as ***He beds himself,** and **We get up** cannot be rendered as ***We raise ourselves,** whereas in Spanish a reflexive pronominal construction is used to express the same action, **Él se acuesta** (literally ***He beds himself**) and **Nos levantamos** (literally ***We raise ourselves**).

Occasionally we find two related English verbs, one used only transitively and the other only intransitively. English uses the intransitive form where Spanish employs a reflexive verb. Spanish may use the same base verb in both transitive and reflexive pronominal constructions. The shift from one meaning to the other is accomplished through changing the noun or pronoun complements, eg **Lo bañé = I bathed him** (transitive) vs **Me bañé = I bathed myself** (reflexive).

TRANSITIVE	INTRANSITIVE and/or REFLEXIVE
raise/levantar	**rise/levantarse**
He raised his hand.	He rises at nine.
Él levantó la mano.	Él se levanta a las nueve.

138

TRANSITIVE	INTRANSITIVE and/or REFLEXIVE
set/poner	**sit down/sentarse**
She set it here.	She sat down (seated herself) here.
Ella lo puso aquí.	Ella se sentó aquí.
lay/poner	**lie/acostarse**
They laid their papers there.	They lay on the couch.
Pusieron sus papeles allí.	Se acostaron en el sofá.

PRONOUNS USED WITH REFLEXIVE PRONOMINAL VERBS
15.2

The Spanish reflexive object pronouns along with their English equivalents are used to show that the object, be it direct or indirect, which they represent is the same person as the subject of the sentence. Hence, they show agreement in person, number, and gender with the subject of the verb.

Spanish and English Forms

SINGULAR		PLURAL	
me	myself	nos	ourselves
te, se	yourself	os, se	yourselves
se	himself	se	themselves
se	herself		
se	itself		

In the 1st and 2nd persons singular and plural, the Spanish reflexive object pronouns are identical in form to the direct and indirect object pronouns. For example, **me** can function as a direct object like in **Carlos me atacó,** as an indirect object like in **Carlos me escribió una carta,** or as a reflexive object like in **No me levanté muy temprano.** In the 3rd persons singular and plural, however, the reflexive object **se** is clearly distinct from either the 3rd person direct or indirect object forms. Syntactically, the reflexive pronouns assume the same position with respect to various verbal forms as do the D.O. and I.O. pronouns. (See §14.5.)

The English reflexive object pronouns are the same as those used reflexively as objects of prepositions. The forms themselves are of some interest because they are compounds, some formed with possessives (eg, **myself**) and others formed with object pronouns (eg, **themselves**).

English reflexive pronoun forms frequently occur not as true reflexives but as intensifiers, used to give emphasis to the subject of a sentence. This can be seen in the examples below. Spanish uses **mismo, misma, mismos, mismas** in association with the subject as pronominal intensifiers.

John did it himself, *or*	Juan mismo lo hizo.
John himself did it.	
I myself saw her, *or*	Yo mismo/misma la vi.
I saw her myself.	
They broke it themselves, *or*	Ellos/Ellas mismos/-as lo rompieron.
They themselves broke it.	

Translate the following English sentences into Spanish using a reflexive pronoun construction. Give all possible word orders.

1. We (usually) go to bed at eleven o'clock. (acostarse)
2. When do they want to get up? (levantarse)
3. We are going to wake up very early. (despertarse)
4. What did they themselves do to avoid trouble?
5. She will probably sit down with me here. (sentarse)
6. We felt very happy yesterday. (sentirse)
7. The leader himself didn't know the way.
8. Don't get angry! (familiar) (enojarse)
9. My mother is getting tired. (cansarse)
10. Don't go near that dog! (formal) (acercarse)

11. We get up at eight o'clock and get dressed. (levantarse, vestirse)
12. The mayor himself joined in the rally.
13. They went to sleep in the living room. (dormirse)
14. She hasn't awakened yet. (despertarse)
15. Katherine, sit down and shut up! (familiar) (sentarse, callarse)
16. They couldn't calm down after the accident. (tranquilizarse)
17. You yourself said so. (formal)
18. I don't want to get sick in Paraguay. (enfermarse)
19. I know he's going to get bored with that class. (aburrirse)
20. If you don't feel well, go to bed early. (familiar) (sentirse, acostarse)

TRANSITIVE AND REFLEXIVE CONTRASTS
15.3

Examine the following English and Spanish transitive and reflexive contrasts. You will see that the reflexive pronouns in the Spanish reflexive sentences actually function as direct objects and that the subject and the direct object are the same person. Only the English sentences using the suffix **-self/-selves** are relatively parallel to the Spanish reflexive examples.

TRANSITIVE:	Ella lo molestó.	She bothered him.
REFLEXIVE :	Ella se molestó.	She got (became) upset.
TRANSITIVE:	Él la cansó.	He tired her. (made her tired)
REFLEXIVE :	Ella se cansó.	She got (became) tired.
TRANSITIVE:	Ella me calló.	She silenced me.
REFLEXIVE :	Ella se calló.	She fell silent.
TRANSITIVE:	Los ocultamos.	We hid them.
REFLEXIVE :	Nos ocultamos.	We hid ourselves.
TRANSITIVE:	Él la curó.	He cured her.
REFLEXIVE :	Él se curó.	He cured himself.

| TRANSITIVE : | Él me divirtió. | He entertained me. |
| REFLEXIVE : | Él se divirtió. | He entertained himself. (He had a good time/had fun.) |

In some instances, the Spanish reflexive pronoun actually functions as an indirect object. Here again the indirect object is the "involved entity" presented in §14.12. For this type of structure, English generally uses a construction made up of POSSESSIVE ADJECTIVE + (**OWN**) + NOUN.

TRANSITIVE :	Te corté el labio.	I cut your lip. (literally **I cut the lip to/for/on you**)
REFLEXIVE :	Me corté el labio.	I cut my (own) lip (literally **I cut the lip to/for/on myself**)
TRANSITIVE :	Te afeitaré la barba.	I will shave your beard.
REFLEXIVE :	Me afeitaré la barba.	I will shave my (own) beard.
TRANSITIVE :	Me quitas la corbata.	You take off my tie (for me).
REFLEXIVE :	Te quitas la corbata.	You take off your (own) tie.
TRANSITIVE :	Ella me puso la blusa.	She put my blouse on me.
REFLEXIVE :	Ella se puso la blusa.	She put on her (own) blouse.

Exercise 2

Translate the following sentences into the other language. Be able to state whether the construction is transitive or reflexive in any given case. In whatever Spanish reflexive constructions you write, state whether the reflexive pronoun actually functions as a direct or as an indirect object.

1. When will the children be quiet? (callarse)
2. No nos acostamos muy temprano en el verano.
3. We got angry because she didn't write to us. (enojarse)
4. Él se quebró la pierna al saltar desde el balcón.
5. They entertained us in Madrid. (agasajar)
6. Federico no quiso valerse de la explicación.
7. That man makes me sick! (enfermar)
8. Josefa los aguardó en compañía de su familia.
9. They aren't going to get up until later. (levantarse)
10. ¿Cuándo se casó tu hermano?
11. Tomorrow I'm going to shave my beard. (afeitarse)
12. Nos pusimos el sombrero y salimos.
13. Aren't you going to wash your hands? (lavarse) (familiar)
14. ¿Quieres que se te quite el apetito?
15. Mary wasn't able to calm them after the accident. (tranquilizar)

Exercise 3

For each of the following Spanish verbs write one original sentence which is transitive and one which is reflexive. Then translate both Spanish sentences into English.

| molestar(se) | fundir(se) | extender(se) | mejorar(se) |
| mojar(se) | secar(se) | preocupar(se) | callar(se) |

SEMANTIC DIFFERENCES
15.4.
Some verbs in Spanish are used non-reflexively with one meaning and reflexively with another. Often the meaning change is very slight between the two usages.

NON-REFLEXIVE	REFLEXIVE
caer = fall	caerse = fall (down)
Las hojas caen en el otoño.	Cuidado, que no te caigas.
comer = eat	comerse = eat up, skip over, omit
Hay que comer para vivir.	Él se comió una pera.
	El orador se comió palabras.
contentar = satisfy	contentarse = make up
Hay que contentar a los demás.	Se contentaron por fin los novios.
decidir = decide	decidirse = make up one's mind
Lo decidieron por voto.	No puedo decidirme entre tantos.
dormir = sleep	dormirse = go to sleep, fall asleep
El niño duerme en el piso.	No pude dormirme anoche.
fijar = fasten	fijarse = pay attention
Fija bien el eje a la sierra.	Fíjate bien en lo que te dicen.
ir = go (with a stated goal)	irse = go away, leave (no stated goal)
Voy a Uruguay en agosto.	¿A qué hora te vas?
llevar = carry, manage	llevarse = take away, carry off
Él lleva encima una pistola.	El personal técnico se llevó el cadáver
Ella lleva las cuentas del casino.	
parecer = seem	parecerse = resemble, look like
Parece que viene lluvia.	Te pareces a tu hermana.
poner = put	ponerse = put on, (also) become
Voy a poner la figura ahí.	Me puse el traje. Se puso enferma.
	ponerse a + INF = begin, start
	Se puso a llorar.

Exercise 4

Translate the following English sentences into Spanish and decide in each case whether a reflexive or a non-reflexive form of the verb is the most appropriate.

1. I can't study because someone took away my books.
2. He can't make up his mind whether he can do it or not.
3. The children fell asleep in the living room.
4. They slept there all night.
5. When are you going away?
6. He resembles (looks like) his father.
7. I don't want to eat that sandwich.
8. Don't put your feet on the table. (familiar)
9. When I started to sing, everyone fell asleep.
10. He seemed to be sick before he fell down.

15.5
There are some verbs in Spanish which historically are used only reflexively since the action expressed can fall only on the subject. Among these are **arrepentirse, fugarse, quejarse, rebelarse, suicidarse.**

Exercise 5

Translate the following English sentences into Spanish, using a reflexive form of the verb in all cases.

1. He bragged about his meeting with the President.
2. Those fanatics believe that everyone should repent.
3. We don't dare (to) speak to him that way.
4. The students have rebelled, and there will be a strike.
5. The general committed suicide after the battle.

RECIPROCAL ACTIONS
15.6.
A reciprocal action is one in which at least two persons do the same thing to each other. Since all reciprocal actions involve two or more agents, the subject and its verb must be in plural form in both English and Spanish.

The following are the formulas for expressing reciprocal actions in the two languages.

ENGLISH	SPANISH
S[plural] + V[plural] + **each other, one another**	(S)[plural] + PRON[reflexive, pl.] + V[plural] + (clarifiers [if any])
They saw one another.	Ellos se vieron.
We greeted each other.	Nos saludamos.
The boys hit one another.	Los muchachos se golpearon.
They will kill each other.	Ellos se van a matar.

Spanish clarifies by gender and number who are the participants in a reciprocal action by tagging the constructions with such phrases as **unos a otros, el uno al otro, la una a la otra,** etc.

Ellos se dieron golpes unos a otros.
Los muchachos se golpearon el uno al otro.
Las mujeres se saludaron la una a la otra.

Note that Spanish reciprocal constructions, if not accompanied by their clarifier tags as illustrated above, are often ambiguous in their meaning. A reciprocal usage could, without a meaningful context or a clarifying tag, be construed as having true reflexive meaning.

Ellos se vieron.	They saw each other. (reciprocal) They saw themselves. (reflexive)
Nos golpeamos.	We hit each other. (reciprocal) We hurt ourselves. (reflexive)

Translate the following sentences into the other language, giving reciprocal constructions in each case.

1. We greeted each other before the contest.
2. Los recién casados se aman muchísimo.
3. We didn't see one another in Panama.
4. Se besaron antes de despedirse.
5. They hated each other so much that they tried to kill one another.
6. Los perros comenzaron a ladrar cuando se vieron.

Sentences with Indefinite Subjects

16.1
Both Spanish and English have ways of expressing ideas impersonally, that is, saying that an action affects everyone in general, not just me, you (to whom I am speaking), us, or them (people we can identify). The subjects of such impersonal sentences are indefinite subjects.

English Indefinite Subjects
English uses the impersonal **one** or generic **you** (unstressed) as indefinite subjects.

> One forgives and forgets.
> You forgive and forget.

> One shouldn't cover that.
> You shouldn't cover that.

> One advances quickly at this institute.
> You advance quickly at this institute.

> One works hard, and what happens? One doesn't make enough money.
> You work hard, and what happens? You don't make enough money.

Spanish Indefinite Subjects
Spanish uses the impersonal reflexive **se** or the indefinite subject **uno(-a)** with the third person singular form of the verb. **Usted** is also used in such sentences, but with impersonal or indefinite force. Indefinite **uno(-a)** and **usted** are the forms which correspond in usage to those of English. In many regions of the Spanish-speaking world, **una** is increasingly preferred by the feminine sex.

> Se perdona y se olvida.
> Uno(-a) perdona y uno(-a) olvida.
> Usted perdona y olvida.

> No se debe cubrir eso.
> Uno(-a) no debe cubrir eso.
> Usted no debe cubrir eso.

> Se avanza rápidamente en este instituto.
> Uno(-a) avanza rápidamente en este instituto.
> Usted avanza rápidamente en este instituto.

Se trabaja duro y ¿qué pasa? Nunca se gana suficiente dinero.
Uno(-a) trabaja duro y ¿qué pasa? Nunca gana suficiente dinero.
Usted trabaja duro y ¿qué pasa? Nunca gana suficiente dinero.

When **se** is used as an impersonal reflexive, it assumes the position of a conjunctive pronoun, that is, it cannot be separated from the verb. In the first sentence of the second group above, if the subject were **él**, the sentence would be rendered as **Él no debe cubrir eso.** **Él**, a subject pronoun, is a disjunctive pronoun and can be separated from its verb. **Se**, however, although it has the meaning of a subject, functions as a true conjunctive pronoun since in **No se debe cubrir eso, se** even displaces the negative **no** from the verb.

16.2

Closely related to sentences with indefinite subjects are those which express actions as taking place in and of themselves with no apparent or explicitly expressed causative agent. Note the following English sentences which express actions that have no apparent cause.

a. The fire went out.   d. The door opened.
b. The train stopped.   e. The windows got broken.
c. The chant ended.   f. The meeting got organized.

Unlike English, Spanish does not express such actions as occurring in and of themselves. Instead, Spanish expresses the apparently causeless English actions with a reflexive construction. The logic of this type of construction is obvious to the English speaker when the subject involves a living being.

Ella se levantó. (She got up, ie, She raised herself.)
Él se acostó. (He went to bed, ie, *He bedded himself.)
El pájaro se bañó. (The bird bathed itself.)

However, the English speaker may have some difficulty seeing the logic of the following sentences since non-living things are involved. Here, Spanish expresses the six English sentences (a) to (f) cited above with **se**, that is, the impersonal reflexive, as if the non-living entities were doing things to themselves.

a. Se apagó el fuego.   d. Se abrió la puerta.
b. Se paró el tren.   e. Se rompieron los cristales.
c. Se acabó el canto.   f. Se organizó la reunión.

Spanish uses the following formula to convey ideas in which actions seem to occur in and of themselves.

(S) + **se** + V [3rd pers. sgl. or pl.] + (S)

El juego se terminó. *or* Se terminó el juego.
Los juegos se terminaron. *or* Se terminaron los juegos.

16.3

Unplanned or Unexpected Occurrences
Spanish uses a special construction to express the idea that someone is affected by an unplanned or an unexpected occurrence. The construction seems to remove the blame for the event from the person affected and to place it upon the thing involved. The structure occurs mostly with the Spanish verbs **escaparse, morirse, ocu-**

rrirse, olvidarse, and romperse, although other verbs can employ the construction as well. The indirect object in such sentences is the *involved entity* explained in §14.12.

Following is the Spanish formula for unplanned or unexpected occurrences.

se + IO + V[3rd pers. sgl. or pl.] + (S)

Se me olvidó el retrato.   Se me olvidaron los retratos.
Se te rompió una pieza del auto.   Se te rompieron unas piezas del auto.
¿Se le escapó el caballo?   ¿Se le escaparon los caballos?
¿Se nos murió la planta?   ¿Se nos murieron las plantas?
Se les ocurrió una idea.   Se les ocurrieron unas ideas.
Se me durmió el niño.   Se me durmieron los niños.

English expresses unplanned or unexpected occurrences more directly, with the following formula:

S + V + DO (or PREP OBJECT)

I forgot the picture.   I forgot the pictures.
You broke a part of the car.   You broke some parts of the car.
Did the horse escape from him?   Did the horses escape from him?
Did our plant die on us?   Did our plants die on us?
An idea occurred to them.   Some ideas occurred to them.
The kid went to sleep on me.   The kids went to sleep on me.

Exercise 1

Render the following sentences into the other language, using the structures presented in this unit. Give all possible versions.

1. One can see my house from here.
2. Se acabó toda su angustia (de ellos).
3. The children escaped from me.
4. De repente se paró la batalla.
5. You don't do that in my house.
6. ¿Cuándo se te rompió el paraguas?
7. A fantastic idea occurred to me last night.
8. Se nos murió el abuelo luego ese mismo año.
9. The class got organized very early.
10. No se aprende nada en este colegio.
11. He forgot to buy the soda.
12. Todas las luces se apagaron después de la catástrofe.
13. One has to think about money these days.
14. Se nos rompieron las cosas que habíamos comprado.
15. You can't concentrate with so much noise.
16. Desde el interior, se escuchó el ruido.
17. The shutters opened and the doors closed in the wind.
18. A los soldados se les escapó el cabo.
19. One shouldn't drink the water in Malaga.
20. No se fuma durante la función.

EXISTENTIAL STRUCTURES IN SPANISH AND ENGLISH
16.4

Spanish uses the verb **haber** in its existential structures while the English formula is **there + be** [3rd pers. sgl. or pl.]. Both these structures state that something exists, but they put virtually no emphasis upon the exact location of the person or thing in question. When an exact location is asked for, Spanish uses its verb **estar** instead of **haber**, and English uses **be** without the apparent subject **there.**

The Spanish Construction with *haber*

There is no stated subject in Spanish constructions expressing mere existence and utilizing the verb **haber**. The affirmative and negative statement, affirmative and negative question, and content question structures freely occur just as they would for any other verb. Existential **haber** is used only in the impersonal 3rd person singular form of the present indicative.

AFFIRMATIVE	: Hay un castillo encima de la montaña.
NEGATIVE	: No hay ningún castillo encima de la montaña.
YES-NO QUEST.	: ¿Hay un castillo encima de la montaña?
NEG. QUEST.	: ¿No hay un castillo encima de la montaña?
CONT. QUEST.	: ¿Qué hay encima de la montaña?

Haber, expressing mere existence, may also occur in tenses other than the present indicative.

IMPERFECT	había un castillo …
PRETERITE	hubo un castillo …
FUTURE	habrá un castillo …
CONDITIONAL	habría un castillo …
PERFECT	haber habido (ha habido, había habido, etc)
MODALS	puede, debe, tiene que + haber

Note: **Haber** expressing existence does not occur in the progressive tense.

16.5
The English Construction

In the English structure, the **there** operates as an "apparent subject." It has no real meaning but serves to occupy the subject position in the affirmative and negative statement, affirmative and negative question, and content question structures. This can be proven by substituting the subject **it** for **there** in these examples.

AFFIRMATIVE	There (It) is a castle on the mountain.
NEGATIVE	There (It) isn't a castle on the mountain.
YES-NO QUEST.	Is there (it) a castle on the mountain?
NEG. QUEST.	Isn't there (it) a castle on the mountain?
CONTENT QUEST.	What is there (it) on the mountain?

In English tenses other than the present, the same structures occur, but the tenses of the verb **be** change.

PAST	There was/were (a castle/castles) on the mountain.
FUTURE	There will be (a castle/castles) on the mountain.
CONDITIONAL	There would be (a castle/castles) on the mountain.

PERFECT   There has/have been (a castle/castles) on the mountain.

MODALS   There can/could/must/should/etc be (a castle/castles) on the mountain.

Note: As is the case in Spanish, the English expressions of existence do not occur in the progressive tense.

16.6

There is one major difference between the English and Spanish structures for expressing mere existence. English consistently distinguishes between a singular and a plural in its verbal forms in the simple present and past tenses, as well as in the present perfect.

There *is* a university in this territory.
There *are* some universities in this territory.

There *was* a university in this territory.
There *were* some universities in this territory.

There *has been* an agreement.
There *have been* some agreements.

Spanish, on the other hand, uses only the 3rd person singular of the verb **haber**, regardless of whether the item in existence is singular or plural.

Hay una universidad (unas universidades) en este territorio.
Había una universidad (unas universidades) en este territorio.
Ha habido un acuerdo (unos acuerdos).

Heard frequently are such erroneous expressions as:

*Antes *habían* dos universidades en este territorio.

Exercise 2

Translate the following sentences, all of which express the mere existence of some person or thing, into the other language.

1. There is a man in my room.
2. ¿Habrá un espectáculo cultural en la zona histórica?
3. Weren't there any oranges in the store?
4. Debe haber un demonio dentro del infeliz.
5. There has been a terrible accident.
6. ¿Dónde habría tantos republicanos?
7. There were several documents on the table.
8. Hay varios discípulos de la reforma cristiana.
9. Will there be a war?
10. ¿No tiene que haber físicos en el laboratorio?
11. When was there a strike at the factory?
12. ¿Ha habido algún acontecimiento decisivo?
13. Can there be a bird in that cage?
14. Hay millares de militares concienzudos en el ejército.

17

English and Spanish Contractions

17.1
Spanish has only two contractions; these are the prepositions **a** and **de** contracted with the definite article **el** to form **al** and **del** respectively.

> **a + el → al**
> Descansemos *al* aire libre.
> El hombre trató de lograrlo *al* instante.
> Se asomaron *al* borde de la fuente.

> **de + el → del**
> Los individuos huyeron *del* bosque.
> Admiramos la colección *del* museo.
> Lo descubrí al extremo de la orilla *del* mar.

17.2
Unlike Spanish, English has many contractions which may occur at any level of speech, from the most formal to the most informal. English contractions can be very difficult for Spanish speakers, whether they are speaking, reading, writing, or listening to English.

Remember that contractions in English are always optional, with the exception of the one occurring between the AUX and the **not** in the negative yes-no question structure **Haven't we been here before?** (Unit 6, §6.10). That contraction is mandatory in English.

Only one contraction per simple sentence is allowed in English. This is a rule which should always be respected. In the following sentence, the underlined segments show where a contraction is theoretically possible **She is not going.** But the sentence can be rendered in contracted form in only one or the other of the two possible ways.

> She's not going *or*
> She isn't going.

17.3.
Classification of English Contractions
There are three major classifications of English contractions.

> Class 1. Contractions which occur between a subject pronoun and the verbs **be** (forms **am, is,** and **are** only, used as an AUX and non-AUX); **have, has,** and **had** (AUX and non-AUX); and modals **will/would**.

150

I'm in school now. (am)
She's working in an atomic plant. (is)†
You've bought a new car. (have)
They'd been living there for years. (had)*
He'll be here in a few minutes. (will)
We'd rather be in Texas. (would)*

†See 17.4 (a), (b), and (c).
*See 17.4 (e).

Class 2. Contractions which occur between a subject noun or interrogative word and the verbs **be** (forms **is, are,** and **was** used as an AUX or non-AUX); **have/has/had** (AUX and non-AUX); and the modals **will/ would.** This type of contraction is less frequent in English.

Mary's in school today. (is)†
Both John and Mae're working in the State Department. (are)
Who's been working here lately? (has)†
Where'll you be this time next year? (will)
What's your name, little boy? (is)†
Billy'd go to Spain if he could. (would)*
†See 17.4 (a), (b), and (c).
*See 17.4 (e).

Class 3. Contractions which occur between the following verb forms: **be** (forms **is, are, was,** and **were** used as an AUX or non-AUX), **have/has/had** (AUX or non-AUX), **do/does/did** (AUX), most of the modal auxiliaries and **not**.

They aren't here now. (are not)
She isn't working here these days. (is not)
We weren't studying much last year. (were not)
I wasn't trying to open your door. (was not)
He hasn't any friends in Florida. (Brit.) (has not)
They haven't gone yet. (have not)
We hadn't seen him for several weeks. (had not)
I don't know your name. (do not)
They didn't know any of the answers. (did not)
She doesn't want to see them now. (does not)
He wouldn't say a thing like that. (would not)
We won't be there when you arrive. (will not)
Why can't you help me? (can not)
They couldn't find their friends. (could not)
We shouldn't have bought so much bread. (should not)

17.4
Confusing Contractions in English
Here are some particularly confusing English contractions.

(a) A contraction like **Mary's** may have the following meanings:
Mary is ... Mary's here and needs to see you.
Mary has ... Mary's done all her work.
The possessive form **Mary's brother is Tom.**

(b) **its** vs **it's**

Its is a possessive adjective. **I don't like its color.**
It's is the contracted form of **it is** or **it has.** **It's an old chair; it's been broken for days.**

(c) **there's** vs **theirs**

There is ... There's a book on the table.
There has ... There's been a terrible accident.
The possessive form **The house is theirs.**

(d) **they're** vs **there** and **their**

They're is the contraction of **they are: They're ready to go.**
There is an adverb of location: **The students are over there.**
Their is a possessive adjective determiner: **They love their children.**

(e) **I'd** and similar contractions: **she'd, he'd, you'd, we'd,** etc.

I would ... I'd be a liar if I told you that.
I had ... I'd told him several times before not to do that.

Exercise 1

Rewrite the following English sentences, making all possible contractions. Some sentences may have at least two versions. In every case, analyze the elements which comprise the contraction and classify each under the appropriate class of contraction outlined above in §17.3.

1. We are not at home now.
2. They have not been traveling much.
3. You would not say a thing like that.
4. Marianne did not come home last night.
5. Your father has not been feeling well.
6. Frederick is trying to do much better work.
7. Who is not studying chemistry this year?
8. They will unlock the door soon.
9. I will not be at home when you arrive.
10. He will buy it if it is not too expensive.
11. She had bought that in Peru.
12. Your brother did not see us.
13. Our sister has not arrived yet.
14. What is he going to say to us?
15. Where will I be able to find you?
16. You should not go out with her.
17. He could not open it with her key.
18. You would have a good time in Yucatan.
19. Your mother is here now.
20. That is not whom I wish to see right now.

Part Three

VERB PHRASE COMPLEMENTATION

COMPLEMENTOS DEL ÁREA VERBAL

"Palabra, sintagma o proposición que, en una oración,
completa el significado de uno o de varios componentes
de la misma e, incluso, de la oración entera."

Diccionario de la Real Academia Española

Adverbs and Prepositions

18.1
Spanish and English adverbs and related prepositional constructions are frequently difficult for both the English speaker and the Spanish speaker. In the following contrastive listings, note that the Spanish adverb is often converted into a prepositional construction with the addition of the preposition **de.** In English, however, the adverb and the prepositional construction are often identical. Nevertheless, in both languages, many exceptions are to be found.

SPANISH		ENGLISH	
ADVERB	PREPOSITION	ADVERB	PREPOSITION
además	además de	besides	besides
antes	antes de	before (time)	before
cerca	cerca de	near, nearby	near
después	después de	afterwards	after
delante	delante de ante	in front before (space)	in front of before
encima	encima de	on top above	on top of above
lejos	lejos de	far (away)	far from
arriba	arriba de	above, upstairs	above
abajo	debajo de bajo	below, beneath downstairs	below, beneath under(neath)
(a)dentro	dentro de	inside within	inside (of) within
atrás detrás	detrás de	behind in back	behind in back of
(a)fuera	fuera de	outside	outside (of)

18.2
In the following English-Spanish adverbial contrasts, note that there are very few troublesome contrastive problems.

Él nunca vino aquí antes.	He never came here before.
Mis tíos viven cerca.	My aunt and uncle live near (nearby).
Después escribieron la crónica.	Afterwards they wrote the chronicle.
La frontera no está lejos.	The border isn't far away.
El recién nacido está arriba.	The newborn (baby) is upstairs.
Nadie está (a)dentro.	No one is inside.
Se oyó un grito afuera.	A scream was heard outside.
La red está abajo.	The net is below (downstairs).

18.3
In the following English-Spanish contrasts in which prepositional constructions are involved, note that in virtually every case contrastive differences appear in both the English and the Spanish renditions.

Él llegó antes de la revolución.	He arrived before the revolution.
Vivo cerca de la plaza pública.	I live near the public square.
Hablé después del representante.	I spoke after the representative.
La caja está arriba de esa otra.	The box is above that other one.
Ella está dentro de la casa.	She's inside the house.
Viven aislados fuera de la ciudad.	They live isolated outside the city.
El cuadro está detrás de la pared verde.	The picture is behind the green wall.

Exercise 1

Translate the following sentences into the other language. Be able to state in each case whether you are dealing with just an adverb or with a prepositional construction. Also be prepared to say whether a significant English-Spanish contrast exists and what the nature of it is.

1. Besides apples, he wants to buy oranges.
2. El interesado está nervioso porque no quiere estar afuera.
3. Before the opera we went to a small café.
4. Rubén se quedó atrás, pero Alejandra se fue delante.
5. I think he was working near that machine.
6. No creíamos que nadie estuviera adentro.
7. After the dance she went home with a friend.
8. Mis amigos están abajo con mis abuelos.
9. I couldn't see him because he was behind the car.
10. ¿Se coloca la materia arriba de o debajo de la superficie?

ADVERB FORMATION IN ENGLISH AND SPANISH
18.4
In both English and Spanish, adverbs are usually derived from adjectives or from nouns.

The English adverb is formed by adding the suffix **-ly** to an adjective.

ADJECTIVE	ADVERB
pleasant	pleasantly
great	greatly
rapid	rapidly
rich	richly

The Spanish adverb is formed in one of two ways:

• By placing the preposition **con** before the noun.

NOUN	ADVERB
mérito	con mérito (meritoriously)
acierto	con acierto (successfully, skillfully)
tristeza	con tristeza (sadly)
gratitud	con gratitud (greatfully)

• By adding the suffix **-mente** to a Class II adjective or to the feminine form of a Class I adjective (see Unit 10). Note that contrary to the Spanish rules for use of the graphic (written) accent, if the adjective has an accent, it is retained in the derived adverb.

ADJECTIVE	ADVERB
peligroso (I)	peligrosamente (dangerously)
fácil (II)	fácilmente (easily)
rápido (I)	rápidamente (rapidly)
especial (II)	especialmente (especially)

18.5
It should be observed that in both Spanish and English certain adjectives assume adverbial force without any change in their form. English, for example, says:

Don't go fast; go slow!
He spoke loud and clear.
She came back quick.

Spanish has numerous examples, among which can be cited:

No puedo verlo muy claro.
Mi carro viejo va muy lento.
Viven feliz en su casita.
Hablaron largo y tendido.

Exercise 2

Give an adverbial equivalent in the other language for these adverbs.

1. con grandeza
2. specially
3. probablemente
4. happily
5. con simpatía
6. easily
7. fríamente
8. sadly
9. con gracia
10. beautifully
11. solamente
12. clearly
13. con pasión
14. fast
15. descuidadamente

PREPOSITIONS AND USES
18.6
The English prepositions **in, on, at,** and **to** versus Spanish **en** are put in perspective here. English employs four locative prepositions **in, on, at,** and **to,** while Spanish generally uses only one, **en.** The Spanish speakers learning English have great difficulty discerning which of the four English prepositions of location they should use. The following guides should prove helpful.

18.7
In (= **en**) is used with objects or people which are found within the confines of some container, or with months and years.

The feather is in the box.	La pluma está en la caja.
The reader is in the library.	El lector está en la biblioteca.
The salt is in the container.	La sal está en el envase.
I work in an assemby plant.	Trabajo en una maquiladora.
He came in July.	Él vino en julio.
We arrived in 1999.	Llegamos en el 1999.
They live in the village.	Ellos viven en la aldea.

18.8
On (= **en**) is used to indicate that an object or person touches the surface of something while not being located within the confines of that something. It is also used for dates and for days of the week. For dates and days, Spanish uses the definite articles **el** and **los.**

I found it on the corner.	Lo encontré en la esquina.
He came on May 3rd.	Él llegó el 3 de mayo.
The picture is on the wall.	El cuadro está en la pared.
I live on this street.	Vivo en esta calle.
A ring is on her finger.	Ella tiene un anillo en su dedo.
There is nothing on the table.	No hay nada en la mesa.

English **on** is also used for most modes of conveyance (ie vehicles which you climb onto), although the person or thing traveling is in reality actually within the confines of the conveyance.

They weren't on that plane.	Ellos no estaban en ese avión.
He arrived on a bus.	Él llegó en un autobús.
Let's celebrate on the ship.	Vamos a celebrar en el barco.
She died on a train.	Ella se murió en un tren.
He was on his bike.	Él estaba en su bicicleta.
There is iron on that truck.	Tienen hierro en ese camión.

But, when small, four-wheeled motor vehicles are the mode of conveyance, English uses **in,** which seems quite logical to the Spanish speaker.

He was in a taxi.	Él estaba en un taxi.
I was born in an ambulance.	Nací en una ambulancia.
She left in a car.	Ella se fue en un auto.

18.9

At (= **en**) is used to indicate the location where an activity takes place, but it does not specify that either people or things are actually within the confines of that place. It is also used like Spanish **a** to mark the time of day an event takes place. It is doubtlessly the most difficult locative preposition for the Spanish speaker when location in space rather than in time is designated.

I saw her at the market.	La vi en el mercado.
He's at the airport.	Él está en el aeropuerto.
Meet me at the station.	Búscame en la estación.
The party was at my house.	La fiesta fue en mi casa.
I bought it at the store.	Lo compré en la tienda.
He was at the doctor's office.	Él estaba en el consultorio del médico.
I work at the university.	Trabajo en la universidad.

But,

She arrived at one.	Ella llegó a la una.
I left at two.	Salí a las dos.

18.10

To (= **en**) is frequently used as a locative preposition in English. Its locative use is derived through semantic confusion with **to**, the English preposition expressing motion through space toward some destination. Since English says **I have gone to Mexico several times,** which expresses movement toward a goal, it has developed over time such expressions as **I have been to Mexico several times,** which expresses mere location. The usage is considered to be standard but is limited in occurrence to the verb **be** in the present perfect or the pluperfect tenses.

I have never been to Spain.	Nunca he estado en España.
He had been to Denmark.	Él había estado en Dinamarca.
I've been to your house repeatedly.	He estado en tu casa repetidas veces.
Who's been to school?	¿Quién ha estado en la escuela?
You haven't been to the port yet.	Ud. no ha estado en el puerto aún.

(Exercise 3)

Translate the following Spanish sentences into English using **in, on, at,** or **to** to render the Spanish locative preposition **en.** More than one choice may be possible in some cases, but in all cases be able to state the reason for your choice of prepositions.

1. ¿Has estado alguna vez en la Costa Azul?
2. El río Tajo se halla en la Península Ibérica.
3. Tus llaves están en mi bolsillo.
4. Creo que te conocí en otra actividad idéntica.
5. ¿Qué tiene Daniel en la mano izquierda?
6. Estábamos en el cine cuando pasó algo misterioso.
7. El perro se sentó en el rincón.
8. No se veía una sola nube en el cielo infinito.
9. Mis amigos nunca han estado en San Juan.
10. El señor que está en el avión es el profesor Santana.

11. Me senté en la silla que estaba en el balcón.
12. La Segunda Guerra Mundial comenzó en 1939 y terminó en 1945.
13. Mi padre enseña inglés en la Universidad de Salamanca.
14. ¿Has estado alguna vez en el pueblo donde nací?
15. El Presidente estaba en un coche cuando fue asesinado.
16. Sandra estaba en el autobús cuando le habló el anciano.
17. Hay muchas páginas en esta unidad.
18. Paquito, ¿qué tienes en la boca?
19. Mi auto no está ni en el garaje ni en la calle sino en la estación de trenes.
20. Querían venir en octubre, pero llegaron el 2 de noviembre.

18.11

The English locative prepositions **in, at,** and **on** appear in a host of idiomatic expressions. The following list, by no means complete, gives some idea of the frequency of such expressions. They were taken from one issue of a local newspaper.

in	**at**	**on**
in a hurry	at all	on account of
in all	at any rate	on fire
in a while	at best/worst	on purpose
in detail	at first	on second thought
in every way	at last	on several occasions
in fact	at least	on the contrary
in favor of	at night	on the left/right
in front/back	at once	on the other hand
in general	at present	on the whole
in many/most ways	at the beginning of	on time
in mind	at the end of	
in no time	at the moment	
in order to	at the side of	
in the afternoon	at this/that time	
in the beginning		
in the end		
in the evening		
in the event of		
in the future		
in the meantime		
in the middle		
in the morning		
in this/that case		
in time for		
in touch		

Exercise 4 (optional)

Examine the English idiomatic expressions using **in, at,** and **on** which appear above and find a Spanish equivalent for each. Use each expression in an English sentence and translate each sentence into Spanish.

CONTRASTS
18.12
Spanish uses **de** and **por** while English uses **in** with time divisions of the day. When a specific time of a specific division of the day is mentioned, Spanish **de** is used for English **in.**

Ella llegó a las ocho de la mañana.	She arrived at eight in the morning.
No salimos hasta las tres de la tarde.	We didn't leave until three in the afternoon.

Spanish **por** is used for English **in** when only the division of the day is mentioned, but no specific hour of that division is involved. **En**, however, is used by some speakers.

Andrés no trabaja por (en) la mañana.	Andrew doesn't work in the morning.
Tengo clases por (en) la tarde.	I have classes in the afternoon.
¿Qué haces por (en) las noches?	What do you do in the evenings?
But,	What do you do *at* night?

Exercise 5

Translate the following sentences into Spanish using **de** and **por** correctly to translate English **in.**

1. My friends have to work in the afternoon.
2. Julio arrived at nine o'clock in the morning.
3. Do you do anything in the evenings? (familiar)
4. What could she be doing at five o'clock in the morning?
5. I have classes in the evenings, but I don't in the afternoons.

18.13
Spanish uses **con** and **de** while English uses **with.** In Spanish, **con** (= **with**) is used to convey the idea of the person or object's being in the company of or associated with another person, object, or abstract entity.

Leonardo llegó con su amigo.	Leonard arrived with his friend.
Siempre tomo café con leche.	I always take my coffee with milk.
Sustituimos lo viejo con lo nuevo.	We replaced the old with the new.

Spanish **de** (= **with/in**) is used to convey the notion of identification, that is, the person or thing can be identified by the phrase following **de.** It is also used to indicate the state in which a person or thing finds itself.

¿Conoces a la chica de los ojos claros?	Do you know the girl with the blue eyes?
La de la falda me gusta más.	I like the one in the skirt more.
Él llegó cubierto de polvo.	He arrive covered with dust.
Ella tiene la cara cubierta de sangre.	Her face is covered with blood.

Translate the following English sentences into Spanish, determining whether to use **con** or **de** to translate English **with** or **in**.

1. The girl in the blue dress is my sister.
2. His shirt was all covered with grease.
3. The man arrived with a large dog.
4. The man with the dog is a friend of mine.
5. Those boys with the long hair smoke marijuana.
6. He came with the beer and spoke to the man in the hat.
7. His face was covered with bandages.
8. My students arrived with their books.
9. It's covered now with a sheet.
10. The car with the new tires is mine.

18.14

English Phrases of Possession or Location vs Spanish Clauses

English generally uses a phrase to indicate possession or identification, whereas Spanish more normally uses a clause. Spanish may also employ an identification phrase introduced by **de** (§18.13).

the young man with the short legs	el joven que tiene las piernas cortas
	el joven de las piernas cortas
the man with the defect in his shoulder	el hombre que tiene el defecto en el hombro
	el hombre del defecto en el hombro
the people with prestige	la gente que tiene prestigio
	la gente de prestigio

English also generally uses a phrase to indicate location, but Spanish prefers a clause.

the women in the store	las mujeres que están en la tienda
the boys in the field	los chicos que están en el campo
the girl in the car	la chamaca que está en el carro

Translate the following English sentences into Spanish using a clause to express possession, identification, or location where English uses a phrase.

1. I want to meet the girl with the new car.
2. The people in the library don't speak Spanish.
3. The book on the table is about Chilean wines.
4. We don't like the house with the blue door.
5. That dog in your house really barks a lot. (familiar)
6. The stores in the country towns are small.
7. We met a woman with a sick husband.

8. The houses on my street are very expensive.
9. Look! The girl at the window is crying. (familiar)
10. The boys with the coin collection live in that building.

18.15
Finally, English generally uses only one preposition before a multiple complement (a complement composed of more than one element), but Spanish repeats the preposition before each element of the complement.

They have a formidable impression of you and me.
Tienen una impresión formidable de ti y de mí.

They promoted him for being honest and humble.
Lo ascendieron por honrado y por humilde.

I want to live with love and respect.
Quiero vivir con amor y con respeto.

Exercise 8
Translate the following sentences into Spanish, being certain to use the preposition before each element of the multiple complement.

1. We spoke to my mother and aunt.
2. I know all the business about your brother and nephew.
3. They came by for my father and mother.
4. My father works with Dr. Smith and Dr. Martin.
5. You can't leave without your hat and coat.

19

The Spanish Personal Accusative

19.1.

In Spanish whenever a noun or a pronoun referring to a person or to a named pet is used as the direct object in a sentence, it must be preceded by **a**, the so-called personal **a** or personal accusative. English has no system for marking personal direct objects, so mastery of correct usage of the Spanish personal accusative is a learning problem for the English speaker studying Spanish.

Examples of the Spanish personal accusative:

No veo a Raquel.
Gabriel no conoce a la señora Dennis.
Mi padre cree que vio a alguien en el patio.
Geraldo nunca visita a nadie.
Acusaron a Milagros de matar a alguien.
¿A quién quiere usted ver, por favor?

19.2

The verb **tener** when it takes a personal direct object is sometimes followed by the personal accusative and sometimes not. Compare the following sets of examples.

Tengo muchos hijos.   Tengo una sobrina en México.

versus,

Ya no tengo *a* nadie.   Tengo *a* mi sobrina conmigo.

Tener may emphasize either *existence* or *possession*. When Spanish speakers say **Tengo una sobrina en México,** they are calling attention to the mere existence of such a person so related to them. **Tener**, then, does not take the personal accusative when it expresses simply the existence of a person from the speaker's viewpoint. But in **Tengo *a* mi sobrina conmigo,** the existence of the niece has already been established. What is actually expressed is possession, and in such cases **tener** is followed by the personal accusative.

19.3

Sometimes in Spanish the direct object noun preceded by the personal accusative occurs as a unit before the verb. In these cases, the direct object is then repeated in

164

pronoun form directly before the verb. This redundant usage of the direct object pronoun was discussed in Unit 14 (§14.10).

A Elena no la conozco.
A tus padres no los he visto por aquí.
Al Presidente de la República lo mataron.
A los habitantes desamparados no los puede ayudar el gobierno.

Exercise 1

Translate the following English sentences into Spanish, making certain to provide the personal accusative where appropriate.

1. We don't want to see your friends now. (familiar)
2. I think John killed someone last night.
3. They want to have at least three children.
4. I know Dr. Johnson, but I don't know his wife.
5. We didn't see anyone on the street.
6. Who(m) are you going to bring to my party? (familiar)
7. They have relatives in Panama.
8. I see some of them (people), but I don't see their cars.
9. Who was with you when you met the ambassador? (familiar)
10. Did someone say something to Dr. Smith?
11. They want to know who(m) we saw in class.
12. My friends don't know anyone in Mexico.
13. We plan to meet a lot of people during our trip.
14. Who(m) did they take to the airport?
15. John brought his little dog to class yesterday.

20

The Spanish
Subjunctive

20.1
In order for English speakers to understand the structural conditions under which the subjunctive is used in Spanish, they must first be able to perceive subordinate clauses and then analyze such clauses as (1) noun clauses, (2) adjective clauses, and (3) adverb clauses.

A subordinate clause is a group of words with the following grammatical characteristics:

(1) It has minimally its own subject and verb. Since every Spanish verb form implies a subject, a simple verb form can constitute a clause.

(2) It makes very little sense alone, as its meaning depends at least partially upon a main clause to which it is somehow attached.

In the following Spanish sentence examples, the subordinate clauses are in italics.

Yo no quiero *que tú cometas una injusticia.*
Él se da cuenta de *que tienes mucho talento.*
Ramón va a buscar a un señor *que le arregle el programa.*
Conozco al profesor *que te proporcionó esa excelente nota.*
Voy a obrar *hasta que agote todas las posibilidades.*
Luis siempre inventa algo *cuando me hace una visita.*

20.2
A subordinate noun clause functions as a noun, that is, it represents *a thing* and answers the question **¿Qué?/What?** In Spanish a subordinate noun clause generally functions as a direct object, but occasionally it assumes the functions of a subject.

In the following discussion, the noun clause, which is italicized, will be shown to represent a thing and to answer the question **¿Qué?/What?**

Yo quiero la paz. (**La paz** is a noun phrase which functions as a direct object. It is the thing I want and answers the question **¿Qué quieres?**)

Yo quiero contribuir. (In this case, **contribuir** is the direct object even though it is a verb. It is the name of the action I want to do. **Contribuir** answers the question **¿Qué quieres?**)

166

Yo quiero *que tú triunfes*. (Here, the subordinate clause, **que tú triunfes,** is the thing I want. Although it is a clause, it is the direct object in this sentence. Since it is the thing I want, it is called a *noun clause*. This noun clause answers the question **¿Qué quieres?**)

Es importante *que te superes*. (This may be restated as **Que te superes es importante.** Nevertheless, **que tú superes** is still a noun clause in that it represents a thing and answers the question **¿Qué es importante?** In this instance, however, the noun clause functions as a subject rather than as a direct object.)

The following are examples of Spanish sentences which contain subordinate noun clauses, all of which are italicized. Note that some of the noun clauses contain indicative verbal forms, others, subjunctive verbal forms.

Supongo *que va a ser muy amoroso con ella*.
Afirmaron *que tienen que estar en la fábrica*.
No creo *que tengas tanta edad como yo*.
Mi padre se alegró de *que estuviéramos en el baile*.
Me fijé en *que tenías fe en la juventud*.
Insisto en *que suprimas todo romanticismo*.
Es práctico *que emplees más seguridad./Que emplees más seguridad* es práctico.

20.3

A subordinate adjective clause functions as an adjective, that is, it describes or somehow modifies a noun or a pronoun. In the following examples, the adjective clauses are italicized.

Voy a construir una villa típica. (**Típica** is a one-word adjective modifying the noun **villa.**)

Voy a construir una villa *que sea típica*. (**Que sea típica** is a subordinate adjective clause modifying **villa. Villa** is the antecedent or modified word of the adjective clause.)

The following are examples of Spanish sentences which contain subordinate adjective clauses. Again, the subordinate adjective clauses are shown in italics, and it will be seen that some of them contain indicative verb forms while others contain subjunctive forms.

Busco a alguien *que me atienda el negocio*.
Lo encerraron en una torre *que se hallaba en la colonia*.
Quiero comprar un animal *que no moleste mucho de noche*.
El año pasado compraron un animal *que molesta mucho*.
Aquí tienes palabra por palabra lo *que digo*.
Necesitamos un puesto *que se encargue de la disciplina*.
Me concedieron el puesto *que se encarga de la disciplina*.

20.4

The subordinate adverbial clause functions as an adverb in that it answers such adverbial questions as **When?, Where?, How?,** etc. The adverbial clauses are italicized.

Alfredo viene *mañana*. (**Mañana** is a one-word adverb telling **when.**)

Alfredo viene *cuando tiene tiempo.*
Alfredo va a venir *cuando tenga tiempo.* (In both sentences, the clause following **cuando** is adverbial since it tells **when.**)

Further illustrative examples follow.

Roberto va a repararlo *con cuidado.* (**Con cuidado** is an adverbial phrase telling **how.**)

Roberto va a repararlo *según tú le digas.* (The italicized clause **según tú le digas** is an adverbial clause, again telling **how.**)

The following are examples of Spanish sentences which contain subordinate adverbial clauses, shown in italics. Some clauses have subjunctive forms and others have indicatives.

Daré un paseo *mientras estés haciendo tus ejercicios.*
Lo midieron *según tú les señalaste.*
Junto dinero *para que mis hijos puedan asistir a la universidad.*
Me lo ordenó *antes de que aumentara el precio.*
Nicolás me lo aseguró *cuando lo vi.*
Nicolás me lo va a asegurar *cuando lo vea.*
Lo comprobaron *sin que nadie presentara pruebas.*

Exercise 1

Examine the following Spanish sentences and identify the subordinate noun, adjective, or adverbial clauses in each. Name the clause type.

1. Siempre noto cierta inquietud mientras cita a la autoridad.
2. Creo que el instrumento está arriba.
3. Está a la venta la tienda que está situada en el barrio.
4. Vamos a retirarnos para que puedas descansar un poco.
5. Es verdad que su reacción fue violenta.
6. Quiero emprender una carrera que responda a mis necesidades.
7. Anoche soñé con el éxito hasta que me desperté.
8. No conocemos a nadie que haya adivinado su suerte.
9. Que la ley de aquí no requiera un castigo fuerte es imposible de entender.
10. Van a insistir en que registremos la propiedad completa.
11. Voy a agradecértelo cuando cambies ese temperamento.
12. Allá está el buque nacional que vimos en el puerto ayer.

Sometimes the verbal form used in the three types of clauses above (noun, adjective, and adverbial) must be a subjunctive. The problem for the English speaker learning Spanish is that of being able to use the Spanish subjunctive actively and correctly. On the other hand, the Spanish speaker learning English will discover that the lack of overt marking in English of the subjunctive is not helpful. English indicative and subjunctive forms of the lexical verb are indistinguishable except in the 3rd person singular (**I insist that he *deposit* more money in the bank**) and in the highly irregular verb **be** (**We demand that she *be* here on time**). English employs alternate structures more frequently than the subjunctive ones. Thus, the formulas used to convey subjunctive ideas in Spanish are at great variance with those used to express similar English concepts.

THE SPANISH SUBJUNCTIVE IN THE NOUN CLAUSE
20.5
A subjunctive verbal form is mandatory in the Spanish noun clause under the following two conditions, both of which must be met in the same sentence.

> (1) There is a different subject between the main clause and the subordinate noun clause.
>> **Yo** quiero que **tú** vayas.
>> **Yolanda** sugiere que **nosotros** salgamos.
>> **Ella** insiste en que **ellos** traigan los resultados.
>> **Tú** no crees que **los políticos** hayan llegado.

> (2) There is a verb in the main clause which can be classified under one of the following three semantic categories:

>> a. A verb of suasion (ie a verb which brings pressure upon the subject of the subordinate noun clause to do or not to do something, for example, **querer, insistir en, prohibir, preferir**).

>> b. A verb of doubt or denial (eg **dudar, no creer, negar**).

>> c. A verb of strong emotion (eg **temer, alegrarse de, sentir, esperar**).

20.6
Main Expressions of Suasion
The following is a fairly complete listing of the main Spanish expressions of suasion. Note that each expression has a meaning which places pressure upon the subject of the subordinate noun clause to do or not to do something. The pressure may be quite intense (eg **mandar**), or it may be relatively light (eg **preferir**). Notice also that the following formula is consistently used in Spanish sentences hosting subordinate noun clauses.

$$(S)_1 + V_1[\text{INDICATIVE}] + \textbf{que} + (S)_2 + V_2[\text{SUBJUNCTIVE}]$$

The wide variety of English structures used to render the Spanish subjunctive will be presented later.

aconsejar:	Te aconsejo que no cedas tu título.
aprobar:	No apruebo que destruyas tu matrimonio.
decir (= tell):	Me dijo que no confundiera la cuestión.
dejar:	No dejes que te amenacen.
desear:	Deseo que te diviertas en Mérida.
es aconsejable:	Es aconsejable que respetemos la tradición.
es importante:	Es importante que instalen un régimen justo.
es necesario:	Es necesario que concluyamos esta discusión.
es preciso:	Es preciso que le advierta de las consecuencias.
es preferible:	Era preferible que no lo compararas con las demás personas.
exigir:	La tribu exige que le demos el respeto debido a su dios.
gustar:	No me gusta que fumes en la habitación.
hacer:	Hizo que aprobara lo decidido.

impedir:	No voy a impedir que lo publiquen en la prensa.
insistir en:	Ella insiste en que acertemos todas las preguntas.
mandar:	El capataz mandó que saliéramos en grupo.
necesitar:	Necesito que tú me ayudes a planificar el estudio.
oponerse a:	La gerencia se opuso a que oganizáramos un sindicato laboral.
pedir:	Pido que se establezca un taller moderno.
permitir:	La época no permite jamás que olvidemos el futuro.
preferir:	Prefiero que te limites a mirar.
prohibir:	Él prohíbe que besen a su hija.
querer:	No querían que las tropas ocupasen el edificio.
rogar:	Ruego que Ud. pese con serenidad la situación.
sugerir:	El líder sugirió que concurriéramos en la doctrina a seguir.

Several of the verbal expressions just presented may be used with an infinitive construction rather than the subjunctive. All of them are indirect object taking verbs, that is, each one may be accompanied by **le a uno.** The most common verbs referred to are **dejar, hacer, mandar, permitir, prohibir.** Each is used below both with a permissible infinitive construction and with a full noun clause subjunctive construction.

dejar(le) a uno:	Mi madre no me deja fumar.
	Mi madre no deja que yo fume.
hacer(le) a uno:	Nos hace sonreír a cada paso.
	Hace que sonriamos a cada paso.
mandar(le) a uno:	Su majestad le mandó partir.
	Su majestad mandó que partiera.
permitir(le) a uno:	No te permito tender la ropa en el patio.
	No permito que tiendas la ropa en el patio.
prohibir(le) a uno:	Te voy a prohibir renunciar a la herencia.
	Voy a prohibirte que renuncies a la herencia.

20.7
English Structures for Verbs of Suasion

Whereas Spanish consistently uses the structure $(S)_1$ + V[INDICATIVE] + **que** + $(S)_2$ + V_2[SUBJUNCTIVE], English has a number of formulas which are used in the translation of sentences with verbs of suasion. Several of the verbs may be used with more than one structure, there being no difference in meaning but merely a change in level of formality.

(1) S + V + DO + **to**-INF: used with main verbs **advise (aconsejar), allow (dejar), ask (pedir), beg (rogar), command (mandar), forbid (prohibir), like (gustar), need (necesitar), permit (permitir), tell (decir),** and **want (querer/desear).**

advise:	I advise you to leave immediately.
allow:	They won't allow me to speak now.
ask:	I ask you to try a little harder.
beg:	She begged us to help her that fateful night.
command:	They commanded us to shoot.
forbid:	I forbid you to see that boy.

like: I don't like you to smoke in the house.
need: Yesterday we needed them to carry the groceries.
permit: She won't permit us to work here.
tell: They told them to get out of town.
want: We want you to be successful.

(2) S + V + DO + LV: used with main verbs **have** [cause] (**hacer**), **let** (**dejar**), and **make** (**hacer**).

have: He had me bring several examples.
let: They won't let us see the puppies.
make: She made us stay in class an extra hour.

(3) S + V + **for** + IO + **to**-INF: used with main verbs like **ask** (**pedir**), **like** (**gustar**), **prefer** (**preferir**), **say** (**decir**), or impersonal verbal phrases like **be advisable** (**es aconsejable**), **be important** (**es importante**), **be necessary** (**es necesario/preciso**), **be preferable** (**es preferible**).

ask: He asked for us to try harder.
like: I don't like for you to drink so much.
prefer: We prefer for them to stay here.
say: She said for them to leave immediately.
be advisable: It is advisable for them not to leave so soon.
be important: It's important for you to get to work on time.
be necessary: It is necessary for them to do all the exercises in the book.
be preferable: It was preferable for us to go by train rather than by bus.

(4) S + V + DO + **from** + LV-**ing**: used with the main verb **prevent** (**impedir**).

prevent: He prevented me from leaving on time.

(5) S + V + POSS ADJ + LV-**ing**: used with main verbs **forbid** (**prohibir**), **like** (**gustar**), **oppose** (**oponerse a**), **prevent** (**impedir**), **recommend** (**recomendar/aconsejar**).

forbid: I forbid your smoking in the house.
like: They don't like my working at night.
oppose: We oppose your becoming governor.
prevent: They prevented his saying anything.
recommend: They recommended our seeing a good lawyer.

(6) S + V + PREP + POSS ADJ + LV-**ing**: used with main verbal expressions **approve of** (**aprobar**), **be opposed to** (**oponerse a**), **insist on** (**insistir en**).

approve of: They approved of our getting married.
be opposed to: She was opposed to his leaving.
insist on: I insist on your telling me.

(7) S_1 + V_1 + **that** + S_2 + V_2[SUBJUNCTIVE]: used with the main verbal expressions **ask** (**pedir**), **command** (**mandar**), **demand** (**exigir**), **insist** (**insistir en**), **prefer** (**preferir**), **propose** (**proponer**),

recommend (recomendar/aconsejar), suggest (sugerir), or impersonal verbal phrases like **be advisable (es aconsejable), be important (es importante), be necessary (es necesario), be preferable (es preferible).**

Note: The above formula (7) is identical to the Spanish subjunctive structure formula, and all of the examples given demonstrate situations where the true subjunctive shown in italics is used in English.

ask:	I ask that he *find* the time to do it.
command:	He commanded that she *open* the door.
demand:	He demanded that she *open* the door.
insist:	They insist that he *work* to earn his expenses.
prefer:	I prefer that you not *be* here so early.
propose:	We propose that he *be* hired now.
recommend:	They recommend that she *decide* immediately.
suggest:	We suggested that he *study* the problem more carefully.
be advisable:	It is advisable that they not *be* here when he arrives.
be important:	It's important that he *see* the professor right away.
be necessary:	It is necessary that she *take* care of the children today.
be preferable:	It's preferable that I *be* with my parents.

However, in the negative transformation of this formula, the negator **not** occurs before the LV[SUBJUNCTIVE] without the use of **do, does,** or **did** found in regular indicative structures. (See §2.10.)

$$S_1 + V_1 + \textbf{that} + S_2 + \textbf{not} + V_2[\text{SUBJUNCTIVE}]$$

I ask that he not find the time to do it.

Exercise 2 (Optional)

Translate all of the English sentences under §20.7 (1–7) into Spanish. Regardless of the structure employed in English to express sentences with main verbs of suasion, note that Spanish consistently uses the $(S)_1 + V_1 + \textbf{que} + (S)_2 + V_2[\text{SUBJ}]$ when main verbs of suasion are involved.

Exercise 3

Translate the following sentences into the other language. Spanish will consistently use its special formula, while English will use one of the formulas under §20.7. If more than one English version of a sentence can be given, provide all versions. **(Optional)** For every translated sentence, provide the structural formula.

1. Nos aconsejaron que no descendiéramos del monte.
2. We forbid them to eat in that restaurant.
3. No van a dejar que él inicie la protesta.
4. They wanted us to bring the food for the party.
5. Es importante que ella examine su conciencia antes de obrar.
6. They made him work with the prisoners.
7. Es preferible que no aluda él al comentario.
8. We need you to help us with this project.
9. Mis padres insisten en que mi hermano estudie medicina.
10. They prevented us from seeing our relatives.

11. No le gusta que juguemos a los dados los domingos.
12. They forbid us to speak Spanish to the children.
13. Hicieron que pagáramos la deuda sin tener suficientes fondos.
14. My father opposed my studying in a foreign country.
15. El presidente insiste en que todos tratemos de probar nuestra habilidad.
16. My parents don't approve of my getting married this year.
17. El general impidió que los soldados atacaran de inmediato.
18. She insists on our being on time for class.
19. Piden que él firme el manuscrito auténtico.
20. I advised them not to work there at night.
21. Mi abuela prefería que sus hijos le hablaran en alemán.
22. She proposes that we study the economic problems of Central America.
23. Querían que atravesáramos la aldea antes de caer la nieve.
24. We suggest that they write a letter to the President.

20.8
Main Verbs and Other Expressions of Doubt or Denial

The following is a fairly complete listing of the Spanish main verbs and other expressions of doubt or denial. As was the case with the main verbs of suasion, Spanish again consistently uses the formula $(S)_1 + V_1 + $ **que** $ + (S)_2 + V_2[\text{SUBJ}]$[1].

¿creer?:	¿Crees que Wilfredo sepa dónde estamos?
dudar:	Dudo que hayan hecho el trabajo completo.
negar:	Niego que la fórmula tenga errores.
poder ser:	Puede ser que se determine pronto la fecha de producción.
es difícil:	Es difícil que estén aquí para la boda.
es dudoso:	Es dudoso que la cifra alcance esa cantidad.
es imposible:	Es imposible que hagan tanta labor.
es improbable:	Es improbable que ese trozo de cobre sea suficiente para la prueba.
es posible:	Es posible que designe a un familiar para el puesto.
es probable:	Es probable que tropiecen con dificultades.
no creer:	No creemos que ellos falten a la exposición.
no es cierto:	No es cierto que hayan fundado un organismo de odio.
no es claro:	No es claro que hayan exagerado sobre su fama.
no es evidente:	No era evidente que existiera un movimiento contrario.
no es seguro:	No es seguro que inicien la reforma total en esta jornada.
no es verdad:	No es verdad que lo haya planteado el historiador.

Non-verbal expressions (English **perhaps, maybe**)

acaso:	Acaso Gilberto tome el Metro para llegar a tiempo.
quizá(s):	Quizá(s) hayan olvidado tu apellido.
tal vez:	Tal vez desaparezca con su novia esta noche.

20.9
Main Verbs and Other Expressions of Strong Emotion

A fairly complete listing of the Spanish main verbs and other expressions of strong emotion follows. As was the case with both the main verbs and expressions of

---

[1] Subjunctive. See footnote (9) on page 26.

suasion, doubt, or denial, Spanish consistently employs the formula $(S)_1 + V_1 +$ **que** $+ (S)_2 + V_2[\text{SUBJ}]$.

alegrarse:	Me alegro (de) que logres tu ilusión de formar un hogar.
doler:	Me duele que se hayan envuelto en la política.
esperar:	Espero que estés dispuesto a ejercer esa profesión.
extrañar:	Me extraña mucho que te manifiestes de esa manera.
sentir:	Siento tanto que nadie haya evitado esa desgracia.
temer:	Temía que él me disparara sin razón.
es absurdo:	Es absurdo que causen tanta confusión.
es bueno:	Es bueno que estés estudiando árabe.
es curioso:	Es curioso que haya llegado acompañado.
es lamentable:	Es lamentable que Ud. tenga esa enfermedad.
es una lástima:	Es una lástima que ella no demuestre más su capacidad.
es malo:	Es malo que piensen hacerte daño.
es raro:	Es raro que el marqués se exponga a la muerte.
es ridículo:	Es ridículo que gastes tanta energía en gritar.
es triste:	Es triste que no tengan mejor criterio.
estar alegre:	Están alegres de que no hayamos perdido el partido.
estar encantado:	Estoy encantado de que puedas lucirte en la recepción.
estar triste:	Estoy triste de que tomes esa decisión.
parecer mentira:	Parece mentira que no sepas leer.
tener miedo:	Tiene miedo de que su sueño malo se convierta en realidad.

(non-verbal)
ojalá: ¡Ojalá (que) se haga un milagro!
            ¡Ojalá hubiera más tiempo para destacarme!

SEQUENCE OF TENSES IN SPANISH SUBJUNCTIVE SENTENCES
20.10

This general principle of the sequence of tenses in Spanish subjunctive sentences is that if the main verb of a Spanish sentence belongs to the present tense family, the subordinate subjunctive verb will generally be either the present or preterite perfect (present perfect) subjunctive. Likewise, if the main verb in the sentence belongs to the past tense family, then the subordinate subjunctive verb will usually be either the imperfect or the pluperfect subjunctive.

Note that in this discussion of the sequence of tenses, the principles apply not only to subjunctive sentences involving noun clauses but to subjunctive sentences containing adjective and adverbial clauses as well.

Main verbs of the present tense family:
    Present indicative: **espero**
    Future indicative: **esperaré, voy a esperar**
    Any imperative (command): **dígale, no le diga**

Main verbs of the past tense family:
    Preterite: **esperé**
    Imperfect: **esperaba**
    Conditional: **esperaría**

20.11
Present Tense Family
When the main verb is of the present tense family, the subordinate verb may express a time subsequent to the main verb.

> Espero (ahora) que vengas dentro de un par de días.
> No creo (ahora) que estén hoy aquí para esa hora.
> Dudo (ahora) que tengan tiempo para hacerlo más tarde.
> Es ridículo (ahora) que te integres a esa organización el mes que viene.

In structures where the main verb is of the present tense family, the subordinate verb may express a time simultaneous with that of the main verb.

> Siento (ahora) que tengas temor de un ataque de nervios (ahora).
> Tampoco creo (ahora) que estén en la facultad (ahora).
> La era exige (ahora) que mantengamos normas positivas y eficaces (ahora).
> Es una lástima (ahora) que ella no tenga mejores sentimientos (ahora).

When the main verb is of the present tense family, the subordinate verb may express a time prior to that of the main verb.

> Parece mentira (ahora) que hayas opinado de esa forma (antes).
> Es posible (ahora) que hayan llamado (antes).
> ¿Crees (ahora) que hayan influido en sus ideales religiosos (antes)?
> Me extraña (ahora) que él no haya cubierto la distancia (más temprano).

Note: It is quite common for some Latin American Spanish speakers not to observe this particular rule for tense sequence. Rather than saying **Me extraña que él no haya cubierto la distancia,** some speakers from the Americas will say **Me extraña que él no cubriera la distancia.**

20.12
Past Tense Family
When the main verb is of the past tense family, the subordinate verb may express a time subsequent to the main verb.

> Yo no creía (entonces) que Juan tuviera motivo de protestar (más tarde).
> Él temía (entonces) que destruyeran el local (luego).
> Sería una lástima que ella figurara en la investigación (finalmente).
> Yo quería (entonces) que él me sacara los cálculos (luego).

When the main verb is of the past tense family, the subordinate verb may express a time simultaneous to that of the main verb.

> El director no creía (entonces) que estuvieran en la conferencia (entonces).
> Era raro (entonces) que la mayoría lo nombrara (entonces).
> Muchos negaron (entonces) que se formara un escándalo (entonces).
> Era preferible (entonces) que ella dejara esas pretensiones (entonces).

When the main verb is of the past tense family, the subordinate verb may express a time prior to that of the main verb.

> Sentía (entonces) que me hubiera transformado en espíritu (antes).
> No era verdad (entonces) que le hubiera sucedido esa tragedia a Ud. (antes).
> ¿Creías (entonces) que yo te hubiera mentido (antes)?
> Temí (entonces) que los niños hubieran pasado hambre (antes).

(Exercise 4)
Translate the following English sentences into Spanish and be certain to observe all the rules concerning the correct sequence of tenses. All of the sentences, when translated, will contain noun clauses, but not all will require a subjunctive verbal form in the subordinate noun clause. Be able to state in each case why a subjunctive form is or is not required.

1. We don't believe that he has arrived yet.
2. I think that she has my keys.
3. He wanted me to bring my friends.
4. They insist on our being here early.
5. Perhaps your father had met the man in South America.
6. I know that he lives near the university.
7. He was sorry that they hadn't seen the film.
8. We believe that they understand all the questions.
9. He is going to have us read a long book in English.
10. Our parents never permitted us to smoke at home.

11. Tell him that his family has arrived.
12. She told me to open the door.
13. It seems to me that the boy is very ill.
14. It seemed a lie that he would say something like that.
15. My mother advised me to study Latin in school.
16. It's a pity that you haven't been able to work.
17. He denied that his children had stolen the money.
18. They said that you had bought a new car.
19. We hoped that you would tell us the truth.
20. I am opposed to your going to the party with them. (familiar)

THE SPANISH SUBJUNCTIVE IN THE ADJECTIVE CLAUSE
20.13
Whether or not a subjunctive verbal form occurs mandatorily in a Spanish adjective clause depends entirely upon the nature of the antecedent of that subordinate clause (ie the noun or pronoun which the subordinate adjective clause modifies).

A subjunctive verbal form is required in the subordinate adjective clause under either of two possible conditions.

(1) The antecedent is imaginary or indefinite in the mind of the speaker at the moment referred to, that is to say the referent has not yet been experienced by the speaker.

Buscamos una casa que tenga jardín. (The house referred to by the adjective clause is in the speakers' minds only. They haven't yet experienced the house in reality. At the moment referred to, in this case the present, the house is an imaginary house.)
Quiero enamorarme de alguien que sepa estimar mis cualidades. (The someone referred to is in the speaker's mind, not in the reality of one's experience at the time the sentence is uttered. The person is, therefore, imaginary and indefinite.)

Vamos a buscar a personas que sean más tranquilas. (The persons mentioned have yet to be found. They are imaginary, indefinite people in the mind of the speaker only, waiting to be found at some future time, if at all.)

But,

¿Ves la estrella a la que se refiere el texto? (This is a definite star. It is being experienced at the time referred to. It is not imaginary; therefore, no subjunctive is used in the adjective clause describing this antecedent.)

(2) The antecedent is negated, that is, it is said not to exist.

No hay nadie que anime una actividad como él.
No hay mal que dure cien años.
No había persona que alzara la vista.

But,

Me indicó a alguien que podía repararlo. (Antecedent is not negated nor is it imaginary or indefinite, so no subjunctive is used.)

20.14

Lo que (= English **what**) is another Spanish structure marking an adjective clause and is accompanied by the subjunctive only in certain instances. In sentences containing this construction, **lo** is the antecedent of the adjective clause introduced by **que.**

(1) If **lo** refers to a definite thing in the speaker's mind, then no subjunctive is used in the adjective clause introduced by **que.**

No percibo lo que pretendes haber logrado.
Ud. no merece lo que recibe en este momento.
No va a ser definitivo lo que prometen hacer.

(2) If **lo** refers to something indefinite in the speaker's mind, to something which is yet to be experienced by the speaker, a subjunctive form must appear in the subordinate adjective clause introduced by **que.**

Voy a rechazar lo que me indiques. (I haven't yet been shown what to reject.)
Tienes que escoger lo que te haga feliz. (I don't know what it is that makes you happy.)

But,

Voy a rechazar lo que me indicas. (I have been shown what to reject.)
Tienes que escoger lo que te hace feliz. (I know what it is that makes you happy.)

(Exercise 5)

Translate the following English sentences involving adjective clauses into Spanish. Be mindful of the rules for the sequence of tenses. Some sentences will require a subjunctive, others will not, but in any case be able to state why you did or did not use a subjunctive form in the subordinate adjective clause.

1. I am looking for the man who wrote this book.
2. He was looking for a house that was comfortable.
3. You should do what he tells you. (He hasn't told you anything yet.)

4. You should do what he tells you. (You have already been told.)
5. There is someone in the hotel who can speak English.
6. There was no one in the hotel who could speak English.
7. Is there anyone in the hotel who can speak English?
8. I met a man who could drink a lot of wine.
9. My parents couldn't believe what they heard.
10. I know I'm not going to believe what I hear. (But, I have not heard anything as yet.)

11. I don't know anyone who can drink that much.
12. They want to buy a car that works well.
13. Last year we bought a car that didn't work well.
14. Did you see the lady who sold this dress? (familiar)
15. I need to see a lady who sells dresses.
16. Do you want to see the lady who sells dresses?
17. They had a dog that barked a lot.
18. They want to buy a dog that barks a lot.
19. They didn't want to buy a dog that barked a lot.
20. He wanted to meet a girl who had a lot of charm.

THE SPANISH SUBJUNCTIVE IN THE ADVERBIAL CLAUSE
20.15

Spanish sentences which host subjunctive forms in the adverbial clause consistently use the formula $(S)_1 + V_1 + \text{ADV EXPRESSION} + (S)_2 + V_2[\text{SUBJUNCTIVE}]$.

Certain adverbial expressions are mandatorily followed by a subjunctive verbal form in the adverbial clause.

a menos que = unless
> No cedo a menos que tú me convenzas.
> No quería obtenerlo a menos que a ti te interesara.

antes (de) que = before
> Establécelo definitivamente antes (de) que deje de ser oportuno.
> Verificamos la respuesta antes (de) que nos pudieran meter en serios problemas.

con tal (de) que/siempre y cuando = provided that
> Tomarán medidas firmes con tal (de) que cese la violencia.
> Felipe hace buen trabajo siempre y cuando le paguen bien.

para que = so that
> Dedujeron el impuesto para que no se aumentara el precio.
> Te di el dinero para que pudieras comprar la provisión.

sin que = without
> Transcurre el tiempo sin que haya ninguna esperanza.
> Abrieron la puerta sin que nadie los viera.

Other adverbial expressions may or may not take the subjunctive depending upon the time relationships between the main clause and the subordinate adverbial clause, or upon the speaker's knowledge of or feeling about the situation described.

20.16
Cuando = when
The indicative is used following **cuando** when no futurity, either in relation to the present or to the past, is implied. **Cuando** + INDICATIVE expresses a usual occurrence which has been experienced in the past or which is routine.

    Cuando Emilia viene, siempre la recibimos con alegría.
    Mi familia se preocupa mucho cuando estoy fuera.
    Cuando su querida madre me llama, siempre salgo de prisa.
    Cuando tengo dinero, compro la mar de cosas que no les doy uso.
    Julia me llamó cuando había llegado a su destino.

    The subjunctive is mandatory after **cuando** when the reference is to future time, either with respect to the present or the past.

    Cuando Emilia venga, vamos a recibirla con alegría. (She has not yet
        arrived at the moment of speaking.)
    ¡Hijo mío!, cuando seas mayor, sabrás más de esos asuntos.
    Vamos a variar cuando sea debido.
    Quiero viajar al exterior cuando estemos preparados.
    Me dijo que me iba a escribir dos letras cuando llegara a Buenos Aires.

20.17
Hasta que = until
The indicative follows **hasta que** when no futurity is implied. **Hasta que** + INDICATIVE, like **cuando** + INDICATIVE, expresses a usual or routine occurrence in either the present or the past.

    Siempre toman la medicina hasta que se sienten mejor.
    El Primer Ministro gobernó con afán hasta que perdió la salud.
    La marcha duró hasta que llegaron al palacio.
    El borrachón siempre consume hasta que no puede más.
    Ella estudió su oficio hasta que lo dominó completamente.

    When the subjunctive follows **hasta que,** the reference is always to future time, either with respect to the past or to the present.

    Tienes que estudiar la lengua hasta que la asimiles bien.
    No quiero disponer del comercio hasta que lo tengamos en completo orden.
    No quería disponer del comercio hasta que no lo tuviéramos en completo
        orden.
    ¡Come, muchacho, hasta que no puedas comer más!

20.18
Mientras = while
Mientras takes the indicative when the reference is to usual or routine occurrences in any time sequence.

    Siempre viajamos por la provincia mientras mamá está aquí.
    Mientras viajábamos por el continente, vimos muchas cosas de valor.
    Me dedico a la pintura mientras ella practica la música.
    Mientras sus hermanos se educaban, él andaba tras la fantasía.

The subjunctive occurs after **mientras** when future time in any time sequence is referred to.

> Vamos a viajar por la provincia mientras mamá esté aquí.
> ¿Qué piensas hacer mientras estés en los Estados Unidos?
> Nos dijo que iba a estar ocupado mientras diéramos la vuelta.
> ¿Qué puedo yo hacer al respecto mientras estén meditando?
> Ella pensaba desviarse a Burgos mientras yo siguiera directo a Madrid.

20.19
En cuanto (tan pronto como) = as soon as
As is the case with the other adverbial expressions of time **en cuanto (tan pronto como)** takes the indicative when usual or routine occurrences are referred to in any time sequence.

> Ella siempre se pone en contacto conmigo en cuanto (tan pronto como) sabe algo distinto.
> Alberto siempre gasta todo su dinero en cuanto (tan pronto como) recibe su jornal.
> Me hiciste falta en cuanto (tan pronto como) te fuiste.
> En cuanto (Tan pronto como) lo veo, me enojo.

However, this adverb of time takes the subjunctive whenever the reference is to the future.

> Mi amiga se va a poner en contacto conmigo en cuanto (tan pronto como) sepa algo distinto.
> Néstor me iba a decir la verdad en cuanto (tan pronto como) las circunstancias le dejaran hacerlo.
> Sé que Alberto va a gastar todo su dinero en cuanto (tan pronto como) reciba su jornal.
> En cuanto (Tan pronto como) lo veas, dile que quiero hablar con él.

20.20
Aunque = even though/although
This is a concessive adverb in which the speakers concede to the listeners the truth of the ideas expressed. An indicative follows **aunque** when the speakers affirm their belief in the truth of what is stated or when they indicate that they know the beliefs held by the listener.

> Es verdad, aunque tú no lo crees. (The speaker knows that the listener does not believe what the speaker holds to be true.)
> Aunque puede tratarlo con desdén, él no va a hacerlo ahora. (The speaker affirms that he knows the person can, indeed, treat someone disdainfully.)
> Aunque trajeron los productos, no repartieron ninguno.
> Ella no va a podernos pagar aunque tiene gran deseo.
> Aunque tenía conocimiento de la industria, no lo nombraron para el cargo.

Aunque is followed by the subjunctive when the speaker is unsure of the truth of what is stated or when there is uncertainty about what the listener might believe.

> Es verdad, aunque no lo creas. (The speaker indicates the lack of knowledge about exactly what the listener thinks. The listener may think it is true or may also think it isn't.)

Aunque pudiera hacerlo, él no va a tratarlo con desdén. (The person discussed may or may not be able to treat someone disdainfully; the speaker simply does not know.)

No van a poder repartir ninguno aunque traigan los productos. (Maybe they will bring the products, maybe not.)

Aunque tenga conocimiento del trabajo, no lo van a nombrar para el cargo.

20.21
Según = according to/how

The indicative follows **según** when some definite or already experienced idea is expressed.

Voy a hacerlo asimismo según me dices. (The speaker has already been told how to do it.)

No pude hacerlo exclusivamente según el maestro me lo explicó.

No quiero ponerlo en el último puesto según tú me explicas.

No puedo creer tu historia de locura según me la cuentas.

Según takes the subjunctive when an indefinite concept or something projected for future time is stated.

Voy a hacerlo asimismo según me digas. (The speaker is not certain how to do it but will do it exactly as instructed.)

Confío en que podré hacerlo según me lo expliques.

Pensaba componerlo según el maestro me explicara.

Ya sé que no voy a creer la historia según me la cuentes.

(Exercise 6)

Translate the following sentences into Spanish. Although all of them host adverbial clauses, some will require subjunctives and others will not. Be careful with tense sequence and be able to state why you used or did not use a subjunctive in each case.

1. He left before we could speak to him.
2. They worked hard until they finished the job.
3. Do you plan to work until you finish the job?
4. His family spent a lot of money so that he could become a doctor.
5. We weren't going to see them unless they came on time.
6. What did you say when you saw him?
7. What are you going to say when you see him?
8. He was reading a book while she was washing clothes.
9. She said she would bring her husband provided you brought yours. (formal)

10. The horse always escapes without anyone seeing it.
11. He used to drink without his girlfriend's knowing it.
12. What are you going to study before we go to class?
13. Although his wife may not know it, he has a girlfriend.
14. Please explain it to me according to how he explained it to you.
15. Although he arrived late, we all went to the party.

16. I was going to write it according to how he wanted it. (But, at the same
    time, I hadn't been told yet how to write it.)
17. I'm going to read that book as soon as I buy it.
18. She went shopping as soon as she received her salary.

Spanish and English
Verb + Relator Constructions

21.1

A relator is a preposition which may function in one of two ways:

(1) As a connector between a conjugated verbal form and a following dependent but non-conjugated verbal form such as an infinitive or a present participle.

> Vienen *a* comer.
> Soñaron *con* ganar.

> They succeeded *in* entering.

(2) As a connector linking a conjugated verbal form with a following noun or pronoun complement.

> Nos acercamos *a* la casa.

> They all laughed *at* him.

Spanish and English occasionally use a relator in a parallel fashion.

Él insistió *en* salir.	He insisted *on* leaving. (same relators)
Él planeó traerlo.	He planned to bring it. (no relators)

Note: In this analysis the **to** of **to bring** is considered the morphological infinitive marker and not a preposition. The verbal form which follows prepositions or relators in English is the present participle **-ing**, while in Spanish, it is the infinitive (see Unit 27).[1]

---

[1] It has long been the custom to describe the infinitive in English as **to** + LV with **to** functioning as the infinitive marker. Such a description makes a further distinction by recognizing a **to**-infinitive and a **bare**-infinitive. However, convincing arguments have been put forth in more recent times to show that **to** is not a morphological infinitive marker but is more defensively described as a preposition followed by an infinitive complement (LV); hence, the base form only of the lexical verb is the true infinitive. The two words, according to this analysis, would constitute a prepositional phrase structure. The following parallel structures are given as just two examples illustrating this analysis:

The testimony led us *to assume your innocence.*
The testimony led us *to the assumption of your innocence.*   (Continued on next page.)

Relator usage more frequently differs from one language to the other as can be seen in the examples which follow.

(3) The relator, if any, appears between a conjugated verb form and a following dependent but non-conjugated verb form.

Comenzó *a* llover. (Spanish uses a relator.)
It began to rain. (English uses no relator if **to rain** is considered the infinitive.)
She succeeded *in* going. (English uses a relator.)
Ella pudo ir./Ella logró ir. (Spanish uses no relator.)

(4) The relator, if any, occurs between a conjugated verb form and a following noun or pronoun complement.

Juegan *a/al* béisbol. (Spanish uses a relator.)
They play baseball. (English uses no relator.)

He looked *for* the wound. (English uses a relator.)
Él buscó la herida. (Spanish uses no relator.)

Ellos se preocupan *por* las masas. (Spanish uses a relator.)
They worry *about* the masses. (English uses a relator also.)

The contrastive analysis of relator usages between English and Spanish often varies according to the particular translation given to lexical items. Note that an obvious relator contrast exists between Spanish and English in these sentences.

Él entró *en* la región.   He entered the region.
Ella se acercó *a* la multitud.   She approached the multitude.

A contrast occurs because **entrar** has been translated **enter** and **acercarse** as **approach.** However, in the following examples, no contrasts occur simply because in this instance **entrar** has been rendered as **go into** and **acercarse** as **go up to.**

Él entró *en* la región.   He went *into* the region.
Ella se acercó *a* la multitud.   She went *up to* the multitude.

In the following sections a classification and analysis of Spanish/English relator contrasts will be found.

My uncle lived *to be one hundred.*
My uncle lived *to the age of one hundred.*

Another very current analysis calls **to** a prepositioned infinitival particle (Huddleston, 128). Whichever of these analyses one subscribes to would account for the absence of **to** in structures such as **Nobody made you go** or **Look at him run** without having to call them "exceptions to the rule" or **bare**-infinitives. If you subscribe to these more recent analyses, then various of the statements made in this unit and the examples given should per force be changed.

RELATORS AND THEIR POSITIONS
21.2

The relator, if any, appears between a conjugated verbal form and a following dependent but non-conjugated verbal form. In these examples, Spanish uses a relator between the verbal forms, whereas English does not if **to** is considered part of the infinitive.

Relator **a**
The relator **a** is found after such verbs as:

acercarse a
Él se acercó a oponerme resistencia.

to approach
He approached to offer me resistance.

acostumbrarse a
Él se acostumbró a dormir durante el día.

to become accustomed to
He became accustomed to sleeping during the day.

aprender a
Ella aprendió a multiplicar con eficacia.

to learn
She learned to multiply effectively.

apresurarse a
Me apresuré a sonar el timbre.

to hurry
I hurried to ring the bell.

atreverse a
Él no se atreve a gastarles una broma pesada.

to dare
He doesn't dare (to) play a practical joke on them.

ayudar a
Ella me ayudó a componer poemas.

to help
She helped me (to) compose poems.

bajar a*
Bajaron a podar el jardín.

to go (come) down
They went (came) down to trim the garden.

comenzar a
Pepe comenzó a empujarlo hacia abajo.

to begin/to start
Pepe began (started) to push him down.

correr a*
Corrieron a salvarme.

to run
They ran to save me.

empezar a
Empezamos a dividir las monedas en partes iguales.

to begin/to start
We began/started to divide the coins in equal parts.

enseñar a
Ella me enseñó a dar discursos notables.

to teach
She taught me to give notable speeches.

inspirar a
Le inspiré a elevar sus pensamientos hasta el máximo.

to inspire
I inspired him to elevate his thoughts to the maximum.

invitar a*
Los invité a definir su posición en torno a la defensa propia.

to invite
I invited them to define their position on self defense.

ir a*
Fueron a rodear el muro.
Van a rodear el muro.

to go/to be going
They went to surround the wall.
They are going to surround the wall.

llamar a*
Nos llamaron a representar el
partido ante el congreso.

to call
They called us to represent the party
before the congress.

llegar a*
Llegaron a recoger sus papeles.
Llegaron a poseer una enorme
fortuna.

to arrive/to manage (come)
They arrived to collect their papers.
They managed (came) to possess an
enormous fortune.

pasar a*
Él pasó a darme la noticia del siglo.

to pass (come) by
He passed (came) by to give me the
news of the century.

ponerse a
Ella se puso a imaginar terribles
sucesos.

to begin/to start
She began (started) to imagine terrible
happenings.

salir a*
Él salió a unirse a la sociedad
moderna.

to leave/to go out
He left (went out) to join modern
society.

subir a*
Ella subió a provocar un disgusto.

to go (come) up
She went (came) up to start a quarrel.

venir a*
Vendrán a prestar ayuda a la grave
pobreza.

to come
They'll come to lend aid to the severe
poverty.

volver a*
Volvieron a pedir la llave.
Volví a llamarte anoche.

to return/to do (something) again
They returned to ask for the key.
I called you again last night.

*The verbs marked with an asterisk are the so-called verbs of motion or attraction. When a noun complement follows them, they are accompanied by the relator **a,** and the English speaker has no difficulty seeing the logic of such usage since it parallels English: **Corrieron a la tienda = They ran *to* the store.** However, Spanish demands that this same relator **a** also be used before dependent infinitive complements. Compare **Corrieron *a* ayudarme** with **They ran *to* help me.** Spanish requires a relator while English uses the **to**-infinitive with no relator. As a result of this, the English speaker will tend to say mistakenly in Spanish ***Corrieron ayudarme.**

Exercise 1

Translate the following sentences into the other language, taking care with the interverbal relator usages in each case.

1. Volveremos a precisar con claridad el procedimiento a seguir.
2. He never became accustomed to eating so late.
3. Subieron a decirnos que nuestro vuelo había llegado.
4. He learned to dance the samba in Rio de Janeiro.
5. El cuerpo de ella comenzó a temblar del miedo.
6. He won't dare (to) leave his wife there.
7. El genio llegó a ignorar la existencia del placer.

8. They began to study Russian last summer.
9. Van a ofrecer una descripción exacta de la escena dolorosa.
10. My father taught me to make wine.

21.3
Relator **de**
The relator **de** is used after such verbs as:

acabar de
Acabo de equivocarme en relación a ellos.

to have just + PAST. PART.
I have just made a mistake about them.

acordarse de
Él se acordó de reducir el margen de error.

to remember
He remembered to reduce the margin of error.

alegrarse de
Me alegro de poder prestar mi colaboración en el caso.

to be happy
I'm happy to be able to lend my collaboration in the case.

cesar de
Ella cesó de ser compasiva.

to quit/to stop + LV-**ing**
She quit (stopped) being compassionate.

cuidar de
Cuidaron de no actuar en contra de la voluntad de la naturaleza.

to take care/to be careful
They took care (were careful) not to act against the will of nature.

dejar de
Ella dejó de satisfacer sus impulsos naturales.

to stop/to quit + LV-**ing**
She quit (stopped) satisfying her natural impulses.

gozar de
Gozan de tomar baños fríos.

to enjoy + LV-**ing**
They enjoy taking cold baths.

haber de
Has de situarlo en la era de lo grandes descubrimientos.

to be + INF
You are to place it in the era of great discoveries.

olvidarse de
Juan se olvidó de marcarlo.

to forget
John forgot to mark it.

terminar de
Terminaron de recoger una cosecha abundante.

to finish + LV-**ing**
They finished gathering an abundant harvest.

tratar de
Enrique trató de atribuir su culpa al egoísmo.

to try/to attempt
Henry tried (attempted) to blame his guilt on egoism.

21.4
Relator **en**
The relator is **en** after such verbs as:

consentir en
Ella consintió en aceptar la responsabilidad.

to consent
She consented to accept the responsibility.

quedar en
Quedaron en revolucionar su operación.

to agree
They agreed to revolutionize their operation.

tardar en/tardarse en

¿Cuánto tarda uno en llegar a El Paso?
Él se tardó mucho en cumplir la misión.

to take x time + INF
to be late in + LV-**ing**
How much time does it take to get to El Paso?
He was very late in completing the mission.

21.5
Relator **que**
The relator **que** is used after such verbs as:

tener que
Tengo que poner más empeño.

to have
I have to be more persistent.

haber que (3rd pers. sgl. only)
Hay que llegar a una conclusión.

one must/it is necessary
One must arrive/It is necessary to arrive at a conclusion.

Exercise 2

Translate the following sentences into the other language, taking care with the interverbal relator usages in each case.

1. One must see it to believe it.
2. Acaban de separarse con dignidad.
3. He had to work last night.
4. Se alegraron de recibir la admiración de los fieles.
5. They agreed to send us the documents.
6. Dejaron de molestarme; por lo tanto soy cordial con ellos.
7. She forgot to bring her books.
8. Trataremos de poner límites a toda acción vulgar.

21.6

English uses a relator between the verbal forms; Spanish uses no relator. Take note of how few instances of this type of contrast there are compared to the large number of cases in which Spanish uses a relator between verbal forms while English does not.

to succeed in
They succeeded in raising the building.

lograr/conseguir
Lograron/Consiguieron levantar la construcción.

to prevent from
I prevented her from leaving.

impedir
Impedí que ella saliera.

to think of/about
He thought of (about) giving a party.

pensar
Él pensó dar una fiesta.

(Little contrast with English)
Él pensó en hacer una fiesta.
Él pensó en dar una fiesta.

21.7

The relator, if any, appears between a conjugated verbal form and a following noun or pronoun complement.

Relator **a**

Spanish uses a relator before a noun or pronoun complement; English uses no relator.

acercarse a
Ella se acercó al edificio.

to approach
She approached the building.

asistir a
Asistimos a la reunión.

to attend
We attended the meeting.

dar a
La construcción da a la calle.

to face
The construction faces the street.

entrar a
Entraron a mi clase.

to enter
They entered my class.

jugar a
Juegan a/al béisbol.

to play
They play baseball.

parecerse a
Te pareces a tu padre.

to resemble/to look like
You resemble (look like) your father.

unirse a
Roberto se unió a la asociación.

to join
Robert joined the association.

21.8

Relator **de**

The relator is **de** between the following verbs and their noun or pronoun complements in Spanish. English uses none.

acordarse de
Me acordé de tu risa.

to remember/to recall
I remembered (recalled) your laugh.

cambiar de
Ella cambió de actitud.

to change
She changed her attitude.

darse cuenta de
No me di cuenta de tu presencia.

to realize/to notice
I didn't realize (notice) your presence.

gozar de
Gocé de la leyenda.

to enjoy
I enjoyed the legend.

olvidarse de
Me olvidé de la frase.

to forget
I forgot the phrase.

partir de
Partieron de España.

to leave (a city or a country)
They left Spain.

salir de
Salieron de mi despacho.

to leave (a confined space)
They left my office.

21.9

Relator **con**

The relator is **con** between verbs like the one following and the noun or pronoun complements. English does not use a relator.

casarse
Él se casó con una europea.

to marry/to get married
He married a European.

21.10
Relator **en**
The relator is **en** between the following verbs and their noun or pronoun complements. English uses no relator.

confiar en
Confío en tu solución.

to trust
I trust your solution.

entrar en (less common than
entrar a)
Entré en el edificio.

to enter
I entered the building.
(No contrast) I went into the building.

fijarse en
Me fijé en su perfil elegante.

to notice/to focus on
I noticed his elegant profile.
(No contrast) I focused on his
elegant profile.

Exercise 3

Translate the following sentences into the other language, taking care with any relators used between the verb and its noun or pronoun complements.

1. I noticed his expression of anxiety.
2. Se acercaron al círculo con curiosidad.
3. We entered the class in order to talk to the professor.
4. El año pasado asistí a clase con diversas preocupaciones.
5. He married a Mexican woman and then they left the country.
6. Me dedico al arte porque gozo de su variedad.
7. The leftists joined the Communist Party.
8. Se olvidó de sus gratos recuerdos de infancia.
9. Suddenly I remembered the name of his friend.
10. No me di cuenta en absoluto del constante eco que producía el viento.

21.11
English uses a relator between a verb and its noun or pronoun complement. Spanish uses no relator.

to ask for
I asked for the address.

pedir
Pedí la dirección.

to listen to
He listened to the testimony.

escuchar*
Él escuchó el testimonio.

to look at
She looked at her face.

mirar*
Ella miró su rostro.

to look for
They looked for a modest home.

buscar*
Buscaron un hogar modesto.

to wait for
We waited for the elections.

esperar*
Esperamos las elecciones.

to pay for
I paid for the passage (fare).

pagar
Pagué el pasaje.

*If the Spanish verbs marked with an asterisk are followed by personal noun complements, such complements must be preceded by **a**. This **a** is not a relator but the so-called "personal accusative" which belongs to the personal direct object, thus marking it as a person rather than a thing. **Miraron el libro,** but **Miraron a los niños.** Complete treatment of the personal accusative was given in Unit 19.

Exercise 4

Translate the following sentences into the other language, taking care with the relators which occur between the verb and its following noun or pronoun complement.

1. Buscamos el tratado de un filósofo contemporáneo que fue citado.
2. He paid for the car with a personal check.
3. Les pedí consideración, pero me la negaron.
4. They waited for the summer with great anticipation.
5. Escuché la versión del nacimiento sagrado, mas no comprendí nada.
6. He always asks for help with his homework.
7. Tengo que esperar la supuesta partida.
8. She always listens to that ridiculous program.
9. No pude pagar la entrada a la función.
10. We are looking for a good apartment on this street.

21.12

Both languages use a relator before a noun or pronoun complement, but the relators are not the same.

contar con
Puedo contar con tu trato amable.

to count on
I can count on your friendly treatment.

cubrir de
Estaba cubierto de una sustancia oscura.

to cover with
It was covered with a dark substance.

consistir en
La población consiste en numerosas divisiones económicas.

to consist of
The population consists of numerous economic divisions.

depender de
Todo depende de mi cansancio en el momento.

to depend on
Everything depends on my fatigue at the moment.

despedirse de
Me despedí de una ilusión perdida.

to say goodbye to
I said goodbye to a lost fantasy.

enamorarse de
Se enamoraron de ese paraíso remoto.

to fall in love with
They fell in love with that remote paradise.

interesarse por
Me intereso por el progreso conti-
nuo de ambos.

to be interested in
I'm interested in the continuous progress of both (of them).

olvidarse de
Me olvidé del asunto original.

to forget about
I forgot about the original matter.

pensar en/de
Pensaron en/Pensaron de ella.

to think of/about
They thought of her/about her.

preocuparse por
Me preocupo por el porvenir de la
religión allí.

to worry (be concerned) about
I worry (am concerned) about the future
of religion there.

quejarse de
Ella se quejó del volumen excesivo
de ruido.

to complain about
She complained about the excessive
volume of noise.

soñar con
Ella soñó con su novio.

to dream about/of
She dreamed about (of) her sweetheart.

Exercise 5

Translate the following sentences into the other language. Relators occur in each
case between the verb and the following noun or pronoun complements, but the
relators are not the same in the two languages.

1. I know that we can count on them.
2. Anoche soñé con un ángel cuyo pelo era dorado.
3. He covered it with honey and then he ate it.
4. No me gusta que comenten de mí a mis espaldas.
5. In California everything depends on the rains.
6. Ese tonto no se queja de nada.
7. We said goodbye to our friends last week.
8. Me preocupo por una mejor enseñanza para todos.
9. He fell in love with a secretary.
10. Usted se olvidó del hecho de que cualquier proyecto necesita una base
    fundamental.

Exercise 6 (Optional)

The following exercise covers all of the relator usages presented in this unit. After
translating each sentence into the other language, state the nature of the relator
contrasts. First, state whether the relator (if any) occurs between a verb and another verb or between a verb and a noun or pronoun complement. Second, state if the
relator occurs in both languages, in neither language, or in one language and not the
other.

1. Where did you learn to speak Spanish? (familiar)
2. Lograron entrar en el espacio por séptima vez.
3. He approached the bird without making noise.
4. Están mirando al agua cristalina debajo del puente.
5. I know that I can't count on her.
6. Anteayer me invitaron a asistir al doble juego final.

7. You don't have to do anything for that class.
8. Estaban esperando el comienzo del prólogo.
9. Students always complain about examinations.
10. Ella trató de deshacerse de todo pecado, pero no pudo hacerlo.
11. He left Uruguay many years ago.
12. ¿Qué vas a pedir este año?
13. They agreed to come tomorrow at eight o'clock.
14. Hay que pensar en una breve preparación antes de continuar.
15. We didn't realize the danger.
16. Se despidieron de la dictadura recién establecida.
17. The little boy laughed at his puppy.
18. Bajaron a ver a los valientes que acababan de regresar.
19. It hasn't stopped snowing yet.
20. Hemos de asistir a una manifestación popular pasado mañana.
21. They are listening to my new records.
22. Adolfo no se atrevió a obligarlos a callar.
23. They came to tell me something sad.
24. No se juega mucho al fútbol americano en Sudamérica.

22

Spanish and English Conditional Sentences and Unreal Comparison

22.1

Both English and Spanish have ways to express a hypothesis and a conclusion to that hypothesis. The clause expressing the hypothesis is often termed the **if-clause** and the conclusion may be called the **result-clause**. The word **if** generally introduces the hypothesis in English, **si** in Spanish. No specific word is required to introduce the conclusion in either language, although **then** may occur in English. In any conditional structure in either language, the protasis (if-clause or hypothesis) may precede the apodosis (then-clause or conclusion) or vice versa without any change of meaning.

Spanish examples of various types of conditional sentences:

> Si ella viene, la veré.
> Si ella viniera, la vería.
> Si ella fue, perdió todo.
> Habría perdido todo, si ella hubiera ido.

English examples of various types of conditional sentences:

> If she comes, I will see her.
> If she came (should come), I would see her.
> If she went, she lost everything.
> She would have lost everything if she had gone.

CONDITIONALS
22.2

Both Spanish and English distinguish quite clearly between neutral conditional sentences and contrary-to-fact sentences.

Neutral conditional sentences state the hypothesis and its conclusion in such a way as to indicate that both are fully capable of realization. It is completely possible that the hypothesis the speaker makes and its accompanying conclusion were fulfilled in past time, are being fulfilled in present time, or will be fulfilled at some future time. In both languages only indicative mood tenses are used in the expression of neutral conditional sentences.

Neutral conditional future time:
SPANISH: **si** + (S) + V[PRES INDIC], (S) + V[PRES or FUT INDIC]

> Si Eustaquio va a San Luis mañana, no digo nada.
> Si Eustaquio no viene el viernes, no verá el juicio.

ENGLISH: **if** + S + V[PRESENT], S + V[FUTURE]

>If Eustace goes to St. Louis tomorrow, I won't say anything.
>If Eustace doesn't come Friday, he won't see the trial.

Neutral conditional present time:
SPANISH: **si** + (S) + V[PRES INDIC], (S) + V[PRES INDIC]

>Si Efraín está aquí, nadie lo sabe.
>Si Alicia habla inglés, debe ser norteamericana.

ENGLISH: **if** + S + V[PRES], S + V[PRES]

>If Ephraim is here, no one knows it.
>If Alice speaks English, she must be North American.

Neutral conditional past time:
SPANISH: **si** + (S) + V[PAST INDIC], (S) + V[PAST INDIC]

>Si José fue a Argentina, gastó mucha plata.
>Si Josefina hablaba con José, no le hablaba en inglés.

ENGLISH: **if** + S + V[any PAST TENSE], S + V[any PAST TENSE]

>If Joseph went to Argentina, he spent lots of money.
>If Josephine was speaking to Joseph, she wasn't speaking to him in English.

Exercise 1

Translate the following neutral conditional sentences into the other language and be able to state in each case whether the sentence refers to the past, present, or future.

1. If you gave him the money, he lost it.
2. Si Josefina viene mañana, nadie va a saberlo.
3. If he has a new car, I want to see it.
4. Si José le dio un regalo a ella, le gustó mucho.
5. Even if he has a watch, he doesn't ever know what time it is.
6. Si escribes tan suave, nadie va a poder leerlo.
7. If he didn't go to class, the professor always knew it.
8. Si usted no vio la corona, era porque no estaba en el museo.
9. If you bring your books, we will translate the story. (familiar)
10. Si te es conveniente, podemos permanecer sentados.

22.3

Contrary-to-fact conditional sentences state the hypothesis and its conclusion in such a way as to imply that what was hypothesized never actually took place in the past nor is it taking place in the present. Since the future has not yet occurred at the moment of speech, there is no such thing as a contrary-to-fact future, but there is a hypothetical future which states that the hypothesis and the conclusion are highly unlikely of realization at any future time. The Spanish contrary-to-fact present and the hypothetical future employ the same verb forms.

Hypothetical future:
SPANISH: **si** + (S) + V[IMPERF SUBJ **-ra, -se**], (S) + V[COND]

Si José fuera/fuese a Argentina, gastaría mucha plata.
Si vinieras/vinieses mañana, celebraríamos.

Note: In the conclusion of hypothetical future conditionals, the **-ra** form of the imperfect subjunctive occasionally occurs as a substitute for the conditional. The usage is considered to be stylized, however: **Si Bolívar volviera/volviese a vivir entre nosotros, ¿qué *pensara* de la actual situación política?**

ENGLISH: **if** + S + V[PAST][1], S + V[COND]
if + S + **were** + **to**-INF, S + V[COND]
were + S + **to**-INF, S + V[COND]
if + S + **should** + LV, S + V[COND]
should + S + LV, S + V[COND]

If Joseph went to Argentina, he would spend a lot.
If Joseph were to go to Argentina, he would spend a lot.
Were Joseph to go to Argentina, he would spend a lot.
If Joseph should go to Argentina, he would spend a lot.
Should Joseph go to Argentina, he would spend a lot.

If you came tomorrow, we would celebrate.
If you were to come tomorrow, we would celebrate.
Were you to come tomorrow, we would celebrate.
If you should come tomorrow, we would celebrate.
Should you come tomorrow, we would celebrate.

Contrary-to-fact present:
SPANISH: **si** + (S) + V[IMPERF SUBJ **-ra, -se**], (S) + V[COND]

Si José tuviera/tuviese tanto dinero, no estaría aquí.
Si Bernardo fuera/fuese francés, no hablaría inglés.
Si vieras/vieses a Juan, no lo conocerías.

Note: Present contrary-to-fact conditionals occasionally take the **-ra** form of the imperfect subjunctive in the conclusion. The usage is again viewed as stylistically motivated: **Si ahora mismo hubiera/hubiese un ataque atómico, la población no *estuviera* preparada.**

ENGLISH: **if** + S + V[PAST], S + V[COND]
V[**were, had**] + S, S + V[COND]

If Joseph had (Had Joseph) so much money, he wouldn't be here.
If Bernard were (Were Bernard) French, he wouldn't speak English.

---

[1] This apparent past tense form of the English verb is really an English subjunctive. The past tense of English and the English subjunctive share the same form with only one exception. The exception is **be** in which the subjunctive is **were** (not **was**) for all persons.

If you saw John, you wouldn't recognize him. (This is the only version possible for this present contrary-to-fact sentence, as the main verb is neither **have** nor **be.**)

Contrary-to-fact past:
SPANISH: **si** + (S) + V[PLUPERF SUBJ **-ra, -se**], (S) +
                     V[COND PERF or PLUPERF SUBJ **-ra** only]

Si José hubiera/hubiese ido a Argentina, habría/hubiera gastado mucha plata.
Si José hubiera/hubiese estado allí, habría/hubiera visto el accidente.

ENGLISH: **if** + S + V[PLUPERF], S + V[COND PERF]
             had + S + V[PAST PART], S + V[COND PERF]

If Joseph had gone (Had Joseph gone) to Argentina, he would have spent a lot of money.
If Joseph had been (Had Joseph been) there, he would have seen the accident.

(Exercise 2)
Translate the following contrary-to-fact and hypothetical future conditionals into the other language. Be able in each case to state whether the time referred to is past, present, or future. Give all versions possible where more than one is acceptable.

1. If I were you, I wouldn't say that.
2. Si acaso vieras a Victoria, no te diría nada ella.
3. Had you given him the money, he would have spent it all. (formal)
4. Si tuvieses tanto dominio propio como yo, estarías mucho más sereno.
5. Were you to bring a book, I would read you a story. (familiar)
6. Si tus amigos hubieran venido directamente, no habrían perdido el rumbo.
7. If you didn't love your mother, you wouldn't send her flowers. (tú)
8. Te enfermarías muy pronto si bebieras esa clase de vino.
9. There wouldn't be so many taxes should he be elected President.
10. Si un rayo llegase a alcanzarnos, no estaríamos vivos.
11. They would have helped me if they had been my friends.
12. Nadie te hubiera descubierto si hubieras guardado silencio.

13. If you met the President tomorrow, what would you say to him? (usted)
14. Si fuese una piedra legítima, ¿cuánto costaría?
15. We would know what time it is had we a clock.
16. Si yo fuera tú, no pagaría la diferencia.
17. He would have told me his name if I had asked (it of) him.
18. Tendrías que comprar un traje nuevo si quisieras salir conmigo.
19. Would you know him were he to enter the room right now? (familiar)
20. No hubieras dicho nada si hubieras estado realmente bajo mi influencia.
21. If you left early tomorrow, you would be in León by noon. (formal)
22. Si salieses con esa muchacha preciosa, su novio lo sabría al minuto.
23. What would they do were there to be another civil war in El Salvador?
24. ¿Dónde estarías ahora si fueras tan indiferente como tu hermano?

22.4

Since conditional sentences tend to be lengthy (they are composed of two clauses) and also because their semantic content deals with ideas which, in fact, are not reflective of reality, native speakers of both languages tend to alter their structure in colloquial speech. None of the following types of conditionals is standard in either language, but they occur in everyday speech with such frequency as to merit some attention. They should not, however, be included in any instructional materials for either the English or the Spanish speaker since grammarians universally view them as unacceptable in the written idiom.

In the present contrary-to-fact conditional in Spanish, the imperfect indicative is frequently found in both the hypothesis and the conclusion.

> ¿Qué hacías si tenías más ventajas?
> (Standard) ¿Qué harías si tuvieras/tuvieses más ventajas?
> Si me daban esa suma de dinero, no sabía qué hacer.
> (Standard) Si me dieran/diesen esa suma de dinero, no sabría qué hacer.
> Si los marcos sobraban de veras, los compraba.
> (Standard) Si los marcos sobraran/sobrasen de veras, los compraría.

In the past contrary-to-fact in English, the conditional perfect often occurs in both the hypothesis and the conclusion.

> What would you have done if he would have seen you?
> (Standard) What would you have done if he had (had he) seen you?
> I would have said something if he would have been there.
> (Standard) I would have said something if he had (had he) been there.
> He would have given me the money if I would have asked.
> (Standard) He would have given me the money if I had (had I) asked.

The past contrary-to-fact in Spanish is sometimes expressed by using the conditional perfect in both the hypothesis and the conclusion.

> No habría hecho una excepción si yo no habría estado allí.
> (Standard) No habría/hubiera hecho una excepción si yo no hubiera/hubiese estado allí.
> Te habría dado el remedio si te habría visto.
> (Standard) Te habría/hubiera dado el remedio si te hubiera/hubiese visto.
> Si me habrían visto, me habrían matado.
> (Standard) Si me hubieran/hubiesen visto, me habrían/hubieran matado.

22.5

Often, simply because the speakers are highly charged emotionally, they will shorten a past contrary-to-fact conditional and use all indicatives in both clauses, simply for emphasis or to indicate rage or grim determination.

> Si en ese momento la veo, la mato.
> (Standard) Si en ese momento la hubiera/hubiese visto, la habría/hubiera matado.

Particularly in Castilian Spanish usage where the **-se** form of the imperfect subjunctive occurs more frequently than does the form in **-ra**, there is a tendency for the **-se** form to appear in the conclusion, particularly in past contrary-to-fact conditionals. The usage is rejected as a hypercorrection.

Si la hubieses visto, no la hubieses reconocido.
(Standard) Si la hubieses/hubieras visto, no la habrías/hubieras reconocido.

UNREAL COMPARISON
22.6
To make an unreal comparison, Spanish has the expression **como si ...** which English renders with **as if/as though ....** The idea which follows either expression is contrary-to-fact and is expressed by the speaker in the first place only as a point of comparison. Unreal comparisons may refer either to present or to past time. Spanish uses the imperfect subjunctive in either **-ra** or **-se** for present unreal comparisons and its pluperfect subjunctive (either in **-ra** or **-se**) for unreal comparison in the past. English uses its past tense (except for **be,** for which the form is **were** in all persons) for present time unreal comparison and its pluperfect for past time unreal comparison.

Unreal comparison present time:

SPANISH: (S) + V[INDIC] + **como si** + (S) + V[IMPERF SUBJ]

    Ella habla como si conociera/conociese a ese hombre ingenioso.
    Él corre como si fuera/fuese un caballo de carrera.

ENGLISH: S + V[INDIC] + **as if (though)** + S + V[PAST]

    She speaks as if she knew that witty man.
    He runs as though he were a race horse.

Unreal comparison past time:

SPANISH: (S) + V[INDIC] + **como si** + (S) + V[PLUPERF SUBJ]

    Hablan como si hubieran/hubiesen vivido durante el Imperio Chino.
    Parecía tan heroico como si hubiera/hubiese conquistado una nación.

ENGLISH: S + V[INDIC] + **as if (though)** + S + V[PLUPERF]

    They speak as though they had lived during the Chinese Empire.
    He appeared as heroic as if he had conquered a nation.

Exercise 3
Translate the following unreal comparisons into the other language and be able to state in each case whether the time referred to is past or present.

    1. Hablas inglés como si lo hubieras estudiado por muchos años.
    2. He smokes as if nothing else were important.
    3. La niña se comió la fruta como si tuviera mucha hambre.
    4. You drink coffee as though you didn't like it very much. (familiar)
    5. Corrieron como si el mismo diablo les persiguiera a ellos.
    6. He explained everything as if he had studied the lesson already.
    7. Norberto hablaba sin expresión, como si estuviera en un trance.
    8. The baby is crying as if you had punished it. (familiar)
    9. El anciano habló muy lento, como si sufriera un dolor intenso.
    10. He is listening as though he were interested in what we are saying.

23

Expressions of Comparison

23.1
Both English and Spanish distinguish between three degrees of comparison for the adjective and the adverb: (1) the positive degree (called absolute degree in some grammars), (2) the comparative degree, and (3) the superlative degree.

	ADJECTIVE		ADVERB	
POSITIVE:	frank	franco	fast	rápido
COMPARATIVE:	franker	más franco	faster	más rápido
SUPERLATIVE:	frankest	el más franco	fastest	el más rápido

DEGREES OF GRADATION
23.2
The positive degree in either language is the simple dictionary form of the adjective or the adverb.

The comparative degree of an adjective or adverb is regularly formed in Spanish by placing the words más or **menos** before the positive form (**más/menos escaso, más/menos lógico, más/menos profundo**).

Several comparative forms, however, are irregular.

POSITIVE	COMPARATIVE
mucho	más
poco	menos
bueno	mejor
malo	peor
grande	mayor *or* más grande
viejo	mayor *or* más viejo
pequeño	menor *or* más pequeño
joven	menor *or* más joven

Note: **Mayor** is used more than **más viejo** when age is the reference. **Más grande** is preferred to **mayor** when physical size is stressed. Similarly, **menor** generally refers to age, while **más pequeño** is more common when the reference is to physical size.

The comparative degree of an English adjective or adverb is formed by adding the suffix **-er** to a word of one syllable, for example, **faster, richer, harder, softer, brighter, bigger, nicer.** (Note: the **g** of **big** is doubled in **bigger** and the **e** of **nice** is dropped in **nicer.**)

Two syllable words ending in the sounds [i], [o], and some ending in the sound [l] also add **-er** to form their comparative forms: **funnier, sillier, yellower, mellower, littler, simpler.**

Other two syllable words generally form the comparative by placing the word **more** before the positive form: **more handsome, more bookish, more standard.**

English adjectives or adverbs of more than two syllables invariably form the comparative by using **more** before the positive form: **more intelligent, more rigorously, more influential.**

Like Spanish, English has several irregularly formed comparatives.

POSITIVE	COMPARATIVE
good (well)	better
bad (badly)	worse
much	more
little	less
far	farther/further

23.3

The superlative degree of comparison in Spanish is formed by placing the definite article **el, la, los,** or **las** before an adjective or adverb in comparative degree form.

Some examples are **el más poderoso, la más bella, los más vivos, las más vitales, los mejores, el más cerca.**

The superlative degree of comparison in English is formed by placing the article **the** before the superlative form of the adjective or the adverb. The superlative form of English adjectives and adverbs is formed as follows:

•The suffix **-est** is added to a positive form of one syllable or to a two syllable positive form ending in the sounds [i], [o], and in many cases [l]: **largest, strongest, fastest, ugliest, yellowest, simplest.**

•The superlative form of other two syllable words or of words of three or more syllables is formed by placing **most** before the positive form: **most even, most intelligent, most influential.**

•The English adjectives and adverbs which have irregular comparative forms also have irregular superlatives.

COMPARATIVE	SUPERLATIVE
better	best
worse	worst
more	most
less	least
farther/further	farthest/furthest

23.4

With respect to Spanish, note that a so-called "absolute superlative" is formed by adding the suffix **-ísimo, -a, -os, -as** to the root of a positive degree adjective or adverb. English would translate this form with **very, exceedingly, extremely, highly,** or **really** + positive adjective/adverb. The Spanish construction never occurs in sentences in which one item or person is compared with another. Some examples of the Spanish absolute superlative are **ancho → anchísimo, generoso → generosísimo, hondo → hondísimo, ilustre → ilustrísimo.**

Exercise 1

Give both the comparative and superlative degree of comparison for the following Spanish and English positive degree adjectives and adverbs.

1. inteligente 2. agudo 3. enfermo 4. lento 5. bueno 6. alto 7. débil
8. valiente 9. joven 10. viejo.

1. wonderful 2. callow 3. expensive 4. filthy 5. careful 6. loud 7. bad
8. simple 9. sunny 10. clear.

23.5

In the comparison of inequality, one item or person is compared with a second item or person. The English and Spanish systems are virtually identical.

He is richer than I (am).	Él es más rico que yo.
They are more intelligent than we (are).	Ellos son más inteligentes que nosotros.
I am happier than she (is).	Soy más feliz que ella.
This is worse than that.	Esto es peor que eso.

When the element following **than** (**que**) is a clause, the two language systems are at considerable variance. In the English system the connective is always **than** when a clause occurs as the second element in the comparison.

He is richer than you think.
He has more friends than we know about.
She has more money than she can spend.
They are better than we thought.

In the Spanish system a number of connectives are involved when the second element of the comparison is a clause. If an adjective or an adverb is found in the first element of the comparison, **de lo que** is the connective used with the following clausal element of the comparison.

Es más rico de lo que tú crees.
Ella sabe más de lo que puede demostrar.
Ese modelo corre más rápido de lo que puedes imaginar.

If a noun is found in the first element of the comparison, **del, de la, de los, de las + que** are the connectives used with the following clausal element of the comparison.

Ellos tienen más dinero del que pueden gastar.
Siento más pena de la que puedo expresar.
Trajeron más libros de los que pueden leer.
Compré más patatas de las que podemos usar.

Translate the following comparisons of inequality into the other language. Take particular care with the connectives used between the first and the second elements of the comparison, especially if the second element is a clause.

1. He has more classes than I (have).
2. La figura tiene más ángulos de los que debe tener.
3. We need less gasoline than they do.
4. Amelia es más alta que su hermana.
5. Texas is poorer than you believe. (familiar)
6. ¿Es tu padre mayor que tu madre?
7. He brought more food than they could eat.
8. Tengo más práctica que usted.
9. They spent more money than we could believe.
10. Ella es más admirable que las demás personas del grupo.

11. She is more intelligent than she thinks.
12. Fumo más cigarrillos de los que debo fumar.
13. We need more sugar than we can buy.
14. Hablan español mejor que nosotros.
15. He spoke worse than anyone would have imagined.
16. Ella ganó más plata de la que pudo gastar.
17. There is more smoke in this room than ever before.
18. Había más ruido en el edificio del que nadie podía creer.
19. Do you write English better or worse than you sister? (familiar)
20. Tomás piensa traer a más visitas de las que podemos atender.

23.6
The superlative degree structures in English and Spanish are shown below.

> He is the fastest boy in the group.
> She is the most naive girl in the class.
> That is the poorest family in the neighborhood.

> Es el muchacho más rápido del grupo.
> Es la muchacha más ingenua de la clase.
> Esa es la familia más pobre del barrio.

In a superlative degree construction in either language, the main noun may be suppressed if it is clearly understood from context. This is the standard process of nominalization presented in §10.11. The article must remain to imply the noun. English may substitute **one**(s) for the suppressed noun, but this is not mandatory.

> Es el ~~muchacho~~ más rápido del grupo.
> He is the fastest (one) in the group.

Es la ~~familia~~ más pobre del barrio.
It's the poorest (one) in the neighborhood.

When stated in the superlative degree, an adjective precedes the noun in English: *the fastest boy, the most pleasant gentleman.* In Spanish the superlative adjective construction normally follows the noun: *el muchacho más rápido, el caballero más agradable.*

Finally, the connectives **in** or **on** of English are rendered as **de** in Spanish.

the tallest man *in* the world   el hombre más alto *del* mundo
the cleanest house *on* the block   la casa más limpia *de* la cuadra

---

Exercise 3

Translate the following comparisons of inequality in the superlative degree into the other language, making nominalized structures where indicated by the items enclosed in parentheses.

1. Usted es el hombre más considerado del grupo.
2. Who is the tallest student in your class? (familiar)
3. Esther es la más sentimental de todas.
4. Are they the most intelligent (men) in the United States?
5. ¿Eres la persona más animada de tu familia?
6. Which is the largest country in South America?
7. Ese lugar tiene el paisaje más maravilloso del estado.
8. Which is the best (wine) in the world?
9. Esa es la peor (tienda) del pueblo.
10. Pepe is the strongest player on the team.
11. Es la chica más extraordinaria de la escuela.
12. They are the poorest people in our neighborhood.

23.7

In superlatives involving modified adverbs, English uses the structure **as** + positive adverb + **as** + modification.

Come as soon as possible.
He spoke as loud as he could.

In modified adverbial superlatives, Spanish uses the structure **lo** + **más** + positive adverb + modification.

Ven lo más pronto posible.
Ella habló lo más alto que pudo.

Exercise 4

Translate the following superlatives involving modified adverbs into the other language, using the structures presented above.

1. Raúl salió lo más pronto posible.
2. He ran as fast as he could.

3. Lo puse lo más alto que pude.
4. They did it as slowly as possible.
5. La joven habló lo más expresivamente que podía.

23.8
The comparison of equality when nouns are involved has the following system in English:

as + much + non-count noun **+ as**
He has as much money as I (have).
She drinks as much milk as they (do).

as + many + count noun **+ as**
They know as many sayings as we (do).
He has as many friends as you.

The Spanish system for comparison of equality when nouns are involved is

tanto/-a + non-count noun **+ como**
Usted tiene tanto dinero como yo.
Bebo tanta leche como ellos.

tantos/-as + count noun **+ como**
Saben tantos dichos como nosotros.
Alicia tiene tantas amistades como tú.

Structures involving adjectives and adverbs in the comparison of equality have the following English system:

as + adjective/adverb **+ as**
He is as poetic as she (is).
He eats as rapidly as a machine.

Note: In English when the auxiliary **do** is needed with the LV, we usually repeat **do** after the comparison noun phrase: **Does he eat as rapidly as you do?**

The Spanish system is as follows:
tan + adjective/adverb **+ como**
Él es tan poético como ella.
Él come tan rápido como una máquina.

(Exercise 5)
Translate the following comparisons of equality into the other language. Keep in mind whether you are dealing with nouns or with adjectives and adverbs.

1. I want to earn as much money as you. (familiar)
2. Alberto tiene unas referencias tan magníficas como cualquiera.
3. They don't know as many Spanish idioms as I do.
4. ¿Tiene ese escrito un sentido tan iluminador como aquél?
5. Our street doesn't have as many trees as yours does.
6. Noé no fuma tanto como yo.
7. Do they sell as much fruit at the supermarket as they do in the market place?

8. El desarrollo bajo su reino fue tan extenso como bajo el anterior.
9. Many Latin Americans don't speak Spanish as fast as the Spaniards do.

10. La vía estrecha no se inclina tanto como la ancha.
11. Do you study as much as your brother does? (familiar)
12. El gobierno militar va a gastar tanto dinero como el civil.
13. I hope to receive as many presents as my sister.
14. No puedo ser tan digno como los otros.
15. Do you know as much as she does? (formal)
16. Ella demuestra tanto cariño como su hermana.
17. My grandmother isn't as nice as my mother.
18. Arizona no tiene tanta población como California.

23.9
Correlative Constructions

The English structure in correlative constructions is **the more/less ... the more/less ....**

The more I study, the less I learn.
The less I work, the more I earn.

The Spanish structure in correlated constructions is **cuanto más/menos ... (tanto) más/menos ...** or **mientras más/menos ... (tanto) más/menos ...**

Cuanto más estudio, (tanto) menos aprendo.
Mientras más estudio, (tanto) menos aprendo.
Cuanto menos trabajo, (tanto) más gano.
Mientras menos trabajo, (tanto) más gano.

Exercise 6

Translate the following correlative constructions into the other language. Give all possible versions.

1. The more I eat, the fatter I get.
2. Cuanto más aprendo, (tanto) menos sé.
3. The more he drank, the sicker he became.
4. Mientras menos leo, (tanto) menos me confundo.
5. The more time I spend with you, the more I like you. (familiar)
6. Cuanto más fumo, (tanto) más me preocupo por mí mismo.
7. The less you spend, the more you will have. (familiar)
8. Mientras más gano, (tanto) más gasto.
9. The less I see her, the happier I am.
10. Cuanto menos te llamo, (tanto) menos sé de ti.

Spanish Integrated Versus English Separable Interrogatives

24.1
Both Spanish and English have interrogative words and expressions, the interrogatives used in content questions. The order of the elements which comprise content questions in both languages has already been presented in Unit 6. In this present unit we will discuss the varieties of the interrogative words and expressions themselves.

Spanish consistently integrates (keeps together) the elements of its interrogatives if they consist of more than one word. English, however, allows the elements of the interrogative unit to be separated, the first element occurring at the beginning of the question and the remaining element being placed as the last item in the question.

Examine the following contrasts involving Spanish integrated and English separable interrogative constructions.

¿De dónde es usted?	*Where* are you *from*?
¿Para qué lo quieres?	*What* do you want it *for*?
¿De qué están hablando?	*What* are they talking *about*?
¿Con qué lo abrió él?	*What* did he open it *with*?
¿Debajo de qué lo viste?	*What* did you see it *under*?
¿Para quién es esto?	*Who(m)* is this *for*?
¿A quién le doy la caja?	*Who(m)* do I give the box *to*?
¿De quién recibió ella eso?	*Who(m)* did she get that *from*?
¿Para cuándo lo pedimos?	*When* did we order it *for*?

Modern English usage recommends that in the case of non-separable interrogatives when the word **who** is preceded by a preposition, it must assume the objective form **whom: From whom did you receive the letter?** However, if the construction with this interrogative is in separable form, **who** is acceptable: **Who did you receive the letter from?** Even though prescriptive grammar recommends **whom** instead of **who** in this last example, few speakers seem to follow this dictate.

Translate the following Spanish interrogative sentences into English. Give both integrated and separable interrogative constructions.

1. ¿Para cuándo los necesitas?
2. ¿De dónde son esos aborígenes?
3. ¿De qué período hablas?
4. ¿A qué vas al extranjero constantemente?
5. ¿Para quién precisamente se señala este punto?
6. ¿Encima de qué casa está el animal?
7. ¿Con quiénes vas al teatro?
8. ¿En qué alternativa estás pensando?
9. ¿Por quién fue escrita la carta?
10. ¿Acerca de qué aspecto son sus opiniones?

Translate the following English interrogative sentences into Spanish. Be sure to give an integrated version of the Spanish interrogative construction.

1. Who(m) did you do for? (familiar)
2. What do we want that for?
3. With whom does she wish to speak?
4. What are you drinking that for?
5. Where is your professor from?
6. What are they writing about?
7. With whom am I going to leave?
8. When do you want it for?
9. What did they find it under?
10. About whom is he going to speak?
11. With whom is she speaking?
12. Where are you coming from?

24.2

Spanish and English simple interrogative words correspond well, except in a few cases which will be illustrated here.

The interrogative for unidentified persons in Spanish is ¿**quién**?; it has a plural form ¿**quiénes**?. Either word functions as the subject in a question. Since English does not designate number or person in its interrogatives, both ¿**quién**? and ¿**quiénes**? are translated by **who** in subject position. If need be, English may distinguish between singular and plural by the addition of the word **all** for the plural.

¿Quién quiere ir?   Who wants to go?
¿Quiénes quieren ir?   Who all want to go?

When ¿**quién**? and ¿**quiénes**? function as either direct or indirect objects, they are preceded by **a**. In the case of direct objects, **a** is the personal accusative. However, the **a** which precedes an indirect object is considered a preposition and is translated with 'to' as seen in the examples below.

DIRECT OBJECT

¿A quién viste?	Who(m) did you see?
¿A quiénes ayudarán?	Who(m) (all) will they help?

INDIRECT OBJECT

¿A quiénes escribieron?	To whom (all) did they write?
	Who(m) (all) did they write to?
¿A quién le diste el dinero?	To whom did you give the money?
	Who(m) did you give the money to?

Standard "correct" English prefers **whom** in the translation, although **who** is acceptable and widely used in these cases, perhaps increasingly more than **whom.** **Whom** is obligatory only after a preposition, as was noted above.

24.3
The interrogative for unidentified things in English is **what.** It has three Spanish equivalents: ¿**qué**?, ¿**cuál**?, and ¿**cuáles**? In sentences involving the verb **ser,** the Spanish speaker employs either ¿**qué**? or ¿**cuál/cuales**? You use ¿**cuál(es)**? when the subject of the question follows a form of **ser,** except when a mere definition is asked for.

¿Cuál es la fecha de hoy?	What is the date today?
¿Cuál es tu número de teléfono?	What is your telephone number?
¿Cuáles son los meses del otoño?	What are the months of autumn?

But,

¿Qué es una visión?	What is a "vision"?
¿Qué es una hipótesis?	What is a "hypothesis"?

In the last two examples, a mere definition is sought. The word **cosa** could be placed after **qué** in each case.

Qué occurs when the subject of the question directly follows the **qué** and both precede the forms of **ser.**

¿Qué fecha sería mejor?	What date would be better?
¿Qué número es mayor?	What number is larger?
¿Qué meses te gustan más?	What months do you like best?
¿Qué cosa es un hipótesis?	What is a hypothesis?

24.4
The English interrogatives **which (one)/which (ones)** are usually rendered in Spanish by ¿**cuál/cuáles**? These interrogatives may refer to either personal or to non-personal objects. In references of this type, the listener is being asked to select one or more elements from a supposed grouping or actual listing of items.

¿Cuál de las afirmaciones prefieres?	Which (one) of the affirmations do you prefer?
¿Cuáles escogieron al azar?	Which (ones) did they choose at random?

Translate the following English interrogative sentences into Spanish using ¿**quién**?, ¿**quiénes**?, ¿**cuál**?, ¿**cuáles**?, and ¿**qué**? correctly.

1. What are the most important cities in the United States?
2. Who did you sell it to? (familiar)
3. What book did you find at the bookstore? (familiar)
4. Which (ones) of your students know Portuguese? (formal)
5. What was the year of his birth?
6. What museum do they want to visit?
7. Who (all) are in the library?
8. What is a kangaroo?
9. Which (one) are you going to buy? (formal)
10. What will be the result of our actions?
11. Whom did he help?
12. What was her problem?

Relative Words
Used Between Clauses

25.1
Both Spanish and English have words which function between clauses as connectors, thus relating one clause to another in some way. Sometimes the connector (or relator) functions as a coordinator; that is to say, it unites two clauses which otherwise would function as totally independent clauses: **I know** *that* **you see me, Yo sé** *que* **me ves.**

On other occasions the connector (or relator) functions as a relative pronoun; it has an antecedent (a word to which it refers) in the main clause of the sentence. In the following examples, the antecedent is italicized and the relative pronoun is in regular type: **She is the** *girl* who(m) **I saw, Ella es la** *muchacha* que **vi.**

25.2
The English subordinating conjunction **that**, always rendered in Spanish by **que**, is used to connect two clauses which have approximately equal weight. Without the subordinating conjunction, the two clauses would function totally independently and would essentially be two separate sentences. For example **I hope that you will come** is composed of **I hope** and **you will come.**

One problem the Spanish speaker has with the English subordinating conjunction **that** is its frequent omission (or suppression) in English. In Spanish the subordinating conjunction **que** is never left out. Compare the English sentences on the left, which contain the conjunction **that**, with those on the right, in which **that** is suppressed. Note, however, that both sets of sentences are wholly grammatical and express exactly the same ideas.

RELATOR EXPRESSED	RELATOR SUPPRESSED
I know that you see me.	I know you see me.
He thinks that we live here.	He thinks we live here.
They believe that I know you.	They believe I know you.
She said that she could do it.	She said she could do it.
Please remember that I need it.	Please remember I need it.

The subordinating conjunction **that** is so frequently omitted in English that a sentence like the following might be totally incomprehensible to the Spanish speaker at first glance: "I know you believe you understand what you think I said, but I'm not sure you realize what you heard is not what I meant."

Translate the English sentence examples given above under "Relators" into Spanish. Note that in each case the Spanish subordinating conjunction **que** must be supplied.

SPANISH AND ENGLISH RELATIVE PRONOUNS
25.3
The following is a contrastive listing of the Spanish and English relative pronouns. They always have an antecedent in the clause preceding the clause which they introduce. Note that the Spanish words are in many cases identical in form to the Spanish interrogative words, but as relative pronouns they never have a written accent mark. Additionally there are prosodic differences.

RELATIVE PRONOUNS	
que	which, that, who, whom
quien, quienes	who, whom
el cual, la cual, los cuales, las cuales	which, that, who, whom
el que, la que, los que, las que	the one who/which/that, the ones who/which/that
lo que, lo cual	what, which
cuyo, cuya, cuyos, cuyas	whose

25.4
Que is the most commonly used relative pronoun of all in Spanish. It can have as its antecedent both people and things of either gender and number.

Ella es la persona que vi.	She is the person (who[m]) I saw.
Son los libros que compré.	They are the books (that) I bought.
Son las señoras que llegaron.	They are the ladies who arrived.

25.5
The relative pronouns **quien** and **quienes** refer only to people. They substitute for **que** only when they are preceded by a preposition.

¿Es ella la persona a quien escribiste?	Is she the person to whom you wrote?
Ellos son los jóvenes con quienes hablé.	They are the young men with whom I spoke.

25.6
El cual, la cual, los cuales, las cuales are used to make their antecedents absolutely clear when confusion might otherwise result. They occur also after compound prepositions (prepositions composed of more than one element, eg,

encima de) or after the prepositions **por** and **sin**.

> El esposo de Elena, el cual estaba presente ...
> (Since **el cual** is marked for gender and number, it is used rather than **que** because it makes clear the fact that Elena's husband and not Elena was present.)

> Las aspiraciones de mis hermanos, las cuales son muy grandes ...
> (**Las cuales** rather than **que** is employed to clarify the fact that the **aspirations**, not the **brothers**, are large.)

> La razón por la cual lo hice ...
> (The reason that I did it ...)

> Su buen humor sin el cual no es el mismo ...
> (His high spirits, without which he's not the same ...)

> El núcleo adentro del cual lo encontré ...
> (The nucleus inside which I found it ...)

25.7

El que, la que, los que, las que are used when the articles **el, la, los,** and **las** are the only antecedents expressed. Invariably these relative pronoun constructions indicate a nominalization, that is, the suppression of a noun between the article and the relator **que**.

La que (= la chica que) lo dijo ...	The one who said it ...
El que (= el hombre que) lo trajo ...	The one who brought it ...
No vi los que (= los libros que) mandaste.	I didn't see the ones you sent.
¿No ves las que (= las revistas que) leí?	Don't you see the ones I read?

25.8

Either **lo que** or **lo cual** may be used to refer to a previously mentioned idea or to a genderless abstraction. **Lo que** is equivalent to the English relative pronoun **what**.

Ya sé lo que quieres.	I already know what you want.
Dime lo que te dijo ella.	Tell me what she told you.
¿No ves lo que trajo él?	Don't you see what he brought?
Lo que pido es esencial.	What I ask for is essential.

    Lo cual is merely an emphatic variation upon **lo que**. It may never, however, begin a sentence. English uses **which** in the translation.

> César no vino, lo cual (lo que) me preocupa.
> Caesar didn't come, which worries me.

> Pusieron las letras en relieve, lo que (lo cual) se ve mejor.
> They made the letters stand out, which looks better.

> Llovió toda la semana, lo cual (lo que) es raro.
> It rained all week long, which is unusual.

25.9

Cuyo, cuya, cuyos, cuyas have as their English equivalent **whose**, a relative possessive pronoun. The Spanish words agree in gender and number with the possessed thing rather than with the possessor just like Spanish possessive adjectives. English **whose** refers back to the possessor (see Unit 11, §11.2).

Cristina, cuyos padres viven muy cerca …
Christine, whose parents live very close by …

El pájaro, cuyo cuello está roto …
The bird, whose neck is broken …

Los aztecas, cuya cultura era única …
The Aztecs, whose culture was unique …

Los niños, cuyas manos están cubiertas de tierra …
The children, whose hands are covered with dirt …

(Exercise 2)

Translate the following English sentences or sentence fragments into Spanish, using the correct relative pronoun constructions.

1. My friend, whose books are on the table …
2. He didn't say anything, which surprised me a lot.
3. The one you know is a Venezuelan girl. (familiar)
4. My grandparents, whose house is in Morelia …
5. That is the man with whom she lives.
6. I didn't understand what he was saying.
7. The building behind which I work …
8. There is someone that I know in Honduras …
9. The Sánchez family, whose house is on the corner …
10. He doesn't want to know what you think about it. (formal)

11. They earned a lot of money, which makes me angry.
12. Do you know the ones (boys) who have the new car? (formal)
13. The house in front of which he fell down …
14. The girls to whom you gave the money spent it all.
15. The students who came late didn't hear what he said.
16. The ones who saw us also saw the professor who is from Nicaragua.
17. I know what I want, but I don't want what I see.
18. Is that the student for whom you wrote the recommendation? (formal)
19. He had a menacing look which frightened her.
20. The man who said that is the one who left early.

25.10

The English relative pronoun system is analyzed somewhat differently from the Spanish system. One must approach the English relative pronouns with the following questions in mind.

• Is the relative's antecedent a person or a thing?
• Does the relative function as a subject or as an object *in its own clause?*
• Can the relative pronoun be omitted?
• If the relative can be suppressed, does this cause another possible arrangement of the relative pronoun construction?
• How many ways are there of expressing the same idea with a variety of relative pronoun constructions?

In the following examples of relative pronoun clausal constructions, note that (∅) indicates the suppression of a relative pronoun which would normally be found introducing the clause.

(1) The relative's antecedent is non-personal; the relative is the subject of its own clause:

>This is the letter that/which came in the mail.
>Here is the book that/which tells the whole story.
>There is the truck that/which killed the little boy.

(2) The relative's antecedent is non-personal; the relative is the object of its own clause:

>This is the letter that/which/(∅) you wanted to read.
>Here is the book that/which/(∅) the professor wrote.
>There is the truck that/which/(∅) I saw go by last night.

(3) The relative's antecedent is personal; the relative is the subject of its own clause:

>He is the man who/that was on the bus.
>They are the boys who/that won the race.
>You are the woman who/that screamed at me.

(4) The relative's antecedent is personal; the relative is the object of its own clause:

>He is the man who(m)/that/(∅) I saw.
>They are the boys who(m)/that/(∅) I met in Zacatecas.
>You are the woman who(m)/that/(∅) they attacked.

(5) The relative's antecedent is non-personal; the relative is the object of a preposition. Note here the great variety of versions permissible in English:

>This is the table under which I found it.
>This is the table which/that/(∅) I found it under.
>
>This is the place about which I spoke.
>This is the pace which/that/(∅) I spoke about.
>
>Here are the dishes for which she came.
>Here are the dishes which/that/(∅) she came for.

(6) The relative's antecedent is personal; the relative is the object of a preposition. Again, note the variety of acceptable versions:

>This is the man about whom I spoke.
>This is the man who(m)/that/(∅) I spoke about.
>
>These are the boys for whom he did it.
>These are the boys who(m)/that/(∅) he did it for.
>
>Do you want to see the girl with whom he worked?
>Do you want to see the girl who(m)/that/(∅) he worked with?

The English relatives **the one(s) who, the one(s) that, the one(s) which,** and (∅) have as their Spanish equivalents **el que, la que, los que, las** que and represent mere nominalizations. They can be used with all the structures and their variations presented above in (1)–(6).

Exercise 3

Rewrite the following English sentences, giving all possible English versions of the original sentences. Be able to classify each sentence under the headings above in (1) through (6) in order to show your knowledge of the type of relative sentence with which you are dealing.

    1. I want to see the person who owns that car.
    2. Does she want to buy the book my father wrote?
    3. We went to the bank which opened yesterday.
    4. Let's say something nice to that Chilean girl we met yesterday.
    5. Are they going to read the letter my mother spoke about?
    6. I don't know the woman who he gave the money to.
    7. Where is the building under which they discovered it?
    8. I'm trying to find the gold watch which I lost at their party.
    9. Do you see the children that are on that bus?
    10. Do you know the students about whom the professor spoke?

(Exercise 4)

Translate the English sentences in Exercise 3 into Spanish. Note that Spanish does not allow the great variety of versions that English permits, nor does it allow any suppression of the relative words.

Exercise 5 (optional)

Write original English sentences using **the one(s) who, the one(s) that, the one(s) which,** and **the one(s) Ø.** Write at least one sentence under each of the headings above (1)–(6) and be able to account for variations upon your original sentences under each heading. Then, translate your English sentences into Spanish. You will be writing a minimum of six English sentences and six Spanish sentence translations of them.

Part Four

SYNTACTIC AND LEXICAL VARIANCES

VARIANTES SINTÁCTICAS Y LÉXICAS

"Cada una de las diversas formas con que se presenta una voz, un fonema, una melodía, etc. . ."

Diccionario de la Real Academia Española

The English and Spanish Imperative Systems

26.1
Both English and Spanish have ways of giving both direct and softened affirmative and negative commands to the addressee(s). The major contrast between the two languages in this regard derives from the fact that English has only one word for the addressee(s): **you** (singular and plural), while Spanish has four words: two familiar, **tú** and **vosotros** and two formal, **usted** and **ustedes.**

In addition to its direct commands, both affirmative and negative, English has a variety of other command structures which are used to soften or attenuate otherwise overly direct or brusk imperatives. Object pronouns always follow the verbal form.

Spanish, on the other hand, has specialized imperative forms for each of its four forms of address in addition to polite or softened commands. Spanish carries the notion of softening or attenuation into the making of requests and criticisms as well. Spanish places object pronouns after the verbal form only in affirmative commands. Unlike English, it places object pronouns before the command form in negative commands. This is explained in detail in §26.6–7.

26.2
The affirmative command structure in English has two forms: the direct command and the less direct, more attenuated, or polite command.

The base form of the English lexical verb is used for direct, affirmative commands:

> Go! Come! Look! Study!
> Work harder! Try it again! Eat all of it! Be here tomorrow!

The modals **can/could** and **will/would** are used periphrastically with **you** along with optional **please** to make these indirect, more polite commands. This structure is normally followed by a question mark since it is phrased as an interrogative. The formula follows:

can/could/will/would + ADDRESSEE + (**please**) + LV

Can you (please) look?
Could you (please) come?
Will you (please) bring them?
Would you (please) eat?

26.3

The negative command structure in English can have two forms as does the affirmative command—a direct command and a less direct one. The negative direct command is formed by using the **do**-auxiliary, a negative marker, and the main verb. Here again a direct object or any other complement follows the lexical verb.

> AUX-**do** + **not*** + LV (*optionally contracted)
>
> Don't go! Don't come! Don't look! Do not enter!
> Don't work too hard! Don't eat all of it! Do not try that again!

A less direct and more polite, negative command may be made by using the modals **can, could, will,** and **would.** **Please** may be optionally added to further soften the command. A direct object or other complement follows the verb, and a question mark ends the sentence. More about indirect commands and attenuation will be found below in section §26.5.

> MODAL-**can/could/will/would** + ADDRESSEE + (**please**) + **not** + LV
>
> Can you (please) not look?
> Could you (please) not come?
> Will you (please) not be here tomorrow?
> Would you (please) not eat all of it?

Object pronouns, both direct and indirect, follow all English command forms.

> Eat it!
> Don't write to him!
> Will you please bring them?
> Would you please not give it to her?

26.4

The Spanish imperative system, like English, can form a less direct, attenuated, or polite command which is the equivalent of the English paraphrase.

> Spanish uses **hacer el favor de** + INF or **hacer el favor de no** + INF
>
> ¡Haz el favor de entrar!   ¡Haz el favor de no entrar!
> ¡Haced el favor de decírmelo!   ¡Haced el favor de no decírmelo!
> ¡Haga(n) el favor de salir pronto! ¡Haga(n) el favor de no salir ahora!
>
> Note: **Hacer el favor de** is frequently heard in an abbreviated form **Favor de (no) ...**

> Also used are ¿**querer** + INF? or ¿**no querer** + INF?
>
> ¿Quieres entrar?   ¿No quieres entrar?
> ¿Queréis decírmelo?   ¿No queréis decírmelo?
> ¿Quiere(n) venir?   ¿No quiere(n) venir?

Translate the following English and Spanish less direct or polite commands into the other language. Use the level of formality and the constructions indicated.

1. Could you please bring some friends? (familiar, plural: querer)
2. ¡Haz el favor de no actuar de esa manera! (will/would)
3. Will you please say something? (formal, singular: querer)
4. ¿Quiere traer aquí la silla? (can/could)
5. Can you stop for a moment? (formal, plural: hacer el favor)
6. Hagan el favor de adoptar la otra resolución. (can/will)
7. Would you not do that again? (familiar, singular: hacer el favor)
8. ¿Por favor, no quieres abrir una ventana? (will, negative)

26.5

Peripherally related to the Spanish attenuated command system is its system for making softened requests and criticisms. The verbs most typically involved in the usage are **querer, deber,** and **poder.** Attenuation is accomplished with these verbs by shifting tenses or mood, going from the present indicative, which is the least attenuated way of stating the request or criticism, through the imperfect indicative and the conditional, to the imperfect subjunctive (**-ra** form) to achieve the maximum softening effect.

Note that the softening of a request or criticism in Spanish may be done for any subject, not only the addressee. In the examples which follow, each verb is listed with examples which go from least attenuated to most attenuated. The appropriate English translations are also presented.

querer
¿Quieres irte?	Will you leave?
¿Querías irte?	Would you leave?
¿Querrías irte?	Would you leave?
¿Quisieras irte?	Would you please leave?

deber
No debes hacerlo.	You must not do it.
No debías hacerlo.	You (really) shouldn't do it.
No deberías hacerlo.	You (really) shouldn't do it.
No debieras hacerlo.	You (really) shouldn't do it.

poder
Puedes decir más.	You can say more.
Podías decir más.	You could say more.
Podrías decir más.	You could say more.
Pudieras decir más.	You could say more.

Give all possible renditions in Spanish for the following English sentences expressing requests and criticisms. Translate English **want, must,** and **can** with the Spanish present indicative tense. Translate English **would like, should,** and **could** each in three ways: (1) the imperfect indicative, (2) the conditional, and (3) the imperfect subjunctive in **-ra** form.

1. You could call a friend. (3 ways) (familiar)
2. You can do better on my examinations.
3. We would like to visit you. (3 ways)
4. Manuel shouldn't spend so much time there. (3 ways)
5. You must not send him the money. (formal)
6. They should buy a new car. (3 ways)
7. One must come to work on time daily.
8. Your pronunciation could be better. (3 ways)
9. I would like to write to your sister. (3 ways)
10. We could visit her in the hospital. (3 ways)

26.6

The Spanish direct commands are all forms of the present subjunctive with the exceptions of **tú** and **vosotros/vosotras** in the affirmative. The normal form for the **tú** affirmative direct command is the same as the 3rd person singular present indicative of the verb.

¡Habla! ¡Come! ¡Vive!

There are, however, eight exceptions:

decir → di	salir → sal
hacer → haz	ser → sé
ir → ve	tener → ten
poner → pon	venir → ven

The form of the negative **tú** command is the 2nd person singular present subjunctive preceded by **no**. There are no exceptions.

¡No hables! ¡No comas! ¡No digas!
¡No vengas! ¡No vayas! ¡No seas conforme!

The form of the affirmative **vosotros/vosotras** command is the infinitive form of the verb with a **-d** marker replacing the final **-r**. There are no exceptions.

¡Hablad! ¡Comed! ¡Vivid! ¡Id! ¡Tened!

The **vosotros/vosotras** negative forms are the second person plural present subjunctive preceded by **no**. Here again, there are no exceptions.

¡No habléis! ¡No comáis! ¡No viváis!
¡No vayáis! ¡No vengáis! ¡No digáis!

The formal **usted/ustedes** affirmative form for direct commands is the 3rd person singular or plural of the present subjunctive. There are no exceptions.

¡Hable! ¡Coman! ¡Viva feliz! ¡Sean prudentes! ¡Tenga cuidado!

The negative form of the formal command with **usted/ustedes** is the same as the affirmative form, only preceded by **no**.

¡No hablen! ¡No coma! ¡No me digan! ¡No sean tontos!

With respect to the Spanish formal direct command, it should be noted that for added politeness, the words **usted** and **ustedes** are used after the command form.

¡Venga usted! ¡No salgan ustedes!

26.7

The position of the indirect and/or the direct object pronouns in Spanish with respect to the direct command forms are outlined as follows:

- For any affirmative direct command, the pronouns follow and attach to the command form in the order IO + DO, if both pronouns occur. If only one object pronoun occurs, it is attached to the verb.

tú	:	¡Háblame!	¡Escríbeselo!
vosotros(-as):		¡Habladme!	¡Escribídselo!
usted	:	¡Hábleme!	¡Escríbaselo!
ustedes	:	¡Háblenme!	¡Escríbanselo!

- For any negative direct command, the pronouns must precede the verbal form, but again in the order IO + DO, if both pronouns occur.

tú	:	¡No me hables!	¡No se lo escribas!
vosotras(-as):		¡No me habléis!	¡No se lo escribáis!
usted	:	¡No me hable!	¡No se lo escriba!
ustedes	:	¡No me hablen!	¡No se lo escriban!

Exercise 3

Give English direct command equivalents for the following Spanish direct commands. Be sure to place the accompanying pronouns in the correct position. Also, state whether the Spanish commands given are **tú, vosotros(-as), usted,** or **ustedes.**

1. ¡No me lo diga!
2. ¡Háganselo a continuación!
3. ¡Tráiganosla en seguida!
4. ¡No lo abandonéis!
5. ¡Confírmelo pronto!
6. ¡Leedla de todos modos para mañana!
7. ¡Póngalo aquí en números redondos!
8. ¡Mándaselas aparte!
9. ¡Prepáramelos para la fiesta únicamente!
10. ¡No me hables en ese tono de voz!

Exercise 4

Give Spanish direct command forms for the following infinitive constructions. The type of command, affirmative or negative, and the subjects **tú, vosotros(-as), usted,** and **ustedes** are all indicated for each infinitive. Be certain to place the pronouns in their correct form, position, and order with respect to the verb.

1. dármelo (vosotros, afirmativo)
2. decirle (tú, negativo)
3. estudiarlo (usted, afirmativo)
4. tenerlos (tú, afirmativo)
5. reunirlas (ustedes, negativo)
6. devolvérmela (vosotros, negativo)

7. escribirle (ustedes, negativo)
8. cargársela (tú, afirmativo)
9. ponerlo (vosotros, negativo)
10. explicármela (ustedes, afirmativo)

11. cantársela (usted, afirmativo)
12. decirlo (tú, afirmativo)
13. hacerlo (usted, negativo)
14. proponérsela (tú, afirmativo)

26.8

The English indirect command system uses the hortative auxiliaries **let** and **let us** (**let's**) to form affirmative statements.

$$\text{let} + DO_1 + LV + DO_2 \,/\, IO$$

> Let him do it.
> Let her speak to him.
> Let your son have it.
> Let's visit your family.
> Let them eat cake.

Modern colloquial English has no regular system for converting an affirmative indirect command into a negative indirect command. Note that if the affirmative command **Let him do it** is made negative, **Don't let him do**, there is a change of meaning equivalent to **Don't permit him to do it.** This in Spanish would be **No le permitas hacerlo** or **No permitas que lo haga.**

When the English subject is **we**, then English can directly convert the indirect affirmative command into a negative version.

> Let's go home. → Let's not go home.

For the other subjects, the best negative version English can provide is by using the modal **may.** This usage is at best rhetorical, poetic, or archaic.

$$\text{may} + S + (\textbf{not/never}) + LV$$

> May you never speak to her again.
> May he always be young.
> May it not keep you from leaving.

26.9

Spanish affirmative indirect commands are formed by using the present subjunctive tense of the verb as was the case with most direct commands. Note, however, that the 1st person plural has a different order for forming indirect commands and an alternate expression using the present indicative instead of the subjunctive.

que + IO/DO +V[PRES SUBJ] + (S)
(for **nosotros/-as**) V[PRES SUBJ] + IO/DO *or*
    vamos a + INF + IO/DO

él/Ariel	Que lo haga él (Ariel).
ella/Ana	Que lo haga ella (Ana).
ellos/ellas/noun (pl.)	Que lo hagan ellos/los muchachos.
nosotros/-as	Hagámoslo *or* Vamos a hacerlo.

The negative indirect command uses the formula:

que + no + IO/DO + V[PRES SUBJ] + (S)
(for **nosotros/-as**) **no** + IO/DO + V[PRES SUBJ]

él/Ariel	Que no lo haga él (Ariel).
ella/Ana	Que no lo haga ella (Ana).
ellos/ellas/noun (pl.)	Que no lo hagan ellas/las muchachas.
nosotros/-as	No lo hagamos.

Exercise 5

Translate the following indirect commands into the other language and make certain that any object pronouns are placed in their correct position.

1. Let them read it tomorrow!
2. ¡Que me lo diga mi padre!
3. Let's go to the movies!
4. ¡Que me lo preste Felícita!
5. Let them bring it to us!
6. ¡No les escribamos!
7. Let's not give it to her.
8. ¡Vamos a decírselo!
9. Let him send it!
10. ¡Que nos lo explique el oficial de policía!

27

The Present Participle and the Infinitive

27.1
The Present Participle
The present progressive tenses in English and Spanish, although formed in corresponding ways (AUX-**be** + LV-**ing** / AUX-**estar** + LV-**ndo**), differ considerably in their usage. Spanish uses the present progressive tense to refer only to the moment of speech, while English, in addition to employing it for that purpose, also uses it to refer to future time. Compare these contrastive examples.

REFERENCE TO THE MOMENT OF SPEECH	REFERENCE TO THE MOMENT OF SPEAKING AS WELL AS THE FUTURE
Estamos trabajando ahora.	We are working now. (PRESENT) We are working (will be working) tonight. (FUTURE)
Están comiendo ahora.	They are eating now. (PRESENT) They are eating (later) in that restaurant. (FUTURE)
¿Estás viviendo aquí ahora?	Are you living here now? (PRESENT) Are you living/Will you be living here next semester? (FUTURE)
Ella está hablando ahora.	She is speaking now. (present) She is speaking/will speak at a conference next month. (FUTURE)
No estoy leyendo nada ahora.	I'm not reading anything now. (PRESENT) I am not reading/won't be reading anything during my vacation. (FUTURE)

Spanish uses the present participles of the verb **ir** and **venir** in their progressive tenses, including the present progressive, only under limited conditions. An example of this limitation is seen in the rendering of English progressive **I'm going/coming.** Spanish uses the simple present indicative tense **Voy/Vengo** in place of the progressive. If the English progressive construction has future reference, then Spanish selects from one of three options: (1) use the simple present indicative with a future indicator **Voy/Vengo la semana próxima**, (2) use the

226

synthetic future tense **Iré/Vendré,** or (3) use the periphrastic future **Voy a ir/ Voy a venir.**

As noted above, the limited use of Spanish verbs **ir** and **venir** in the progressive tense does not exclude them, however, from serving as auxiliaries in progressive constructions. Examples include **Voy hablando mejor** and **Vengo trayendo libros.** Several other verbs are used as auxiliaries in the same manner in progressive constructions. **Andar** and **seguir** frequently occur, as in **Ando trabajando mucho** and **Sigo estudiando idiomas.** (See §3.5.)

(Exercise 1)
Give the best possible translation for the following English sentences which use the present progressive tense. You may have more than one possible Spanish translation for some of the sentences.

1. He is working in the factory now.
2. Are you having dinner with us tomorrow? (plural, formal)
3. Where is she studying next semester?
4. They are coming to my house tomorrow night.
5. Is anyone looking at us right now?
6. What is she doing tomorrow morning?
7. Whom are you bringing to my party Saturday night? (formal)
8. Are their parents living in New York?

9. When are the students leaving for Peru?
10. What is he doing with the computer?
11. Where are we going after the game?
12. What language are they writing?
13. Is that man speaking Spanish or English?
14. If it's agreeable to you, I'm using your car tonight. (familiar)
15. He's studying for an exam now.
16. She's not going to classes today.

THE SPANISH INFINITIVE VS THE ENGLISH PRESENT PARTICIPLE
27.2
After prepositions, Spanish consistently uses the infinitive, while English uses the present participle. This contrast is very difficult for both the English speaker and the Spanish speaker to master in the target language.

¿Adónde vas después de comer?	Where are you going after eating?
Ella salió sin explicar sus motivos.	She left without explaining her motives.
Tomo leche antes de acostarme.	I drink milk before going to bed.
Sirve para tratar metal.	It's for treating metal.

•The expression **al** + INF in Spanish is equivalent to English **upon** + LV-**ing.**

Al abrir la puerta, lo oí todo.	Upon opening the door, I heard everything.
Al salir, vi a mi amiga.	Upon leaving, I saw my friend.
Siempre me salían las lágrimas al pensar en ello.	I always shed tears upon thinking about it.

Translate the following English sentences into Spanish, being sure to use an infinitive after the preposition.

1. I never go there without buying something.
2. Upon entering, I saw that there was no one there.
3. After seeing her, he realized that she was his sister.
4. One needs a key for opening that safe.
5. You deserve that for being so stupid. (familiar)
6. What did you see upon opening the window? (formal)
7. I dreamed about being a famous athlete.
8. She always worries about gaining weight.
9. Before buying it, we should have examined it.
10. I want to work instead of studying mathematics.
11. I didn't count on losing so much money.
12. He'll never learn to speak Spanish without studying more.

Translate the following Spanish sentences into English, being sure to use a present participle after the preposition.

1. ¿Qué vas a hacer después de terminar los estudios?
2. Al verla, me escondí debajo de la escalera.
3. No sé qué va a hacer ella al recibir las noticias.
4. Para ser tan pequeño, tu hermano tiene mucha fuerza.
5. Me preocupa morir de cáncer, y voy a dejar de fumar.
6. Pensamos en abrir una tienda con las últimas novedades en artículos de vestir.
7. ¿Qué definición puedo usar para explicar ese término literario?
8. No quiero llegar a la fiesta sin llevar algo.
9. No vas a creer lo que oí al escuchar su interpretación del suceso.
10. Debes buscar un plan determinado en vez de empezar sin nada.
11. Algunos hombres sueñan con alcanzar la gloria.
12. Antes de demostrarle nuestra satisfacción, averigüemos lo que él opina.

27.3

Certain main verbs of English are followed by the infinitive, while others take the present participle. There is no infallible way of determining which main verbs govern which type of dependent verbal form. Since both lists of main verbs are only representative—and these in no way pretend to be complete—it is clear that the Spanish speaker will have to work hard to master an extensive system.

MAIN VERBS TAKING THE **to**-INFINITIVE		MAIN VERBS WHICH TAKE THE PRESENT PARTICIPLE	
agree (**I agree to take it.**)		admit (**I admit taking it.**)	
claim	need	advise	keep
demand	offer	appreciate	mind
expect	plan	avoid	postpone
fail	pretend	consider	practice
forget	promise	delay	recall
hate	refuse	deny	recollect
hesitate	resolve	enjoy	resent
hope	seem	finish	risk
intend	tend	dislike	stop
long	want	imagine	suggest

27.4
Nominalization of Verbs

The nominalization of verbs in English and Spanish is accomplished through totally different processes in each language. To nominalize (make a noun out of) a verb in Spanish, the masculine singular definite article **el** is placed before the infinitive.

To nominalize a verb in English, not the infinitive but the present participle is used with nominal force where noun phrases normally appear.

No me gusta el nadar.	I don't like swimming.
El quejarse no vale nada.	Complaining isn't worth anything.
El renunciar no resuelve nada.	Resigning doesn't solve anything.

Exercise 4

Translate the following sentences into the other language.

1. They don't like waiting for us.
2. El verte así feliz es un encanto.
3. Hiding in your room isn't going to solve a thing.
4. El fumar mariguana está prohibido en este país.
5. Drinking wine helps one's digestion..
6. El mirar así tu reloj no hará pasar el tiempo con más rapidez.
7. Running stimulates the heart.
8. El querer tanto a tu amado podría resultar muy peligroso.
9. Losing weight is not easy in my family.
10. El saber que triunfaste me sirve verdaderamente de estímulo.

27.5

English regularly uses its present participle as an adjective, placing it directly after the noun it modifies, as in **the girl watching TV ..., the man eating the apple ..., the birds singing in the trees ....**

Spanish, on the other hand, avoids using the present participle with adjectival force and instead requires an adjective clause introduced by **que** in its place.

The man looking for the secretary is our professor.	El hombre que busca a la secretaria es nuestro profesor.

| He died from a shot penetrating his heart. | Él murió de un tiro que le penetró el corazón. |
| Who is that girl looking through the window? | ¿Quién es esa chica que mira por la ventana? |

Exercise 5

Translate the following sentences into Spanish. Use an adjective clause in Spanish where English uses the present participle as an adjective modifier.

1. Do you know that boy swimming in the river? (formal)
2. The people eating in the restaurant were Chileans.
3. Who is that man smoking a cigar?
4. The students studying Spanish are in my classes.
5. All the professors teaching here earn a lot of money.
6. You have to meet the girl living in my apartment. (familiar)
7. I have to say something to the children playing in my yard.
8. The black cat climbing the tree isn't mine.
9. The people praying are members of our church.
10. Don't say anything to that girl chewing gum.

27.6

Whenever Spanish expresses an action as perceived, there being also a stated object in the sentence, it is more usual to use an infinitive construction, although some verbs allow a present participle also.

The English construction for expressing perceived actions closely parallels the Spanish. The LV (without **to**) is used in these structures. Unlike Spanish, however, English may use the present participle in most instances also. The same verbs are involved in English as in Spanish; these include **watch, hear, feel,** and **see**.

Lo observé abrir la puerta.	I watched him open/opening the door.
Él me oyó salir.	He heard me leave/leaving.
Te sentí tocarme/tocándome.	I felt you touch/touching me.
Los vimos escapar.	We saw them escape/escaping.
Vi a Jorge cortar/cortando el árbol.	I saw George cut/cutting down the tree.

Exercise 6

Translate the following perceived action sentences into the other language. Give both infinitive and present participial construction when applicable.

1. When did you see them talking with us?
2. ¿No oíste al maestro hacer la comparación?
3. He felt her touching his face.
4. No te oí llamarme en el hospital.
5. In India we saw many people die on the streets.
6. Nos despertamos cuando oímos al perro ladrando.
7. Where were you when you saw the car burning? (familiar)
8. Vi al hombre abrir la puerta con una llave.

27.7

Certain English present participial usages, particularly those expressing physical postures or positions of people or things and normally expressed in Spanish by a reflexive verb in an active structure, take the past participle in corresponding Spanish passive structures.

She was standing on the corner.	Ella estaba parada en la esquina.
I was sitting in the living room.	Yo estaba sentado(-a) en la sala.
He is lying down in his room.	Él está acostado en su recámara.
They were sleeping.	Estaban dormidos (*also* Estaban durmiendo).
The dog was hiding under my bed.	El perro estaba escondido debajo de mi cama.

Exercise 7

Translate the following sentences into the other language using the present participle for position or posture in English and the past participle for the same in Spanish.

1. He didn't see me hiding in the corner.
2. Quiero que le diga al juez donde usted estaba parado.
3. Were you just lying down, or were you asleep? (familiar)
4. El perro está dormido sobre mi cama.
5. Where were you sitting? (formal)
6. No me vio aunque estaba parado cerca de él.
7. Was she standing next to you or was she sitting down? (familiar)
8. David estaba escondido en su aposento.

28

Verb Contrasts

28.1

One particular language might express the whole of a given reality by utilizing just one solitary word, while another language may have two or even more different words to render the same thought. English **be** in contrast with Spanish **ser** and **estar** are excellent examples of this phenomenon. The copula **be** covers both permanent and temporary aspects of a descriptive quality in English, whereas Spanish uses **ser** for characteristics considered permanent and **estar** for those considered temporary or changeable. This particularly important contrast and others similar to it are presented in this unit.

28.2

There are many instances where English expresses a certain concept with more than one verb, and Spanish has only one word to describe the particular action. The most frequently used of these are listed here.

Do and **make** are used for Spanish **hacer.** **Do** generally implies that the subject is involved in an action, but no emphasis is placed upon the final product which may result from that action.

> They do a lot of work outside the home.
> Ellos hacen mucho trabajo fuera de la casa.

> What does she plan to do with those roots?
> ¿Qué piensa hacer ella con esas raíces?

> I don't do anything when forced to.
> No hago nada obligado.

Make usually expresses an action which culminates in a product or emotional state that is the direct result of the action.

> The bakery makes over a million loaves of bread yearly.
> La panadería hace sobre un millón de panes al año.

> What are they making with that huge machine?
> ¿Qué están haciendo con esa máquina tan inmensa?

> I don't like it when the students make noise.
> No me gusta cuando los estudiantes hacen ruido.

Say and **tell** are used for Spanish **decir**. **Tell** is almost always used with an indirect object; it expresses the imparting of information by the speaker to the listener. When it occurs without an indirect object, **tell** means the same as **relate** or **recount** and then has the meaning of Spanish **contar**.

They told me where to find the opposite type of blood.
Me dijeron donde encontrar el tipo opuesto de sangre.

They told us to go also.
Nos dijeron que fuéramos también.

We told them the truth.
Les dijimos la verdad.

My aunt used to tell (us) lots of strange, true stories.
Mi tía nos decía (contaba) muchos cuentos extraños y verdaderos.

Say generally does not occur with an indirect object; when it does, **tell** can usually be substituted for it. The usual meaning of **say** is to utter something, the emphasis being upon the utterance rather than upon its being imparted to a listener.

He said, "I ache all over!"
Dijo, —¡Me duelen hasta las entrañas!

What did they say about the ninth inning?
¿Qué dijeron de la novena entrada?

The politician even said a number of surprising things.
Incluso el político dijo unas cuantas cosas sorprendentes.

Exercise 1

Translate the following Spanish sentences into English using the correct English verb, be it **do, make, say,** or **tell.**

1. ¿Qué van a hacer tus amigos andaluces esta semana?
2. ¿Quién hizo el pan que está en la mesa?
3. ¿Qué les dijo ese llamado experto?
4. Cuando lo vi anteayer, no me dijo nada de la crítica.
5. La criada siempre les cuenta historias de pasiones secretas.
6. Mi abuela dice que tenemos que resistir toda clase de tentaciones.
7. Mis hermanos no hacen nada sino quejarse siempre.
8. Puesto que nadie sabe hacer comida china, comeremos fuera.
9. Benito le dijo, —¡Ganaste por votación unánime!
10. Nos dijeron ayer que habían estado descansando.

28.3

The exact inversion of the phenomenon that was described in the above section is seen in other cases. This is particularly noticeable in those cases where Spanish expresses a concept with more than one verb while English has but one word to describe an action. A typical example is where **saber** and **conocer** are used for English **know.**

Saber is used to indicate the knowledge of facts. It is also used to express the ability or knowledge of how to do something.

> ¿Sabes dónde está la copia perfecta que mencionaron?
> Do you know where the perfect copy is that they mentioned?

> No sé hacer ese tipo de dibujo, pero mi hermanito sí lo sabe.
> I don't know how to make that kind of drawing, but my little brother does.

> Ella no sabe cuantas personas hicieron la misma observación.
> She doesn't know how many people made the same observation.

> Mi hermana sabe nadar muy bien.
> My sister knows how to (can) swim very well.

Conocer is generally used to express personal acquaintanceship, ie to know another person. It also renders the concept of familiarity with a location or a plan. In addition, **conocer** expresses the recognition of a person, place, or thing.

> Juan no conoce a mi profesor de inglés.
> John isn't acquainted with (doesn't know) my English professor.

> Quiero trabajar en Venezuela porque conozco bien ese país.
> I want to work in Venezuela because I know that country well.

> No conozco ese sistema para desarrollar la memoria.
> I don't know that system for developing your memory.

> Tus amigos conocen este barrio, ¿verdad?
> Your friends know this neighborhood, don't they?

Dejar and **salir** can be used for English **leave.** **Dejar** is equivalent to English **leave** in the sense of leaving something behind, either accidentally or intentionally.

> ¿Mi libro? Debo de haberlo dejado en la biblioteca.
> My book? I must have left it in the library.

> No me dejaron más que un breve recado.
> They didn't leave me more than a short note.

> El cartero no ha dejado ninguna carta hoy.
> The mailman didn't leave any letters today.

Salir is equivalent to English **leave** in the sense of exiting from a room, a city, or even a country. When the meaning is that of exiting, English uses no linking preposition while spanish does: **He left the room** vs **Salió** *del* **cuarto.** When the meaning is that of departure for some destination, both languages use a connecting preposition: **He left** *for* **Costa Rica = Salió** *para* **Costa Rica.**

> Salieron del salón de clase a las ocho y media.
> They left the classroom at eight-thirty.

> ¿Cuándo vamos a salir de esta soledad?
> When are going to leave this lonely place?

> No sé cuándo salieron para Buenos Aires.
> I don't know when they left for Buenos Aires.

Pensar and **creer** are used for English **think.** **Pensar** expresses the actual thought processes that go on in the brain, or thoughts about a person or thing. When followed by an infinitive, it is used to express the intention of doing something.

> Sencillamente pienso mejor en inglés que en español.
> I simply think better in English than in Spanish.

> Él no piensa mucho en su novia.
> He doesn't think often about his girlfriend.

> Pensamos hacer un viaje corto a Santo Domingo.
> We intend (plan) to take a short trip to Santo Domingo.

Creer renders English **think** in the sense of holding a belief or a conviction of some kind. In this usage, **creer** can be translated by either English **think** or **believe.**

> Susana no cree que sepas hablar alemán.
> Susan doesn't think (believe) that you know how to speak German.

> No creemos que ella haya llegado todavía.
> We don't think (believe) that she has arrived yet.

> Muchas personas no creen en un Ser Supremo.
> Many people don't believe in a Supreme Being.

Hacerse, llegar a ser, ponerse, and **volverse** can all be used to represent English **become.** **Hacerse** is equivalent to English **become** and occasionally English **get.** The "becoming" takes place through conscious effort, hard work, or even "pushiness" on the part of the agent of the action.

> Se hizo rico por sus anhelos de triunfar.
> He became (got) rich because of his desire to succeed.

> Ese general se hizo presidente después del golpe de estado.
> That general became president after the coup.

Llegar a ser expresses English **become** in the sense of achieving goals after a long time. Great energy may or may not be devoted to the fulfilling of the goals which are achieved only with the passage of time.

> Esa profesora por fin llegó a ser la directora de la facultad.
> That professor at last became head of the faculty.

> Isabel llegó a ser reina de Castilla en el siglo XV.
> Isabel became queen of Castile in the 15th century.

Ponerse renders English **become** or **get** when the subject has little or no control over the state entered, which is usually physical, mental, or emotional.

> Tu mujer se puso furiosa al ver lo que habías hecho.
> Your wife became (got) furious when she saw what you had done.

> Él bebió mucho vino y se puso muy alegre.
> He drank a lot of wine and became (got) happy.

Volverse often occurs with the adjective **loco(-a)** (= English **go/become crazy/mad**), but it can occur with other adjectives as well with the English meaning of **turn** + ADJ.

> Se volvió loca al ver morir a sus hijos.
> She went crazy upon seeing her children die.

> Primero el hombre se volvió rebelde y luego, hasta violento.
> First the man turned rebellious and immediately following, even violent.

(Exercise 2)

Translate the following English sentences into Spanish using the correct verbs **saber, conocer, dejar, salir, pensar, creer, hacerse, llegar a ser, ponerse,** or **volverse.**

1. She went crazy when she saw the ghost.
2. We don't think that they will be here tomorrow.
3. I don't know your nephew, but I know your niece.
4. She knows how to prepare an excellent meal.
5. He should think more about his studies.
6. Are you going to leave a tip for the waiter?
7. When did they leave this city?
8. He became famous through his important discoveries.
9. They became disappointed after hearing the news.
10. After many difficulties, he became President of the United States.

11. He studied at Harvard and became a professor of philosophy.
12. Peter the Cruel became king after many civil wars.
13. Be careful! I think he has a gun.
14. He knows how to speak Arabic very well.
15. Do you know (are you acquainted with) this park? (formal)
16. She turned pale after hearing the news.
17. Do you believe that they know we are students? (familiar)
18. He struggled to become somebody.
19. I don't know this plan very well.
20. They left for San Francisco after leaving me a message.

SER AND ESTAR
28.4

The important contrast between the use of **ser** and **estar** in Spanish, when English has but one verb **be**, has been given its own section in this text because of its great significance to the English speaker learning Spanish. A different but excellent and thorough treatment of the topic can be found in Gili Gaya's *Curso superior de sintaxis española*. In it he makes the following initial comment:

> La finísima diferencia en el empleo de uno y otro verbo [ser y estar] es una de las cualidades más destacadas de la lengua española. Expresa un matiz de las oraciones atributivas, difícil de percibir con precisión para los extranjeros cuya lengua no conoce más que un solo verbo copulativo (§44).

Generally speaking, Spanish **ser** and **estar** have mutually exclusive usages. There are two exceptions, however, to this fact: (1) with the expression of certain types of "location," and (2) in constructions involving predicate adjectives.

Most grammars limit their descriptions to the two most common Spanish copulas as attributing permanent qualities to a complement when **ser** is used and as attributing temporary qualities when **estar** is used. This is correct as far as it goes, but there are other important factors also involved in the selection between **ser** and **estar.** Apart from its function as a copula, **ser** is used as an auxiliary with lexical verbs which impart an imperfective aspect to the description or mention of an action. **Ser**, then, must be classified as an actional auxiliary. The **estar** auxiliary has two distinct functions. When it is used with a past participle, it describes the state of being or resultant condition of its complement. The perfective aspect is what has been highlighted by the use of **estar.** It is also used with the gerundial (**-ndo**) to form the progressive aspect of verbal tenses.

28.5
The exclusive uses of **ser** are:

(1) To express what something is made of.
   Mis reloj es de oro.
   Esta silla no es de madera; es de metal.
   Mi suéter es de lana, y no de algodón.

(2) To express possession.
   La casa es de mis primos.
   Las flores son de mi abuela.
   Este auto es de Jaime.

(3) With any predicate noun, thus identifying the subject.
   El señor Gómez es el nuevo gerente.
   Claudia es mexicana, pero su esposo es italiano.
   Berta es una actriz famosa.

(4) To express the time of day.
   ¿Qué hora es?
   Son las ocho.
   Aún no eran las cuatro y media cuando llegamos.

(5) To state some impersonal expressions.
   Es importante que estés aquí a tiempo.
   Es triste que te tengas que ir.
   Es imposible que salgas a estas horas.

(6) To express the origin of a person or thing.
   ¿De dónde son tus padres?
   La viuda es de Zaragoza, España.
   Esta chaqueta es de Argentina.

(7) To form the actional passive (see Unit 29).
   El marqués fue bien recibido en Nueva Granada.
   Las puertas serán abiertas por el portero.
   El cuadro fue terminado por otro pintor.

(8) To express the occurrence of events, the emphasis being upon their taking place rather than upon their precise location.

La fiesta es a las siete y treinta.
No sabemos dónde es la reunión.
Mi cumpleaños es en noviembre.
En Sudamérica, el invierno es en junio.

28.6

The exclusive uses of **estar** are:

(1) To express the location of people, places, or things, provided that a true location rather than a happening or event is involved.
Puebla está cerca de México, D. F.
Estábamos a alrededor de quince kilómetros al este de aquí.
¿Dónde están las columnas de que me hablaste?

(2) To express the **estar** passive, a construction in which a past participle follows the verb and expresses a resultant condition of the action expressed by the lexical verb (see Unit 29).
La comida ya está preparada.
La estructura estaba rodeada de flores.
El piso está todo cubierto de polvo.

(3) To voice some impersonal expressions.
¿Está bien si doy un informe en relación al renacimiento?
Está claro que nadie sabe quién es.

(4) As an AUX to form progressive (or durative) tenses.[1]
Los abogados están juzgando la moral del ciudadano.
¡Qué estás haciendo ahí!
La gente estaba saliendo de la iglesia.

28.7

One of the two exceptions to the mutually exclusive use of **ser** and **estar** was stated to be when a predicate adjective is involved (§28.4). Either of the two copulas may occur with a predicate adjective, but the meaning from the English viewpoint will always be different with each separate verb.

When **ser** is used with a predicate adjective, the subject has the inherent quality of or is characterized by the predicate adjective.

Mi padre es rico.
Humberto es muy alto
Su abuelo es viejo. (He is chronologically old.)
La sangre es roja. (Blood is usually a red substance.)
El cielo es azul. (The sky is usually thought of as blue.)

The use of **estar** plus a predicate adjective indicates that the subject is in the condition described by the predicate adjective, and this condition is usually open to change. The subject may also be conceived of as somewhat distinct on a certain occasion from our usual concept of it. It may have changed or become a certain way which is out of the ordinary. Often its sensual perception is emphasized in the usage, ie the subject may be shown to taste, look, feel, or seem to be a certain way

---

[1] Although this is not an exclusive use since Spanish can employ other auxiliaries as well, **estar** is found the most frequently. (See Unit 3, §3.5.)

on a certain occasion.

> El agua está fría. (Describes the condition of the water which is subject to change.)
> ¡Qué gordo estás! (You've gained weight; you look fat. You've changed from my concept of your usual weight.)
> Estoy muy aburrida. (Describes the condition in which I find myself.)
> Ricardo no está enfermo. (His condition.)
> ¡Qué linda está la casa! (It is all prettied up; it looks unusually nice. It's different.)

28.8

The permanent or temporary characteristics of any element being described are tellingly evident in interrogative structures using **ser** and **estar.** The structure **¿Cómo + ser?,** whose English equivalent is **What is X like,** asks the listener to give the permanent characteristics of a person, place, or thing.

> ¿Cómo es tu madre? (What is she like? tall? short? nice?)
> ¿Cómo es Ecuador? (What is it like? large? rich? densely populated?)
> ¿Cómo es la clase? (What is it like? hard? easy?)

On the other hand, the structure **¿Cómo + estar?,** whose English equivalent would be **How is X?,** asks the listener to give the condition the subject is in.

> ¿Cómo están tus padres? (Are they well? sick?)
> ¿Cómo está el profesor? (Is the professor happy? ill?)

Exercise 3

A predicate adjective is used in each of the following Spanish paired sentences. Try to give the English meaning and the conditions under which each sentence might be uttered. In each pair there is some difference of meaning, often slight, often considerable, based upon the usages of **ser** and **estar** with the predicate adjective.

1. El profesor es aburrido.
2. El profesor está aburrido.

3. La manzana es verde.
4. La manzana está verde.

5. Mi hermana es lista.
6. Mi hermana está lista.

7. La comida italiana es muy sabrosa.
8. La comida italiana está muy sabrosa.

9. Ese hombre es muy entretenido.
10. Ese hombre está muy entretenido.

11. Mi madre es muy callada.
12. Mi madre está muy callada.

13. Mi padre es un enfermo mental.
14. Mi padre está enfermo.

15. Ese aparato es malo.
16. Ese aparato está malo.

17. La niña es triste.
18. La niña está triste.

19. La puerta fue cerrada por el portero.
20. La puerta estaba cerrada.

21. Los gatos son muy limpios.
22. Los gatos están muy limpios.

23. El profesor es loco.
24. El profesor está loco.

25. Fue muerto.
26. Estaba muerto.

Exercise 4

Try to state in English the circumstances under which each of the following utterances might be made by the Spanish speaker. Why would the speaker use **ser** rather than **estar** in any given case and vice versa?

1. ¡Qué azul está el cielo hoy!
2. ¡Qué viejo soy!
3. ¡Qué feo es ese carro!
4. ¡Qué roja está esta sangre, doctor!
5. ¡Qué viejo estoy al mirarme en el espejo!
6. ¡Qué bonita está ella con el pelo así!
7. La leche estaba muy cara el mes pasado.
8. En mi país la leche es muy cara.
9. ¡Qué brillante está la luna esta noche!
10. La luna no es tan brillante como el sol.
11. Esos señores son muy amables.
12. ¡Qué amables estaban con los niños enfermos!
13. ¿Cómo son los profesores de esta facultad?
14. ¿Cómo están los profesores hoy después de la fiesta de anoche?

(Exercise 5)

Translate the following English sentences into Spanish and be able to justify your usage of **ser** and/or **estar** in each case.

1. My class is large, but his is small.
2. She's sick today, but she says she will be here tomorrow.
3. How is your brother today? (familiar)
4. What is your professor like? (familiar)
5. All of our friends are from Santafé de Bogotá.
6. Where are all of your friends? (formal)
7. My uncle is a lawyer, and his wife is a professor.
8. The carpet is (made of) nylon.
9. The windows were open when we arrived.
10. The door was opened by the little boy.

11. The party is going to be (take place) in my apartment.
12. My wrist watch is broken.
13. Roses are red and violets are blue.
14. It was already eleven o'clock, and I was tired.
15. That man is very stubborn.
16. I am bored simply because this class is boring.
17. His birthday is in the fall.
18. Elizabeth is furious because we are not ready.
19. Where are the tourists who are from Nicaragua?
20. What are they doing there?

29

Passive Constructions

29.1

In its simplest form, an English passive sentence is one in which the grammatical subject (person or thing being discussed) is also the logical object (receiver of the action) in the sentence. In such a construction, the subject does not act, rather, it receives the action performed by the agent (doer) of the action, which may be expressed or merely implied from the context.

The basic parts of an English passive sentence are (1) the subject, which is the person or thing being discussed and the receiver of the action, (2) the verb phrase, which always includes a form of AUX-**be** used in any tense plus the past participle, and (3) the agent, which is the performer of the action and may be optionally expressed or omitted.

SUBJECT	VERB PHRASE	AGENT
My father	was elected	(by a majority)
His students	are tested	(by him)
The rebels	will be executed	(by the firing squad)
No problems	have been encountered	(---)
They	are being attacked	(---)

29.2

Only transitive verbs may be used in passive voice structures, and a small group among these normally do not allow a passive transformation. **Have** is the most common of the group while others are **become, fit, hold, lack, resemble suit,** etc. A passive voice construction is not possible when there is co-reference between subject and object in the active voice sentence (ie reflexive, reciprocal, or possessive pronouns in the object noun phrase).

REFLEXIVE: She could see herself in the mirror ≠ *Herself could be seen in the mirror.

RECIPROCAL: We saw each other faintly in the rain ≠ *Each other was seen faintly in the rain.

POSSESSIVE: In answer to the question, the student shook his head ≠ *His head was shaken by the student in answer to the question.

29.3

An indirect object may occur in an English passive sentence if the verb in the sentence allows it in the equivalent active sentence. Depending upon the nature of the verb, there may be only a single version of the English passive sentence containing an indirect object, or there may be a second alternate passive version.

English verbs which allow the introduction of an indirect object into a passive sentence and occasion a single version of that sentence are the verbs which in active sentences permit only the S + V + **to/for** + IO construction. No agents are expressed in the following examples.

> The book was described to us. (Not possible *We were described the book)
> The procedure will be explained to me.
> The incident will be reported to her.
> It was never mentioned to him.
> The assignments have been returned to the students.

English verbs which allow the introduction of an indirect object into a passive sentence and which occasion two alternate passive versions of the sentence are the verbs which in active sentences permit not only S + V + DO + **to/for** + IO (He gave the book to me), but also the alternate S + V + IO + DO (He gave me the book). These are such verbs as **bring, give, lend, mail, offer, owe, pay, read, sell, send, show, teach, tell, throw,** and **write.** Verbs of this type can be transformed in the passive with either the direct object in the subject position or the indirect object in the subject position (see §14.14). Expression of the agent is optional.

ACTIVE:	They brought us some food. ⇒
PASSIVE:	Some food was brought to us (by them) (D.O. subject).
	We were brought some food (by them) (I.O. subject).

ACTIVE:	My mother will tell a story to the children. ⇒
PASSIVE:	A story will be told to the children (by my mother) (D.O. subject).
	The children will be told a story (by my mother) (I.O. subject)

ACTIVE:	I have written a letter for Robert. ⇒
PASSIVE:	A letter has been written for Robert (by me) (D.O. subject).
	Robert has been written a letter (by me) (I.O. subject).

Exercise 1

Change the following English active sentences into English passive ones. If an indirect object is involved and two versions of the passive sentence are possible, give both.

1. Jonathan wrote a very significant novel last summer.
2. The President will give a medal to the hero. (2)
3. The children have eaten all the apples.
4. The boss will suggest a new plan to the employees.
5. My parents sent me some money in July. (2)
6. He drank a whole bottle of gin.
7. She visits the children every summer.

8. The professor had offered them a better grade. (2)
9. They will describe a new system to the general.
10. His father lent him some money. (2)

29.4
Three types of passive voice sentences are generally described in many Spanish grammars. These are (1) the passive with **ser** + PAST PARTICIPLE, the actional form, (2) the passive with **estar** + PAST PARTICIPLE, the state of being form, and (3) the **se** passive, whose verb is active in Spanish but is rendered by the passive construction in English. The **se** passive is called the passive reflexive (pasiva-refleja) by the Royal Spanish Academy.

(1) La noticia era ya conocida por/de todos.
    The news was already known by everyone.

(2) Está/Estaba prohibido.   It is/was forbidden.

(3) Se firmó la paz.   The peace was signed.
    Se han vendido setenta.   Seventy have been sold.
    Se les atacó en la casa.   They were attacked at home.
    Se le dieron a él varias tareas.   He was given various tasks.
                                   Various tasks were given (to) him.

Although Spanish grammar has three ways of expressing the sense of passivity, this does not mean that there will be a direct correspondence with the English passive structures in all instances. The Spanish passive voice is used much less frequently than it is in English, and there are many restrictions attached to it. The sense of the English passive structure will as often as not be rendered in Spanish through active sentences, impersonal sentences, reflexive verb forms, or other non-passive voice means. If a choice between using the active or the passive voice can be made, use the active construction preferably in Spanish since it is more idiomatic and is the one used by native speakers in most normal speech activities. On this point the Academy gives the following advice:

Las lenguas francesa e inglesa emplean la pasiva … en proporciones mucho mayores que la nuestra [española]. Conviene que los traductores tengan en cuenta esta preferencia, para no cometer faltas de estilo y aun incorrecciones gramaticales. Por otra parte, el empleo creciente de la pasiva refleja e impersonal contribuye a limitar la frecuencia de la pasiva con **ser** (*Esbozo*, §3.12.9).

29.5
The Spanish **ser** passive construction closely parallels the English simple passive formula and may be used to translate English passive sentences so long as these do not contain indirect object subjects or human subjects whose verbs imply the subjects' voluntary or involuntary involvement in the action. The basic parts of the Spanish **ser** passive are (1) the subject, which is the person or thing discussed and also the receiver of the action, (2) the verb phrase, which always includes a form of AUX-**ser** used in any tense and followed by the past participle of the LV agreeing in gender and number with the subject, and (3) the agent or performer of the action, which is optionally expressed. The agent is introduced by **por** or **de,** with **por** being increasingly preferred.

SUBJECT	VERB PHRASE	AGENT
Mi padre	fue atacado	(por un perro)
Ella	es perdonada	(por su abuela)
Los ladrones	serán acusados	(por la policía)
Nosotras	hemos sido elegidas	(---)

29.6

In **ser** passive sentences, the recipient of the action is emphasized in deference to the agent. Although the agent may or may not be overtly expressed, it can usually be implied from the context. The tendency of the Spanish speaker to avoid passive construction, particularly in speech, is probably due to the fact that the passive is subject to a number of restrictions, which are outlined in the subsequent sections. Note that the restrictions applicable to Spanish **ser** passive constructions do not necessarily apply to the English passive.

- In a **ser** passive sentence, what was an indirect object in the active version of the sentence cannot be used as the subject of the passive version.

    El jefe me dio cincuenta pesos ⇒ *Yo fui dado cincuenta pesos por el jefe.

- A **ser** passive sentence cannot have a human subject which, because of the inherent characteristics of the verb, is in any way involved in the action of the sentence.

    Sus consejos nos agradaron. ⇒ *Fuimos agradados por sus consejos.

- Active sentences using verbs of perception (eg **escuchar, ver, oír, sentir,** etc) are rarely passivized in Spanish .

    La joven no oyó nada sino la noche silenciosa. ⇒ *Nada no fue oído por la
    joven sino la noche silenciosa.

- The **ser** passive is used freely with inanimate subjects as long as a human agent is expressed or implied.

    Un alma espiritual busca lugares solitarios. ⇒ Lugares solitarios son busca-
    dos por un alma espiritual.
    La noticia me sorprendió. ⇒ *Fui sorprendido/-a por la noticia.

- All the perfect tenses can be used in **ser** passive sentences.

    El hombre ha sido elegido por sus seguidores en el partido.
    Esa gloriosa obra había sido comenzada en el siglo XV.
    Me pregunto si su obra habrá sido presentada antes de que la necesiten.
    Ya la casa habría sido pintada por mí, si yo hubiera tenido el tiempo.
    Si a estas alturas sus orígenes no han sido comprobados por los científicos,
        no los serán nunca.
    Si la categoría hubiera sido anunciada por los jueces, la joven se habría
        inscrito.

- The present and imperfect tenses are used in **ser** passives only when describing a sustained, habitual, or repeated action. They are never used with conclusive verbs for describing a momentary one-time action.

> Germán es respetado por todos. Gloria era respetada en su pueblo.
> (not possible) *La puerta es abierta por el guardia ahora.
> (not possible) *La hoja era vuelta por él.

One exception to this restriction is its usage in the historical present.

> Puerto Rico es descubierto por Cristóbal Colón en 1493.

Exercise 2

Change the following active Spanish sentences into passive ones, using **ser** + PAST PARTICIPLE. If a change is not possible due to some restriction placed on **ser** passives, leave the sentence as is.

1. Sus vecinos la estiman mucho.
2. En todas partes la gente conoce esa noticia.
3. Lo conocían bien en su pueblo.
4. Llamamos a la puerta para avisar nuestra llegada.
5. Apenas llegó el aviso, se dio la noticia.
6. Unos desconocidos atacan y roban a un anciano.
7. La madre tenía ansias de ver a su hijo.
8. Los oficiales habían firmado el acuerdo antes de marcharse.
9. Ellos tenían nociones sobre este asunto, pero las desconozco.
10. Habré terminado mis estudios antes del verano.

29.7

The **estar** passive, the state of being passive which describes the condition, state, location, or posture of a person or thing, is used in describing the result or ultimate effect of a completed action. Since English uses only **be** for both state of being and actional passives (whereas Spanish has both **estar** and **ser**), the English speaker will have to take special care in discerning the differences in usage in Spanish. These differences were covered in detail in the previous Unit 28.

The basic parts of the Spanish **estar** passive sentence are the same as those for the **ser** passive: the subject, the verb phrase, and the optional agent. Subjects and agents function as they do in the **ser** passive.

Estar + PAST PARTICIPLE is used with transitive verbs and is generally found in the simple tenses only—present, imperfect, preterite.

> El libro está impreso ya.
> La estructura estaba hecha.
> El edificio estuvo situado junto a la carretera.

Estar cannot be used with the perfect tenses in the passive since the mere choice of **estar** over **ser** indicates prior perfectivety of the action being alluded to.

> *El libro ha estado impreso ya.

The **estar** passive is used in the present and the imperfect tenses with conclusive verbs such as **acabar, arrancar, lanzar, mandar, ordenar, pagar,**

prohibir, resolver, etc.

    El nadar desnudo está/estaba prohibido.

Inceptive reflexive verbs like **adormecerse, arrepentirse, avergonzarse, dormirse, enfadarse, enojarse, entristecerse, sentarse,** etc, which express the beginning of an action, can be used with **estar** passive in the present and the imperfect tenses without the reflexive pronoun.

    Las niñas están/estaban sentadas.

An agent may accompany an **estar** passive verb phrase when the past participle refers to a durative or non-conclusive action or condition concurrent with the speech activity.

    El programa está/estaba/estuvo garantizado por el gobierno.

Exercise 3

Change the following sentences into the passive by using **estar** + PAST PARTICIPLE. The resulting constructions will express states or conditions which are the result of any actions which might have occurred to the subjects or objects in the original sentences.

1. Un jardín de flores rodeaba mi casa en las afueras de la ciudad.
2. Escondieron a sus mujeres antes de llegar el enemigo.
3. Clemente se levantó muy temprano.
4. Tu tío envejeció mucho.
5. Mi hermana administra la tienda de sombreros.
6. El genio resolvió el dilema.
7. La familia gobierna sus acciones.
8. Todos se habían dormido cuando llegué.

29.8

Possible ambiguities often arise between English and Spanish passive sentences using **be** and **ser/estar.** Frequently, what would appear syntactically to be passive constructions, when examined in light of their morphology, turn out to be attributive structures utilizing a copula. Spanish sentences are less susceptible to this confusion than are English sentences, since the choice of **ser** over **estar** and vice versa in Spanish will dispel ambiguities in most cases.

    In English there is no difficulty if a past participle and an attributive adjective derived from a same verb have different forms. When used in passive constructions no ambiguity occurs.

    a. The door was opened. (past participle)
    b. The door was open. (adjective)

In sentence (a), an agent is strongly implied and the action occurring to the door is stressed. The sentence is a true passive. In sentence (b), no agent is expressed or implied. Furthermore, no action is expressed. The sentence is merely a reflection of the state the door was in, and **open** is an attributive adjective joined to its subject by the copula **was.**

    However, if the past participle and attributive adjective derived from the same verb are identical in form, ambiguity may result, particularly if the sentence occurs out of context. Note these examples.

> c. The house was surrounded.
> d. The door was closed.

In example (c), it is impossible to say whether the intended meaning is a passive one, stressing an agent and the action which happened to the house, or whether the mere condition of the house is emphasized. Likewise, in sentence (d), either action (the closing of the door) or condition (the state in which the door was found) could be implied.

Ambiguity as in the preceding English examples cannot occur in Spanish since the **estar** passive denotes a resultant state or condition and the **ser** passive describes an action. In Spanish both sentences would have to be framed in one or the other of these structures. The English sentences which were determined to be actional passive would be rendered in Spanish as **ser** passive constructions, whereas a stative meaning would call for the **estar** passive.

> c. The house was surrounded.   (actional) La casa fue sitiada.
> (stative)   La casa estaba sitiada.
>
> d. The door was closed.   (actional) La puerta fue cerrada.
> (stative)   La puerta estaba cerrada.
>
> e. The prices were reduced.   (actional) Los precios fueron reducidos.
> (stative)   Los precios estaban reducidos.

In addition to the choice between actional **ser** and stative **estar,** differences in intended meaning are further clarified when the **por** + AGENT structure is added in Spanish. This is vividly illustrated in these two contrasting sentences, (f) and (g).

> f. La mercancía *es pesada por* el comerciante. (participial phrase)
> g. Esa mujer *es pesada por* su manera de ser. (adjectival phrase)

29.9

Spanish s e passive, the third type of passive structure mentioned before, occurs with transitive verbs and is used when the performer (agent) of the action's identity is unknown, is deemed unimportant, or is deliberately concealed. In dealing with the s e passive, one must consider whether the recipients of the action are inanimate or animate, but in either case, only third person subjects, both singular and plural, occur in this type of construction due to its impersonal character (cf. Unit 16).

29.10

Spanish *se* Passive with Inanimate Recipients

The information communicated when the s e passive is used with inanimate recipients is that an action is being done to something, but no mention is made of the agent (performer) of that action. Consider the following examples, both of which will be discussed from a grammatically analytical point of view.

> Aquí se alquilan habitaciones.   (?)Aquí se alquila habitaciones.
> (s e passive)   (active impersonal)

In the first sentence, s e would seem to function as a reflexive pronoun, as the sentence could have the literal translation of ***Here rooms rent themselves.**

English would translate the sentence with its true passive construction **Rooms are rented here.** In the second sentence, **se** acts as an impersonal, indefinite subject or as a passive particle, giving the sentence the literal translation of **Here one/ someone rents rooms.** Again, English would use the true passive rendition of **Rooms are rented here** or more commonly **Rooms for rent.**

Native Spanish speakers tend to prefer the first version, **Aquí se alquilan habitaciones,** in which the inanimate recipient and the verb agree, simply because such subject-verb agreement is so characteristic of Spanish grammar. Nevertheless, Spanish speakers may disagree concerning which sentence is the most acceptable. The Academy recommends using the first construction, calling it more traditional, but it does not reject the second.

Gili Gaya has observed a certain preference for postpositioning the inanimate noun recipient of the action in these constructions. Moreover, with verbs which are already reflexive in their normal usage *(verbos siempre pronominales),* we cannot say ***Se se acostumbra a todo** or ***Se se despeina con ese viento.** In these cases the impersonal **se** is substituted by indefinite **uno/una: Uno se acostumbra a todo** and **Se despeina una con ese viento.**

In the following examples, **se** passive sentences are shown to be capable of transformation into true passives in Spanish, as long as no agent is mentioned. The sentences have been gleaned from various well-known Spanish grammars, including that of the Academy.

SE PASSIVE	**SER** PASSIVE
Se alquilan coches.	Los coches son alquilados.
Se han descubierto sus trampas.	Han sido descubiertas sus trampas.
Se cometieron muchos atropellos.	Muchos atropellos fueron cometidos.
Se suspende la sesión.	La sesión es suspendida.
Se edifican muchas casas en este barrio.	Muchas casas son edificadas en este barrio.
La paz se aceptó.	La paz fue aceptada.
Se venden botellas.	Las botellas son vendidas.
La pared se hundió con el peso de la techumbre.	La pared fue hundida con el peso de la techumbre.
Los pájaros se alborotaron por el ruido.	Los pájaros fueron alborotados por el ruido.
Se firmó la paz.	La paz fue firmada.
Se han divulgado estas noticias.	Estas noticias han sido divulgadas.

Exercise 4

Change the following Spanish sentences into **se** passives. In all cases the recipients are inanimate.

1. Anuncian muchas actividades sociales a través de la televisión.
2. Expresaron su plena satisfacción por la excelencia del vino.

3. Temen otra guerra internacional.
4. Organizaron el Décimo Festival Juvenil.
5. Rechazaron el nuevo modo de aplicación.
6. Vieron en la obra detalles análogos a la poesía de Darío.
7. Observaron las estrellas durante varias horas.
8. Celebraron innumerables fiestas este año.
9. No saben el origen del lenguaje.
10. Estudian literatura universal en esta clase.

29.11

Spanish *se* Passive with Animate Recipients

When animate recipients are involved, the Spanish structure used for inanimate recipients must be modified. With inanimate recipients, we can say **Se alquila(n) habitaciones** with the English true passive translation of **Rooms are rented (by someone)/Rooms for rent.** But when the recipients are animate, we cannot say ***Se asesinó el dictador,** or ***Se asesinaron los dictadores,** as these would have the English translations of **The dictator assassinated himself,** and **The dictators assassinated themselves** (or **each other**), respectively. The following constructions must then be used, and in each, **se** functions as an indefinite subject or passive particle. The English translation will perforce be a true passive.

> Se asesinó al dictador. (Literally **Someone assassinated the dictator**) rendered passively in standard English as **The dictator was assassinated.**
>
> Se asesinó a los dictadores. (Literally **Someone assassinated the dictators**) rendered passively in standard English as **The dictators were assassinated.**

In our discussion of the Spanish true passive construction (using **ser**), it was pointed out that the **ser** passive cannot be used with indirect objects. ***Ella fue dada un libro** is an ungrammatical translation of **She was given a book.** Spanish has only the **se** passive option for expressing English passives in which indirect objects occur, as can be seen in the following examples. Note that no agent can be mentioned in **se** passive sentences with animate recipients, be they direct or indirect objects, just as was the case in constructions with inanimate objects.

> Se le dio un libro.   She was given a book.
>   A book was given to her.
> Se les dio varios libros.   They were given several books.
>   Several books were given to them.

(Exercise 5)

Render the following English passive constructions into Spanish, choosing among all three Spanish passive equivalents. Remember, however, that only impersonal **se** can be used when the English sentence contains an indirect object.

1. My parents were mentioned in the letter.
2. The President has been assassinated.
3. They were hanged in the public square.

4. These documents will be studied with care.
5. My friend will be appointed Secretary of State.
6. She is considered (to be) an excellent teacher.
7. The children will be served ice cream at the party.
8. He hasn't been recommended for the position.
9. You will be given a gift at the reception. (familiar)
10. Nothing had been said to me.

11. Her parents weren't told the whole truth.
12. We weren't invited to your wedding. (familiar)
13. Several letters have been sent to them.
14. Those men will be taken to jail.
15. No one had been found in the building.
16. A Mexican meal will be prepared at the reunion.
17. A new governmental program was announced.
18. All the apples have been sold.
19. We will be brought a car early in the morning.
20. Poor children aren't given a good education.

29.12

It has been stated that English makes much more frequent use of the passive than does Spanish. Although Spanish has three manners for expressing the sense of passive voice structures, the language demonstrates a tendency to reject the passive in preference to the more dynamic, animated verbal structure of the active sentence. This frequent lack of direct correspondence between the two languages in this respect should be carefully kept in mind.

The preference for the active voice is illustrated in these examples: **The novel was written by Rómulo Gallegos** can be expressed in Spanish as **La novela fue escrita por Rómulo Gallegos** (passive), but it would be more natural to say **Rómulo Gallegos escribió la novela** (active) or **La novela la escribió Rómulo Gallegos** (active voice with a change of focus).

We include here some very common examples where the two languages are at odds with one another. English expresses the thought passively, while Spanish expresses the same thought more naturally in the active voice.

PASSIVE	ACTIVE
I was seated next to the guests.	Me sentaron al lado de los invitados.
We are interested in linguistics.	Nos interesa la lingüística.
That officer was detested by everyone.	Todos detestaban a ese oficial.
She was changed into a new person.	Se transformó en una nueva persona.
We were shown the way.	Nos enseñaron el camino.
He was awarded a consolation prize.	Le otorgaron un premio de consolación.
That role will be played by the understudy.	El suplente desempeñará ese papel.
The children are awakened at seven o'clock.	A los niños los despiertan a las siete.

He was being haunted by his past.	A él lo perseguía su pasado.
We are encouraged to continue with the project.	Nos animamos a continuar con el proyecto.
Elementary details are not forgotten the same as more complicated ones.	Uno no se olvida de los detalles elementales al igual que de los más complicados.
Indispensable information has been transmitted by the station.	La estación ha transmitido informaciones indispensables.
A control mechanism must be established.	Debe establecerse un mecanismo de control.

Thorough inspection of the above pairs of sentences will provide an additional dimension to the many differences that exist between the Spanish and the English passive systems.

Exercise 6

Translate the following sentences into the other language. Many of the English sentences as phrased are ambiguous; indications have been made as to the focus to be used in Spanish.

1. The children were hidden in the old building. (state: estar)
2. Mi casa, en Barcelona, estaba rodeada de un jardín de rosas.
3. That type of book is read only by scholars. (action: ser)
4. No sabemos quién será elegido presidente en la actualidad.
5. I saw that the windows were closed when I entered the room. (state: estar)
6. La puerta derecha debiera estar cerrada.
7. My brother was injured in an accident. (action: ser)
8. El edificio estará terminado para fines de mes.
9. An important program will be presented this evening. (action: se)
10. Los cuarenta cuentos de horror fueron escritos por un solo autor.
11. My composition is written. It will be read by my professor. (state: estar, action: ser)
12. Las curvas serán eliminadas de la carretera.
13. I knew they were there because the lights were turned on. (state: estar)
14. Esta estructura será elevada a la altura de la otra.
15. This painting will have to be finished by another artist. (action: ser)

Affirmative Words and their Negative Counterparts

30.1
As was seen earlier in Unit 6, the negation systems of English and Spanish function differently on a syntactic level. There is also a morphological difference, which can be observed in the lexical forms listed in the following columns. These examples of Spanish and English affirmative words and their negative counterparts represent but a sample inventory of what is available in a complete lexicon. You will note that the third column gives the English word form which is used when the verb is independently negated.

AFFIRMATIVE TERMS	NEGATIVE TERMS	NEGATED ENGLISH VERB
Vi a … **alguien** I saw … **someone/somebody**	No vi a … **nadie** I saw … **no one/nobody**	I didn't see … **anyone/anybody**
Vi … **algo** I saw … **something**	No vi … **nada** I saw … **nothing**	I didn't see … **anything**
Vi … **algún(o)/alguna** **algunos/algunas** **uno/una, unos/unas** I saw … **some** **someone/somebody**	No vi … **ningún(o)/ninguna** **ningunos/ningunas** I saw … **none** **no one/nobody**	I didn't see … **any** **anyone/anybody**
Voy … **siempre/algún día** I will go … **always/some day**	No voy … **nunca/jamás** I will go … **never**	I won't go … **ever**
O vas **o** vienes. **Either** go **or** come.	**Ni** vas **ni** vienes. **Neither** go **nor** come.	**Either** don't go **or** don't come.

AFFIRMATIVE TERMS	NEGATIVE TERMS	NEGATED ENGLISH VERB
Voy **también**.	No voy **tampoco**.	
I am going **also/too/as well**	**Neither** am I going.*	I am not going **either**.

*Note the inversion of the AUX-**am** with the subject pronoun. Whenever **neither** or any other negative adverb or adverbial phrase initiates a clause, subject/AUX inversion is compulsory. The failure to make this inversion is a frequently committed error among Spanish speakers learning English.

30.2
There are two rules which apply to the use of negative words in Spanish.

(1) If a negative word (other than **no**) precedes the verb, no other negative word is required in the sentence, although some may occur if so desired since double negatives are a valid part of Spanish syntax. When the negative word precedes the verb, the verb is fully negated.

> Nadie vio la sombra.
> Nada se puede presumir en este caso.
> Nunca (Jamás) iré por esos horizontes.
> Ningún hombre puede comprobarlo.
> Yo tampoco estoy en disposición de hablar.
> Ni Héctor ni Marta estarán expuestos al peligro.

(2) If a negative word other than **no** follows the verb, then the word **no** must precede the verb; this results in the use of two negative forms in this type of Spanish negative sentence. Note that the following sentences have the same meaning as those listed under rule (1) above.

> No vio nadie la sombra.
> No se puede presumir nada en este caso.
> No iré por esos horizontes nunca/jamás.
> No puede comprobarlo ningún hombre.
> Yo no estoy en disposición de hablar tampoco.
> No estarán ni Héctor ni Marta expuestos al peligro.

In the first set of sentences above, only one negative element is present. In the second set, two negative elements occur. English allows the first type of construction with just one negative but never the second with two negatives. An English speaker's approach to a sentence with two negatives would be to logically assume that a second negative cancels the first, hence the statement reverts to a positive assertion.

Exercise 1

Give two negative versions of the following Spanish affirmative sentences. These are examples in which (1) a negative word other than **no** precedes the verb, and (2) **no** precedes the verb, and a negative word other than **no** follows the verb.

1. Alguien estaba en mi cuarto cuando entré.
2. Algún día iremos a vivir en Puerto Rico.

3. Algo llegó hoy para ti en la correspondencia.
4. Alguien quiere verte a las ocho mañana.
5. Yo también tengo amigos en Acapulco.
6. O mi hermano o mi hermana van a procurarlo.
7. Siempre pienso en ser una persona ejemplar.
8. Alguien quiere hablarte ahorita.
9. Un animal pasó por debajo de la puerta.
10. Anoche dejaron algo sobre la mesa.
11. También voy a ver a mi novia.
12. O el gato o el perro están en la sala.

30.3
The rules for negation in English are two; they are outlined here.

(1) An English affirmative sentence may be made negative by using a negative word or phrase somewhere in the sentence, usually before the verb.

He always goes to Spain.
He *never* goes to Spain.

Something is under the table.
Nothing is under the table.

Either William or Jenifer knows how to do it.
Neither William *nor* Jenifer knows how to do it.

(2) English has an alternate way of making affirmative sentences negative. If the verb is already negated, that is, if the word **not** or the contracted form **-n't** occurs in the sentence, one of the affirmative words listed in the first section (§30.1) of this unit under column three must be used. Unlike Spanish, English does not allow more than one negative element to appear in a negative sentence. In some types of non-standard speech, double negatives are found; however, this usage is frowned upon since it is considered ungrammatical.

STANDARD	NON-STANDARD
He always goes to Spain.	
He doesn't *ever* go to Spain.	*He don't never go to Spain.
Something is under the table.	
There isn't *anything* under the table.	*There ain't nothing under the table.
I want to see someone about it.	
I don't want to see *anyone* about it.	*I don't want to see nobody about it.

30.4
We have drawn from the list of affirmative and negative word examples given in §30.1. to demonstrate their various uses in contrastive contexts. It will be noted that many of the examples have alternate ways of expressing the same contexts. English sentences utilizing negated verbs are preceded by a bullet (•).

AFFIRMATIVE	NEGATIVE
Alguien está aquí.	*Nadie* está aquí.
Someone/Somebody is here.	*No one/Nobody* is here.
	There is *no one/nobody* here.
	•There isn't *anyone/anybody* here.
Hay *algo* sobre la mesa.	*Nada* hay sobre la mesa.
	No hay *nada* sobre la mesa.
Something is on the table.	*Nothing* is on the table.
	There is *nothing* on the table.
	•There isn't *anything* on the table.
Siempre voy a España.	*Nunca/Jamas* voy a España.
	No voy a España *nunca/jamás*.
I *always* go to Spain.	I *never* go to Spain.
	•I don't *ever* go to Spain.
Algún día iré a España.	*Nunca/Jamás* iré a España.
	No iré a España *nunca/jamás*.
Someday I'll go/I'm going to Spain.	I'll *never* go/I'm *never* going to Spain.
	•I won't *ever* go to Spain./ I'm not *ever* going to Spain.
Algún señor/*Un* señor lo sabe.	*Ningún* señor lo sabe.
	No lo sabe *ningún* señor.
Some man/*A* man knows it.	*No* man knows it.
	No one knows it.
	Nobody knows it.
	There is *no* man who knows it.
	There is *nobody* who knows it.
	There is *no one* who knows it.
	•There isn't *any* man who knows it.
	•There isn't *anybody* who knows it.
	•There isn't *anyone* who knows it.
Nosotras vamos *también*.	*Tampoco* vamos nosotras.
	No vamos nosotras *tampoco*.
We are going *too*. We're going *also*.	*Neither* are we going. (See §30.1 note, page 254.)
	•We're not going *either*.
Va *o* Héctor *o* Marta.*	*Ni* Héctor *ni* Marta van.*
	No van *ni* Héctor *ni* Marta.*
Either Hector *or* Martha is going.	*Neither* Hector *nor* Martha is going.
	• (There is no version possible here using an affirmative word with a negative verb.)

*Note: Also heard are **Van o Héctor o Marta; Ni Héctor ni Marta va; No va ni Héctor ni Marta,** none of which is accepted by the Academy. Observe closely the differences in verb agreement between Spanish and English in these examples, another illustration of the different ways the two languages have of viewing a same situation. Since either one of the two alternatives or none is involved in the action, English uses the singular form of the verb instead of the plural.

Exercise 2

Rewrite the following English sentences by negating the verb and using an affirmative word with the negated verb.

1. Did no one see the man?
2. Nothing was in the mailbox.
3. They never speak Portuguese to me.
4. Has no one heard the news?
5. We never have good parties at school.
6. No children were at the movie.
7. Neither *are we* going to the meeting. (Note SUBJ/AUX inversion.)
8. Is neither he nor she going?

Exercise 3

Translate the following Spanish negative sentences into English, giving two versions for each: (1) with a negative word accompanying the verb, and (2) with a negated verb accompanied by an affirmative word with negative bias.

1. Nadie hace el trabajo en esta casa.
2. Nada sucede en la asociación.
3. Mis padres nunca prestan atención a los lujos.
4. Ningún estudiante tiene rasgos de enfermedad mental.
5. Yo no tengo tan amplia imaginación tampoco.
6. Jamás conduces por esa ruta.
7. No te concedo nada.
8. No voy a referirme a nadie.
9. No quiero verla de nuevo nunca.
10. No creo en la justicia tampoco.
11. No quiero luchar con nadie.
12. Esa oración no tiene ningún sujeto.

31

Admirative Expressions

31.1

Both English and Spanish have formulas by which they can express admiration, surprise, or contempt.

What a sensation!	¡Qué sensación!
How horrible!	¡Qué horror!
How fast you run!	¡Cuán rápido corres!

The Spanish formulas for admirative expressions used as noun intensifiers are more consistent and simpler than those of English. The two systems are compared below with examples.

An admirative expression of a singular **count noun**[1] is formed as follows:

ENGLISH: **what** + (INDEF. ART.) + (ADJ) + NOUN
What a man!
What speed it has!
What a novel!
What a difficult course!

SPANISH: **qué** + NOUN + (**tan/más** + ADJ)
¡Qué hombre!
¡Qué velocidad tiene!
¡Qué novela!
¡Qué curso tan (más) difícil!

An admirative expression of a **non-count noun**[1] or of a plural noun is formed as outlined in the following formulas:

ENGLISH: **what** + (ADJ) + NOUN
What men!
What strong women!
What books!
What good coffee!

---

[1] See Unit 13 (§13.1) for information on count and non-count nouns.

SPANISH: **qué** + NOUN + (**tan/más** + ADJ)
¡Qué hombres!
¡Qué mujeres más (tan) fuertes!
¡Qué libros!
¡Qué café más (tan) bueno!

The admirative expression of an adjective, an adverb, or a verb in English has this formula:

how + ADJ	How beautiful!
how + ADV	How quickly they answered!
how + S + V	How you talk!

In Spanish admirative expressions with adjectives and adverbs use a different formula from the expressions with verbs.

qué/cuán + ADJ/ADV	¡Qué rápido! ¡Cuán falso!
cómo + V + (S)	¡Cómo hablas (tú)!
	¡Cómo corre (Juan)!

Exercise 1

Translate the following admirative expressions into the other language. Be able to determine in each case whether you are dealing with count nouns, non-count nouns, or with adjectives, adverbs, and verbs.

1. ¡Qué rápido corre tu carro!
2. What a tall boy John is!
3. ¡Qué bien sabes tus lecciones!
4. What good wine!
5. ¡Cómo me preocupa esa señora!
6. How slowly you work! (familiar)
7. ¡Qué sutil es ese sabor!
8. What bad beer they served us!
9. ¡Qué dura e intolerable es esta vida!
10. How well you teach Spanish! (formal)

31.2

Two additional forms of admirative expressions are frequently used. One form is found in English, and you often hear the other in Spanish. The first example may be difficult for the Spanish speaker, and the other would trouble the English speaker.

Colloquial English sometimes uses an affirmative yes-no question structure (but always with descending intonation) to express admiration. An interjection of some type usually accompanies this usage, for example **Man!, Wow!, Boy!, Gosh!**, etc. Of course, Spanish speakers may be confused by the English yes-no question structures being used in this way, so they should be taught to recognize the meaning of such utterances.

Man! Does he speak Spanish well!	¡Qué bien habla español!
Wow! Is this food (ever) delicious!	¡Qué deliciosa está esta comida!

Boy! Does he say romantic things!	¡Qué cosas tan (más) románticas dice!
Gosh! Did she get annoyed!	¡Qué molesta se puso!

Spanish uses a **lo** + ADJ/ADV construction for English **how** when the English word introduces an assertive subordinate clause following the main clause.

You don't know *how hard* we worked.	No sabes *lo duro* que trabajamos.
If you knew *how ugly* he is, ...	Si supieras *lo feo* que es, ...
I want you to tell me *how far* it is.	Quiero que me digas *lo lejos* que está.
I hope you know *how difficult* it is.	Espero que sepas *lo difícil* que es.

Exercise 2

Translate the following admirative sentences into the other language, drawing from all the structures presented in this unit when appropriate.

1. You don't know how fast I can run! (formal)
2. ¡Qué rápido corría ese tren!
3. Don't they see how bad he is!
4. ¡Qué furiosa se puso la profesora!
5. She won't tell you how ridiculous it is! (familiar)
6. ¡Qué bonita va a ser la casa de ellos!
7. I don't want to know how handsome he is!
8. ¡Qué chica más bonita la que vimos en la playa!
9. Isn't she beautiful!
10. ¡Qué contento está mi hermano!

Elliptical Verbal Usages and Verification Tags

ELLIPTICAL VERBAL USAGES
32.1
Spanish usually answers simple affirmative or negative yes-no questions with a simple **sí** or **no.**

¿Vives en San Francisco?	Sí.
¿Vas a venir mañana?	No.

English may follow the Spanish model, but it also has the option of employing the auxiliary verbal system in answering such yes-no questions. In addition to a simple **yes** or **no** response, the use of a substitute pronoun for the subject of the statement combined with a corresponding auxiliary serves as an anaphoric elliptical echo of the original statement.

YES-NO QUESTION	AFFIM. RESPONSE	NEG. RESPONSE
Is your father working?	Yes, he is.	No, he isn't.
Does she live here?	Yes, she does.	No, she doesn't.
Did your friends go?	Yes, they did.	No, they didn't.
Will they come home?	Yes, they will.	No, they won't.
Would your brother like her?	Yes, he would.	No, he wouldn't.
Has she studied French?	Yes, she has.	No, she hasn't.
Had they come early? (British)	Yes, they had.	No, they hadn't.
Do you have a book?	Yes, I do.	No, I don't.
Have you a book? (British)	Yes, I have.	No, I haven't.
Should the boy be here?	Yes, he should.	No, he shouldn't.
Can your friends come?	Yes, they can.	No, they can't.

The structure for the affirmative response is seen as:

Yes, S[PRONOUN] + AUX[**be, do, have,** or MODAL]

The structure for the negative response is shown as:

No, S[PRONOUN] + AUX[**be, do, have,** or MODAL]** + **not**

Mandatory contraction with **not of all auxiliaries except **am** and **must.**

Exercise 1

Give both affirmative and negative elliptical responses for the following English yes-no questions.

    1. Are you rich? (Two different pronouns are possible.)
    2. Were your parents here yesterday?
    3. Is he working at the plant this month?
    4. Were you in school last semester?
    5. Did the students try to do the work?
    6. Have you a car in the city? (British)
    7. Do they have many friends in Honduras? (American Eng.)
    8. Have your friends left yet?
    9. Has your brother written to your family?
    10. Had they ever been there before?
    11. Will the professor help me?
    12. Would they like to see the old part of the city?
    13. Can you show me the exercises?
    14. Should we wait for them?
    15. Am I really sick?

32.2

In compound sentences, English often uses an elliptical verbal construction in the second sentence segment in order to avoid repeating the verb which occurred in the first segment. As in the case of elliptical responses to the positive or negative yes-no questions, only the auxiliary is left in the second sentence.

Observe the following examples:

They can't go, but I can.
He likes his car, and so do I. (or **and I do too**)
He doesn't like his car, and I don't either. (or **and neither do I**)
I reside in Chicago, and he does too. (or **and so does he**)
I don't reside in Miami, and she doesn't either. (or **and neither does she**)

He'll be here tomorrow, but I won't.
He would've helped you, and so would've I. (or **and I would've too**)
They haven't been to Spain yet, but I have.
I hadn't met her before, but they had.

Spanish expresses this type of construction with a simple subject plus **sí** or **no,** or with a similar nonverbal construction, as can be seen in these examples.

Ellos no pueden ir, pero yo sí.
A él le gusta su carro y a mí también.

A él no le gusta su carro, ni a mí tampoco.
Yo resido en Chicago y él también.
Yo no resido en Miami, ni ella tampoco.
Él estará aquí mañana, pero yo no.
Él te hubiera ayudado y yo también.
No han estado en España aún, pero yo sí.
Yo no la había conocido antes, pero ellos sí.

Exercise 2

Translate into English the following Spanish sentences which use a verbal ellipsis in the second clause of the compound sentence.

1. Rey está en casa, pero Providencia no.
2. Estábamos traduciendo del latín y ellos también.
3. Yolanda no es bonita, ni su hermana tampoco.
4. El príncipe no fue asesinado, pero el conde sí.
5. Ella no piensa en ti, pero yo sí.
6. Yo tengo muchas preocupaciones, pero mi padre no.
7. Mi madre siempre mantiene el mismo peso, pero mi tía no.
8. Ellos no hablaban de sus virtudes y nosotros tampoco.
9. Ella no padecía de nada, pero él sí.
10. Yo he visto a Roberto, pero tú no.
11. Casi nadie había hecho la tarea, pero Paulina sí.
12. Ellos no tenían deseos de llegar, pero yo sí.
13. Ella no tiene voto, pero mi hermana sí.
14. Ellas no aparecen en la lista publicada, pero yo sí.
15. Pablo no diría ni siquiera la mitad del misterio, ni ella tampoco.
16. Yo no pude abrir la puerta, pero ellos sí.
17. Este libro habla de la evolución, pero ese otro no.
18. Ellos no podían trasladarse al Mediterráneo, pero tú sí.
19. Mis padres no vivían en la nueva urbanización, ni yo tampoco.
20. Nadie más te ha visto esa mirada, pero yo sí.

32.3

Finally, English may make an ellipsis of its infinitive in the second clause of a compound sentence. This is done by removing the lexical verb and leaving behind only the **to** particle of the infinitive phrase. Such an ellipsis is again done in order to avoid the repetition of the verb which already occurs in the first clause. Spanish must repeat the infinitive or bring it to mind with the substitute verb **hacer.**

ENGLISH EXAMPLES:

We haven't read it yet, but we plan to (...) tomorrow.
He wants to write a book, and he hopes to soon.
She didn't leave a message, but she's going to tonight.
I haven't met them, but I expect to at the party.

SPANISH EXAMPLES:

Aún no lo hemos leído, pero pensamos *hacerlo* mañana.
Él quiere escribir un libro y espera hacerlo pronto.
Ella no dejó ningún recado, pero va a dejar uno esta noche.
No los he conocido, pero espero conocerlos en la fiesta.

Exercise 3

Translate the following sentences into English. Make an elliptical construction for the infinitive which occurs in the second segment of the compound sentence.

1. No han traído los noventa libros, pero piensan traerlos esta noche.
2. Quiero decírtelo y voy a hacerlo cuando te vea.
3. No nos hemos dirigido al profesor, pero tenemos que hacerlo mañana.
4. No puedo hablarte ahora, pero necesito hablarte más tarde.
5. Debo escribir una composición y voy a hacerlo esta tarde.
6. No le hemos contado la historia, pero esperamos contársela dentro de poco.

VERIFICATION TAGS
32.4

In any language, a speaker may make a statement (affirmative or negative) for which a confirmation is solicited from the listener. To accomplish this, the speaker appends a so-called "verification tag" to the statement. The Spanish system for verification tags called **preguntas retóricas** is relatively simple. The English system is more complex as you will see in the next section.

In Spanish, if the tagged statement is affirmative, either of the tags **¿no?** or **¿verdad?** may be used.

Zoraida viene esta noche, ¿verdad?/¿no?
Esa técnica es confusa, ¿verdad?/¿no?
Vicente va a Santo Domingo a vivir, ¿verdad?/¿no?
Ella llegó a las siete ¿verdad?/¿no?

If the tagged statement in Spanish is negative, only **¿verdad?** may be used.

Zoraida no viene esta noche, ¿verdad?
Esa técnica no es confusa, ¿verdad?
Vicente no va a Santo Domingo a vivir, ¿verdad?
Ella no llegó a las siete ¿verdad?

Exercise 4

Determine which tags, **¿verdad?**, **¿no?**, or both, could be used with the following Spanish affirmative and negative statements.

1. Los críticos de drama no vienen esta noche, _____
2. Su colección contiene muchas figuras de cristal, _____
3. Juanillo no fue a Uruguay, _____

4. Tus amigos siempre llegan con alegría, _____
5. Ellos no van a estar en la fiesta el sábado, _____
6. Los Estados Unidos de América es un país muy rico, _____
7. Venezuela se encuentra al lado de Colombia, _____
8. Mis padres no conocen a tus padres, _____
9. La ciudad más grande del mundo pronto será México, _____
10. No fumas a diario, _____

32.5
English Tags

The English verification tag system is more complicated than that of Spanish. In English the verification tag restates an affirmative statement as a negative question and a negative statement as an affirmative question. The tense remains the same, but the verb phrase of the statement is reduced to the first auxiliary verb or to **do** if no other auxiliary is present. When the main verb of a sentence is any form of **be** or **have,** these are repeated in the tag. The subject of the tagged statement is mandatorily restated as a pronoun in the tag itself, just as in the case of the elliptical responses to English yes-no questions. As was explained in Unit 6, some mandatory contractions occur in negative responses. The intonation pattern is usually a falling contour ($\downarrow$) or step down on the last word of the negative tag and the affirmative tag. This intonation is seen to be rather problematic for Spanish speakers.

AFFIRMATIVE STATEMENT	NEGATIVE TAG
	AUX** + **not** + S[PRONOUN] $\downarrow$
	Mandatory contraction with **not.
He is here,	isn't he?
They live here,	don't they?
Susan will arrive on time,	won't she?
Your son has been working,	hasn't he?
You had been sick,	hadn't you?
The cause would be lost,	wouldn't it?
We met your father,	didn't we?
John should visit her,	shouldn't he?
Your parents have a car,	don't they?
(British)	haven't they?

NEGATIVE STATEMENT	AFFIRMATIVE TAG
	AUX + S[PRONOUN] $\downarrow$
They aren't here,	are they?
She doesn't live here now,	does she?
Janice won't arrive on time,	will she?
My son hasn't been working,	has he?
Harry hadn't been sick,	had he?
The cause wouldn't be lost,	would it?
They didn't see your cousin,	did they?
Our friends can't come home,	can they?
Her father doesn't have a car,	does he?

Write the correct verification tag for the following affirmative and negative statements.

1. You have a house in the country, _____?
2. You didn't bring a car to school today, _____?
3. You see my friends on the corner, _____?
4. She is an American student, _____?
5. They aren't working in Europe this summer, _____?
6. They are your cousins from Argentina, _____?
7. Your uncle wasn't living in Guatemala, _____?
8. The children had been sick with the measles, _____?
9. Your little girl hasn't seen a circus, _____?
10. His nieces will be here for the whole month, _____?
11. Your brother wouldn't do a thing like that, _____?
12. They know Spanish very well, _____?
13. Your sister can write English, _____?
14. She couldn't open the window, _____?
15. The professor lives near the university, _____?
16. The school is on this block, _____?
17. Those boys had given her a ride home, _____?
18. All the students know the material, _____?
19. Your nephew has to pay a huge fine, _____?
20. Your party is going to be a huge success, _____?

Por versus Para

33.1

A variety of English words are used to translate the two Spanish prepositions **por** and **para.** The English speaker has more difficulty than the Spanish speaker determining whether to use **por** or **para** since both forms serve as translations of **for.** The native Spanish speaker, in choosing between the two, can be guided by numerous indications put forth in modern grammars. Gili Gaya, to cite a familiar one, would classify **por** as a causal preposition and **para** as a preposition denoting aim, purpose, or result. He further states: "En nuestros días se ha consumado casi totalmente la distinción entre el sentido final de **para** y el causal de **por**" (Gili Gaya *Curso superior*, §193).

When reading the following section, keep in mind that Spanish speakers often use these two prepositions more on the basis of their feelings for them than on the basis of any dictates of grammatical rules. The following discussion, moreover, should prove helpful to both language speakers.

USES OF **POR**

33.2.

In the paragraphs which follow, we have outlined the most frequent situations which require use of the preposition **por** together with plausible equivalent translations in English. At the end of the section, you will find a list of common idiomatic expressions utilizing **por** along with an explanation of its usage followed by an infinitive.

Por is used:

(1) To express the agent in true passive constructions—English uses **by.** (See Unit 29.)

Ese edificio fue diseñado por un conocido arquitecto.
That building was designed by a well-known architect.

Don Quijote fue escrito por don Miguel de Cervantes Saavedra.
Don Quixote was written by Miguel de Cervantes Saavedra.

La sexta versión fue bien recibida por todos.
The sixth version was well received by all.

(2) To express the manner or means by which something is accomplished—English uses **by, through.**

Lo logró por la pura fuerza.
He accomplished it by sheer force.

Conseguí el trabajo por un amigo.
I got the job through a friend.

(3) To express a motive—English uses **because of, out of, due to.**

Ella no fue a la manifestación principalmente por miedo.
She didn't go to the demonstration principally because of (out of) fear.

No pudimos salir por la lluvia.
We were unable to leave due to the rain.

(4) To express the act of going for something or someone. The verbs most commonly used with this meaning of **por** are such verbs of motion as **ir, venir, mandar, enviar, volver, regresar,** and **pasar.** English uses **for.**

Regresamos por el resto de las cosas.
We returned for the rest of the things.

No pude pasar por ti anoche.
I was unable to come by for you last night.

(5) To express an opinion of someone or something—English uses **as.**

Indudablemente le tienen a él por loco.
Undoubtedly they consider him (as) crazy.

Absolutamente todos lo rechazaron por ladrón.
Absolutely everyone rejected him as (because he was) a thief.

(6) To express duration of time or distance—English uses **for.**

Se suscribió ella por un año a la revista *Buen Hogar*.
She subscribed for one year to the *Good Housekeeping* magazine.

Viajamos por más de cien kilómetros.
We traveled for more than one hundred kilometers.

(7) To express movement **along, through,** or **by**, or to express imprecise time as **in.**

Paseamos por la Gran Vía.
We strolled along the Gran Vía.

El tren pasó por el túnel.
The train passed through the tunnel.

Entraron por esa ventana.
The entered through/by that window.

No hago nada por las mañanas.
I don't do anything in the mornings.

(8) To express the exchange of one item for another—English uses **for**.

    Le di a él mucho dinero por el carro.
    I gave him a lot of money for the car.

    Ni me dieron las gracias por el favor que les hice.
    They didn't even thank me for the favor I did them.

(9) To express occurrences in a sequence—English uses **by, for**.

    Iban preguntando casa por casa.
    They went around asking house by house.

    Aquí tienes lo que dijo ella, palabra por palabra.
    Here's what she said, word for word.

(10) To express whatever unit of measure is being used—English uses **per, a.**

    Los compré en tres dólares por docena.
    I bought them at three dollars a/per dozen.

    Él gana más de sesenta mil dólares por año.
    He earns more than $60,000 a year.

(11) To express the term **times** in math problems involving multiplication.

    Dos por dos son cuatro.
    Two times two is four.

    ¿Cuántos son cinco por cuatro?
    How much is four times five?

(12) To express on behalf of someone or in place of someone—English uses **for.**

    Naturalmente todo lo hacemos por nuestro país.
    Naturally we do it all for our country.

    Él habló por su padre, que tuvo que asistir a otra reunión.
    He spoke for (in place of) his father, who had to attend another meeting.

(13) **Por** + INF expresses something remaining to be done.

    Todavía nos quedan detalles pendientes por hacer.
    We still have some details left to do.

    No nos dejaron mucho por hacer.
    They didn't leave us much to do.

(14) **Por** is used in a variety of Spanish idiomatic expressions. We list here some of the most common ones.

por ahora	for now/for the present
por cierto	certainly/incidentally
por Dios	for heaven's sake
por eso	for that reason/therefore
por favor	please
por fin	at last/finally
por lo menos	at least

por lo visto	apparently
por poco	almost, nearly
por supuesto	of course

USES OF **PARA**
33.3

Although the listing is not as long as that for **por**, we have included here the most common usages of the preposition **para** along with their equivalencies in English. A careful study of this and the preceding section should benefit the English speaker greatly in knowing when to use **por** and when to use **para**.

Para is used:

(1) To express the person or thing for which something is intended—English uses **for.**

Aquí tengo una carta para ti.
Here is a letter for you.

No pienso traer nada para ella.
I don't plan to bring anything for her.

(2) To express an unexpected comparison—English uses **for.**

Usted habla español muy bien para (ser) extranjero.
You speak Spanish very well for (being) a foreigner.

Para ser mayo hace mucho frío.
It's very cold for May.

(3) **Para** is used to express English **only to** or **not/never to.**

Salió el sol para esconderse luego detrás de las nubes.
The sun came out only to be hidden later behind the clouds.

Ella se fue a Brasil para no volver nunca.
She went off to Brazil never to return.

(4) To express a time deadline—English uses **by.**

Tenemos que terminar de imprimir el libro para mañana.
We have to finish printing the book by tomorrow.

Le dije a él que me lo trajera para el miércoles.
I told him to bring it to me by Wednesday.

(5) To express the purpose of or reason for an action (**para** + INF = **to/in order to**), or to express an actual destination (**para** + GOAL = **for**).

Harás lo que sea necesario para lograr tus fines.
You will do whatever is necessary (in order) to achieve your goals.

Saldremos para el Perú mañana.
We shall leave for Peru tomorrow.

(6) **Estar para** + INF expresses the concept of **being about to** or **being on the verge of** doing something. **Estar a punto de** is also used; however,

many speakers prefer **por** in this context instead of **para.** The use of **por** is very colloquial and not generally condoned by grammarians.

Estamos para/por salir.
We are about to leave.

Yo no quería decir más porque ella estaba para/por llorar.
I didn't want to say more because she was on the verge of crying.

Exercise 1

Translate the following English sentences into Spanish. Be able in every case to state by number the reason for your choice of **por** or **para.**

1. You speak English very well for being a foreigner.
2. I went along the street, but they went through the park.
3. What are you going to do in the evenings? (plural, formal)
4. We have to spend a lot of money in order to travel.
5. Is this package for you or for me? (familiar)
6. How much did they give you for the horse? (familiar)
7. She read this difficult book page by page.
8. Because of the lack of water, we almost died of thirst.
9. They attacked him as (being) a rebel.
10. I returned for the car, but nobody was there.
11. That picture was painted by El Greco.
12. We are about to leave. We have to be there by seven o'clock.
13. He entered a monastery never to leave again.
14. They were here for two hours, and they brought candy for the kids.
15. Mrs. Martínez sacrifices herself for her son.
16. I don't want to speak for (on behalf of) my brother.
17. May I exchange this dictionary for another one?
18. Dinner remained to be prepared.
19. How much do you earn an/per hour? (familiar)
20. I found out through my sister that you had been ill. (familiar)
21. For a professor of languages, you seem to know a lot about physics. (formal)
22. At last they arrived. They had bought flowers for my sister.
23. Apparently we will finish it by tomorrow.
24. We came by for Mary, but she couldn't come with us on account of being ill.
25. In order to arrive on time, we had to run through the library.

34

Verbal Expressions
Using Spanish
Dar, Hacer, and Tener

34.1

The Spanish verb **tener** is combined with many words to form common expressions of everyday use in the language. Many of these combinations may be considered idiomatic by the native English speaker since the English equivalent uses the verb **be** to express the same idea and not **have.**

SPANISH	ENGLISH
tener + NOUN	**be** + ADJECTIVE
x años (tener 8 años)	x years old (be 8 years old)
la bondad de	kind enough to
calor	hot
celos	jealous
cuidado	careful
frío	cold
ganas de + INF	desirous of (*also* feel like) + **V-ing**
hambre	hungry
miedo	afraid
prisa	hurried (*also* in a hurry) + INF
razón	right
no … razón	wrong
sed	thirsty
sueño	sleepy
suerte	lucky

34.2

Like tener, the verb **dar** combines with many words to form common usage expressions. Spanish often uses this verb with the indirect object pronoun plus a noun to express English **make one feel a certain way: Eso me da calor, That makes me feel warm.**

I.O. **da(n)** + NOUN	**it makes** D.O. + ADJECTIVE
me/te/le da calor	it makes me/you/him/her hot
celos	jealous
deseos de + INF	desirous of + **V-ing**
frío	cold
ganas de + INF	feel like + **V-ing**

272

I.O. **da** + NOUN	**it makes me/you/him/her** + ADJECTIVE
gusto + INF	happy (to)
hambre	hungry
miedo	afraid
(la) razón	right
satisfacción	pleased
sed	thirsty
sueño	sleepy

Modification of the Spanish nouns and English adjectives used in the Spanish **dar** and **tener** expressions is possible. Since English uses adjectives in the expressions presented here and in §34.1 above, an adverb such as **very** or similar can be used as a modifier. Spanish, on the other hand, uses nouns in the expressions, so the adjective **mucho/-a** or similar is used as the modifier.

I'm very cold.	Tengo mucho frío.
You are very jealous.	Tienes muchos celos.
It makes him very thirsty.	Le da mucha sed.
It makes them very afraid.	Les da mucho miedo.

Exercise 1

Translate the following sentences containing idiomatic expressions into the other language.

1. Tu perro me da miedo.
2. He was hungry when he arrived.
3. El niño le tenía miedo a su abuelo.
4. The cold makes the children hungry.
5. ¿Tiene diez años tu hermano?
6. Saying that doesn't make you right.
7. Ella no tiene ganas de ir al cine con nosotros.
8. We're fine; we're not hot nor cold.
9. El trabajar aquí bajo el sol me da sed.
10. This book on Mexico makes me feel like visiting that country.

34.3

The verb **hacer** is used in Spanish to express both weather conditions and duration of time. English again uses **be** in its equivalent expressions.

Weather conditions and other meteorological phenomena, as expressed in the two languages, are very similar in their respective structures.

hacer[3rd pers. sgl.] + NOUN	**it is** + ADJECTIVE
hace calor	it is hot
brisa	breezy
fresco	cool
frío	cold
sol	sunny
buen/mal tiempo	nice/bad (weather)

34.4

The structures used by Spanish and English to express time duration are very different simply because of the point of view taken by each language. Spanish tends to view expressions of time duration as statements that the action is still going on, regardless of whether the points of view are present or past. English, on the other hand, views the actions as existing in a period of time stretching backwards into some earlier time, a past with current relevance.

Time duration beginning in the past and continuing up until and including the present has distinct structures in the two languages. Spanish uses the present tense of both the main verb and the verb **hacer.** English uses the present perfect or the present perfect progressive of the main verb.

hace + x-TIME + **que** + V[PRES] *or*
V[PRES] + **desde hace** + x-TIME

S + V[PRES PERF] *or* [PRES PERF PROG] + **for** + x-TIME

Hace dos años que ella vive aquí.
Ella trabaja aquí desde hace seis meses.

She has lived here for two years.
She has been working here for six months.

For time duration beginning somewhere in the past and ending somewhere in the past (time wholly in the past), Spanish uses the imperfect tense of both the main verb and the verb **hacer.** English uses the pluperfect or the pluperfect progressive tense of the main verb.

hacía + x-TIME + **que** + V[IMPERF] *or*
V[IMPERF] + **desde hacía** + x-TIME

S + V[PLUPERF] + **for** + x-TIME *or*
S + V[PLUPERF PROG] + **for** + x-TIME

Hacía cinco años que ella vivía aquí.
Ella trabajaba aquí desde hacía seis meses.

She had lived here for five years.
She had been working here for six months.

In order to convey the concept of x-TIME ago, Spanish uses the present tense of **hacer** and the preterite or imperfect of the main verb. English uses the past tense of the verb in conjunction with the word **ago.**

hace + x-TIME + **que** + V[PRET] *or* [IMPERF]
or V[PRET] *or* [IMPERF] + **hace** + x-TIME

S + V[PAST] + x-TIME + **ago**

Hace dos años que él vivió aquí.
Él vivió aquí hace dos años.
Él vivía aquí hace dos años.

He lived here two years ago.

Exercise 2

Translate the following sentences into the other language. Give all possible versions when more that one is acceptable.

1. I don't like it when it is hot.
2. Hace dos semanas que estaba aquí mi hermano.
3. I think it is windy there.
4. No hace sol hoy, pero tampoco hace frío.

5. We have been studying here for five hours.
6. Eloisa tocaba el piano desde hacía mucho tiempo.
7. The firemen arrived ten minutes ago.
8. Fumo desde hace dieciocho años.
9. It's always good weather in California.
10. Tuve que tomar ese examen hace un mes.
11. How long have you been studying Spanish? (plural, formal)
12. Antes de ir a Costa Rica, hacía un año que yo estudiaba español.
13. We left Chile several weeks ago.
14. No hace mucho tiempo que ella cambió su apariencia por completo.
15. She was sick because she had been drinking for a long time.
16. Hace fresco esta mañana, pero va a hacer calor esta tarde.
17. I had been working in Bolivia for several years.
18. Hace quince años que tu padre está en Los Ángeles.
19. That boy has been taking drugs for a long time.
20. Llegó la carga hace una hora.

35

Spanish Constructions with Gustar, Faltar, and Similar Verbs

35.1
Spanish syntax as concerns the usage of certain verbs, among which are **gustar** and **faltar,** is very difficult for the English speaker since it is at such great variance with the English ways of expressing the same concepts.

Me gustas (tú).	I like you.
Me faltan cinco pesos.	I need five pesos. (Five pesos are missing.)

Other major Spanish verbs that resemble **gustar** and **faltar** and are used in the same structures are **doler, encantar, fascinar, importar, interesar, quedar, hacerle falta a uno,** etc.

For the English speaker to best perceive the syntax required for these verbs in Spanish, it is helpful to think of them as corresponding to English **be + -ing** or some similar construction.

doler = be hurting, be painful
encantar = be enchanting
faltar = be lacking, be missing
fascinar = be fascinating
gustar = be pleasing
importar = be important, care about
interesar = be interesting
quedar = be remaining, left over
hacerle falta a uno = be lacking, be needing

The following diagram shows the syntax required with these Spanish verbs. Also shown are literal paraphrases using **be + -ing.** These paraphrases *should not be considered grammatical equivalents.*

Obviously, any native English speaker will recognize that the English paraphrases for the Spanish sentences in the following diagram are meaningful, but they are not standard English. You would never find them used in normal English utterances.

276

INDIRECT OBJECT (INDIVIDUAL AFFECTED)	VERB (3RD PERS. SGL. or PL.)	SUBJECT (SINGULAR or PLURAL)
me to me	**duele** it is hurting/painful	**la garganta** the throat
te to you	**encantan** they are enchanting	**las latinas** the Latin girls
le to him/her/you	**falta** it is lacking	**dinero** money
nos to us	**fascinan** they are fascinating	**los estudios** the studies
les to them/you all	**gusta** it is pleasing	**la casa** the house
me to me	**hace falta** it is lacking	**el tiempo** the time
te to you	**importan** they are important	**tus amigos** your friends
le to him/her/you	**interesa** it is interesting	**la literatura** literature
nos to us	**queda** it is remaining/left	**mucho por hacer** a lot to do

35.2

The following would be acceptable English renditions of the above English paraphrases of the Spanish sentences. It will be noted, moreover, that they deviate considerably from the Spanish syntactical specifications.

Me duele la garganta.	=	My throat hurts. My throat is sore. I have a sore throat.
Te encantan las latinas.	=	You love Latin girls. You are enchanted by Latin girls. Latin girls captivate you.
Le falta dinero.	=	He/She needs/lacks money. You need/lack money. You are missing money.
Nos fascinan los estudios.	=	Studies fascinate us. We are fascinated by the studies.
Les gusta la casa.	=	They like the house. They are pleased with/by the house.
Me hace falta el tiempo.	=	I lack the time. I don't have the time. I need the time.
Te importan tus amigos.	=	Your friends matter to you. You care about you friends.

		Your friends are important to you.
Le interesa la literatura.	=	Literature interests him/her/you. He/She is interested in literature. You are interested in literature.
Nos queda mucho por hacer.	=	We have a lot remaining/left to do.

35.3

A comparison of the above Spanish and English constructions reveals that the English subject is usually rendered in Spanish as the indirect object: *I like the house = Me* **gusta la casa.** Further observations show a difference in the function of the noun phrase **the house/la casa.** In English it functions as a direct object of the verb, whereas in Spanish, it is the subject of the verb: **I like** *the house* = **Me gusta** *la casa.*

Note should be taken that the Spanish verbs involved in these constructions tend to be defective. They occur only in certain of their possible forms. In the examples given, they appear only in the 3rd persons singular and plural, depending upon the subject, which is stated last: **Me gusta la casa/Me gustan las casas.**

If the Spanish indirect object is expressed as a noun rather than as a pronoun, it must be accompanied by a redundant disjunctive prepositional object construction (cf §14.12). This may also be done with an indirect object pronoun for purposes of emphasis or contrast.

A Reinaldo *le* duele la garganta.
A mis padres *les* encanta la música clásica.
Al gobierno *le* faltan los fondos económicos para hacerlo.
A ti y a Delia *os* fascinan las flores delicadas.
A mí *me* gusta la clase de castellano. (emphasis)
¿A ti *te* hace falta la inteligencia? (emphasis)
A él/ella/Ud. *le* importan los problemas del mundo. (emphasis)
A nosotros *nos* interesan tus planes para el futuro. (emphasis)
A ellos/ellas/Uds. *les* queda una hora para terminarlo. (emphasis)

Exercise 1

Examine each of the following English sentences and then translate each one into Spanish. In every case, be able to state how the elements which form the normal English construction are converted into the elements forming the Spanish sentence.

1. We don't like cats and dogs.
2. Do you need (lack) paper? (formal, plural)
3. I don't care what you think about me. (familiar)
4. They have sore feet.
5. I have twenty dollars left.
6. Do you like my car? (formal)
7. Isn't money important to your uncle? (formal)
8. What do we need (lack) now?
9. My friend has only one cigarette left.
10. My sister has a pain in her chest.
11. My brother doesn't like Hawaii.

12. The students don't matter to the teacher.
13. My elbow huts.
14. We have several questions remaining to be answered.
15. I'm not interested in your problems. (familiar, plural)
16. He's fascinated by the physical sciences.
17. Mexican movies captivate me.
18. Contemporary world problems interest them.

36

Miscellaneous Contrasts

36.1

The usage of determiners and quantifiers frequently varies from language to language; however, these variations are minor between English and Spanish and involve mostly the word order. This is the case with Spanish **cierto, medio**, and **otro** vis-à-vis English **certain, half**, and **another.** Whereas English says **a certain, one-half/a half,** and **another** + NOUN, Spanish says only **cierto, medio,** and **otro** without an indefinite article.

A certain man arrived.	Cierto hombre llegó.
He needs a certain book.	Él necesita cierto libro.
I drank a half gallon.	Bebí medio galón.
She bought one half kilo.	Ella compró medio kilo.
I want another car.	Quiero otro carro.
Another dog died.	Otro perro murió.

Note: Informal English usage has **half a gallon** as an alternate of **a half gallon.**

In a situation requiring the augmentatives **más/more**, Spanish uses the formula NUMBER + ITEM + **más.** English reverses the Spanish formula and uses NUMBER + **more** + ITEM.

I need one more book.	Necesito un libro más.
Five more girls arrived.	Llegaron cinco muchachas más.
May we eat three more candies?	¿Nos podemos comer tres caramelos más?
One more friend came.	Vino un amigo más.

NUMERICAL CONTRASTS
36.2.

Ciento is the Spanish count number equivalent to English **one-hundred.** Although one rarely hears it in everyday speech, the correct way to count in Spanish is **noventa-y-ocho, noventa-y-nueve, ciento** not (**cien**), **ciento uno,** and so forth. Considered incorrect by some people are the common expressions **Éramos más de cien** and **cien por cien; ciento,** not **cien,** is the more correct word.

When **ciento** is used with numbers larger than itself or when used as a numerical determiner, regardless of the gender of the following noun, **ciento** assumes the shortened form **cien.**

Llegaron cien soldados.
Más de cien mujeres vieron la aparición.
Cien mil personas votaron por el candidato.
Pagaron cien millones justos en compensaciones.

With the exception of **cien,** the multiple-hundred determiners in Spanish (**doscientos/-as, trescientos/-as**) agree in gender and number with the nouns which they modify. As usual, there is no such agreement in English.

doscientas mujeres	two-hundred women
quinientos hombres	five-hundred men
setecientos libros	seven-hundred books
novecientas pesetas	nine-hundred pesetas

36.3

Spanish **mil** and English **one thousand**, or **a thousand**, show slight variation in their usage also. Whereas English says **one (a) thousand**, Spanish says only **mil**. The native English speaker will then tend to say incorrectly ***un mil** in Spanish.

Neither language pluralizes the word for 1,000 when it is preceded by a specific number, nor is it inflected in Spanish for gender.

dos mil personas	two thousand perople
ocho mil ejemplares	eight thousand copies
sesenta mil dólares	sixty thousand dollars

The plurals of both ciphers, **miles** and **thousands**, occur only when no specific number of thousands is indicated, just a general amount. Both have an **of/de** construction.

miles de personas	thousands of people
miles de dólares	thousands of dollars

36.4

Spanish **un millón** and English **one million**, or **a million**, have similar contrasts as do **mil** and **thousand.** There should be no error-inducing tendencies between Spanish **un millón** and English **one (a) million.** However, when used with a specific number larger than one, Spanish **millón** has a plural, while English continues to use the singular form. The Spanish speaker must guard against an ungrammatical statement like **The population exceeds ten *millions.**

dos millones	two million
ocho millones	eight million
ochenta millones	eighty million

When followed by a noun, Spanish uses a construction with **de**, while English does not.

un millón de soldados	a million soldiers
tres millones de animales	three million animals
veinte millones de pesos	twenty million pesos

Both languages use the plural of 1,000,000 when no specific number of millions is specified.

millones de carros	millions of cars
millones de personas	millions of people

36.5

The English word **one**, due to its multiple classifications as a noun numeral, adjective, and pronoun, is interchanged with indefinite article **a** in certain combinations (see §36.2,4).

The Spanish number for **one** has three forms when it functions as a true numeral: **uno, un,** and **una.**   **Uno** is the count number which occurs in the counting sequence **uno, dos, tres,** etc, and it also serves as the masculine numerical pronoun, for example: **Tengo uno** 'I have one,' **Voy a comer uno** 'I am going to eat one,' and **Solo quiero ver a uno de ustedes** 'I only want to see one of you.'

Un, an apocopated form of **uno**, is the masculine numerical adjective, used only before either singular or plural nouns of the masculine gender.

un hombre	one man
veintiún dólares	twenty-one dollars
ciento un soldados	one-hundred (and) one soldiers

Una is the feminine numerical adjective, used only before either singular or plural nouns of the feminine gender.

una mujer	one woman
veintiuna casas	twenty-one houses
mil y una noches	a thousand (and) one nights

36.6

Spanish constructions involving **todo** in its various forms and English **all, every, each,** and **everything** contrast mainly in their employment with singular or plural nouns and in whether the noun is accompanied by a determiner or not.   English says **all** + NOUN[Plural], where Spanish says either **todos/-as** + DEFINITE ARTICLE + NOUN[Plural] or **todo/-a** +NOUN[Singular].

All professors are crazy.	Todos los profesores son locos.
	Todo profesor es loco.
All Americans are rich.	Todos los americanos son ricos.
	Todo americano es rico.
All men are mortal.	Todos los hombres son mortales.
	Todo hombre es mortal.

In cases where English **all** and **everything** are in any way modified or when they serve as direct objects, Spanish would use a **todo** construction accompanied by a redundant **lo** in the equivalent situation.

All you say is true.	Todo *lo* que dices es verdad.
I have all I need.	Tengo todo *lo* que necesito.
She ate it all.	Ella se *lo* comió todo.
He bought it all.	Él *lo* compró todo.

| She bought everything there was. | Ella compró todo *lo* que había. |
| I want to see everything. | Quiero ver*lo* todo. |

Translate the following sentences into the other language, bearing in mind the contrasts presented so far in this unit.

1. He is going to bring everything.
2. Todo lo que usted hizo no significa nada.
3. He is looking for a certain man.
4. Vamos a comer media caja de dulces.
5. She lost three more dollars there.
6. Vamos a cubrir dos temas más en esa categoría.
7. We have visited a hundred countries.
8. Queremos averiguar por qué perdieron más de seiscientas mil pesetas.
9. He bought one-hundred twenty-one books.
10. El niñito puede contar hasta doscientos.
11. Two million people died in that war.
12. Las palabras de Ud. tienen cierto matiz de pureza.
13. There were thousands of cars on the highway.
14. Había millones de individuos afectados por la enfermedad.
15. Does she still have everything she brought?
16. ¿Quieres mostrarme todo lo que compraste?
17. Do you think you know it all? (familiar)
18. Todo perro es peligroso a veces.
19. Every machine works well.
20. Todas las banderas están igualmente visibles.

36.7

Time-duration and time-when are signaled differently in the two languages under study. Spanish uses **todo/-a + el/la** and **todos/-as + los/las** to represent each time span respectively. English must use two different structures to signal the same two periods of time: **all ___ (long)** and **every (each)**. By simply converting the singular **todo/-a el/la** to the plural **todos/-as los/las**, Spanish can indicate that an activity which takes place throughout the duration of a specific time period can take place also at specific intervals (time-when) spread out over time. English has a more complicated system by which to effect this conversion. Different words must be used in English: **all ___ long** becomes either **each** or **every** + TIME ELEMENT.

The following contrastive examples illustrate this difference.

| Él trabaja todo el día. | He works all day (long). |
| Él trabaja todos los días. | He works each/every day. |

| Estudian toda la semana. | They study all week long. |
| Estudian todas las semanas. | They study each/every week. |

| Enseño todo el año. | I teach all year (long). |
| Enseño todos los años. | I teach each/every year. |

| Hay clase toda la mañana. | There is class all morning long. |
| Hay clase todas las mañanas. | There is class each/every morning. |

DATES IN ENGLISH AND SPANISH
36.8
The systems used in the expression of dates in English and Spanish are at considerable variance with one another, and the possibility of error on the part of both the English and Spanish speaker is quite high.

In the English system to state what today's date is, two different structures may be used.

> (1) **the** + DATE[ordinal] + **of** + MONTH
> the 12th of January
> the 22nd of May
> the 1st of October

> (2) MONTH + DATE[ordinal]
> February 3rd
> June 2nd
> April 1st

To state on what particular date something happened, two alternate structures are used also.

> (1) S + V + **on the** + DATE[ordinal] + **of** + MONTH
> He arrived on the 20th of March.
> They left on the 2nd of November.

> (2) S + V + **on** + MONTH + DATE[ordinal]
> He arrived on March 20th.
> They left on November 2nd.

In the Spanish system to state what today's date is, only one structure is commonly used.

> **el** + DATE[cardinal] + **de** + MONTH
> el dos de mayo
> el cinco de abril

There is one exception which should be noted. The first of any month in Spanish is expressed by the ordinal number **el primero** and not by the cardinal number **uno.** In this respect the two systems coincide.

el primero de noviembre	the first of November
el 1ro de enero	the 1st of January

In order to state on what date something happened in Spanish, again we have only one structure.

> (S) + V + **el** + DATE[cardinal] + **de** + MONTH

> Juan llegó el ocho de febrero.
> Yo la vi el cinco de junio.
> Ellas salieron el primero de octubre.

36.9
A comparison of the two linguistic systems for the expression of dates reveals several important contrasts that should be carefully observed.

(1) English uses ordinal numbers while Spanish uses the cardinal numbers (except for the 1st, **el primero**, of any month). The Spanish speaker must therefore become adept at using the English ordinal number system and learn that **one** becomes **first, two** becomes **second, three** becomes **third, four** becomes **fourth,** etc. Compound numbers follow the same system in English, that is **21** becomes **21st, 22** becomes **22nd, 23** becomes **23rd, 24** becomes **24th,** and so on.

(2) Finally, English uses **on** while Spanish employs the definite article **el** for expressing on what date something happened. English capitalizes months of the year and days of the week, while Spanish uses lower-case letters for both.

Exercise 2

Translate the following sentences into the other language, being mindful of the structural contrasts presented in §36.7–9 of this unit.

1. Marcelino vino el cinco de julio. (two ways)
2. He has to work all summer long.
3. Mi cumpleaños es el treinta de diciembre. (two ways)
4. We go to the mountains every summer.
5. ¿Tienes que trabajar todas las noches?
6. I am going to be in Brazil all year (long).
7. ¿Dónde vas a estar el primero de setiembre? (two ways)
8. Today is the 4th of July.
9. Tenemos enseñanza individual todas las mañanas a las ocho.
10. I'm going to be in my office all morning (long).
11. ¿Por qué tengo que estar de punta en blanco todas las tardes?
12. I have a Spanish class every semester.
13. Nos despedimos de ustedes y les deseamos bienandanza para el año 2000.
14. We take leave now, wishing you good fortune for the new century.

*　　*　　*

♦ clave ∞ key ♦ key ∞ clave ♦ clave ∞ key ♦ key ∞ clave ♦

♦ KEY ∞ CLAVE ♦ CLAVE ∞ KEY ♦ KEY ∞ CLAVE ♦ CLAVE ∞ KEY ♦

♦ clave ∞ key ♦ key ∞ clave ♦ clave ∞ key ♦ key ∞ clave ♦

♦ KEY ∞ CLAVE ♦ CLAVE ∞ KEY ♦ KEY ∞ CLAVE ♦ CLAVE ∞ KEY ♦

♦ clave ∞ key ♦ key ∞ clave ♦ clave ∞ key ♦ key ∞ clave ♦

*　　*　　*

KEY TO THE EXERCISES

NORMS USED IN THE KEY

In translating the Spanish verb phrases found in the exercises when these have no expressed subjects showing gender and/or person, for example, the third person singular indicative and subjunctive forms of the Spanish verb in all tenses, the subject could be rendered in English with any of the following personal pronouns: **he, she, it,** or **you.** By the same token, when translating the English personal pronoun **you** plus a verb into Spanish, it could be rendered **tú, usted, ustedes, vosotros,** or **vosotras** followed by the corresponding verb form. For example, sentence number 10 of exercise 6.1 *Have you been waiting for the bus?* was translated as: "¿Has estado esperando el autobús?" It could have be translated also as: ¿Ha estado esperando usted el autobús?, ¿Han estado esperando ustedes el autobús?, or ¿Habéis estado esperando vosotros/-as el autobús? This same variety of alternates is given also for the possessives: Spanish **su** + NOUN could be **your/his/ her/their**, and English **your** + NOUN could be **tu/su/vuestro(-a).**

Loísta usage is employed in the Spanish versions for all direct object pronouns in the exercises with the exception of exercises 14.7, 14.8, and 14.9.

Alternate translations of the exercises often are indicated in the Key. An attempt to include all possible variations has not been made since that would be very impractical as concerns length; nevertheless, an endeavor is made to use the most frequently heard forms of expression. When an alternate phrase is given, this is generally shown by separating the various possibilities by a slash line (/). Examples: **There were many innocent people who did not know the danger they were in/the risk they were running; No me gustan/No van conmigo las fiestas desenfrenadas (desordenadas).** A slash line (/) is also used when an exercise calls for various answers, all framed in the same pattern. Example: **hemos amado/temido/vivido; unos/unas cuantos/-as.** Alternate words or forms of words (and sometimes phrases) are usually enclosed in parentheses, as can be seen in the second example above. Other examples are: **Para todos ustedes traigo este regalo (presente); Some ate (were eating) while others waited (were waiting) to eat.** Note should be taken that on occasion, due to orthographic requisites which could lead to misreading of the text, these slash/parenthesis patterns are not always observed.

In this Key the exercise numbers of each unit (eg **1.2, 1.3**) are followed by various other numbers enclosed in parentheses (eg §1.4–5). These other numbers indicate the sections of the text which the exercises deal with. The notation **1.2** (§1.4–5) indicates that Exercise 2 of Unit 1 covers text sections 4 and 5.

Those exercises which require the writing of original answers or other such similar tasks will not be found in the Key. Examples: **Exercise 1.1** "Write original English and Spanish sentences patterned after the structural types illustrated in each of the examples given in the paragraphs above," **Exercise 2.1** "Select ten regular verbs other than those already mentioned and give all of their forms," or **Exercise 5.3** "From your readings or experiences, cite other verbal examples like those listed above where Spanish and English morphological ranges differ."

PART ONE KEY
BASIC SYNTAX AND VERBAL FORMS

1

BASIC WORD ORDER IN ENGLISH AND SPANISH

1.1 (No key)

1.2 (§1.4–5) 1. Hará Juan el trabajo./Juan hará el trabajo. 2. Salieron del autobús cuatro de mis amigos./Cuatro de mis amigos salieron del autobús. 3. No llegaron los invitados hasta después de las diez./Los invitados no llegaron hasta pasadas las diez. 4. Tiene Freddy mi libro, y lo saben sus padres./Freddy tiene mi libro, y sus padres lo saben.

5. Están sobre el escritorio tus papeles./Tus papeles están sobre el escritorio. 6 Me mostró la casa un vendedor de voz fuerte./Un vendedor de voz fuerte me mostró la casa. 7. No vio Joseph a nadie en la estación esta mañana./Joseph no vio a nadie en la estación esta mañana. 8. Cantaban los pájaros, pero no podía oírlos la niña sorda./Los pájaros cantaban, pero la niña sorda no podía oírlos.

1.3 (§1.6) 1. Muchas personas alquilan casas. 2. Alquilan casas muchas personas. 3. Anoche se marchó (se fue) nuestra hija. 4. No está en su oficina mi padre. 5. Una carta traje para ti. 6. Para todos ustedes traigo este regalo (presente). 7. Tu hermana les dio la caja a mis amigos. 8. Su hermana les dio a mis amigos la caja.

9. Muchas personas compraron ese libro. 10. Compraron ese libro muchas personas. 11. La semana próxima terminan las clases. 12. Están en casa los muchachos. 13. Mostraron los ejemplos al maestro (a la maestra). 14. Al maestro (A la maestra) le mostraron los ejemplos. 15. Dos hombres le vendieron un reloj a la muchacha. 16. Dos hombres le vendieron a la muchacha un reloj.

2

THE VERB FORMS OF ENGLISH

2.1 (No key)

2.2 (§2.6) 1. proving, proven 2. controlling, controlled 3. dyeing, dyed 4. committing, committed 5. trying, tried 6. traveling, traveled 7. worrying, worried 8. preferring, preferred 9. lying, lied 10. comparing, compared 11. trafficking, trafficked 12. laying, laid 13. programing, programed 14. saying, said 15. worshiping, worshiped.

2.3 (§2.7) A. 1. sneezes [ɪz] rule (c) 2. swims [z] rule (b) 3. cooks [s] rule (a) 4. prefers [z] rule (b) 5. cries [z] rule (b) 6 strives [z] rule (b) 7. searches [ɪz] rule (c) 8. slaps [s] rule (a) 9. goes [z] rule (b) 10. skates [s] rule (a) 11. judges [ɪz] rule (c) 12. passes [ɪz] rule (c) 13. coughs [s] rule (a) 14 sings [z] rule (b) 15. sews [z] rule (b)

B. 1. tested [ɪd] rule (c) 2. lived [d] rule (b) 3. sobbed [d] rule (b) 4. learned [d] rule (b) 5. cashed [t] rule (a) 6. seemed [d] rule (b) 7. preceded [ɪd] rule (c) 8. raised [d] rule (b) 9. conveyed [d] rule (b) 10. cracked [t] rule (a) 11. paid [d] rule (b) 12. guaranteed [d] rule (b) 13. tried [d] rule (b) 14. dragged [d] rule (b) 15. breathed [d] rule (b).

2.4 (Appendix I) Note: Verbs enclosed in parenthesis appear in more than one column since they have alternate forms.

(1)	(2)	(3)	(4)	(5)	(6)
beat	abide	beseech	begin	arise	(bet)
bend	become	bring	drink	awake	bid (*offer*)
(bet)	bind	buy	ring	be	burst
build	bleed	can	shrink	bear (*carry*)	cast
burn	breed	catch	sing	bear (*birth*)	cost *intr.*
(cleave) *tr.*	(chide)	creep	sink	beget	cut
cleave *intr.*	cling	deal	(spin)	bid (*order*)	hit
cost *tr.*	come	(dream)	spring	bite	hurt
(dream)	dig	feel	stink	blow	let
dwell	feed	flee	swim	break	put
gild	fight	hear	wring	(chide)	(quit)
gird	find	keep		choose	rid
hang *law*	fling	kneel		(cleave) *tr.*	set
have	(get)	leave		do	shed
heave	grind	lose		draw	shut
(hew)	hang	may		drive	slit
lay	heave *naut.*	mean		eat	split
lean	hold	(quit)		fall	spread
leap	lead	say		fly	thrust
learn	(light)	seek		forbid	
lend	meet	sell		forget	
(light)	read	shoe		forsake	
make	run	sleep		freeze	
pay	shine	sweep		(get)	
rend	shoot	teach		give	
(saw)	sit	tell		go	
send	slide	think		grow	
(shave)	sling	weep		(hew)	
smell	slink			hide	
(speed)	(speed)			know	
spell	(spin)			lade	
spend	spit			lie	
spill	split			mow	
spoil	stand			ride	
(stave)	(stave)			rise	
(stew)	stick			(saw)	
	sting			see	
	strike			sew	
	string			shake	
	swing			(shave)	
	win			shear	
	wind			show	

(5)
slay
smite
sow
speak
steal
(stew)
stride
strive
swear
swell
take
tear
thrive
throw
tread
wake
wear
weave
write

3
THE FORMS OF REGULAR VERBS IN SPANISH

3.1 (§3.3–6) (Patterned as illustrated) 1. amamos, temimos, vivimos 2. amáis, teméis, vivís 3. (yo) amaba, temía, vivía 4. (él) amaría, temería, viviría 5. amarás, temerás, vivirás 6. amen, teman, vivan 7. (ella) ame, tema, viva 8. amáramos, temiéramos, viviéramos 9. amareis, temiereis, viviereis 10. amasen, temiesen, viviesen 11. he amado/temido/vivido 12. habías amado/temido/vivido 13. (Vd.) hubo amado/temido/vivido 14. (Uds.) habrán amado/temido/vivido 15. hayáis amado/temido/vivido 16. hubiéremos amado/temido/vivido 17. (yo) hubiera amado/temido/vivido 18. amemos, temamos, vivamos 19. (yo) hubiese amado/temido/vivido 20. ama, teme, vive.

3.2 (§3.7) 1. conseguimos, conseguir 2. secan, secar 3. escoja, escoger 4. apacigüemos, apaciguar 5. argüí, argüir 6. llega, llegar 7. zurciste, zurcir 8. encogen, encoger 9. apagó, apagar 10. recogí, recoger 11 trabajo, trabajar 12. mengua, menguar 13. averigües, averiguar 14. saco, sacar 15. convences, convencer 16. proseguí, proseguir 17. sequemos, secar 18. venza, vencer 19. coges, coger 20. toqué, tocar 21. sigue, seguir 22. amortiguo, amortiguar 23. zanje, zanjar 24. rezo, rezar

3.3 (§3.7–8) 1. arranqué 2. (él) distinga 3. colguemos 4. escojamos 5. esparza 6. averigüemos 7. freí 8. (yo) pague 9. remolcaron 10. bruñendo 11. consigamos 12. sentaos 13. oyeron 14. volvámonos 15. refriendo

4

THE FORMS OF IRREGULAR VERBS IN SPANISH

4.1 (§4.2–5) 1. cierro, acuesto, pierdo, (group A1), hiervo (group B1), sigo (group C1), vuelvo (group A1) 2. cierra, acuesta, pierde, (group A1), hierve (group B1), sigue (group C1), vuelve (group A1) 3. cerramos, acostamos, perdemos, (group A4), hervimos (group B3), seguimos (group C3), volvemos (group A4) 4. cierran, acuestan, pierden, (group A1), hierven (group B1), siguen (group C1), vuelven (group A1) 5. cierres, acuestes, pierdas, (group A1), hiervas (group B1), sigas (group C1), vuelvas (group A1) 6. (él/ella) cierre, acueste, pierda, (group A1), hierva (group B1), siga (group C1), vuelva (group A1) 7. cierren, acuesten, pierdan, (group A1), hiervan (group B1), sigan (group C1), vuelvan (group A1).

4.2 (§4.2–5) 1. sugieres, mueres, mientes, duermes (group B1) 2. sugirió, murió, mintió, durmió (group B2a) 3. sugiere, muere, miente, duerme (group B1) 4. sugiramos, muramos, mintamos, durmamos (group B2b) 5. sugirieran, murieran, mintieran, durmieran (group B2a) 6. sugiriésemos, muriésemos, mintiésemos, durmiésemos (group B2a) 7. sugiriereis, muriereis, mintiereis, durmiereis (group B2)

4.3 (§4.2–5) 1. present indicative 3rd person plural, group A, verb root stressed 2. gerund, group B, verb root followed by stressed **-ie-** 3. present indicative 3rd person pl., group A, verb root stressed 4. gerund, group C2, stressed **-ie-** in syllable following root 5. present subjunctive 1st pers. pl., group B, verb root followed by stressed **-a-** 6. present indicative 3rd pers. pl., group B, verb root stressed 7. imperative 1st pers. pl., group A, no change, verb root unstressed 8. preterite 3rd pers. sgl., group C, stressed **-io** in syllable following root 9. preterite 3rd pers. sgl., group A, no change, verb root unstressed 10. preterite 3rd pers. pl., group B, verb root followed by stressed **-ie** 11. pres. subj. 2nd pers. sgl., group C, stressed root vowel 12. imperfect subjunctive I, 1st pers. pl., group B, verb root followed by stressed **-ie** 13. present subjunctive 1st or 3rd pers. sgl., group A, verb root stressed 14. preterite 1st pers. sgl., group A, no change, verb root unstressed 15. future indicative 3rd pers. pl., group A, no change, verb root unstressed.

4.4 (§4.7–10) 1. satisfaga, satisfagamos, satisfagáis; satisfaz/satisface, satisfagan 2. nazca, nazcamos, nazcáis; nace, nazcan 3. reluzca, reluzcamos, reluzcáis; reluce, reluzcan 4. oponga, opongamos, opongáis; opón, opongan 5. se atenga, nos atengamos, os atengáis; atente, aténganse 6. convenga, convengamos, convengáis; convén, convengan 7. prevalga, prevalgamos, prevalgáis; prevale, prevalgan 8. sobresalga, sobresalgamos, sobresalgáis; sobresal, sobresalgan 9. caiga, caigamos, caigáis; cae, caigan 10. incluya, incluyamos, incluyáis; incluye, incluyan.

4.5 (§4.11–12) 1. trajiste, trajéramos, trajesen 2. dijiste, dijéramos, dijesen 3. hiciste, hiciéramos, hiciesen 4. quisiste, quisiéramos, quisiesen 5. viniste, viniéramos, viniesen 6. condujiste, condujéramos, condujesen 7. supiste, supiéramos, supiesen 8. hubiste, hubiéramos, hubiesen 9. pudiste, pudiéramos, pudiesen 10. pusiste, pusiéramos, pusiesen 11. estuviste, estuviéramos, estuviesen 12. tuviste, tuviéramos, tuviesen.

4.6 (Patterned as illustrated) 1. andar: (yo) ande, andemos 2. leer: (yo) lea, leamos 3. corregir: (yo) corrija, corrijamos.

4.7 (Appendix III)

(a)	caber	(b)	poner	(c)	decir
	haber		salir		hacer
	poder		tener		
	querer		valer		
	saber		venir		

4.8 (Appendix III)

(a) STEM **u**		(b) STEM **i**	(c) STEM **a**
andar	poder	bendecir	traer
caber	poner	dar	
conducir	producir	decir	
deducir	saber	hacer	
estar	(ser)	querer	
haber	tener		
(ir)			

4.9 (Appendix III)

e/i → ie	o/u → ue	c → zc	Ø → ig	Ø → oy
adquirir	avergonzar	conducir	caer	dar
empezar	colgar	conocer	oír	estar
pensar	dormir	deducir	roer	ir (v + oy)
perder	forzar	lucir	traer	ser
querer	jugar	placer		
sentir	poder	producir		
	torcer			
	volver			

Ø → g	ec → ig	u → uy	ab → eØ	e → i
poner	bendecir	construir	haber	reír
salir	decir	incluir	saber	seguir
tener				
valer				
venir				

ab → ep	Ø → y	c → g	o → ue	Ø → e
caber	errar	hacer	oler	ver
saber				

5

THE SPANISH IMPERFECT–PRETERITE CONTRAST

5.1 (§5.1–3) 1. Te estuve esperando/Te esperé hasta que cerraron el edificio. 2. As was her custom, she seldom left the house. 3. No mirábamos el camino cuando un camión cruzó delante de nosotros. 4. Some ate (were eating) while others waited (were waiting) to eat. 5. Nunca nevaba, pero siempre hacía mucho frío. 6. Angela used to sing in that nightclub. (**before** 'antes' is not translated since *anterioridad* is shown in the modal) 7. Cuando éramos (más) jóvenes, mi hermano me molestaba mucho. 8. They weren't doing anything when I saw them. 9. Antes más gente viajaba por tren que por avión. 10. I arrived in class at eight (o'clock); the others were already there.

5.2 (§5.4–6) 1. Anoche fuimos al teatro. 2. There were many innocent people who did not know the danger they were in/the risk they were running. 3. Ella estudió para la prueba (el examen) por lo menos hasta las diez. 4. They came up to me, greeted me, and left without saying another word. 5. Nunca supe el nombre de ella. 6. The young lady wanted to buy the chain but didn't since it was priced too high. 7. Llovía y nadie caminaba por las calles. 8. I had to work all day long to derive some benefits. 9. Mi hermano los conocía bien; los conoció en Santafé de Bogotá. 10. Isabel was very afraid upon seeing the twenty-five loose animals. 11. Yo no llevaba (tenía) puesta la camisa y luego hizo frío. 12. William was nauseated and refused to eat anything. 13. Yo no te podía oír porque había mucho ruido. 14. There was a strike in the company because the administrator didn't want/refused to pay anyone enough (sufficiently).

5.3 (No key)

5.4 (§5.1–6)
A. Por la mañana, a mediodía y al ocaso, <u>resonaban</u> leves pisadas en las estancias del piso bajo. <u>Hablaban</u> un hidalgo y un mozuelo. El hidalgo se <u>hallaba</u> sentado en un pozo del patio; el mozuelo frente a él, <u>iba comiendo</u> unos mendrugos de pan que <u>había sacado</u> del seno. Tanta <u>era</u> la avidez con que el rapaz <u>yantaba</u>, que el hidalgo <u>sonrió</u> y le <u>preguntó</u> si tan sabroso, tan exquisito <u>era</u> el pan que <u>comía</u>. <u>Aseguró</u> el muchacho que de veras tales mendrugos <u>eran</u> excelentes, y entonces el hidalgo, sonriendo como por broma—mientras <u>había</u> una inenarrable amargura allá en lo más íntimo de su ser—le <u>tomó</u> un mendrugo al muchachito y <u>comenzó</u> a comer.
B. Cuando Colón <u>llegó</u> al nuevo mundo, <u>cambió</u> el nombre que <u>tenían</u> los indígenas y les <u>dio</u> otro nombre. Colón <u>creyó (creía)</u> que <u>iba</u> a llegar a la India, pero no <u>fue</u> así. Cuando <u>llegó</u>, Colón <u>observó</u> que los indios <u>vivían</u> en pequeños pueblos y que <u>eran</u> muy pobres. La tierra, sin embargo, <u>era</u> muy hermosa, pero no <u>tenía</u> las riquezas que los españoles <u>querían</u> encontrar. Colón no <u>estaba</u> nada satisfecho, pero como <u>tenía</u> que escribirles a sus benefactores, los Reyes Católicos, <u>decidió</u> exagerar bastante, pues <u>sabía</u> que los reyes nunca <u>iban</u> a ver esas tierras. Aunque <u>estaba</u> cansado después de su viaje por el Atlántico, <u>salió</u> de las islas para continuar sus expediciones en busca de oro.

5.5 (§5.1–6) El salón donde me encontraba era muy amplio. Las ventanas eran largas y estrechas (angostas) y estaban a tal distancia del piso (suelo), que eran completamente inaccesibles desde adentro. Unos débiles rayos de luz se filtraban por los cristales y daban suficiente claridad a los objetos más prominentes; la vista se esforzaba inútilmente por alcanzar las esquinas más remotas de la estancia o las oquedades del techo abovedado. Las paredes estaban cubiertas de oscuras cortinas. El mobiliario era abundante, antiguo y gastado. Había muchos libros e instrumentos musicales esparcidos al rededor, pero que no daban ninguna vitalidad a la escena. Sentí que respiraba una atmósfera de pesar. Un ambiente de honda e irredimible tristeza pesaba sobre todo aquello.

Cuando entré, Usher se levantó del sofá donde se hallaba recostado y me saludó con una calidez que al principio me pareció de una cordialidad exagerada. Sin embargo, una mirada a su rostro me convenció de su sinceridad. Nos sentamos, y por unos momentos, mientras él callaba, lo miré con mitad lástima, mitad asombro. Difícilmente podía admitir que aquél que tenía en frente había sido el compañero de mi niñez.

6
BASIC SENTENCE STRUCTURE IN ENGLISH AND SPANISH

6.1 (§6.1–5) 1. negative statement, simple past, My parents didn't see that movie. AUX-**do** preterite with LV in base form 2. content question, simple past, ¿Cuándo te preguntó él por el dinero? LV preterite 3. negative yes-no question, past perfect progressive, Hadn't you been touring the library when I arrived? main verb in **-ing** and two AUX-**have** (preterite) and **be** (past participle) 4. negative yes-no question, simple present, ¿No necesitan ellos (ellas) ayuda en su trabajo? LV inflected 5. affirmative statement, simple future, We'll eat lunch today at someplace nearby. AUX-**will** used with LV in base form 6. content question, present progressive, ¿Qué están haciendo ahorita/ahora (mismo)? inflected AUX-**estar** used with LV in **-ndo** form 7. affirmative yes-no question, future progressive, Will you (all) be studying some foreign language? main verb in **-ing** form used with two AUX, **will** and **be** (base form) 8. negative statement, past perfect, No habíamos gastado mucha gasolina. LV in past participle form with AUX-**haber** (imperfect) 9. negative yes-no question, past progressive, Weren't they helping him yesterday until very late? AUX-**be** inflected with LV in **-ing** form 10. affirmative yes-no question, present perfect progressive, ¿Has estado esperando el autobús? two AUX, inflected **haber** and **estar** in past participle form, are followed by LV in **-ndo** form.

6.2 (No key)

6.3 (§6.6–11) 1. preterite perfect progressive, content question, INTERROG + VP ↓ 2. simple past, negative statement, S + AUX(optional contraction) + **not** + VR 3. simple present, negative yes-no question, **no** + VP + S ↑ 4. future progressive, affirmative yes-no question, AUX + S + VR ↑ 5. present progressive, negative statement, S + **no** + VP 6. present perfect, negative statement, S + AUX (optional contraction) + **not** + VR 7. simple present, affirmative statement, S + VP 8. perfect conditional, content question, INTERROG + AUX + S + VR ↓ 9. simple present, affirmative yes-no question, VP + S ↑ 10. simple past, negative yes-no question, AUX(mandatory contraction) + **not** + S + VR ↑

6.4 (§6.6–11) 1. content question 2. affirmative yes-no question 3. negative statement 4. affirmative statement 5. negative yes-no question 6. content question

7. affirmative yes-no question 8. negative statement 9. affirmative statement 10. negative yes-no question

6.5 (§6.6–11) 1. Eng. negative statement has **not** after the AUX, Mis padres no han estado pagando impuestos. 2. Span. places the negative marker before any AUX, I won't (will not) work here any more. 3. Eng. places the S between the AUX and VR. The example sentence is used by many Spanish speakers and is considered quite acceptable. Grammar purists discourage the structure and recommend the following: ¿Están estudiando francés los alumnos? 4. Span. yes-no questions place the entire VP before the S, Have you worked here before? 5. Eng. places **not** between the AUX and VR, ¿No había conocido usted antes a esa chamaca? 6. Span. places negative **no** before the VP in affirmative statements, Your brother will not (won't) be helping us. 7. Eng. content questions put the S between the AUX and VR, ¿Con quién estaba hablando el profesor? (The same comment about acceptability applies here as in example 3.) 8. Span. content questions have the VP before the S, What would Poland have done about that?

6.6 (§6.6–11) 1. simple past, affirmative statement, S + VP ↓ 2. past perfect, negative yes-no question, **no** + VP ↑ 3. past perfect, affirmative yes-no question, AUX + S + VP ↑ 4. present progressive, affirmative yes-no question, AUX + VR + (S) ↑ 5. future perfect progressive, negative yes-no question, AUX (mandatory contraction) + **not** + S + VR ↑ 6. future perfect, affirmative statement, S + VP ↓ 7. conditional, affirmative yes-no question, AUX + S + VR ↑ 8. past perfect progressive, negative statement, S + **no** + VP ↓ 9. present progressive, content question, INTERROG + AUX + S + VR ↓ 10. past perfect, content question, INTERROG +VP + S ↓

11. present perfect, affirmative yes-no question, AUX + S + VR ↑ 12. simple past, affirmative yes-no question, VP + S ↑ 13. past perfect progressive, content question, INTERROG + AUX + S + VR ↓ 14. past progressive, affirmative statement, S + VP ↓ 15. simple past, negative statement, S + AUX(optional contraction) + **not** + VR ↓ 16. preterite perfect, content question, INTERROG + VP + S ↓ 17. past perfect, negative yes-no question, AUX (mandatory contraction) + **not** + S + VR ↑ 18. past (imperfect) progressive, content question, INTERROG + VP + (S) ↓ 19. past perfect progressive, negative statement, S + AUX (optional contraction) + **not** + VR ↓ 20. simple past (preterite), negative yes-no question, **no** + VP + S ↑

6.7 (§6.6–11) 1. simple past, affirmative statement, S + VP ↓; Ellos(-as) vieron una película (un filme) esta tarde, S + VP ↓ 2. simple present, content question, INTERROG + VP + S ↓; Where are the police moving those robbers (thieves) to? INTERROG + AUX + S + VR ↓ 3. present progressive, negative yes-no ques-tion, AUX (mandatory contraction) + **not** + S + VR ↑; ¿No estás trabajando en la biblioteca? **no** + VP ↑ 4. past perfect, negative statement, S + **no** + VP ↓; The sages (learned people) had not discussed the phenomenon. S + AUX + **not** + VR↓ 5. simple present, affirmative yes-no question, AUX + S + VR ↑; ¿Los estudiantes (alumnos) traen sus libros todos los días? S + VP ↑ / ¿Traen los estudiantes sus libros todos los días? VP + S ↑ 6. preterite perfect, negative statement, S + **no** + VP ↓; The tourists haven't seen the cathedral. S + AUX (optional contraction) + **not** + VR ↓ 7. future perfect, affirmative statement, S + VP ↓; Él habrá ido a su casa entre las nueve o las diez. S + VP ↓ 8. conditional, negative yes-no question, **no** + VP ↑; Wouldn't you consider something like that for me? AUX (optional contraction) + **not** + S + VR ↑ 9. past progressive, content question, INTERROG + AUX + S + VR ↓; ¿A qué hora estuviste (estabas) viendo televisión anoche? INTERROG + VP ↓ 10. past progressive, affirmative yes-no question, VP + S ↑; Were trains continually leaving from the station? AUX + S + VR ↑ 11. past perfect, negative statement, S + VP ↓; Mi jefe no había visto a su secretaria ese día. S + **no** + VP ↓ 12. future, content question, INTERROG + VP ↓; Who will you play with/With whom will you play next season? INTERROG + AUX + S + VR ↓

6.8 (§6.12–13) 1. He *did* go to Ecuador last year. 2. They don't want to see you now. 3. They saw the accident. 4. My mother does *not* speak Spanish. 5. She *does* sing in the choir every Sunday. 6. We do *not* know the answer. 7. Our priest *did* work in Uruguay for some time. 8. The men didn't come on time.

9. La comida sí estaba sabrosa. 10. A pesar de la mucha neblina, el avión pudo aterrizar. 11. La suerte sí que favoreció a nuestro equipo. 12. Desde la montaña sí se divisa la llanura. 13. Esta sugerencia cuenta con el beneplácito del grupo. 14. Esa rosa sí que tiene un bello color. 15. A esta muchacha sí que le crece mucho el pelo. 16. Me apeno de su pronta partida de ella.

6.9 (§6.12, 14) 1. They *do* have a house in the country. Present, affirmative, emphatic statement 2. Have you friends in town? Present, affirmative question (British) 3. My parents didn't have any money at the time. Past, negative statement 4. Why do you have a problem with my suggestion? Present, content question 5. Haven't you a large dog? Present, negative question (British) 6. Had we some food left over? Past, affirmative question (British) 7. When have I the time to do it? Present, content question (British) 8. She hasn't any choice in the matter./She has no choice in the matter. Present, negative statement 9. You had class today, hadn't you? Past, affirmative question (British) 10. Didn't you have a book or two when I saw you? Past, negative question.

7
ENGLISH PHRASAL VERBS

7.1 (§7.2–4) 1. reduce, reducir 2. consider, considerar 3. erect, erigir 4. demolish, demoler 5. resemble 6. examine, examinar 7. delete 8. occupy, ocupar 9. cancel, cancelar 10. require, requerir 11. retract, retractar 12. invent, inventar 13. omit, omitir 14. submit, someter 15. display, desplegar 16. humiliate, humillar 17. discuss, discutir 18. execute, ejecutar 19. review, revisar 20. encounter, encontrar 21. delay, dilatar 22. continue, continuar 23. stop 24. represent, representar 25. tolerate, tolerar.

7.2 (§7.2–4)

break away	disengage oneself (desentenderse de), escape (escapar), start too soon (in racing).
break down	crush (derrumbar), overcome (opposition), separate into parts (detallar), analyze (analizar), go out of working order, give way to tears or emotion, have a physical or nervous collapse.
break in	force in, interrupt (interrumpir), train or tame (entrenar), break in shoes (amoldar).

break off	put a sudden stop to (suspender), discontinue (descontinuar), stop being friendly or intimate, become parted or divided (desprenderse), desist suddenly (desistir, detenerse).
break *on	(The authors know of no phrasal verb commonly used which combines these two elements.)
break out	escape (escapar), begin suddenly, arise or spring up (estallar), appear in eruptions (salirle a uno salpullido).
break up	dissolve and separate (separar), disperse (dispersar), dismantle (desmantelar), dissolve (disolver), end a meeting (acabarse, terminarse), end a relationship (separarse), be broken up (emotionally), be overcome with laughter.

(Note: No attempt will be made from here on to give all possible meanings and uses of the phrasal verb combinations that result grammatically acceptable. Only a few of the most common ones will be cited. A more extensive listing can be found in any good dictionary.)

keep away	remove (mantener alejado/distante, alejarse).
keep down	oppress (oprimir, sojuzgar), restrict (restringir, limitar).
keep in	control or contain, (no dejar salir, mantener dentro).
keep off	keep off the grass (prohibido pisar el césped, tener a raya).
keep on	continue (continuar, seguir), one's clothing (no quitarse).
keep out	exclude (no dejar entrar, prohibida la entrada, permanecer fuera).
keep up	continue (continuar, proseguir), maintain the pace (ir al paso de), remain informed about (mantenerse al tanto de), remain in good order or condition (conservar).
pull away	move away (apartarse), move ahead (dejar atrás, alejarse, distanciarse.)
pull down	demolish (echar abajo, derribar), degrade (rebajar), reduce (reducir).
pull in	restrain (retener).
pull off	take off (quitar), carry out (llevar a cabo).
pull on	dress (ponerse), tug at (tirar de).
pull out	take out (sacar).
pull up	stop (pararse, detenerse).
put away	save (guardar), imprison (encarcelar), institutionalize (meter en un manicomio), consume (comer).
put down	let go of (soltar), suppress (sofocar, reprimir), write down (apuntar) include (poner en la lista), criticize (poner por los suelos, desprestigiar, difamar).
put in	insert (meter), install (instalar), present (presentar), plant (sembrar).
put off	postpone (aplazar, diferir, posponer), make wait (hacer esperar).
put on	dress (ponerse), affect (afectar), pretend (fingir).

put out	extinguish (apagar), publish (publicar), display (sacar, mostrar).
put up	build (levantar, construir), can, preserve by sealing in a can (envasar), nominate (nominar, proponer), lodge (hospedar, alojar).
run away	flee (fugarse), stampede (salir en desbandada).
run down	knock down (atropellar), capture (dar con, encontrar), disparage (hablar mal de), exhaust (agotar), review (repasar)
run in	insert (insertar), arrest (detener).
run off	print (tirar), drive off (echar de), write (redactar rápidamente).
run on	continue (continuar), chatter (hablar sin cesar), elapse (pasar el tiempo).
run out	be exhausted (acabarse, agotarse), expire (expirar), (salir corriendo).
run up	let accumulate (dejar que se acumulen), prices (hacer subir), flag (izar).
take away	remove (quitar, sacar), subtract (restar), carry away (llevarse), separate (separar).
take down	write down (anotar), remove (quitar), disassemble (desarmar).
take in	accept (tomar, aceptar), lodge (alojar), understand (comprender), include (abarcar), deceive (engañar), earn (ganar).
take off	remove (quitar), amputate (amputar), deduct (rebajar), make fun of, imitate (imitar).
take on	assume (asumir), employ (contratar, emplear), load (recibir), accept (aceptar).
take out	remove (sacar), a license (sacar), a person (sacar a pasear).
take up	raise (llevar arriba), pick up (levantar), shorten (acortar).
throw away	dispose of (desechar), hurl (arrojar), waste (desperdiciar), squander (despilfarrar), discard (deshacerse de).
throw down	demolish (demoler, echar por tierra, abandonar armas).
throw in	add (añadir, dar demás), interject (intercalar).
throw off	reject (desechar), emit (despedir, emitir), give up (renunciar).
throw on	dress hurriedly (echarse encima).
throw out	discard (echar fuera, tirar), reject (rechazar).
throw up	vomit (vomitar), abandon (abandonar), raise (alzar, edificar), relinquish (renunciar).

7.3 (§7.1–5) 1. Entonces caí en cuenta del aspecto gracioso de la historia. comprehend/comprender 2. Por favor, ¿puedo mirar tu libro ya que olvidé el mío? 3. No me gustan/No van conmigo las fiestas desenfrenadas (desordenadas). 4. Yo debiera estar pendiente de mi madre ya que ha estado enferma. 5. Mi esposa no tolera (soporta) que yo fume. tolerate/tolerar 6. Les visitamos (inesperadamente)/

Pasamos a visitarlos el viernes pasado por la noche. 7. Sencillamente no puedes huir de (esquivar) tus obligaciones. evade/evadir 8. Mis amigos se llevan muy bien con mi esposo. 9. Trató de escaparse del tiburón. 10. Si corrieras un poco más rápido, me alcanzarías.

11. Recuerdo con agrado mi niñez. 12. El Presidente desea abolir (suprimir) muchas agencias restrictivas. abolish/abolir 13. ¿Cuándo por fin terminarás tus tareas escolares? 14. A pesar de los problemas, continuamos con nuestros planes. 15. El profesor (La profesora) planea reunirse con nosotros mañana. 16. ¿Cómo compensaremos por el tiempo perdido? 17. Hoy no me siento con ánimos para salir. 18. Él no aprobará el curso a menos que se mantenga a la par con sus compañeros de clase (los otros estudiantes) 19. Uno debe estar atento a los carros cuando cruza la carretera. 20. ¿Cómo puedo librarme de ir (¿Cómo puedo evitar tener que ir) a Monterrey? avoid/evitar.

7.4 (§7.7) 1. crédito por intercambio 2. camioneta 3. campaña de limpieza 4. calendario de audiciones 5. puesto de vigilancia 6. venta de liquidación 7. juego eliminatorio 8. elección de desempate 9. hora de despegue 10. huelga de brazos caídos 11. espectáculo de premios 12. botella desechable

13. auto (carro) de fuga 14. pedidos para llevar 15. examen de reposición 16. separar mercancía (sistema de apartado) 17. oración corrida 18. nominación directa 19. hora de salida 20. trabajo de retoque 21. incidencia de bajas (tasa de deserción escolar) 22. ejercicio de calentamiento 23. jugada de anotación (en fútbol) 24. servi-auto (servi-carro)

7.5 (§7.8) 1. Guillermo compró una camioneta Ford nueva. 2. Él hizo varios ejercicios de plancha (varias planchas), y luego comenzó a levantar pesas. 3. Hubo un tremendo choque en cadena en la autopista anoche. 4. El profesor (La profesora) siempre nos da hojas (notas) informativas. 5. El mendigo pedía una limosna. 6. Le dieron a ella una gran fiesta de despedida antes de salir para Venezuela. 7. Pablo es muy presumido (un verdadero exhibicionista), pero aún así es una gran persona. 8. El gobierno sufrió un serio revés económico.

9. Necesito reacción (contrarreacción) de todo el mundo antes de proseguir. 10. Ella sufrió una crisis nerviosa, y tuvieron que hospitalizarla. 11 La película (El filme) resultó una gran desilusión para todos nosotros. 12. Lo despidieron (corrieron) porque tuvo una riña con su patrón. 13. En ese banco ha habido tres asaltos en lo que va del mes. 14. Personas como ellas tienen demasiadas inhibiciones. 15. La mayor parte de los actores del cine emplean suplentes para las escenas de peligro. 16. Previenen un aumento sustancioso de fondos.

8

MODAL AUXILIARIES AND THEIR EQUIVALENTS

8.1 (§8.4–6) 1. I can help you. 2. She isn't able to see you now. 3. (physical ability **can/could** are not used in present perfect tense) 4. When can you bring it? 5. Were you able to see the mountain from there? 6. The students are able/will be able to be here by nine o'clock. 7. We couldn't read the message. 8. I was able to explain it to you before, but I'm not able to now.

8.2 (§8.4–6) 1. No puedo verte. 2. ¿Sabían ellos leer alemán en ese entonces (para ese tiempo)? 3. Ellos no pudieron (fueron capaces de) traerlo. 4. ¿Qué podíamos hacer? 5. ¿Sabes escribir bien? 6. Yo podía ir contigo. 7. Pudieron irse (marcharse/salir) temprano. 8. ¿No podía él (era capaz él de) lograr nada? 9. Él no es capaz de ayudarnos./Él no puede ayudarnos. 10. ¿Quién era capaz de hacerlo? (possession) ¿Quién fue capaz de hacerlo? (demonstration)

8.3 (§8.7) 1. ¿Puedo/¿Me permites visitarla mañana? 2. No puedes/No te permito ir a Santiago este fin de semana. 3. Tu hermano puede traer a un amigo si quiere./Le permito a tu hermano traer a un amigo si quiere. 4. Los niños no podían jugar afuera./A los niños no les permitieron jugar afuera. 5. ¿Cuándo podemos (nos permites) ver tu carro (auto) nuevo? 6. ¿No puedo tener (No me permites) un poco más de tiempo para estudiar? 7. Los niños no pueden jugar en la calle./A los niños no les permiten jugar en la calle. 8. ¿Cuándo puedo (me permites) pintar la casa?

8.4 (§8.8) 1. ¿Quiere(s)/Quería(s)/Querría(s)/Quisiera(s) abrir la puerta, por favor? ¿Puede(s)/Podía(s)/Podría(s)/Pudiera(s) abrir la puerta, por favor? Haz/Haga el favor de abrir la puerta. Ten/Tenga la bondad de abrir la puerta, por favor. Sé/Sea tan amable de abrir la puerta, por favor. (Also) ¿Me abre(s) la puerta, por favor?
2. (Verb forms patterned as sentence 1) ... darme algún/un dinero para el auto? Haz (Haga) el favor ... / Ten (Tenga) la bondad ... / Sé (Sea) tan amable de darme algún/un dinero para el auto. (Also) ¿Me da(s) algún/un dinero para el carro?
3. (Verb forms patterned as sentence 1) ... explicarme la asignación? Haz (Haga) el favor ... / Ten (Tenga) la bondad ... / Sé (Sea) tan amable de explicarme la asignación. (Also) ¿Me explica(s) la asignación?
4. (Verb forms patterned as senence 1) ... traerme una caja de gaseosas? Haz (Haga) el favor ... / Ten (Tenga) la bondad ... / Sé (Sea) tan amable de traerme una caja de gaseosas. (Also) ¿Me trae(s) una caja de gaseosas?
5. ¿Quieren/Queréis/ Querían/Queríais/ Querrían/Querríais/ Quisieran/Quisierais cerrar los ojos unos segundos? ¿Pueden/Podéis/ Podían/Podíais/ Podrían/Podríais/ Pudieran/Pudierais cerrar los ojos unos segundos? Hagan/Haced el favor de cerrar los ojos unos segundos. Tengan/Tened la bondad de cerrar los ojos unos segundos. Sean/Sed tan amables de cerrar los ojos unos segundos. (not the 'Also' structure)
6. (Verb forms patterned as sentence 5) ... decir unas (pocas) palabras en la reunión. Hagan (Haced) el favor ... / Tengan (Tened) la bondad ... / Sean (Sed) tan amables de decir unas (pocas) palabras en la reunión. (not the 'Also' structure)
7. (Verb forms patterned as sentence 5) ... entregarme sus/vuestros libros ahora. Hagan (Haced) el favor ... / Tengan (Tened) la bondad ... / Sean (Sed) tan amables de entregarme sus/vuestros libros ahora. (Also) ¿Me entregan/entregáis sus/vuestros libros ahora?
8. (Verb forms patterned as sentence 5) ... sentarse/-os por favor? Hagan (Haced) el favor ... / Tengan (Tened) la bondad ... / Sean (Sed) tan amables de sentarse/-os por favor. (not the 'Also' structure).

8.5 (§8.9–11) 1. Ese señor será un arquitecto famoso. 2. Los indígenas de este valle habrán sido bajos de estatura. 3. Esa anciana tendrá mucho dinero. 4. El asesino habrá estado en este mismo sitio. 5. Habrá un teléfono por aquí. 6. Mi padre no estará en su oficina después del día doce. 7. No habrán tenido/No tendrían suficiente gasolina para llegar.

8.6 (§8.9–11) 1. Debes (de) estar/Estarás muy cansado/-a. 2. They must have had a problem with the car. 3. Deben (de) haber traído muy poco dinero. 4. Juanita must pronounce Russian very well because she has a good ear. 5. Él no debe tener/Él no tendrá muchas amistades aquí. 6. Last night there must have been a big fire downtown. 7. Ese muchacho no debe saber (no sabrá) la respuesta. 8. How happy that man must be! 9. La tribu sería (debe de haber sido) muy pequeña. 10. It must have been Mrs. Méndez who called.

8.7 (§8.12–13) 1. The woman could/may/might know how to speak Chinese./Maybe (Perhaps) the woman speaks Chinese. 2. ¿Dónde estará él a estas horas? / ¿Dónde él puede estar a estas horas? 3. She may/might not have enough money./Maybe (Perhaps) she doesn't have enough money. 4. ¿Puede ser que/¿Es posible que él sea el nuevo profesor de español? 5. Couldn't a crisis come up (arise)? 6. Puede ser que/Es posible que/Tal vez/Quizá(s) mi sobrino se vaya mañana por la noche. (Acaso/A lo mejor mi sobrino se va mañana por la noche.) 7. They may/might not know you. 8. Puede ser que/Es posible que/Tal vez/ Quizá(s) él no sea tan inteligente como tú. (Acaso/A lo mejor él no es tan inteligente como tú.)

8.8 (§8.14) 1. By this time my cousin should be home already. 2. Él no debería de/debiera de necesitar ayuda. 3. We shouldn't meet (find) anybody (anyone) tonight. 4. ¿Cuándo debería de/debiera de partir el tren? 5. They should arrive very tired. 6. Uno(-a)/Ud. debería de/debiera de conocer a todos sus estudiantes dentro de pocos días.

8.9 (§8.15–16) 1. May you never hear what they have told me. 2. Que siempre tengas dinero suficiente. 3. May they not be here when I arrive./I hope that they aren't here when I arrive. 4. Que viva Ud. en paz. 5. I hope you/ May you marry a witch! 6. Que no los veamos nunca jamás. 7. I *will* accomplish the impossible. 8. Sí que alcanzaremos nuestra meta./*Vamos* a alcanzar nuestra meta. 9. The man would not (wouldn't) cooperate. 10. No quiero soportar insultos.

8.10 (§8.18) 1. ¿Quiere(s)(n)/Queréis que traiga a mis parientes? / ¿Traigo a mis parientes? 2. Shouldn't we return before she arrives? 3. ¿Debe él decirnos la verdad? 4. Shall we dance? 5. ¿Debemos escribirle a él una carta? / ¿Le escribimos a él una carta? 6. Shouldn't I deny him a permit? 7. ¿Deben estar jugando ellos(as) en la calle? 8. Shall/ Should we stay up all night? 9. ¿Cuándo debemos llegar? / ¿Cuándo llegamos? 10. Shall/Should we buy a new model?

8.11 (§8.19) 1. Debías/Deberías/Debieras ver esa película (ese filme). 2. You should (ought to) go see him in his office. 3. No debíamos/deberíamos/debiéramos beber tanta cerveza. 4. (preferred version) What time should they arrive? 5. Él no debía/debería/debiera gastar tanto dinero (tanta plata). 6. You shouldn't/ought not pay so much attention to them. 7. Yo debía/debería/debiera comprar un auto (carro) nuevo este año. 8. Shouldn't we invite them to the party?

8.12 (§8.20) 1. Usted debía/debería/debiera ver a un médico. 2. We had better please (are supposed to please) our parents. 3. ¿Debían/Deberían/Debieran ayudarte con el proyecto? 4. Where are they supposed to live during the winter? 5. Yo no debía/debería/debiera decir nada acerca de ello. 6. You should/ had better be thinking about what you are going to answer. 7. ¿No debíamos/deberíamos/debiéramos estar trabajando ahora? 8. You had better sell (are supposed to sell) that old picture (painting).

8.13 (§8.21) 1. You mustn't smoke. 2. Mi padre no debe trabajar tan duro. 3. My mother doesn't have (hasn't got) to work much. 4. No tienes que fumar. 5. When must we leave/When do we have to leave/When have we got to leave the hotel? 6. ¿No tiene Vd. que hablar francés con ella? 7. You must visit/You have to visit/You have got to visit your companions (mates). 8. Tenemos que ir allí más a menudo. 9. We mustn't ponder over that anymore. 10. ¿Cuándo tenemos que estar allá?

8.14 (§8.22) 1. We are to call them when we arrive. 2. Hay que verlo para creerlo. 3. It is necessary to/ One must/ You should wind it for it to work well. 4. Han de traer varias muestras. 5. This summer I have to teach a class on classical philosophy. 6. Es un empleo (trabajo) horrible porque uno tiene que (hay que) levantarse tan temprano. 7. I suppose it will be necessary to take care of her as usual. 8. Hubo que comprar una casa. 9. You had to confess everything to me, but you didn't say anything. 10. Habrá que emplear la fuerza.

PART TWO KEY
THE COMPLEX NOUN PHRASE

9
NOUNS AND ARTICLES

9.1 (§9.1–4) 1. masculine, rule 9.2i 2. feminine, rule 9.3i 3. fem., rule 9.3iv 4. masc., rule 9.2iii 5. fem., cannot be determined by a rule 6. masc., cannot be determined by a rule 7. masc, cannot be determined by a rule 8. masc., rule 9.2iv 9. masc., rule 9.2iv 10. masc., rule 9.2vii 11. fem., rule 9.3ii 12. masc./fem., rule 9.4iii 13. fem., rule 9.3iii 14. fem., rule 9.3iii 15. masc., rule 9.2v 16. masc., rule 9.2iii 17. fem., rule 9.3iii 18. fem., rule 9.3iii 19. masc., rule 9.2vi 20. masc., rule 9.2viii.

9.2 (§9.6) 1. columnas, rule i 2. bueyes, rule ii 3. andaluces, rule iii 4. consejos, rule i 5. los miércoles, rule v 6. cordobeses, rule iv (Note the elimination of the accent.) 7. alelíes, rule ii 8. pies, rule i 9. peces, rule iii 10. alemanes, rule ii (Note the elimination of the accent.) 11. clases, rule i 12 caracteres, rule ii (Note: Stress shifts to penult in plural.)

9.3 (§9.7) 1. singers [z], rule iii 2. racks [s], rule ii 3. cylinders [z], rule iii 4. snaps [s], rule ii 5. hats [s], rule ii 6. churches [ız], rule i 7. thrushes [ız], rule i 8. fools [z], rule iii 9. toys [z], rule iv 10. flies [z], rule iv 11. classes [ız], rule i 12. clashes [ız], rule i 13. stations [z], rule iii 14. grudges [ız], rule i 15. geese [gis], rule v 16. knives [z], rule v 17. breezes [ız], rule i 18. men, rule v 19. potatoes [z], rule iii 20. threads [z], rule iii.

9.4 (§9.8–11) 1. El roble es un árbol muy importante en Portugal. (singular noun representative of species) 2. It's obvious that you don't know anything about French cooking. (nouns used in general sense) 3. Vamos a viajar por el oeste (la parte occidental) de Francia. (classified noun in indirect address) 4. I took off my shoes and put on my sandals. (article of clothing takes possessive adjective) 5. Él quiere visitarnos el 4 de julio. (exact date) 6. Don't you know Professor Serrano? (classified noun in indirect address) 7. Los pulmones están muy cerca del corazón. (organs of the body) 8. I don't want to walk to jail with you. (often referred to place) / I don't want to walk to the jail with you. (both persons know the identity of the thing) 9. Son las nueve y tengo que irme a casa. (time of day) 10. On Mondays I don't go downtown until late. (day of the week) 11. En otro tiempo se consideraba la Tierra plana. (element of nature) 12 We read the sad story of Diana the Huntress. (epithet) 13. Juan se cortó el brazo en el accidente. (body part; identity or event is known) 14. I don't want to buy any house on Riviera Street. (classified noun) 15. Viven en la ignorancia y en la pobreza porque carecen de dinero. (abstract nouns spoken of in general sense) 16. Some go to heaven and others go to hell. (often referred to places) 17. El doctor Brown habló con el doctor Smith en la reunión. (classified nouns in indirect address; identity of event is known) 18. You students think that you know it all. (apposition) 19. Se fueron el sábado, pero piensan volver el domingo. (days of the week) 20. I opened my eyes when Professor Roscoe sat down beside me. (body part; classified noun in indirect address)

9.5 (§9.12) 1. I want to look for (some) history documents in/at the library. (plural article frequently omitted) 2. El padre de él es hombre de negocios (negociante). (unmodified singular predicate noun of profession) 3. These gentlemen are Brazilians. (plural form of an adjective of nationality) 4. El tío de ella es un médico muy bueno (modified predicate noun of profession) 5. Oswald is an engineer. (unmodified singular predicate noun of profession) 6. Todos tus amigos son estudiantes. (plural form of predicate noun of profession) 7. Is your uncle Guatemalan? (singular adjective of nationality) 8. Ella es italiana. (singular adjective of nationality) 9. The dog ate a bone and some scraps of meat. (used before singular and plural nouns) 10. Cantinflas era un comediante mexicano muy famoso. (modified adjective of nationality) 11. They are well-known actors. (plural predicate noun of profession) 12. Mis padres son franceses. (plural adjective of nationality)

10
DESCRIPTIVE AND LIMITING ADJECTIVES

10.1 (§10.1–4) 1. portugués, portuguesa, portugueses, portuguesas, Class III 2. poco, poca, pocos, pocas, Class I 3. holgazán, holgazana, holgazanes, holgazanas, III 4. tercer(o), tercera, terceros, terceras, I 5. chino, china, chinos, chinas, I 6. remolón, remolona, remolones, remolonas, III 7. superior, superiores, II 8. mal(o), mala, malos, malas, I 9. activista, activistas, II 10. infantil, infantiles, II 11. permanente, permanentes, II 12. profesional, profesionales, II 13. chiquitín, chiquitina, chiquitines, chiquitinas, III 14. hablador, habladora, habladores, habladoras, III 15. capaz, capaces, II 16. común, comunes, II 17. santo (san), santa, santos, santas, I 18. patán, patana, patanes, patanas, III.

10.2 (§10.1–4) 1. pobre, pobres, Class II 2. moderno, moderna, modernos, modernas, Class I 3. francés, francesa, franceses, francesas, III 4. inteligente, inteligentes II 5. primer(o), primera, primeros, primeras, I 6. alemán, alemana, alemanes, alemanas, III 7. pequeño, pequeña, pequeños, pequeñas, I 8. racial, raciales, II 9. español, española, españoles, españolas, III 10. útil, útiles, II

10.3 (§10.5–8) 1. Leo el mismo libro. 2. Llegaron en un avión grande. 3. Él necesita otro vaso. 4. Perdiste una reunión importante. 5. Ella vino a mi casa tres veces./Ella vino tres veces a mi casa. 6. Quiero una taza de té caliente.
7. Venden arroz fortificado en ese almacén. 8. Hubo una huelga general en la segunda fábrica. 9. Unos (Algunos) amigos viven en el quinto piso. 10. Compré el primer libro con mis pesetas españolas. 11. El mismo hombre resolvió tres problemas difíciles. 12. Esta máquina complicada no costó tanto dinero.

10.4 (No key)

10.5 (§10.9–10) 1. Él es un empleado viejo. Él es un viejo empleado. 2. Él llegó en un nuevo carro. Él llegó en un carro nuevo. 3. Es un pobre país. Es un país pobre. 4. Busco cierta respuesta. Busco una respuesta cierta. 5. Contiene leche pura. Él lo abrió a pura fuerza. 6. Entre mi propia ropa, tengo ropa propia para el trabajo. 7. Ella tiene manos grandes. Es una gran maestra.

10.6 (§10.11) 1. If I can't buy a new car, then I'll buy a used one. 2. La línea verde está cerca de la amarilla. 3. I don't have any good ones left. 4. Voy a comprar unas frutas dulces porque no me gustan las agrias. 5. The book on the table is a very valuable one. 6. Los conocidos nuevos siempre son más interesantes que los viejos. 7. Poor people are often forced to beg for money from the rich. 8. Busco un clima más templado porque el de aquí es muy fresco.

10.7 (§10.12) 1. No tengo palabras para explicarte lo cómica (graciosa) que es esa película. 2. The interesting thing (part) is that they had already received the communication. 3. Lo malo es que tengo que levantarme tan temprano. 4. Someday I am going to tell you how much I have suffered in this life. 5. No puedes imaginar lo mal que él lee. 6. Do whatever you want with what you have.
7. Lo de Susana no es tan serio como lo de su madre. 8. I don't like that novelist because of the revolutionary aspect of his style. 9. Lo regañé por lo ridículo de sus acciones. 10. The business about your father is sad, but what you did is worse. 11. Lo que hago con mi tiempo es asunto mío. 12. Nobody has discovered (found out) how bad (evil) she is.

11
POSSESSIVE AND DEMONSTRATIVE ADJECTIVES AND PRONOUNS

11.1 (§11.1–2) (Note: In answers 1, 5, 7, 8, and 9, although grammatically correct, the **su/suyo** demonstrative adjectives would more likely be understood as **your** instead of **his, her** or **their**; see §11.2. A better rendition is the third periphrastic answer.) 1. su primo, el primo suyo, el primo de ella (preferred) 2. mi aventura, la aventura mía 3. nuestra tía, la tía nuestra 4. tus cigarrillos (cigarros), los cigarrillos (cigarros) tuyos 5. sus hermanos, los hermanos suyos, los hermanos de ellos/de ellas 6. su perro, el perro suyo, el perro de usted 7. su abuela, la abuela suya, la abuela de él 8. su tío, el tío suyo, el tío de ustedes 9. sus patas, las patas suyas, las patas de él/de ella 10. vuestro bolígrafo, el bolígrafo vuestro.

11.2 (§11.3) 1. Es mía. 2. I saw his. 3. Conocí a los tuyos/suyos/vuestros. 4. They wounded yours. 5. Disfrutamos la nuestra. 6. Stop yours. 7. Se fumaron los suyos (los de ellos/de ellas). 8. She/He defended theirs. 9. Él ha terminado el suyo. 10. We grow/grew ours.

11.3 (§11.3) 1. Mi secretaria está hablando con la tuya 2. Their cousins want to meet ours. 3. Su esposa está con la tuya. 4. Our money was all spent along with his. 5. La copia de ella llegó junto con la nuestra. 6. Your nephew is fighting with mine. 7. Nuestros ciudadanos son mejores que los de ellos. 8. Their parents don't know yours. 9. El papá de ustedes quiere ver al de ella. 10. His books seem to be locked up with mine.

11.4 (§11.4) 1. No quiero comprar esos plátanos. 2. The director is not going to use those actors over there in the comedy. 3. Mis padres dicen que van a vender aquella casa. 4. They wouldn't let me cross that field; therefore, I'm going up this path. 5. Me dieron cinco dólares por este reloj viejo. 6. In that government these deputies formed an independent junta (council). 7. Durante ese tiempo, nadábamos en este río todos los días. 8. This monk wants to speak to (with) that lady over there. 9. Estos libros son viejos, pero esos libros son muy nuevos. 10. If you want to buy this company, you should contact that owner.

11.5 (§11.5) 1. I don't like these; let's buy those. 2. Éste es muy buen amigo de ese otro. 3. (no rewrite possible) 4. Éste llegó ayer, pero aquél llegó anteayer. 5. (no rewrite possible) 6. Aquéllos convencen al pueblo, pero éstos, no. 7. Before buying this one, you should see those. 8. (no rewrite possible) 9. He brought me these, but I can only answer that one today. 10. Insistió en que aceptáramos éstos, pero no ésos.

12
EXPRESSIONS OF POSSESSION

12.1 (§12.1–2) 1. el hermano de mi padre 2. our friends' kindness 3. el hijo de su hermano/el hijo del hermano de él 4. the dangers of my profession 5. los zapatos de los niños 6. my mother's kitchen 7. los vestidos de las niñas 8. your parents' advice 9. la oficina de la secretaria 10. the girls' skirts 11. el hogar nuevo de Chris 12. the women's girls 13. la fábrica de los padres de ella 14. Verdi's opera 15. las patas del gato 16. the Jews' enemies

12.2 (12.3) A. ¿De quién es esta revista? ¿De quién son estas revistas? ¿De quiénes son estas revistas? ¿A quién pertenece esta revista? ¿A quién pertenecen estas revistas? ¿A quiénes pertenecen estas revistas?

B. Whose book is this? Whose books are these? Whose is this book? Whose are these books? Who(m) does this book belong to? Who(m) do these books belong to? To whom does this book belong? To whom do these books belong?

12.3 (No key)

13
PARTITIVE CONSTRUCTIONS

13.1 (§13.1–3) 1. No queremos leer muchos libros. *count* 2. Pon/Ponga(n)/Poned un poco de azúcar en la fruta. *non-count* 3. Él piensa que puede contar con unos cuantos amigos en Brasil. *count* 4. Por favor, cómprame unos cigarrillos (cigarros). *count* 5. Ella vertió mucha agua en el vaso. *non-count* 6. ¿Por qué no trajeron algunas (unas cuantas) cervezas? *count* 7. Pocos europeos viven en Paraguay. *count* 8. ¿Quiere(s)(n)/Queréis zumo (jugo) de naranja? *non-count* 9. Por favor, cómpreme un poco de queso. *non-count* 10. ¿Gasta mucha gasolina tu/su/vuestro auto (carro)? *non-count* 11. ¿Tienen ellos muchos parientes en Ecuador? *count* 12. Vamos a visitar algunos (unos) amigos en Mendoza. *count*

13.2 (§13.1–3) 1. I have some uncles (aunts and uncles) in Colombia. *count* 2. Does the professor of the academy have many children? *count* 3. Some women use (wear) a lot of expensive perfume. *non-count* 4. Tonight my wife is going to serve a little soup. *non-count* 5. Where can we buy (some) wheat? *non-count* 6 There are few catholics in our homeland. *count* 7. Didn't you tell me to bring (some) olive oil? *non-count* 8. His/Her/Your chest filled up with lots (a lot) of

blood, *non-count* 9. When are you going to lend me some art magazines? *count*
10. I have a few dollars in my pocket. *count* 11. A good diet includes some fruit among other foods. *non-count* 12. This spring the professor assigned a lot (lots) of reading. *non-count*

14
ENGLISH AND SPANISH PERSONAL PRONOUNS

14.1 (§14.2) (The identification of pronouns in this exercise is for practice purposes only. A subject pronoun accompanying a verb is redundant in a number of the cases. See §3.6, also §1.4.) 1. yo 2. ellos, ellas, ustedes 3. tú 4. vosotros, vosotras 5. yo, él, ella, ello, usted 6. yo, él, ella, ello, usted 7. él, ella, ello, usted 8. nosotros, nosotras 9. yo.

14.2 (§14.2) 1. he, she, it 2. I, you, he, she, it, we, they 3. I, you, we, they 4. I, you, he, she, it, we, they 5. I, you, he, she, it, we, they 6. I 7. he, she, it 8. you, we, they 9. you, we, they.

14.3 (§14.3) 1. Hay una carta para ti (usted) sobre la mesa. 2. Creo (Me parece) que recibiste una carta para mí. 3. Ellos/Ellas no saben nada de (sobre) nosotros/nosotras. 4. Él quiere ir conmigo. 5. ¿Desea tu madre vivir contigo? 6. Ella no sabe hacer nada por sí misma. 7. Ellos/-as no pudieron decirnos nada de (sobre) sí mismos/ellos mismos/ellas mismas.
8. El tren pasaba debajo de ellos/ellas. 9. Él me enseñó esta poesía. ¿Sabe usted algo de (sobre) ella? 10. Él murió en Puerto Rico. No sé nada más de ello.
11. La caja estaba debajo de la silla cuando me senté en ella. 12. Mis padres viven cerca de ti (de Vd.). 12. Parecía estar muy satisfecho consigo mismo. 14. Me gustaría estudiar contigo.

14.4 (§14.3) 1. Don't you know anything about it? 2. No one wants to share with me. 3. Does anyone want to paint with us? 4. Does the married couple live near you or far from you (far away)? 5. The tree fell on (on top of) it. 6. That governor is always talking about himself. 7. Juana isn't going to tell me anything about it.
8. They announced that the prize was for me. 9. Cecilia does everything by herself. 10. The stranger could depend on us more. 11. I can't celebrate this occasion with you. 12. I don't please him for her, I do it for myself. 13. They are not going to let us go out (leave) without them. 14. What trust are they going to place in him if they hear him talking to himself?

14.5 (§14.4) 1. A nosotros nos gusta él. DO 2. A él no lo conociste (DO); la conociste a ella. DO 3. A mí nunca me vio antes. DO 4. A ellos les escribí (IO), pero a él, no. IO 5. A ella no le importa. IO 6. Él te mandó las flores a ti. IO 7. A nosotros ella nunca nos dijo la verdad. IO 8. A él lo mordió el perro (DO), pero a mi sólo me ladró. IO 9. Él me va a vender todo a mí. IO 10. Estamos por visitarla a ella ahora mismo. DO A ella estamos por hacerle la visita ahorita. IO.

14.6 (§14.5) 1. Conjunctive pronoun may precede or follow entire verbal unit if the last unit is a dependent infinitive; Sé que no van a decirme nada. 2. (Same as 1) Tienes que hacerlo cuando puedas. 3. Conjunctive pronoun precedes verbal unit in negative commands (no other position possible) 4. Conjunctive pronoun follows verbal unit in affirmative commands (no other position possible) 5. (Same as 4) 6. Conjunctive pronoun must precede conjugated verbs (no other position possible). 7. (Same as 6) 8. Conjunctive pronoun may precede or follow entire verbal unit if the last unit is a dependent **-ndo** form; Jorge no está facilitándome mucha ayuda con este proyecto. 9. Conjunctive pronoun (first **te**) may precede or follow entire verbal unit if the last unit is a dependent **-ndo** form; (second **te**) conjunctive pronoun must precede conjugated verbs; ¿Quién te estaba acompañando cuando te vi esta mañana? 10. Conjunctive pronoun must precede the conjugated verb (no other position possible) 11. (Same as 10) 12. Conjunctive pronoun follows verbal unit in affirmative commands (no other position possible); and conjunctive pronoun may precede or follow entire verbal unit if the last unit is a dependent infinitive; No puedo hablarte en este momento. 13. (Same as 3) and (Same as 6 and same as 1); No te he dicho todavía todo lo que quiero decirte. 14. (Same as 6); conjunctive pronoun must follow a non-dependent infinitive (no other position possible) 15. Conjunctive pronoun must follow a non-dependent **-ndo** form and conjunctive pronoun must precede conjugated verbs (no other position possible).

14.7 (§14.7–9) 1. Los veo. Les veo. 2. La conozco. 3. Él los ve. 4. No la conozco. 5. Él lo conoce. Él le conoce. 6. Él las vio. 7. Ellos los conocen. Ellos les conocen. 8. Las vimos. 9. La quiero. 10. Ella lo vio. 11. No lo conocemos. No le conocemos. 12. Ellos no la ven.

14.8 (§14.7–9) 1. No necesito verlo(-la) mañana./No necesito verle mañana./ No lo (la) necesito ver mañana./No le necesito ver mañana. (Note: The **lo** (**le**) options represent **leísmo** usage) 2. Él la está estudiando ahora mismo./Él está estudiándola ahora mismo. 3. ¿Dónde la pusiste? 4. ¡Tráelo mañana! 5. ¡No los pongas ahí! 6. ¿Cuándo lo tenemos que ver? / ¿Cuándo le tenemos que ver? / ¿Cuándo tenemos que verlo? / ¿Cuándo tenemos que verle? 7. Él las está tratando de llamar./Él está tratando de llamarlas. 8. ¡No lo coman! 9. ¡No los fuméis! 10. La conozco bien.

11. ¿Dónde la conoció él? 12. ¿Quieren visitarme en España? / ¿Me quieren visitar en España? 13. ¿No los quiere usar? / ¿No quiere usarlos? 14. Él nos está atacando./Él está atacándonos. 15. ¡Bébelo! 16. No la he visto hoy. 17. ¿Tenemos que guiarlos? / ¿Tenemos que guiarles? / ¿Los tenemos que guiar? / ¿Les tenemos que guiar? 18. ¿Las están leyendo? / ¿Están leyéndolas? 19. Él no lo quiere escribir./Él no quiere escribirlo. 20. ¡No me molestes!

14.9 (§14.10) (Note: The **lo** (**le**) options represent **leísmo** usage.) 1. No vemos a Alejandro./A Alejandro no lo (le) vemos. 2. No conocen a nuestro alcalde./A nuestro alcalde no lo (le) conocen. 3. ¿No vas a traer a tu madre? / ¿A tu madre no la vas a traer? 4. ¿No conocen ellos (ellas) a tu/su/vuestro padre? / ¿A tu/su/vuestro padre no lo (le) conocen ellos (ellas)? 5. No veo a Norma./A Norma no la veo. 6. ¿No hemos conocido a su esposa? / ¿A su esposa no la hemos conocido?

14.10 (§14.7, 14.11) 1. me (IO), the book (DO) 2. everything (DO), to us (IO) 3. him (IO), some cigarettes (DO) 4. some new plans (DO), to them (IO) 5. my mother (IO), some candy (DO) 6. you (IO), a couple of dollars (DO) 7. her (IO), Portuguese (DO) 8. a new approach (DO), to the employees (IO) 9. them (IO), a very long letter (DO) 10. your friend (DO), to me (IO)

14.11 (§14.11) 1. ¡Tráeme la taza! 2. Él nos va a dar el dinero./Él va a darnos el dinero. 3. ¡No les preste Ud. su auto (carro)! 4. Él nos va a ofrecer un soborno./Él va a ofrecernos un soborno. 5. Me debes mucho dinero (mucha plata). 6. Él les pagó cinco dólares por el abrigo. 7. Léenos el cuento. 8. Poco a poco él les está vendiendo todos sus libros./Poco a poco él está vendiéndoles todos sus libros. 9. No le muestre a ella esos papeles. 10. Él nos tiene que enseñar inglés./Él tiene que enseñarnos inglés.

11. Les escribí una carta larga. 12. Explícale a él la lección. 13. Él me estaba hablando de su madre./Él estaba hablándome de su madre. 14. No nos devuelva esa copia. 15. Les preferimos enseñar estos artículos./Preferimos enseñarles estos artículos. 16. ¿Cuándo me va él a decir donde vive? / ¿Cuándo va él a decirme donde vive? 17. El profesor les está enseñando swahili ahora./El profesor está enseñándoles swahili ahora. 18. ¡No nos envíe pesos; envíenos dólares! 19. ¡Préstame el dinero o no me vuelvas a hablar más! / ¡Préstame el dinero o no vuelvas a hablarme más! 20. Les voy a sugerir algo interesante./Voy a sugerirles algo interesante.

14.12 (§14.12) 1. Creo que él le está escribiendo una carta a su novia. 2. Él siempre les ofrece tequila a sus amigos. 3. ¡No le des a Henry tanto dinero (tanta plata)! 4. A Berta él le va a explicar el incidente./Él va a explicarle a Berta el incidente. 5. Les mostraron este libro a sus colegas. 6. Tengo que enseñarles lenguas extranjeras a mis estudiantes.

14.13 (§14.13) 1. Él no me lo contó. (el chiste) / Él no me la contó. (la broma/chanza) 2. Ella quiere traérmelos./Ella me los quiere traer. 3. Él se las está explicando a ella./Él está explicándoselas a ella. 4. ¡No se lo traiga(s) a ella! 5. Dáselas a él. 6. Él no me lo ofreció. 7. Ella se lo va a leer a ellos(-as) (el cuento) / Ella va a leérsela a ellos(-as) (la historia). 8. Se lo enseñaron a ella. 9. ¿Quién te las vendió? 10. ¡No se lo preste(s) a él! 11. Envíeselo Vd. a ella. 12. Me las devolvieron.

14.14 (§14.14) 1. She is reading us a story./She is reading a story to us. 2. Don't you want to return the book to me? (Structure [b] with verb restriction 'return') 3. Susan will give it to you when she sees you. 4. I lent it to him/her/you/them last year. 5. Ephrem never introduced her to us. 6. I am not going to suggest any new plan to you. 7. When can I teach you French? / When can I teach French to you? 8. I can't explain it to them. 9. Marianne showed me her recently painted house./Marianne showed her newly painted house to me. 10. They never sent it to you. 11. Tell us the rest of the story./Tell the rest of the story to us. 12. Don't throw that ball to me./Don't throw me that ball. 13 Julio still hasn't written it down for him/her/you/them. 14. Who sent you that lovely diamond?/ Who sent that lovely diamond to you?

15

REFLEXIVE AND RECIPROCAL ACTIONS

15.1 (§15.1–2) 1. Acostumbramos a acostarnos a las once./Nos acostumbramos a acostar a las once. 2. ¿Cuándo quieren levantarse? / ¿Cuándo se quieren levantar? 3. Vamos a despertarnos bien temprano./Nos vamos a despertar bien temprano. 4. ¿Qué hicieron ellos(-as) mismos(-as) para evitar problemas? 5.

Probablemente ella se sentará aquí conmigo.   6. Nos sentimos muy contentos ayer. 7. El guía mismo no conocía el camino.   8. ¡No te enojes!   9. Mi madre se está cansando./Mi madre está cansándose.   10. ¡No se acerque usted a ese perro!

11. Nos levantamos a las ocho y nos vestimos.   12. El alcalde mismo se unió al mitin.   13. Se durmieron en la sala.   14. Ella no se ha despertado todavía.   15. Katherine, ¡siéntate y cállate!   16. No podían tranquilizarse después del accidente./ No se pudieron tranquilizar después del accidente.   17. Usted mismo(-a) lo dijo así. 18. No quiero enfermarme en Paraguay./No me quiero enfermar en Paraguay.   19. Sé que él va a aburrirse con esa clase./Sé que él se va a aburrir con esa clase.   20. Si no te sientes bien, acuéstate temprano.

15.2 (§15.2–3)   1. ¿Cuándo se callarán los niños? reflexive   2. We don't go to bed very early in the summer. transitive   3. Nos enojamos porque ella no nos escribió. reflex. DO & transitive   4. He broke his leg jumping from the balcony. trans.   5. Ellos nos agasajaron en Madrid. trans.   6. Frederick didn't want to take advantage of the explanation. trans.   7. ¡Ese hombre me enferma! trans.   8. Josefa waited for them with her family. trans.   9. No van a levantarse hasta más tarde. reflex., DO   10. When did your brother get married? trans.   11. Mañana voy a afeitarme la barba. reflex. IO   12. We put our hats on and left. trans. & intrans. 13. ¿No vas a lavarte las manos? reflex. IO   14. Do you want it to spoil your appetite? trans. & trans. (Do you want to lose your appetite?), trans. & trans.   15. María no pudo tranquilizarlos después del accidente. trans.

15.3 (No key)

15.4 (§15.2–4)   1. No puedo estudiar porque alguien se llevó mis libros. (non-reflexive, reflexive)   2. Él no puede decidirse si puede hacerlo o no. (reflexive, non-reflexive)   3. Los niños se durmieron en la sala. (reflexive)   4. Durmieron allí toda la noche. (non-reflexive)   5. ¿Cuándo te marchas? / ¿Cuándo se marcha? / ¿Cuándo os marcháis? (reflexive)   6. Él se parece a su padre. (reflexive)   7. No quiero comerme ese emparedado. (reflexive)   8. No pongas tus pies sobre la mesa. (non-reflexive)   9. Cuando comencé a cantar, todos se durmieron. (non-reflexive, reflexive)   10. Parecía estar enfermo antes de caerse. (non-reflexive, reflexive)

15.5 (§15.5)   1. Él se jactó de su reunión con el presidente.   2. Esos fanáticos creen que todo el mundo debe arrepentirse.   3. No nos atrevemos a hablarle a él de esa manera.   4. Los estudiantes se han sublevado (se sublevaron) y habrá una huelga.   5. El general se suicidó después de la batalla.

15.6 (§15.6)   1. Nos saludamos antes del concurso.   2. The newlyweds love one another (each other) very much.   3. No nos vimos en Panamá.   4. They kissed (each other) before saying goodbye.   5. Se odiaban tanto que trataron de matarse el uno al otro.   6. The dogs began barking when they saw each other.

16
SENTENCES WITH INDEFINITE SUBJECTS

16.1 (§16.1–3)   1. Se puede ver mi casa desde/de aquí./Uno (Usted) puede ver mi casa desde/de aquí.   2. All their anguish (suffering) ended.   3. Se me escaparon los niños.   4. Suddenly the battle stopped (ceased).   5. En mi casa no se hace eso./Uno (Usted) no hace eso en mi casa. 6. When did your umbrella break? 7. Anoche se me ocurrió una idea fantástica. 8. Our grandfather died (on us) later that same year. 9. Se organizó la clase muy temprano. 10. One doesn't learn anything in this school./You don't learn anything in this school. 11. Se le olvidó a él comprar la gaseoso. 12. All the lights went out after the catastrophe. 13. Se tiene que pensar en el dinero hoy en día./Uno (Usted) tiene que pensar en el dinero hoy en día. 14. The things we had bought got broken. 15. No se puede concentrar con tanto ruido./Uno (Usted) no puede concentrar con tanto ruido. 16. From inside one/you could hear the noise. 17. Las persianas se abrían (se abrieron) y las puertas se cerraban (se cerraron) con el viento. 18. The corporal escaped from the soldiers. 19. En Málaga no se debe tomar el agua./Uno (Usted) no debe tomar el agua en (de) Málaga. 20. One/You shouldn't smoke during the performance.

16.2 (§16.4–6) 1. Hay un hombre en mi habitación (recámara). 2. Is there (Will there be) a cultural event in the historical zone? 3. ¿No había naranjas en la tienda? 4. There must be a demon inside the poor man. 5. Ha habido un terrible accidente. 6. Where could there be so many republicans? 7. Había varios documentos sobre la mesa. 8. There are several disciples (followers) of the Christian reform. 9. ¿Habrá una guerra? 10. Shouldn't there be some physicists in the laboratory? 11. ¿Cuándo hubo una huelga en la fábrica? 12. Has there been any significant event happening? 13. ¿Habrá un pájaro en esa jaula? 14. There are thousands of conscientious soldiers in the army.

17
ENGLISH AND SPANISH CONTRACTIONS

17.1 (§17.2–3) 1. We're not at home now [l]. We aren't at home now [3]. 2. They've not been traveling much [l]. They haven't been traveling much [3]. 3. You'd not say a thing like that [l]. You wouldn't say a thing like that [3]. 4. Marianne didn't come home last night [3]. 5. Your father's not been feeling well [2]. Your father hasn't been feeling well [3]. 6. Frederick's trying to do much better work [2]. 7. Who's not studying chemistry this year? [2], Who isn't studying chemistry this year? [3] 8. They'll unlock the door soon [l]. 9. I'll not be at home when you arrive [l]. I won't be at home when you arrive [3]. 10. He'll buy it if it's not too expensive [1 & 1]. He'll buy it if it isn't too expensive [1 & 3]. (Since this is a complex sentence, two contractions are possible.) 11. She'd bought that in Peru [l]. 12. Your brother didn't see us [3]. 13. Our sister's not arrived yet [2]. Our sister hasn't arrived yet [3]. 14. What's he going to say to us? [2], 15. Where'll I be able to find you? [2], 16. You shouldn't go out with her [3]. 17. He couldn't open it with her key [3]. 18. You'd have a good time in Yucatan [l]. 19. Your mother's here now [2]. 20. That's not whom I wish to see right now [l]. That isn't who(m) I wish to see right now [3].

PART THREE KEY
VERB PHRASE COMPLEMENTATION

18
ADVERBS AND PREPOSITIONS

18.1 (§18.1–3) 1. Además de manzanas, él desea (quiere) comprar naranjas. (periphrastic prep. construction vs simple prep. in English) 2. The interested party is nervous because he does not want to be outside. (adverb construction in both languages) 3. Antes de la ópera fuimos a un pequeño café. (periphrastic prep. construction vs simple prep. in English) 4. Reuben stayed behind, but Alexandra went ahead. (adverb construction in both languages) 5. Creo que él trabajaba cerca de esa máquina. (periphrastic prep. construction vs simple prep. in English) 6. We didn't believe that anyone was inside. (adverb construction in both languages) 7. Después del baile ella se fue a casa con un(a) amigo(-a). (periphrastic prep. construction vs simple prep. in English, plus a simple prep. phrase in both languages at the end) 8. My friends are downstairs with my grandparents. (adverb construction in both languages) 9. Yo no podía verlo porque él estaba detrás del auto/carro. (periphrastic prep. construction vs simple prep. in English) 10. Do you (Does one) put the material (matter *chem.*) above or below the surface? (simple prep. vs periphrastic prep. constr. in Span.)

18.2 (§18.4–5) 1. greatly (grandly) 2. especialmente 3. probably 4. felizmente (alegremente) 5. affectionately (kindly) 6. fácilmente 7. coldly 8. con tristeza/tristemente 9. gracefully 10. bellamente (hermosamente) 11. only 12. claramente 13. passionately 14. rápidamente 15. carelessly.

18.3 (§18.6–10) 1. Have you ever been to the Côte d'Azur? 2. The Tagus River is found in the Iberian Peninsula. 3. Your keys are in my pocket. 4. I believe I met you at (in) another identical affair (activity). 5. What does Daniel have in his left hand? 6. We were in the movie theater (at the movies) when something mysterious happened. 7. The dog sat (down) in the corner. 8. Not a single cloud was seen in the endless sky. 9. My friends have never been in (to) San Juan. 10. The gentleman on the airplane is Professor Santana.

11. I sat down in the chair that was on the balcony. 12. The Second World War started in 1939 and ended in 1945. 13. My father teaches English at the University of Salamanca. 14. Have you ever been to (in) the town where I was born? 15. The President was in an automobile when he was assassinated. 16. Sandra was on the bus when the old man spoke to her. 17. There are many pages in this unit. 18. Paquito, what do you have in your mouth? 19. My car isn't in the garage nor on the street but at the train station. 20. They wanted to come in October, but they arrived on November 2.

18.4 (§18.11) **in:** de (con) prisa; en todo (total); en un momento/dentro de un rato; en detalle/con detalles; de todas maneras/en todos los aspectos; de hecho; a favor de; delante de (al frente)/detrás de (tras); en general; de muchas maneras; en mente; en seguida/de inmediato/sin demora; a fin de/para; en (por) la tarde; al (en el) principio; al final; en (por) la tarde/al atardecer; en caso de (que); en el futuro; mientras tanto; en (por) el medio/en medio de; en (por) la mañana; en este/ese caso; a tiempo de/para; en comunicación/en contacto.

at: del todo/en absoluto/siquiera algo; de todos modos/de todas formas; en el mejor de los casos, cuando mejor/en el peor de los casos, a lo peor; al principio, en un principio; por fin; por lo menos; de noche/en (por) la noche; en seguida/de inmediato; ahora/actualmente/en el presente/al presente; al principio de; al final de; en (por) el momento/por ahora; al lado de; en este/ese (aquel) momento.

on: por motivo de/debido a/por causa de; en llamas; a propósito/adrede; pensándolo bien; en varias ocasiones; de lo contrario/al (por el) contrario; a la izquierda/a la derecha; por (de) otra parte/por otro lado; en general/considerándolo todo/tomando en cuenta todo; a tiempo.

18.5 (§18.12) 1. Mis amigos tienen que trabajar por (en) la tarde. 2. Julio llegó a las nueve de la mañana. 3. ¿Haces algo por (en) las noches? 4. ¿Qué podría estar haciendo ella a las cinco de la mañana? 5. Tengo clases por las noches pero no por las tardes.

18.6 (§18.13) 1. La muchacha del traje azul es mi hermana. 2. Su camisa estaba toda cubierta de grasa. 3. El hombre llegó con un perro grande. 4. El hombre del perro es amigo mío. 5. Esos muchachos de los cabellos largos fuman marihuana (mariguana/marijuana). 6. Él vino con la cerveza y le habló al hombre del sombrero. 7. La cara de él estaba cubierta de vendajes. 8. Mis estudiantes llegaron con sus libros. 9. Ahora está cubierto con una sábana. 10. El carro (automóvil) de las llantas nuevas (los neumáticos nuevos) es mío.

18.7 (§18.14) 1. Deseo conocer a la muchacha que tiene el carro (automóvil) nuevo. 2. La gente que está en la biblioteca no habla español. 3. El libro que está sobre la mesa trata de vinos chilenos. 4. No nos gusta la casa que tiene la puerta azul. 5. Ese perro que está en tu casa sí que ladra mucho. 6. Las tiendas que se encuentran en los pueblitos son pequeñas. 7. Conocimos a una señora que tiene el esposo enfermo. 8. Las casas que están en mi calle son muy costosas. 9. ¡Mira! La muchacha que está en la ventana está llorando. 10. Los muchachos que tienen la colección de monedas viven en ese edificio.

18.8 (§18.15) 1. Hablamos con mi madre y con mi tía. 2. Sé todo lo de tu hermano y lo de tu sobrino. 3. Pasaron a recoger (buscar) a mi padre y a mi madre. 4. Mi padre trabaja con el doctor (la doctora) Smith y con el doctor (la doctora) Martin. 5. No puedes irte sin el sombrero y sin el abrigo.

19
THE SPANISH PERSONAL ACCUSATIVE

19.1 (§19.1–3) 1. No queremos ver ahora a tus amigos. 2. Creo que Juan mató a alguien anoche. 3. Quieren tener, por lo menos, tres hijos. 4. Conozco al doctor Johnson, pero no conozco a su esposa. 5. No vimos a nadie en la calle. 6. ¿A quién vas a traer a mi fiesta? 7. Tienen parientes (familia) en Panamá. 8. Veo a algunos de ellos, pero no veo sus autos (carros). 9. ¿Quién te acompañaba cuando conociste al embajador? 10. ¿Alguien le dijo algo al doctor Smith? 11. Quieren saber a quién (quiénes) vimos en la clase. 12. Mis amigos no conocen a nadie en México. 13. Pensamos conocer a mucha gente durante nuestro viaje. 14. ¿A quién (quiénes) llevaron al aeropuerto? 15. Juan trajo su perrito a la clase ayer. (No **a** since it is not a named pet.)

20
THE SPANISH SUBJUNCTIVE

20.1 (§20.1–4) 1. mientras cita a la autoridad, adverbial clause 2. que el instrumento está arriba, noun clause 3. que está situada en el barrio, adjective clause 4. para que puedas descansar un rato, adverbial clause 5. que su reacción fue violenta, noun clause 6. que responda a mis necesidades, adjective clause 7. hasta que me desperté, adverbial clause 8. que haya adivinado su suerte, adjective clause 9. que la ley de aquí no requiera un castigo fuerte, noun clause 10. que registremos la propiedad completa, noun clause 11. cuando cambies ese temperamento, adverbial clause 12. que vimos en el puerto ayer, adjective clause.

20.2 (§20.7) (1) Te aconsejo que te vayas inmediatamente. No dejan que yo hable ahora. Te pido que te esfuerces un poco más. Ella nos rogó que le ayudáramos esa noche fatídica. Mandaron que disparáramos. Te prohíbo que veas a ese muchacho. No me gusta que fumes en la casa. Ayer los necesitamos para que nos cargaban la compra (de comistibles). Ella no nos permite que trabajemos aquí. Les dijeron que se fueran del pueblo. Queremos que tengas éxito.

(2) Él hizo que yo trajera varios ejemplos. No dejan que veamos los cachorros (perritos). Ella hizo que nos quedáramos en la clase una hora adicional.

(3) Él nos pidió que nos esforzáramos más. No me gusta que bebas tanto. Preferimos que ellos se queden aquí. Ella les dijo que se fueran inmediatamente. Es aconsejable que no se vayan ellos tan pronto. Es importante que llegues al trabajo a tiempo. Es necesario que hagan ellos todos los ejercicios del libro. Era preferible que nos fuéramos en tren en vez de en autobús.

(4) Él me impidió que saliera a tiempo.

(5) Te prohíbo que fumes en la casa. No les gusta que yo trabaje de noche. Nos oponemos a que usted llegue a ser gobernador. Impidieron que él dijera algo. Recomendaron que viéramos a un buen abogado.

(6) Aprobaron que nos casáramos. Ella se opuso a que él se fuera. Insisto en que me lo digas.

(7) Le pido a él que busque el tiempo para hacerlo. Él mandó que ella abriera la puerta. Él exigió que ella abriera la puerta. Insisten en que él trabaje para ganar su sustento. Prefiero que no estés aquí tan temprano. Proponemos que lo contraten a él ahora. Recomiendan que ella decida inmediatamente. Le sugerimos a él que estudiara el problema con más cuidado. Es aconsejable que ellos no estén aquí cuando él llegue. Es importante que él vea al profesor ahora mismo. Es necesario que ella cuide de los niños hoy. Es preferible que yo esté con mis padres.

20.3 (§20.5–7)

Formula 1	S + V + DO + **to**-INF
Formula 2	S + V + DO + LV
Formula 3	S + V + **for** + IO + **to**-INF
Formula 4	S + V + DO + **from** + LV-**ing**

Formula 5   S + V + POSS ADJ + LV-**ing**
Formula 6   S + V + PREP + POSS ADJ + LV-**ing**
Formula 7 S_1 + V_1 + **that** + S_2 + V_2[SUBJUNCTIVE]

1. They advised us not to climb down from the mountain. (formula 1)/They recommended our not climbing down from the mountain. (formula 5) 2. Les prohibimos que coman en ese restaurante. (all Spanish answers have the formula $(S)_1$ + V_1[INDICATIVE] + que + $(S)_2$ + V_2[SUBJ]) 3. They won't allow him to start the protest. (formula 1) 4. Querían que trajéramos (trajésemos) la comida para la fiesta. (same as 2) 5. It is important for her to examine her conscience before acting. (formula 3)/It's important that she examine her conscience before acting. (formula 7) 6. Lo obligaron a que trabajara con los presos (confinados) 7. It is preferable for him not to refer to the comment. (formula 3)/It is preferable that he not refer to the comment. (formula 7) 8. Necesitamos que nos ayude(s) con este proyecto. 9. My parents insist on my brother's studying medicine. (formula 6)/My parents insist that my brother study medicine. (formula 7) 10. Impidieron que viéramos a nuestros parientes. 11. He/She doesn't like for us to shoot dice on Sundays. (formula 3)/ He/She doesn't like us to shoot dice on Sundays. (formula 1) 12. Nos prohíben que les hablemos español a los niños. 13. They made us pay the debt without our having sufficient funds. (formula 2) 14. Mi padre se opuso a que yo estudiara en el extranjero. 15. The president insists on our all trying to demonstrate (show) our ability. (formula 6) /The president insists that we all try to show (demonstrate) our ability (formula 7) 16. Mis padres no aprueban que me case este año./Mis padres no están de acuerdo con que me case este año. 17. The general prevented the soldiers from attacking immediately. (formula 4) 18. Ella insiste en que lleguemos (estemos) a tiempo para la clase. 19. They ask that he sign the authentic manuscript. (formula 7) /They asked for him to sign the authentic manuscript. (formula 3) 20. Les aconsejé que no trabajaran allí de (por la) noche. 21. My grandmother preferred for her children to speak to her in German. (formula 3) /My grandmother preferred that her children speak to her in German. (formula 7) 22. Ella propone que estudiemos los problemas económicos de América Central. 23. They wanted us to pass through the village before the snow fell/before it snowed. (formula 1) 24. Sugerimos que le escriban una carta al presidente.

20.4 (§20.10–12) 1. No creemos que él haya llegado todavía. (doubt) 2. Creo que ella tiene mis llaves. (noun clause, satisfies condition [1] for different subjects but not [2] verbs of suasion, doubt/denial, or strong emotion) 3. Él quería que yo trajera a mis amistades (amigos). (suasion) 4. Insisten en que estemos aquí temprano. (suasion) 5. Tal vez tu padre haya conocido al hombre en Sudamérica (América del Sur). (doubt) 6. Sé que él vive cerca de la universidad. (noun clause, but not verb of doubt) 7. Él sintió que no hubieran visto la película. (strong emotion) 8. Creemos que entienden todas las preguntas. (noun clause, but not verb of doubt) 9. Él va a hacer que leamos un libro grande (extenso) en inglés. (suasion) 10. Nuestros padres no permitieron nunca que fumáramos en casa. (suasion) / Nuestros padres no nos permitieron nunca fumar en la casa. (**permitir** allows the use of an infinitive instead of the subjunctive §20.6).

11. Dile (Dígale) a él que ha llegado su familia. (noun clause, but not verb of suasion, etc.) 12. Ella me dijo que abriera la puerta. (suasion) 13. Me parece que el niño está muy enfermo. (noun clause, but not verb of doubt) 14. Parecía mentira que él dijera algo como eso. (strong emotion) 15. Mi madre me aconsejó que estudiara latín en la escuela. (suasion) 16. Es una lástima que no hayas podido

trabajar. (strong emotion) 17. Él negó que sus hijos hubieran robado el dinero. (denial) 18. Dijeron que había(s) comprado un auto (carro) nuevo. (noun clause, but not verb of suasion, etc.) 19. Esperábamos que nos dijera(s) la verdad. (strong emotion) 20. Me opongo a que vayas a la fiesta con ellos. (suasion).

20.5 (§20.13–14) 1. Busco al hombre que escribió este libro. (antecedent is not indefinite) 2. Él buscaba una casa que fuera cómoda. (antecedent is yet to be found) 3. Debe(s) hacer lo que él le (te) diga. (antecedent **lo** as yet unknown) 4. Debe(s) hacer lo que él le(te) dice. (antecedent **lo** is known) 5. Hay alguien en el hotel que sabe hablar inglés. (antecedent is known) 6. No había nadie en el hotel que supiera hablar inglés. (antecedent is negated) 7. ¿Hay alguien en el hotel que sepa hablar inglés? (antecedent is yet to be found) 8. Conocí a un hombre que pudo beber mucho vino. (antecedent known) 9. Mis padres no podían creer lo que oyeron. (antecedent **lo** is known) 10. Sé que no voy a creer lo que oiga. (antecedent **lo** has not been heard yet)

11. No conozco a nadie que pueda beber tanto. (antecedent is negated) 12. Quieren comprar un auto (carro) que corra bien. (antecedent is yet to be bought) 13. El año pasado compramos un auto (carro) que no corría bien. (antecedent is known) 14. ¿Viste a la dama que vendió este vestido? (antecedent is known) 15. Necesito ver a una dama que venda vestidos. (antecedent not yet unknown) 16. ¿Quiere(s) ver a la dama que vende vestidos? (antecedent is known) 17. Tenían un perro que ladraba mucho. (antecedent known) 18. Quieren comprar un perro que ladre mucho. (antecedent is yet to be found) 19. No querían comprar un perro que ladrara mucho. (antecedent is negated) 20. Él quería conocer a una muchacha que tuviera mucho encanto. (antecedent as yet unknown)

20.6 (§20.15–21) 1. Se fue (Salió) antes de que pudiéramos hablar con él. (mandatory §20.15) 2. Trabajaron fuerte hasta que terminaron el trabajo. (no future reference) 3. ¿Piensa(s) trabajar hasta que termine(s) el trabajo? (future reference) 4. La familia de él gastó mucho dinero para que pudiera llegar a ser médico. (future reference) 5. No íbamos a verlos a menos que no vinieran (llegaran) a tiempo. (mandatory) 6. ¿Qué dijiste cuando lo viste? (no future reference) 7. ¿Qué vas a decir cuando lo veas? (future reference) 8. Él leía un libro mientras ella lavaba ropa. (no future reference) 9. Ella dijo que traería a su marido (esposo) con tal de que usted trajera al suyo. (mandatory)

10. El caballo siempre se fuga sin que nadie lo vea. (mandatory) 11. Él bebía (acostumbraba beber) sin que su amiga lo supiera. (mandatory) 12. ¿Qué vas a estudiar antes (de) que vayamos a clase? (mandatory) 13. Aunque su esposa no lo sepa, él tiene una novia. (concessive unsure truth) 14. Por favor, explícamelo según él te lo explicó. (idea already expressed) 15. Aunque él llegó tarde, fuimos todos a la fiesta. (concessive truth) 16. Yo iba a escribirlo según él lo quisiera. (projected for future time) 17. Voy a leer ese libro en cuanto (tan pronto como) yo lo compre. (projected for future time) 18. Ella fue de compras en cuanto (tan pronto como) recibió su salario. (routine occurrence)

21

SPANISH AND ENGLISH VERB + RELATOR CONSTRUCTIONS

21.1 (§21.1–2) 1. We will specify clearly again (We will specify again with clarity) the procedure to be followed. 2. Él nunca se acostumbró a comer tan tarde. 3. They came up to tell us that our flight had arrived. 4. Él aprendió a bailar la samba en Río de Janeiro. 5. Her body started to tremble from (with) fear. 6. Él no se atreverá a dejar a su esposa allí. 7. The genius managed to ignore the existence of pleasure. 8. Comenzaron a estudiar ruso el verano pasado. 9. They are going to give an exact description of the sorrowful scene. 10. Mi padre me enseñó a hacer vino.

21.2 (§21.3–5) 1. Hay que/Uno tiene que verlo para creerlo. 2. They have just separated (broken up) with dignity. 3. Él tuvo que trabajar anoche. 4. They were happy to receive the admiration of the faithful. 5. Quedaron en enviarnos los documentos. 6. They stopped teasing (annoying/bothering) me; consequently, I'm friendly with them. 7. Ella se olvidó de traer sus libros. 8. We will try to put (place) limits on all vulgar actions (any/every vulgar action).

21.3 (§21.6–10) 1. Me fijé en la expresión de ansiedad de él. 2. They approached the circle with curiosity. 3. Entramos a la clase para hablar con el profesor. 4. Last year I attended class with various preoccupations (worries). 5. Se casó con una mexicana (mejicana) y luego salieron del país. 6. I devote myself to the arts (I dedicate myself to artistic pursuits) because I enjoy their diversity. 7. Los izquierdistas se unieron al partido comunista. 8. You/He/She forgot about your/his/her pleasant childhood memories. 9. De pronto me acordé del nombre del amigo de él. 10. I didn't notice at all the constant echo produced by the wind/that the wind caused.

21.4 (§21.11) 1. We looked for the study (treatise) by a contemporary philosopher which was cited. 2. Él pagó por el carro con un cheque personal. 3. I asked them for consideration but they denied it to me. 4. Esperaban el verano con gran expectación (anticipación). 5. I listened to the version of the holy birth, but I did not understand anything. 6. Él siempre pide ayuda con sus tareas escolares. 7. I have to wait for the supposed departure. 8. Ella siempre escucha ese programa ridículo. 9. I couldn't pay for the ticket to the performance. 10. Buscamos un buen departamento (apartamento/piso) en esta calle.

21.5 (§21.12) 1. Sé que podemos contar con ellos. 2. Last night I dreamed about a golden haired angel (an angel whose hair was golden). 3. Él lo cubrió de miel y luego se lo comió. 4. I don't like for people to comment about me behind my back. 5. En California todo depende de las lluvias. 6. That character (clown/fool) doesn't complain about anything. 7. Nos despedimos de nuestros amigos la semana pasada. 8. I am concerned about a better education for everyone. 9. Él se enamoró de una secretaria. 10. You forgot about the fact that any project needs a fundamental basis.

21.6 (§21.1–12) 1. ¿Donde aprendiste a hablar español? (between conjugated verb and a dependent verb form, relator used in Spanish only) 2. They succeeded in entering space for the seventh time. (between conjugated verb and a dependent verb form, relator used in English only) 3. Él se acercó al pájaro sin hacer ruido. (between verb and complement, Spanish only) 4. They are looking at the crystal clear water under the bridge. (between verb and complement, both languages) 5. Sé que no puedo contar con ella. (between verb and complement, both languages) 6. Day before yesterday I was invited to attend the last double header game. (no relator in English, Spanish uses one between conjugated verb and dependent verb form and between verb and complement) 7. No tiene(s)(n)/tenéis que hacer nada para esa clase. (between conjugated verb and a dependent verb, in Spanish) 8. They were waiting for the beginning of the prologue. (between verb and complement, English only) 9. Los estudiantes siempre se quejan de los exámenes. (between verb and complement, both languages) 10. She tried to rid herself of (get rid of) all sin, but she couldn't do it. (between conjugated verb and a dependent verb form in Spanish only, between verb and complement in both languages) 11. Él salió de Uruguay hace muchos años. (between verb and complement, Spanish only) 12. What are you going to ask for this year? (between conjugated verb and dependent verb form in Spanish, between verb and complement in English) 13. Quedaron en venir mañana a las ocho. (between conjugated verb and a dependent verb form, Spanish only) 14. One/You must think about a brief preparation before continuing. (between verb and complement, both languages) 15. No nos dimos cuenta del peligro. (between verbal unit and complement, Spanish only) 16. They said good-bye to the recently established dictatorship. (between verbal unit and complement, both languages) 17. El niñito se rió de su perrito. (between verb and complement, both languages) 18. They went (came) down to see the brave men who had just returned. (between conjugated verb and dependent verb form, Spanish only) 19. No ha dejado de nevar todavía. (between conjugated verb and dependent verb form, Spanish only) 20. We are supposed to attend a demonstration by the people day after tomorrow. (between conjugated verb and dependent verb form and between verb and complement, both used in Spanish only) 21. Escuchan mis discos nuevos. (between verb and complement, English only) 22. Adolf didn't dare force them to be quiet. (between conjugated verb and dependent verb form and verb and complement, Spanish only) 23. Vinieron a contarme algo triste. (between conjugated verb and dependent verb form, Spanish only) 24. American football isn't played much in South America./They don't play much American football in South America. (between verb and complement, Spanish only)

22
SPANISH AND ENGLISH CONDITIONAL SENTENCES AND UNREAL COMPARISON

22.1 (§22.2) 1. Si le diste/dio/distéis el dinero a él, lo perdió. (past) 2. If Josephine comes tomorrow, nobody will know it. (future) 3. Si él tiene un auto (carro) nuevo, lo quiero ver. (present) 4. If José gave her a present, she liked it a lot (very much). (past) 5. Aun teniendo un reloj/Aun cuando tiene un reloj, él nunca sabe la hora. (present) 6. If you write so lightly, no one (nobody) will be able to read it. (future) 7. Si él no iba a clase, el profesor siempre lo supo. (past) 8. If you didn't see the crown, it was because it wasn't in the museum. (past) 9. Si traes tus libros, traduciremos la historia (el cuento). (future) 10. If it is convenient for you, we can stay seated. (present)

22.2 (§22.3) 1. Si yo fuera/-se tú, no diría eso. (present) 2. If by chance (perchance) you saw Victoria,/If by chance (perchance) you were to see Victoria,/ Were you perchance to see Victoria,/If you should see Victoria by chance,/Should you see Victoria perchance, she wouldn't tell you anything (she wouldn't say anything to you). (future) 3. Si Ud. le hubiera/-se dado el dinero, él lo habría/ hubiera gastado todo. (past) 4. If you had as much self-control/Had you as much self-control as I have, you would be much calmer. (present) 5. Si trajeras/-ses un libro, te leería un cuento. (future) 6. If your friends had come directly/Had your friends come directly, they wouldn't have lost their way. (past) 7. Si no amaras (amases) a tu madre, no le mandarías flores. (present) 8. You would become ill (get sick) very soon if you drank/if you were to drink/were you to drink/if you should drink/should you drink that grade of wine. (patterned as 2, future) 9. No habría tantos impuestos, si lo eligieran/-sen presidente. (future) 10. If a bolt of lightning struck us/If a bolt of lightning were to strike us/Were a bolt of lightning to strike us/etc. (patterned as 2 & 8), we wouldn't be alive. (future) 11. Me habrían/ hubieran ayudado si hubieran/-sen sido mis amigos. (past) 12. Nobody would have found you out if you had (had you) kept quiet. (past)

13. Si encontrara/-se al presidente mañana ¿qué le diría Ud.? (future) 14. If it were (Were it) a real stone, how much would it cost? (present) 15. Sabríamos la hora si tuviéramos/tuviésemos un reloj. (present) 16. If I were you (?Were I you), I wouldn't pay the difference. (present) 17. Él me habría/hubiera dicho su nombre si se lo hubiera/-se preguntado. (past) 18. You would have to buy a new dress (suit) if you wanted to go out with me/if you were to go out with me/etc. (patterned as 2 & 8, future) 19. ¿Lo conocerías si él entrara/-se en la sala ahora mismo? (future) 20. You wouldn't have said anything if you had (had you) really been under my influence. (past) 21. Si Ud. saliera/-se temprano mañana, estaría en León para el mediodía. (future) 22. If you went out with that gorgeous girl/If you were to go out with that gorgeous girl/etc (patterned as 2 & 8), her boyfriend would know about it in a minute. (future) 23. ¿Qué harían, si hubiera/-se otra guerra civil en El Salvador? (future) 24. Where would you be now if you were (were you) as indifferent as your brother is? (present)

22.3 (§22.6) 1. You speak English as if you had studied it for many years. (past) 2. Él fuma como si nada más fuera/-se importante. (present) 3. The child ate the fruit as if she were very hungry. (past) 4. Bebes (Tomas) el café como si no te gustara/-se mucho. (present) 5. They ran as if the devil himself were chasing them. (past) 6. Él explicó todo como si ya hubiera/-se estudiado la lección. (past) 7. Norbert spoke without expression, as if he were in a trance. (past) 8. El bebé llora como si lo hubieras/-ses castigado. (present) 9. The old man spoke very slowly as if he were suffering intense pain. (past) 10. Él escucha como si le interesara/-se lo que decimos. (present)

23
EXPRESSIONS OF COMPARISON

23.1 (§23.1–4)

COMPARATIVE	SUPERLATIVE
1. más/menos inteligente	el/la más inteligente
2. más/menos agudo/-a	el/la más agudo/-a
3. más/menos enfermo/-a	el/la más enfermo/-a
4. más/menos lento/-a	el/la más lento/-a
5. mejor, peor	el/la mejor
6. más/menos alto/-a	el/la más alto/-a
7. más/menos débil	el/la más débil
8. más/menos valiente	el/la más valiente
9. menor (*or* más/menos joven)	el/la menor (*or* el/la más joven)
10. mayor (*or* más/menos viejo/-a)	el/la mayor (*or* el/la más viejo/-a)

COMPARATIVE	SUPERLATIVE
1. more wonderful	the most wonderful
2. callower	the callowest
3. more expensive	the most expensive
4. filthier	the filthiest
5. more careful	the most careful
6. louder	the loudest
7. worse	the worst
8. simpler	the simplest
9. sunnier	the sunniest
10. clearer	the clearest

23.2 (§23.5) 1. Él tiene más clases que yo.   2. The figure has more angles than it should have. 3. Necesitamos menos gasolina que ellos. 4. Amelia is taller than her sister. 5. Tejas es más pobre de lo que crees. 6. Is your father older than your mother? 7. Él trajo más comida de la que ellos podían comer. 8. I have more practice than you (have). 9. Gastaron más dinero del que podíamos creer. 10. She is more admirable than the rest of the people in the group.

11. Ella es más inteligente de lo que ella cree. 12. I smoke more cigarettes than I should. 13. Necesitamos más azúcar de la que podemos comprar. 14. They speak Spanish better than we do. 15. Él habló peor de lo que cualquiera hubiera/-se imaginado. 16. She earned more money than she could spend. 17. Hay más humo en este salón del que nunca antes hubo. 18. There was more noise in the building than anyone could believe. 19. ¿Escribes el inglés mejor o peor que tu hermana? 20. Thomas plans on bringing more visitors than we can take care of.

23.3 (§23.6) 1. You are the most considerate man in the group. 2. ¿Quién es el/la estudiante más alto(-a) de tu clase? 3. Esther is the most sentimental of all (the girls). 4. ¿Son ellos los más inteligentes de los E.U.A. (Estados Unidos de América)? 5. Are you the liveliest person in your family? 6. ¿Cuál es el país más grande de Sudamérica (América del Sur)? 7. That place has the most wonderful scenery in the state. 8. ¿Cuál es el mejor del mundo? 9. That is the worst one in town. 10. Pepe es el jugador más fuerte del equipo. 11. She is the most extraordinary girl in school. 12. Son las personas más pobres de nuestro vecindario.

23.4 (§2.7) 1. Raúl left as soon as possible. 2. Él corrió lo más rápido que pudo. 3. I put (placed) it as high as I could. 4. Lo hicieron lo más despacio posible. 5. The young girl spoke as expressively as she could.

23.5 (§23.8) 1. Quiero ganar tanto dinero como tú. 2. Albert has as magnificent references as anyone. 3. Ellos/-as no saben tantas frases idiomáticas en español como yo. 4. Does that document have as illuminating a meaning as the other one does? 5. Nuestra calle no tiene tantos árboles como la tuya/suya/vuestra. 6. Noah doesn't smoke as much as I do. 7. ¿Venden tantas frutas en el supermercado como en la plaza del mercado? 8. Development under his/her/your reign was as extensive as under the former (one). 9. Muchos hispanoamericanos no hablan español tan rápido como los españoles.

10. The narrow road doesn't slope as much as the wide one does. 11. ¿Estudias tanto como tu hermano? 12. The military government will spend as much money as the civilian one did. 13. Espero recibir tantos regalos (presentes) como mi hermana. 14. I can't be as worthy as the others. 15. ¿Sabe tanto como ella? 16. She shows as much affection as her sister (does) 17. Mi abuela no es tan buena como mi madre. 18. Arizona doesn't have as many people (much population) as California does.

23.6 (§23.9) 1. Cuanto (Mientras) más como, (tanto) más me engordo. 2. The more I learn, the less I know. 3. Cuanto (Mientras) más él bebía, (tanto) más enfermo se puso. 4. The less I read, the less confused I become. 5. Mientras (Cuanto) más tiempo paso contigo, (tanto) más me gustas. 6. The more I smoke, the more I worry about myself. 7. Mientras (Cuanto) menos gastes*, (tanto) más tendrás. (***mientras** + future reference requires the subjunctive mood) 8. The more I earn, the more I spend. 9. Mientras (Cuanto) menos la veo, (tanto) más feliz estoy. 10. The less I call you, the less I know about you.

24

SPANISH INTEGRATED AND ENGLISH SEPARABLE INTERROGATIVES

24.1 (§24.l) 1. When do you need them for?/For when do you need them? 2. Where are those aborigines from?/From where are those aborigines? 3. What period are you talking about?/About what period are you talking? 4. What do you constantly go abroad for?/For what do you constantly go abroad? 5. Who(m) exactly is this point meant for?/For whom exactly is this point meant? 6. What house is the animal on top of?/On top of what house is the animal? 7. Who(m) are you going to the theater with?/With whom (all) are you going to the theater? 8. What alternative are you thinking about?/About what alternative are you thinking? 9. Who(m) was the letter written by?/By whom was the letter written? 10. What aspect are your/his/her/their opinions about?/About what aspect are your/his/her/their opinions?

24.2 (§24.l) 1. ¿Para quién lo hiciste? 2. ¿Para qué queremos eso? 3. ¿Con quién quiere ella hablar? 4. ¿Para qué bebes (bebe Ud.) eso? 5. ¿De dónde es tu/su/vuestro profesor (vuestra profesora)? 6. ¿Sobre (Acerca de) qué escriben ellos/-as? 7. ¿Con quién voy a salir? 8. ¿Para cuándo lo quieres/queréis (lo quiere Ud.)? 9. ¿Debajo de qué lo encontraron? 10. ¿Sobre quién (De quién) va él a hablar? 11. ¿Con quién habla ella? 12. ¿De dónde vienes/venís (viene Ud.)?

24.3 (§24.2–4) 1. ¿Cuáles son las ciudades más importantes de los Estados Unidos de América? 2. ¿A quién (quiénes) se lo vendiste? 3. ¿Qué libro encontraste en la librería? 4. ¿Quiénes de sus estudiantes saben portugués? 5. ¿Cuál fue el año del nacimiento de él? 6. ¿Qué museo quieren visitar ellos? 7. ¿Quiénes están en la biblioteca? 8. ¿Qué es un canguro? 9. ¿Cuál va a comprar? 10. ¿Cuál será el resultado de nuestras acciones? 11. ¿A quién (quiénes) ayudó él? 12. ¿Cuál fue (era) el problema de ella?

25
RELATIVE WORDS USED BETWEEN CLAUSES

25.1 (§25.2) 1. Sé que me ve(s)(n)/veis. 2. Él piensa (cree) que vivimos aquí. 3. Creen que te/lo/la/os conozco. 4. Ella dijo que podía hacerlo. 5. Por favor, recuerda/-e que lo necesito.

25.2 (§25.3–9) 1. Mi amigo(a), cuyos libros están sobre la mesa... 2. Él no dijo nada, lo cual (lo que) me sorprendió mucho. 3. La que conoces es una muchacha venezolana. 4. Mis abuelos, cuya casa está en Morelia... 5. Ese es el hombre con quien ella vive. 6. No entendí lo que él decía. 7. El edificio detrás del cual trabajo... 8. Hay alguien que (a quien) conozco en Honduras... 9. La familia Sánchez, cuya casa está en la esquina... 10. Él no quiere saber lo que usted piensa al respecto (de ello).

11. Ganaron mucho dinero, lo cual (lo que) me enfada. 12. ¿Conoce Vd. a los que tienen el auto (carro) nuevo? 13. La casa delante de la cual él se cayó... 14. Las chicas a quienes les diste el dinero lo gastaron todo. 15. Los estudiantes que llegaron tarde no oyeron lo que él dijo. 16. Los que nos vieron también vieron al profesor, quien es de Nicaragua (el cual es de Nicaragua). 17. Sé lo que quiero, pero no quiero lo que veo. 18. ¿Es ése (ésa) el (la) estudiante para quien escribió Ud. la recomendación? 19. Él tenía una mirada amenazadora la cual (lo cual) la asustó. (**lo cual** can be used if reference is made to "the fact of his looking menacing" as the antecedent and not to the look itself **la mirada**) 20. El hombre que dijo eso es el que se fue temprano.

25.3 (§25.10) 1. I want to see the person *that* owns that car (example 3 personal clause subject) 2. Does she want to buy the book *that/which* my father wrote? (example 2 non-personal clause object) 3. We went to the bank *that* opened yesterday (example 1 non-personal clause subject) 4. Let's say something nice to that Chilean girl *who(m)/that* we met yesterday. (example 4 personal clause object) 5. Are they going to read the letter about *which* my mother spoke?/Are they going to read the letter *which/that* my mother spoke about? (example 5 non-personal prepositional object) 6. I don't know the woman to *whom* he gave the money/I don't know the woman *whom/that/Ø* he gave the money to (example 6 personal prepositional object) 7. Where is the building *which/that/Ø* they discovered it under? (example 5 non-personal prepositional object) 8. I'm trying to find the gold watch *that*/Ø I lost at their party (example 2 non-personal clause object) 9. Do you see the children *who* are on the bus? (example 3 personal clause subject) 10. Do you know the students who(m)/that/Ø the professor spoke about. (example 6 personal prepositional object)

25.4 1. Quiero ver a la persona que es dueña de ese auto (carro). 2. ¿Quiere ella comprar el libro que escribió mi padre? 3. Fuimos al banco que se inauguró ayer. 4. Digamos algo agradable a la chilena que conocimos ayer. 5. ¿Van a leer la carta de la cual habló mi madre? 6. No conozco a la mujer a la cual él le dio el dinero. 7. ¿Dónde está el edificio debajo del cual lo descubrieron? 8. Trato de encontrar el reloj de oro que perdí en la fiesta de ellos(-as). 9. ¿Ve(s)(n)/Veis a los niños que están en ese autobús? 10. ¿Conoce(s)(n)/Conocéis a los estudiantes de quienes el profesor habló? (Note: In interrogative sentences 9 and 10, the verbs may be followed by their corresponding pronoun subjects.)

PART FOUR KEY
SYNTACTIC AND LEXICAL VARIANCES

26
THE SPANISH AND ENGLISH IMPERATIVE SYSTEMS

26.1 (§26.2–4) 1. ¿Queréis traer unos/-as amigos/-as? 2. Will/ Would you please not act that way? 3. ¿Quiere decir algo, por favor? 4. Can/Could you bring the chair here? 5. Hagan el favor de pararse un momento. 6. Can/Will you please adopt the other resolution? 7. ¡Haz el favor de no hacer eso otra vez! 8. Won't you please open a window?

26.2 (§26.5) 1. Podías/Podrías/Pudieras llamar a un amigo. 2. Puede/Puedes/Pueden/Podéis salir mejor (hacer mejor trabajo) en mis exámenes. 3. Queríamos/Querríamos/Quisiéramos visitarte(-lo/-la/-los/-os). 4. Manuel no debía/debería/debiera pasar tanto tiempo ahí. 5. No debe enviarle el dinero a él. 6. Ellos/-as debían/deberían/debieran comprar un auto (carro) nuevo. 7. Uno/-a debe venir a trabajar (al trabajo) a tiempo todos los días. 8. Tu/Vuestra/Su pronunciación podía/podría/pudiera ser (**estar** 'ahora en esta ocasión') mejor. 9. Yo quería/querría/quisiera escribirle a tu/vuestra/su hermana. 10. Podíamos/Podríamos/Pudiéramos visitarla en el hospital.

26.3 (§26.6–7) 1. Don't tell it to me! (usted) 2. Do it for him/her/them next (immediately afterwards)! (ustedes) 3. Bring her/it to us immediately! (usted) 4. Don't leave (abandon) him/it! (vosotros/-as) 5. Confirm (Verify) it soon! (usted) 6. Read it anyway for tomorrow! (vosotros/-as) 7. Put (Place) it here in round figures! (usted) 8. Send them to him/her/them separately! (tú) 9. Prepare (Fix) them for me only for the party! (tú). 10. Don't speak to me in that tone of voice! (tú).

26.4 (§26.6–7) 1. dádmelo 2. no le digas 3. estúdielo 4. tenlos 5. no las reúnan 6. no me la devolváis 7. no le escriban 8. cárgasela 9. no lo pongáis 10. explíquenmela 11. cántesela 12. dilo 13. no lo haga 14. propónsela

26.5 (§26.8–9) 1. ¡Que lo/la lean ellos(-as) mañana! 2. Let my father tell it to me. 3. Vamos al cine. 4. Let Felicita lend it to me. 5. ¡Que nos lo/la traigan ellos (ellas)! 6. Let's not write (to) them. 7. Que no se lo/la demos a ella. 8. Let's tell it to him/her/them. 9. ¡Que lo/la envíe él! 10. Let the police officer explain it to us.

27

THE PRESENT PARTICIPLE AND THE INFINITIVE

27.1 (§27.1) 1. Él está trabajando en la fábrica ahora. 2. ¿Van a cenar con nosotros mañana? 3. ¿Dónde estudiará ella el próximo semestre? / ¿/Dónde va ella a estudiar el próximo semestre? 4. Vienen/Vendrán/Van a venir a mi casa mañana por (en) la noche. 5. ¿Nos está mirando alguien en este momento (ahorita)? 6. ¿Qué hará/Qué va a hacer ella mañana por (en) la mañana? 7. ¿A quién(es) traerá/va a traer Ud. a mi fiesta el sábado en la noche? 8. ¿Están viviendo los padres de ellos en Nueva York? / ¿Los padres de ellas viven en Nueva York?

9. ¿Cuándo se van/se irán/van a irse los estudiantes para el Perú? 10. ¿Qué hace/está haciendo él con la computadora (el computador)? 11. ¿Adónde vamos/ iremos después del juego? 12. ¿En qué idioma escriben/están escribiendo ellos(as)? 13. ¿El hombre habla/está hablando en español o en inglés? 14. Si estás de acuerdo, usaré/voy a usar tu auto (carro) esta noche. 15. Él está estudiando para un examen ahora. 16. Ella no va a ir/no va/no irá a clases hoy.

27.2 (§27.2) 1. No voy ahí nunca/Nunca voy ahí sin comprar algo. 2. Al entrar, vi que ahí no había nadie. 3. Luego de verla, él se dio cuenta de que era su hermana. 4. Uno/-a necesita una llave para abrir esa caja fuerte. 5. Te lo mereces por ser tan estúpido(-a). 6. ¿Qué vio Ud. al abrir la ventana? 7. Yo soñaba con ser un(a) atleta famoso(-a). 8. Ella siempre se preocupa por (de) aumentar de peso. 9. Antes de comprarlo, debiéramos haberlo revisado. 10. Quiero trabajar en vez de estudiar matemática. 11. No conté con perder tanto dinero. 12. Él nunca aprenderá español sin estudiar más.

27.3 (§27.2) 1. What are you going to do after finishing your studies? 2. Upon seeing her, I hid underneath the stairs. 3. I don't know what she will do upon receiving the news. 4. For being so small, your brother is very strong. 5. I'm worried about dying of cancer, and I'm going to stop smoking. 6. We are thinking of (about) opening a store with the latest in clothing fashions. 7. What definition can I use for explaining that literary term? 8. I don't want to arrive at the party without taking something. 9. You're not going to believe what I heard upon listening to his/her/their interpretation of what happened. 10. You should look for some fixed plan instead of starting without anything. 11. Some men dream of attaining heavenly bliss. 12. Before showing him our satisfaction, let's find out what he thinks.

27.4 (§27.3–4) 1. El esperarnos no les gusta (a ellos/-as). 2. Seeing you happy like this is a delight. 3. El esconderte/-se/-os en tu/su/vuestra habitación no resuelve nada. 4. Smoking marijuana is prohibited (forbidden) in this country. 5. El beber vino le ayuda a uno(a) en la digestión. 6. Looking at your watch like that won't make the time pass any more quickly. 7. El correr estimula el corazón. 8. Caring so much for your beloved could turn out very dangerous. 9. El perder peso/El rebajar no es fácil en mi familia. 10. Knowing that you succeeded truly (really) gives me encouragement (encourages me/motivates me).

27.5 (§27.5) 1. ¿Conoce Ud. a ese muchacho que nada en el río? 2. Las personas que estaban comiendo en el restaurante eran chilenos. 3. ¿Quién es ese hombre que se fuma un puro (cigarro)? 4. Los estudiantes que estudian español es-

tán en mis clases. 5. Todos los profesores que enseñan aquí ganan mucho dinero.
6. Tienes que conocer a la muchacha que vive en mi departamento (apartamento,
piso). 7. Tengo que decirles algo a los niños que están jugando en mi patio. 8. El
gato negro que está trepando el árbol no es mío. 9. Las personas que rezan son
miembros de nuestra iglesia. 10. No le digas nada a esa muchacha que mastica
(masca) chicle.

27.6 (§27.6) 1. ¿Cuándo los viste hablar/hablando con nosotros? 2. Didn't
you hear the teacher make/making the comparison? 3. Él la sintió tocar/tocando su
cara. 4. I didn't hear you call/calling me at (in) the hospital. 5. En la India vimos a
muchas personas morir/muriendo en las calles. 6. We woke up when we heard the
dog bark/barking. 7. ¿Dónde estabas cuando viste el auto (coche) quemarse/qu-
emándose? 8. I saw the man open/opening the door with a key.

27.7 (§27.7) 1. Él no me vio escondido/-a en el rincón./Él no vio que yo
estaba escondido(-a) en el rincón. 2. I want you to tell the judge where you were
standing. 3. ¿Estabas solo acostado(-a) o estabas dormido(-a)? 4. The dog is
sleeping on my bed. 5. ¿Dónde estaba Ud. sentado(-a)? 6. He didn't see me
although (even though) I was standing near him . 7. ¿Estaba ella parada al lado tuyo
o estaba sentada? 8. David was hiding in his room.

28
VERB CONTRASTS

28.1 (§28.2) 1. What are your Andalusian friends going to do this week? 2.
Who made the bread that is on the table? 3. What did that so-called expert tell
you/them (say to you/them)? 4. When I saw him day before yesterday, he said
nothing (didn't say anything) about the review. 5. The maid always tells them
stories about secret passions. 6. My grandmother says that we have to resist all
kinds (sorts) of temptation. 7. My brothers/My brothers and sisters do nothing but
complain all the time. 8. Since no one knows how to make Chinese food, we will
eat out. 9. Benito said to him/her, "You won by a unanimous vote." 10. They told
us yesterday that they had been resting.

28.2 (§28.3) 1. Se volvió loca cuando vio al (el) fantasma. 2. No creemos
que estarán aquí mañana. 3. No conozco a tu/su/vuestro sobrino, pero sí a tu/su/
vuestra sobrina. 4. Ella sabe como preparar una comida excelente. 5. Él debería
pensar más en sus estudios. 6. ¿Va(s)/Vais a dejarle una propina al camarero
(mozo/mesero)? 7. ¿Cuándo salieron de esta ciudad? 8. Se hizo famoso por sus
importantes descubrimientos. 9. Se pusieron desanimados/-as luego de oír la
noticia. 10. Luego de muchas dificultades llegó a ser presidente de los Estados
Unidos de América (E.U.A.).
11. Él estudió en Harvard y llegó a ser profesor de filosofía. 12. Pedro el Cruel
llegó a ser rey después de muchas guerras civiles. 13. ¡Ten/Tenga(n)/Tened
cuidado! Creo que él tiene una pistola. 14. Él sabe hablar árabe muy bien. 15.
¿Conoce usted este parque? 16. Se puso pálida después de oír la noticia. 17.
¿Crees que saben que somos estudiantes? 18. Él luchó mucho por hacerse gente.
19. No conozco bien este plan. 20. Salieron para San Francisco luego de dejarme
un recado (mensaje).

28.3 (§28.4–8) 1. The professor is boring. (an opinion) 2. The professor is bored. (with his work) 3. The apple's natural color is green. 4. The apple is unripe. (not ripened) 5. My sister is bright (clever). 6. My sister is ready. (to go somewhere) 7. Italian food is very good. (in general) 8. This (particular) Italian food is very good. 9. That man is very entertaining. 10. That man is very amused (busy/distracted). 11. My mother is very quiet (by nature)./My mother is a quiet person. 12. My mother is too quiet (now). 13. My father is mentally ill. 14. My father is (feeling) sick (now). 15. That apparatus is bad. (inferior quality or condition) 16. That apparatus is not working (now). 17. She is a sad girl (by nature). 18. The girl feels sad (now). 19. The door was closed by the doorman. 20. The door was closed. (we found it closed) 21. Cats are very clean animals. (by nature) 22. The cats look very clean. (they've been recently cleaned) 23. The professor is crazy/mad. (his normal character) 24. The professor is acting crazy. (our impression from what he just said) 25. He was killed. 26. He was dead.

28.4 (§28.4–8) 1. How blue the sky is today in comparison with other days. 2. I've just realized how old I actually am. 3. The car is really ugly, no other way of describing it. 4. This blood appears very red in comparison with other types of blood. 5. As I look in the mirror I realize my (advanced) age. 6. She is exceptionally pretty with that particular hairdo. 7. This month the price of milk has gone down (in comparison with last month). 8. In my country milk is always expensive (no matter which month). 9. The moon is shining exceptionally bright tonight. 10. By nature the moon is never as bright as the sun. 11. Those gentlemen have the reputation of being very friendly. 12. How friendly they were around the sick children! 13. In general, how would you describe the professors of this faculty? 14. How are the professors feeling today after last night's party?

28.5 (§28.4–8) 1. Mi clase es grande, pero la de él es pequeña. 2. Está enferma hoy, pero dice que estará aquí mañana. 3. ¿Cómo está tu hermano hoy? 4. ¿Cómo es tu profesor? 5. Todos nuestros amigos son de Santafé de Bogotá. 6. ¿Dónde están todos sus amigos? 7. Mi tío es abogado y su señora es profesora. 8. La alfombra es hecha de nailon (nilón). 9. Las ventanas estaban abiertas cuando llegamos. 10. La puerta fue abierta por el niño.

11. La fiesta será en mi apartamento (departamento, piso). 12. Mi reloj de pulsera está roto. 13. Las rosas son rojas y las violetas son azules. 14. Ya eran las once, y yo estaba cansado(-a). 15. Ese hombre es muy testarudo. 16. Estoy aburrido(-a) simplemente porque esta clase es aburrida. 17. El cumpleaños de él es en el otoño. 18. Elizabeth está furiosa porque no estamos listos(-as). 19. ¿Dónde están los turistas que son de Nicaragua? 20. ¿Qué hacen ellos ahí?

29

PASSIVE CONSTRUCTIONS

29.1 (§29.1–3) 1. A very significant novel was written by Jonathan last summer. 2. A medal will be given to the hero by the President./The hero will be given a medal by the President. 3. All the apples have been eaten by the children. 4. A new plan will be suggested to the employees by the boss. (despite indirect object, verb allows only one version) 5. Some money was sent to me in July by my parents./I was sent some money by my parents in July. 6. A whole bottle of gin was drunk by him. 7. The children are visited by her every summer. 8. They had been offered a better grade by the professor./A better grade had been offered to them by the professor. 9. A new system will be described to the general by them. (verb allows only one version) 10. He was lent some money by his father./Some money was lent to him by his father.

29.2 (§29.5–6) 1. Ella es muy estimada por sus vecinos. 2. Esa noticia es conocida por la gente en todas partes. 3. Era bien conocido en su pueblo. 4. (not possible) 5. La noticia fue dada apenas llegó el aviso. 6. Un anciano fue atacado y robado por unos desconocidos. 7. (not possible) 8. El acuerdo había sido firmado por los oficiales antes de marcharse. 9. (not possible) 10. Mis estudios habrán sido terminados (por mí) antes del verano.

29.3 (§29.7) 1. Mi casa en las afueras de la ciudad estaba rodeada de un jardín de flores. 2. Sus mujeres estaban escondidas antes de llegar el enemigo. 3. Clemente estaba (estuvo) levantado desde muy temprano. 4. Tu tío estaba muy envejecido. 5. La tienda de sombreros está administrada por mi hermana. 6. El dilema estaba resuelto por el genio. 7. Sus acciones están gobernadas por la familia. 8. Todos estaban dormidos cuando llegué.

29.4 (§29.9–10) 1. Se anuncian muchas actividades sociales a través de la televisión. 2. Se expresó la plena satisfacción por la excelencia del vino. 3. Se teme otra guerra internacional. 4. Se organizó el Décimo Festival Juvenil. 5. Se rechazó el nuevo modo de aplicación. 6. Se vieron en la obra detalles análogos a la poesía de Darío. 7. Se observaron las estrellas durante varias horas. 8. Se celebraron innumerables fiestas este año. 9. No se sabe el origen del lenguaje. 10. Se estudia literatura universal en esta clase.

29.5 (§29.4–11) 1. Mis padres estaban mencionados en la carta. 2. El presidente ha sido asesinado./Se ha asesinado al presidente. 3. Se les ahorcó en la plaza pública./Fueron ahorcados en la plaza pública. 4. Se estudiarán estos documentos cuidadosamente/ Estos documentos serán estudiados cuidadosamente. 5. A mi amigo(-a) se le nombrará secretario(-a) del estado./Mi amigo(-a) será nombrado(-a) secretario(-a) del estado. 6. A ella se le considera una maestra excelente./Es considerada una maestra excelente. 7. A los niños se les servirá helado (nieve/mantecado) en la fiesta. 8. A él no se le ha recomendado para el puesto./Él no ha sido recomendado para el puesto. 9. Se te dará un regalo en la recepción. 10. No se me había dicho nada.

11. A los padres de ella no se les dijo toda la verdad. 12. No se nos invitó a tu boda./No estábamos invitados a tu boda./No fuimos invitados a tu boda. 13. Se les han enviado varias cartas. 14. A esos hombres se les llevará a la cárcel./Esos hombres serán llevados a la cárcel. 15. No se había encontrado a nadie en el edificio. 16. Se preparará una comida mexicana (mejicana) en la reunión./Será preparada una comida mexicana (mejicana) en le reunión. 17. Se anunció un nuevo programa gubernamental./Un nuevo programa gubernamental fue anunciado. 18. Se han vendido todas las manzanas./Todas las manzanas han sido vendidas. 19. Se nos traerá un carro temprano en la mañana. 20. A los niños pobres no se les da una buena educación.

29.6 (§29.5–11) 1. (ambiguous) Los niños estaban escondidos en el viejo edificio. 2. My house in Barcelona was surrounded by a rose garden. (state) 3. Ese tipo de libro es leído sólo por los letrados. 4. We don't know at the present time who will be elected president. (action) 5. Vi que las ventanas estaban cerradas cuando entré en el cuarto. 6. The door on the right should be closed. (state) 7. Mi hermano fue herido en un accidente. 8. The building will be finished by the end of the month. (state) 9. Esta noche se presenta un programa importante. 10. The forty horror stories were written by a single author. (action) 11. Mi composición está escrita. Será leída por el profesor. 12. The curves will be eliminated from the road (highway). (action) 13. Yo sabía que estaban ahí porque las luces estaban encendidas. 14. This structure will be raised to the height of the other one. (action) 15. Esta pintura (Este cuadro) tendrá que ser terminada(-o) por otro artista (pintor).

30
AFFIRMATIVE WORDS AND THEIR NEGATIVE COUNTERPARTS

30.1 (§30.1–2) 1. Nadie estaba en mi cuarto cuando entré./No había nadie en mi cuarto cuando entré. 2. Nunca iremos a vivir en Puerto Rico./No iremos nunca a vivir en Puerto Rico. 3. Nada llegó para ti en la correspondencia hoy./No llegó nada para ti hoy en la correspondencia. 4. Nadie quiere verte a las ocho mañana./ No quiere verte nadie a las ocho mañana. 5. Tampoco tengo yo amigos en Acapulco./No tengo tampoco amigos en Acapulco. 6. Ni mi hermano ni mi hermana van a procurarlo./No van ni mi hermano ni mi hermana a procurarlo. 7. Nunca pienso en ser una persona ejemplar./No pienso nunca en ser una persona ejemplar. 8. Nadie quiere hablarte ahorita./No quiere hablarte nadie ahorita. 9. Ningún animal pasó por debajo de la puerta./No pasó ningún animal por debajo de la puerta. 10. Nada dejaron sobre la mesa anoche./Anoche no dejaron nada sobre la mesa. 11. Tampoco voy a ver a mi novia./No voy tampoco a ver a mi novia. 12. Ni el gato ni el perro están en la sala./No están ni el gato ni el perro en la sala.

30.2 (§30.3–4) 1. Didn't anyone (anybody) see the man? 2. There wasn't anything in the mailbox. 3. They don't ever speak Portuguese to me. 4. Hasn't anyone (anybody) heard the news? 5. We don't ever have good parties at school. 6. There weren't any children at the movie. 7. We aren't going to the meeting either. 8. Isn't either he or she going?

30.3 (§30.4) 1. Nobody does the work in this house./There isn't anyone who does the work in this house. 2. Nothing happens in the association./There isn't anything that happens in the association. 3. My parents never pay attention to luxuries./My parents don't ever pay attention to luxuries. 4. No student has traits (signs) of mental illness./There isn't any student who has traits (signs) of mental illness. 5. Neither do I have such a broad imagination. (Note: The subject and auxiliary verb are inverted after a negative adverb in initial position) I don't have such a broad imagination either. 6. You never drive by that route./You don't ever drive by that route. 7. I concede (grant) nothing to you./I don't concede (grant) anything to you. 8. I will refer to no one (nobody)./I won't refer to anyone (anybody). 9. I never want to see her again./I don't want ever to see her again. 10. Neither do I believe in justice. (AUX/subject inversion) I don't believe in justice either. 11. I want to fight with no one./I don't want to fight with anyone. 12. That sentence has no subject./That sentence doesn't have any subject.

31
ADMIRATIVE EXPRESSIONS

31.1 (§31.1) 1. How fast your car runs! adverb 2. ¡Qué niño más/tan alto es Juan! count noun 3. How well you know your lessons! adverb 4. ¡Qué vino más bueno! non-count 5. How that lady worries me! subject + verb 6. ¡Qué lento (despacio) trabajas! adverb 7. How subtle (delicate) that flavor is! adjective 8. ¡Qué cerveza tan mala nos sirvieron! non-count 9. How hard and intolerable this life is! adjectives 10. ¡Qué bien enseña el español! adverb

31.2 (§31.2) 1. ¡No sabe lo rápido que puedo correr! 2. Boy! Did that train run fast! 3. ¡No ven lo malo que es él! 4. Wow! Did the professor ever get annoyed! (Note: **Ever**, used occasionally in the English translations, is an intensifier.) 5. ¡Ella no te dirá lo ridículo que es! 6. Boy! Is their house ever going to be pretty! 7. ¡No quiero saber lo guapo que es él! 8. Man! What a pretty girl we saw on the beach! 9. ¡Qué bella es ella! 10. Gosh! Is my brother happy!

32
ELLIPTICAL VERBAL USAGES AND VERIFICATION TAGS

32.1 (§32.1) 1. Yes, I am./Yes, we are; No, I'm not./No, we're not. 2. Yes, they were; No, they weren't. 3. Yes, he is; No, he isn't. 4. Yes, I was./Yes, we were; No, I wasn't./No, we weren't. 5. Yes, they did; No, they didn't. 6. Yes, I (we) have; No, I (we) haven't. 7. Yes, they do; No, they don't. 8. Yes, they have; No, they haven't. 9. Yes, he has; No, he hasn't. 10. Yes, they had; No, they hadn't. 11. Yes, he will; No, he won't. 12. Yes, they would; No, they wouldn't. 13. Yes, I (we) can; No, I (we) can't. 14. Yes, we should; No, we shouldn't. 15. Yes, you are; No, you aren't. (Note the change in pronoun focus.)

32.2 (§32.2) 1. Ray is at home, but Providencia isn't. 2. We were translating from Latin, and they were too. 3. Yolanda isn't pretty, and her sister isn't either (and neither is her sister). (There are several such examples of subject AUX inversion in this exercise; see p. 254, Note.) 4. The prince wasn't assassinated, but the count was. 5. She doesn't think about you, but I do. 6. I have a lot of worries, but my father doesn't. 7. My mother always keeps her same weight, but my aunt doesn't. 8. They weren't speaking of your/his/her/their virtues, and we weren't either (and neither were we). 9. She wasn't suffering from anything, but he was. 10. I have seen Roberto, but you haven't. 11. Almost no one had done the homework, but Pauline had. 12. They weren't anxious to arrive, but I was. 13. She doesn't have a vote, but my sister does. 14. They don't appear on (in) the published list, but I do. 15 Pablo wouldn't tell even half of the mystery, and she wouldn't either (and neither would she). 16. I couldn't open the door, but they could. 17. This book speaks of evolution, but that other one doesn't. 18. They weren't able to move to the Mediterranean, but you were. 19. My parents didn't live in the new extension, and I didn't either (and neither did I). 20. No one else has seen that look in you, but I have.

32.3 (§32.3) 1. They haven't brought the ninety books, but they plan to tonight. 2. I want to tell it to you, and I'm going to when I see you. 3. We haven't spoken to the professor, but we have to tomorrow. 4. I can't talk to you now, but I need to later. 5. I ought (have) to write a composition, and I'm going to this afternoon. 6. We haven't told him/her/you the story, but we hope to shortly (soon).

32.4 (§32.4) 1. ¿verdad? 2. ¿verdad/no? 3. ¿verdad? 4. ¿verdad/no? 5. ¿verdad? 6. ¿verdad/no? 7. ¿verdad/no? 8. ¿verdad? 9. ¿verdad/no? 10. ¿verdad?

32.5 (§32.5) 1. (Am.) don't you?/(Brit.) haven't you?↓ 2. did you?↓ 3. don't you?↓ 4. isn't she?↓ 5. are they?↓ 6. aren't they?↓ 7. was he?↓ 8. hadn't they ↓ 9. has she?↓ 10. won't they?↓ 11. would he?↓ 12. don't they?↓ 13. can't she?↓ 14. could she?↓ 15. doesn't he/she?↓ 16. isn't it?↓ 17. hadn't they?↓ 18. don't they?↓ 19. (Am.) doesn't he?/(Brit.) hasn't he?↓ 20. isn't it?↓

33
POR VERSUS PARA

33.1 (§33.1–3) 1. Hablas inglés muy bien para ser extranjero. [2] 2. Fui por la calle, pero ellos fueron por el parque. [7] 3. ¿Qué van a hacer por las noches? [6] 4. Tenemos que gastar mucho dinero para poder viajar. [5] 5. ¿Es este paquete para ti o para mí? [1] 6. ¿Cuánto te dieron por el caballo? [8] 7. Ella leyó este libro difícil página por página. [9] 8. Por la falta de agua [3], por poco nos morimos de sed. [14] 9. Lo atacaron por ser rebelde. [5] 10. Regresé por el auto (carro) pero no había nadie ahí. [4] 11. Ese cuadro fue pintado por El Greco. [1] 12. Estamos por (para) salir./Estamos a punto de salir. [6] Tenemos que estar allá para las siete. [4] 13. Él entró a un monasterio para nunca más salir. [3] 14. Estuvieron aquí por dos horas [6] y trajeron bombones (dulces) para los chamacos. [1] 15. La Sra. Martínez se sacrifica por su hijo. [12] 16. No quiero hablar por mi hermano. [12] 17. ¿Puedo/¿Me permite cambiar este diccionario por otro? [8] 18. La cena (comida) quedó por preparar. [13] 19. ¿Cuánto ganas por hora? [10] 20. Supe por mi hermana que habías estado enfermo(-a). [2] 21. Para ser profesor(-a) de idiomas (lenguas) Ud. parece saber mucho de la ciencia física. [2] 22. Por fin llegaron. [14] Habían comprado flores para mi hermana. [1] 23. Aparentemente lo terminaremos para mañana. [4] 24. Pasamos por María [4], pero no pudo venir con nosotros por estar enferma. [3] 25. Para llegar a tiempo [5], tuvimos que correr por dentro de la biblioteca. [7]

34
VERBAL EXPRESSIONS USING SPANISH
DAR, HACER, AND TENER

34.1 (§34.1–2) 1. Your dog makes me afraid (scares me). 2. Él tenía hambre cuando llegó. 3. The child was afraid of his grandfather. 4. El frío les da hambre a los niños. 5. Is your brother ten years old? 6. El decir eso no te da la razón. 7. She doesn't feel like going to the movies with us. 8. Estamos bien; no tenemos ni calor ni frío. 9. Working here in the sun makes me thirsty. 10. Este libro sobre México me da ganas de visitar ese país.

34.2 (§34.3–4) 1. No me gusta cuando hace calor. 2. My brother was here two weeks ago. 3. Creo que hace viento allí. 4. It's not sunny today, but it isn't cold either (but neither is it cold). 5. Hace cinco horas que estamos estudiando aquí. 6. Eloise had played the piano for a long time./Eloise had been playing the piano for a long time. 7. Hace diez minutos que llegaron los bomberos. 8. I have smoked for eighteen years./I have been smoking for eighteen years. 9. Siempre hace buen tiempo en California. 10. I had to take that examination a (one) month ago. 11. ¿Cuánto tiempo hace que estudian Uds. español? 12. I had studied Spanish for a (one) year before going to Costa Rica./I had been studying Spanish for a (one) year before going to Costa Rica. 13. Hace varias semanas que salimos de Chile. 14. She changed his appearance completely not too long ago. 15. Estaba enferma porque hacía mucho tiempo que ella bebía. 16. It's cool this morning, but it's going to be hot this afternoon. 17. Yo trabajaba en Bolivia desde hacía varios años. 18. Your father has been in Los Angeles for fifteen years. 19. Hace mucho tiempo que ese muchacho usa estupefacientes (drogas/narcóticos). 20. The cargo arrived an hour ago.

35
SPANISH CONSTRUCTIONS WITH GUSTAR, FALTAR AND SIMILAR VERBS

35.1 (§35.1–3) 1. No nos gustan los gatos ni los perros. 2. ¿Les hace falta papel? 3. No me importa lo que piensas de mí. 4. Les duelen los pies. 5. Me quedan veinte dólares. 6. ¿Le gusta mi auto (carro)? 7. A su tío, ¿no le importa el dinero? 8. ¿Qué nos hace falta ahora? 9. A mi amigo(-a) le queda sólo un cigarrillo. 10. A mi hermana le duele el pecho. 11. A mi hermano no le gusta Hawaii. 12. Al maestro (A la maestra) no le importan los estudiantes. 13. Me duele el codo. 14. Nos quedan varias preguntas por contestar. 15. No me interesan vuestros problemas 16. A él le fascinan las ciencias físicas. 17. Me encantan las películas mexicanas. 18. A ellos (ellas) les interesan los problemas mundiales contemporáneos.

36
MISCELLANEOUS CONTRASTS

36.1. (§36.1–6). Él va a traerlo todo. 2. All that you did doesn't mean anything. 3. Él busca a cierto hombre. 4. We are going to eat half a box of candy. 5. Ella perdió tres dólares más ahí. 6. We are going to cover two more topics in that category. 7. Hemos visitado cien países. 8. We want to find out why they (you, pl.) lost more than six-hundred thousand pesetas. 9. Él compró ciento veintiún libros. 10. The little boy can count up to two hundred. 11. Dos millones de personas murieron en esa guerra. 12. Your words have a certain nuance (shade/touch) of purity. 13. Había miles de autos en la carretera. 14. There were millions of individuals affected by the sickness. 15. ¿Todavía tiene ella todo lo que trajo? 16. Do you want to show me everything you bought? 17. ¿Crees que lo sabes todo? 18. All dogs are dangerous sometimes. 19. Toda máquina trabaja bien. 20. All the flags are equally visible.

36.2. (§36.7–9). 1. Marcelino came on the 5th of July./Marcelino came on July 5th. 2. Él tiene que trabajar todo el verano. 3. My birthday is (on) the 30th of December./My birthday is (on) December 30th. 4. Vamos a las montañas todos los veranos. 5. Do you have to work every night? 6. Voy a estar en Brasil todo el año. 7. Where are you going to be on the 1st of September?/Where are you going to be on September 1st? 8. Hoy es el 4 de julio. 9. We have individual teaching every morning at eight o'clock. 10. Voy a estar en mi oficina toda la mañana. 11. Why do I have to be all dressed up (dressed in my best finery) every afternoon? 12. Tengo una clase de español todos los semestres. 13. We take leave of you and wish you good fortune in the year 2000. 14. Nos despedimos ahora y les deseamos bienandanza para el siglo nuevo.

PRINCIPAL FORMS OF IRREGULAR VERBS IN ENGLISH

The following is a fairly complete listing of the English irregular verbs. This list does not include verbs formed by prefixing. If in doubt, consult a dictionary for the principal parts of those such verbs.

BASE	PRETERITE	PARTICIPLE	BASE	PRETERITE	PARTICIPLE
abide	abode/abided	abode/abided	cut	cut	cut
arise	arose	arisen	deal	dealt	dealt
awake	awoke	awaken	dig	dug	dug
be	was, were	been	do	did	done
bear	bore	borne *(carry)*	draw	drew	drawn
bear	bore	born *(birth)*	dream	dreamed/dreamt	dreamed/dreamt
beat	beat	beaten	drink	drank	drunk
become	became	become	drive	drove	driven
beget	begot/begat	begotten	dwell	dwelt	dwelt
begin	began	begun	eat	ate	eaten
bend	bent	bent	fall	fell	fallen
beseech	besought	besought	feed	fed	fed
bet	bet/betted	bet/betted	feel	felt	felt
bid	bade *(order)*	biden	fight	fought	fought
bid	bid *(offer)*	bid	find	found	found
bind	bound	bound	flee	fled	fled
bite	bit	bitten	fling	flung	flung
bleed	bled	bled	fly	flew	flown
blow	blew	blown	forbid	forbad(e)	forbidden
break	broke	broken	forget	forgot	forgotten
breed	bred	bred	forsake	forsook	forsaken
bring	brought	brought	freeze	froze	frozen
build	built	built	get	got	got, gotten *(US)*
burn	burned/burnt	burned/burnt	gild	gilded	gilded/gilt
burst	burst	burst	gird	girded/girt	girded/girt
buy	bought	bought	give	gave	given
can	could	----------	go	went	gone
cast	cast	cast	grind	ground	ground
catch	caught	caught	grow	grew	grown
chide	chid	chidden/chid	hang	hung	hung
choose	chose	chosen	hang	hanged *(law)*	hanged *(law)*
cleave *tr.*	clove/cleft	cloven/cleft	have	had	had
cleave *intr*	cleaved	cleaved	hear	heard	heard
cling	clung	clung	heave	heaved	heaved
come	came	come	heave	hove *(naut)*	hove *(naut)*
cost *tr.*	costed	costed	hew	hewed	hewed/hewn
cost *intr.*	cost	cost	hide	hid	hidden
creep	crept	crept	hit	hit	hit

BASE	PRETERITE	PARTICIPLE	BASE	PRETERITE	PARTICIPLE
hold	held	held	shut	shut	shut
hurt	hurt	hurt	sing	sang	sung
keep	kept	kept	sink	sank	sunk
kneel	knelt	knelt	sit	sat	sat
know	know	known	slay	slew	slain
lade	laded	laden	sleep	slept	slept
lay	laid	laid	slide	slid	slid
lead	led	led	sling	slung	slung
lean	leaned/leant	leaned/leant	slink	slunk	slunk
leap	leaped	leaped/leapt	slit	slit	slit
learn	learned/learnt	learned/learnt	smell	smelled/smelt	smelled/smelt
leave	left	left	smite	smote	smitten
lend	lent	lent	sow	sowed	sown
let	let	let	speak	spoke	spoken
lie	lay	lain	speed *tr.*	speeded	speeded
light	lit/lighted	lit/lighted	speed *intr*	sped	sped
lose	lost	lost	spell	spelled/spelt	spelled/spelt
make	made	made	spend	spent	spent
may	might	---------	spill	spilled/spilt	spilled/split
mean	meant	meant	spin	spun/span	spun
meet	met	met	spit	spat	spat
mow	mowed	mown/mowed	split	split	split
pay	paid	paid	spoil	spoiled/spoilt	spoiled/spoilt
put	put	put	spread	spread	spread
quit	quit/quitted	quit/quitted	spring	sprang	sprung
read [rid]	read [rɛd]*	read [rɛd]*	stand	stood	stood
rend	rent	rent	stave	stove/staved	stove/staved
rid	rid	rid	steal	stole	stolen
ride	rode	ridden	stick	stuck	stuck
ring	rang	rung	sting	stung	stung
rise	rose	risen	stink	stank	stunk
run	ran	run	strew	strewed	strewed/strewn
saw	sawed	sawed/sawn	stride	strode	stridden
say [se]	said [sɛd]	said [sɛd]	strike	struck	struck
see	saw	seen	string	strung	strung
seek	sought	sought	strive	strove	striven
sell	sold	sold	swear	swore	sworn
send	sent	sent	sweep	swept	swept
set	set	set	swell	swelled	swollen
sew	sewed	sewn	swim	swam	swum
shake	shook	shaken	swing	swung	swung
shave	shaved	shaved/shaven	take	took	taken
shear	sheared	shorn	teach	taught	taught
shed	shed	shed	tear	tore	torn
shine	shone	shone	tell	told	told
shoe	shod	shod	think	thought	thought
shoot	shot	shot	thrive	throve	thriven
show	showed	shown	throw	threw	thrown
shrink	shrank	shrunk	thrust	thrust	thrust

BASE	PRETERITE	PARTICIPLE
tread	trod	trodden
wake	woke	woken/waked
wear	wore	worn
weave	wove	woven
weep	wept	wept
win	won	won
wind	wound	wound
wring	wrang	wrung
write	wrote	written

* The base form of **read** has the pronunciation of [rid], but the remaining two forms, although spelled like the base, have the pronunciation of [rɛd]. This is confusing even for the native English speaker, who must rely on context to know which form is intended, the base form or the past tense.

Appendix II

VERB TENSE TERMINOLOGY

Grammatical nomenclature has long been a point of disagreement among many language scholars. Various modern grammarians have broken with classical tradition and employ their own terminology. Linguists have devised yet a different metalanguage. And, as mentioned un Unit 3 (§3.9), Spanish and English terminologies do not always correspond. Following is a listing of the verb tense terms used throughout this manual, along with corresponding terminology prevalently found in other sources.

MANUAL TERM	ALSO CALLED	LA REAL ACADEMIA	OTHER SPANISH GRAMMARIANS
NON-FINITE			
infinitive *amar/love*	* * *	infinitivo	* * *
gerund *amando* *loving*	present participle; imperfective participle; **-ing** form	gerundio	gerundio de presente; participio de presente
past participle *amado/loved*	perfective participle	participio	participio pasivo (*o* pretérito)
INDICATIVE MOOD			
present *amo/I love*	simple present	presente	presente imperfecto
imperfect *(yo) amaba* *I loved*	* * *	pretérito imperfecto	copretérito;imperfecto
preterite *amé/I loved*	simple past; past preterit(e)	pretérito indefinido	pretérito; pretérito perfecto absoluto
future *amaré* *I will love*	* * *	futuro imperfecto	futuro; futuro simple; futuro absoluto
conditional *(yo) amaría* *I would love*	* * *	potencial simple	condicional simple; pospretérito; futuro hipotético

MANUAL TERM	ALSO CALLED	LA REAL ACADEMIA	OTHER SPANISH GRAMMARIANS
PERFECT TENSES			
preterite perfect *he amado* *I have loved*	present perfect; present anterior; past indefinite	pretérito perfecto	antepresente; pretérito perfecto actual; perfecto
pluperfect *(yo) había amado* *I had loved*	past perfect; imperfect anterior	pretérito plus-cuamperfecto	antecopretérito; pluscuamperfecto; antepretérito
anterior pre-terite *hube amado* *I had loved*	preterit(e) per-fect; preterit anterior	pretérito anterior	antepretérito
future perfect *habré amado* *I will have loved*	future anterior	futuro perfecto	futuro compuesto; antefuturo
conditional perfect *(yo) habría amado* *I would have loved*	conditional anter-ior	potencial com-puesto	condicional com-puesto; ante-pospretérito; antefuturo hipotético

IMPERATIVE MOOD

imperative *ama (tú)* *love*	commands	imperativo pre-sente	imperativo

SUBJUNCTIVE MOOD

Note: The terminology for the subjunctive tenses is essentially the same as that for the tenses in the indicative mood with the word 'subjunctive' (subjuntivo) appended.

Appendix III

LIST OF PRINCIPAL IRREGULAR VERBS IN SPANISH

Only the tenses in which irregularities of some type occur are listed. Irregular forms are presented in **bold type,** while the regular forms are shown in standard type.

adquirir
PRESENT — **adquiero, adquieres, adquiere,** adquirimos adquirís, **adquieren**
PRES . SUBJUNC . — **adquiera, adquieras, adquiera,** adquiramos, adquiráis, **adquieran**
IMPERATIVE — **adquiere, adquiera,** adquiramos, adquirid, **adquieran**

andar
PRETERITE — **anduve, anduviste, anduvo, anduvimos, anduvisteis, anduvieron**
IMPERF . SUBJ . I — **anduviera, anduvieras, anduviera, anduviéramos, anduvierais, anduvieran**
IMPERF . SUBJ . II — **anduviese, anduvieses, anduviese, anduviésemos, anduvieseis, anduviesen**

asir
PRESENT — **asgo,** ases, ase, asimos, asís, asen
PRES . SUBJUNC . — **asga, asgas, asga, asgamos, asgáis, asgan**

avergonzar
PRESENT — **avergüenzo, avergüenzas, avergüenza,** avergonzamos, avergonzáis, **avergüenzan**
PRETERITE — **avergoncé,** avergonzaste, avergonzó, avergonzamos, avergonzasteis, avergonzaron
PRES . SUBJUNC . — **avergüence, avergüences, avergüence, avergoncemos, avergoncéis avergüencen**
IMPERATIVE — **avergüenza, avergüence, avergoncemos,** avergonzad, **avergüencen**

bendecir
PRESENT — **bendigo, bendices, bendice,** bendecimos, bendecís, **bendicen**
PRETERITE — **bendije, bendijiste, bendijo, bendijimos, bendijisteis, bendijeron**
PRES . SUBJUNC . — **bendiga, bendigas, bendiga, bendigamos, bendigáis, bendigan**
IMPERF . SUBJ . I — **bendijera, bendijeras, bendijera, bendijéramos, bendijerais, bendijeran**
IMPERF . SUBJ . II — **bendijese, bendijeses, bendijese, bendijésemos, bendijeseis, bendijesen**
IMPERATIVE — **bendice, bendiga, bendigamos,** bendecid, **bendigan**
GERUND — **bendiciendo**

caber
PRESENT — **quepo,** cabes, cabe, cabemos, cabéis, caben
PRETERITE — **cupe, cupiste, cupo, cupimos, cupisteis, cupieron**
FUTURE — **cabré, cabrás, cabrá, cabremos, cabréis, cabrán**

340

CONDITIONAL   **cabría, cabrías, cabría, cabríamos, cabríais, cabrían**
PRES . SUBJUNC .   **quepa, quepas, quepa, quepamos, quepáis, quepan**
IMPERF . SUBJ . I   **cupiera, cupieras, cupiera, cupiéramos, cupierais, cupieran**
IMPERF . SUBJ . II   **cupiese, cupieses, cupiese, cupiésemos, cupieseis, cupiesen**
IMPERATIVE   cabe, **quepa, quepamos,** cabed, **quepan**

caer

PRESENT   **caigo,** caes, cae, caemos, caéis, caen
PRETERITE   caí, **caíste, cayó,** caímos, **caísteis, cayeron**
PRES . SUBJUNC .   **caiga, caigas, caiga, caigamos, caigáis, caigan**
IMPERF . SUBJ . I   **cayera, cayeras, cayera, cayéramos, cayerais, cayeran**
IMPERF . SUBJ . II   **cayese, cayeses, cayese, cayésemos, cayeseis, cayesen**
IMPERATIVE   cae, **caiga, caigamos,** caed, **caigan**
GERUND   **cayendo**
PARTICIPLE   **caído**

colgar

PRESENT   **cuelgo, cuelgas, cuelga,** colgamos, colgáis, **cuelgan**
PRETERITE   **colgué,** colgaste, colgó, colgamos, colgasteis, colgaron
PRES . SUBJUNC .   **cuelgue, cuelgues, cuelgue, colguemos,colguéis, cuelguen**
IMPERATIVE   **cuelga, cuelgue, colguemos,** colgad, **cuelguen**

conducir

PRESENT   **conduzco,** conduces, conduce, conducimos, conducís, conducen
PRETERITE   **conduje, condujiste, condujo, condujimos, condujisteis,
                   condujeron**
PRES . SUBJUNC .   **conduzca, conduzcas, conduzca, conduzcamos, conduzcáis,
                   conduzcan**
IMPERF . SUBJ . I   **condujera, condujeras, condujera, condujéramos, condujeseis,
                   condujeran**
IMPERF . SUBJ . II   **condujese, condujeses, condujese, condujésemos, condujeseis,
                   condujesen**
IMPERATIVE   conduce, **conduzca, conduzcamos,** conducid, **conduzcan**

conocer

PRESENT   **conozco,** conoces, conoce, conocemos, conocéis, conocen
PRES . SUBJUNC .   **conozca, conozcas, conozca, conozcamos, conozcáis, conozcan**
IMPERATIVE   conoce, **conozca, conozcamos,** conoced, **conozcan**

construir

PRESENT   **construyo, construyes, construye,** construimos, construís, **construyen**
PRETERITE   construí, construiste, **construyó,** construimos, construisteis, **construyeron**
PRES . SUBJUNC .   **construya, construyas, construya, construyamos, construyáis,
                   construyan**
IMPERF . SUBJ . I   **construyera, construyeras, construyera, construyéramos, constru-
                   yerais, construyeran**
IMPERF . SUBJ . II   **construyese, construyeses, construyese, construyésemos, cons-
                   truyeseis, construyesen**
IMPERATIVE   **construye, construya, construyamos,** construid, **construyan**

dar

PRESENT   **doy,** das, da, damos, dais, dan
PRETERITE   **di, diste, dio, dimos, disteis, dieron**
PRES . SUBJUNC .   **dé,** des, **dé,** demos, deis, den

IMPERF . SUBJ . I	**diera, dieras, diera, diéramos, dierais, dieran**
IMPERF . SUBJ . II	**diese, dieses, diese, diésemos, dieseis, diesen**

decir

PRESENT	**digo, dices, dice,** decimos, decís, **dicen**
PRETERITE	**dije, dijiste, dijo, dijimos, dijisteis, dijeron**
FUTURE	**diré, dirás, dirá, diremos, diréis, dirán**
CONDITIONAL	**diría, dirías, diría, diríamos, diríais, dirían**
PRES . SUBJUNC .	**diga, digas, diga, digamos, digáis, digan**
IMPERF . SUBJ . I	**dijera, dijeras, dijera, dijéramos, dijerais, dijeran**
IMPERF . SUBJ . II	**dijese, dijeses, dijese, dijésemos, dijeseis, dijesen**
IMPERATIVE	**di, diga, digamos,** decid, **digan**
GERUND	**diciendo**
PARTICIPLE	**dicho**

deducir

PRESENT	**deduzco,** deduces, deduce, deducimos, deducís, deducen
PRETERITE	**deduje, dedujiste, dedujo, dedujimos, dedujisteis, dedujeron**
PRES . SUBJUNC .	**deduzca, deduzcas, deduzca, deduzcamos, deduzcáis, deduzcan**
IMPERF . SUBJ . I	**dedujera, dedujeras, dedujera, dedujéramos, dedujerais, dedujeran**
IMPERF . SUBJ . II	**dedujese, dedujeses, dedujese, dedujésemos, dedujeseis, dedujesen**

dormir

PRESENT	**duermo, duermes, duerme,** dormimos, dormís, **duermen**
PRETERITE	dormí, dormiste, **durmió,** dormimos, dormisteis, **durmieron**
PRES . SUBJUNC .	**duerma, duermas, duerma, durmamos, durmáis, duerman**
IMPERF . SUBJ . I	**durmiera, durmieras, durmiera, durmiéramos, durmieseis, durmiesen**
IMPERF . SUBJ . II	**durmiese, durmieses, durmiese, durmiésemos, durmieseis, durmiesen**
IMPERATIVE	**duerme, duerma, durmamos,** dormid, **duerman**
GERUND	**durmiendo**

empezar

PRESENT	**empiezo, empiezas, empieza,** empezamos, empezáis, **empiezan**
PRETERITE	**empecé,** empezaste, empezó, empezamos, empezasteis, empezaron
PRES . SUBJUNC .	**empiece, empieces, empiece, empecemos, empecéis, empiecen**
IMPERATIVE	**empieza, empiece, empecemos,** empezad, **empiecen**

errar

PRESENT	**yerro, yerras, yerra,** erramos, erráis, **yerran**
PRES . SUBJUNC .	**yerre, yerres, yerre,** erremos, erréis, **yerren**
IMPERATIVE	**yerra, yerre,** erremos, errad, **yerren**

escoger

PRESENT	**escojo,** escoges, escoge, escogemos, escogéis, escogen
PRES . SUBJUNC .	**escoja, escojas, escoja, escojamos, escojáis, escojan**
IMPERATIVE	escoge, **escoja, escojamos,** escoged, **escojan**

estar

PRESENT	**estoy, estás, está,** estamos, estáis, **están**
PRETERITE	**estuve, estuviste, estuvo, estuvimos, estuvisteis, estuvieron**
PRES . SUBJUNC .	**esté, estés, esté,** estemos, estéis, **estén**
IMPERF . SUBJ . I	**estuviera, estuvieras, estuviera, estuviéramos, estuvierais, estuvieran**

IMPERF. SUBJ. II **estuviese, estuvieses, estuviese, estuviésemos, estuvieseis,**
estuviesen
IMPERATIVE **está, esté,** estemos, estad, **estén**

forzar

PRESENT **fuerzo, fuerzas, fuerza,** forzamos, forzáis, **fuerzan**
PRETERITE **forcé,** forzaste, forzó, forzamos, forzasteis, forzaron
PRES. SUBJUNC. **fuerce, fuerces, fuerce, forcemos, forcéis, fuercen**
IMPERATIVE **fuerza, fuerce, forcemos** forzad, **fuercen**

haber

PRESENT **he, has, ha, hemos,** habéis, **han**
PRETERITE **hube, hubiste, hubo, hubimos, hubisteis, hubieron**
FUTURE **habré, habrás, habrá, habremos, habréis, habrán**
CONDITIONAL **habría, habrías, habría, habríamos, habríais, habrían**
PRES. SUBJUNC. **haya, hayas, haya, hayamos, hayáis, hayan**
IMPERF. SUBJ. I **hubiera, hubieras, hubiera, hubiéramos, hubierais, hubieran**
IMPERF. SUBJ. II **hubiese, hubieses, hubiese, hubiésemos, hubieseis, hubiesen**
IMPERATIVE **hé, haya, hayamos,** habed, **hayan**

hacer

PRESENT **hago,** haces, hace, hacemos, hacéis, hacen
PRETERITE **hice, hiciste, hizo, hicimos, hicisteis, hicieron**
FUTURE **haré, harás, hará, haremos, haréis, harán**
CONDITIONAL **haría, harías, haría, haríamos, haríais, harían**
PRES. SUBJUNC. **haga, hagas, haga, hagamos, hagáis, hagan**
IMPERF. SUBJ. I **hiciera, hicieras, hiciera, hiciéramos, hicierais, hicieran**
IMPERF. SUBJ. II **hiciese, hicieses, hiciese, hiciésemos, hicieseis, hiciesen**
IMPERATIVE **haz, haga, hagamos,** haced, **hagan**
PARTICIPLE **hecho**

incluir

PRESENT **incluyo, incluyes, incluye,** incluimos, incluís, **incluyen**
PRETERITE incluí, incluiste, **incluyó,** incluimos, incluisteis, **incluyeron**
PRES. SUBJUNC. **incluya, incluyas, incluya, incluyamos, incluyáis, incluyan**
IMPERF. SUBJ. I **incluyera, incluyeras, incluyera, incluyéramos, incluyerais,**
incluyeran
IMPERF. SUBJ. II **incluyese, incluyeses, incluyese, incluyésemos, incluyeseis,**
incluyesen
IMPERATIVE **incluye, incluya, incluyamos,** incluid, **incluyan**

ir

PRESENT **voy, vas, va, vamos, vais, van**
IMPERFECT **iba, ibas, iba, íbamos, ibais, iban**
PRETERITE **fui fuiste, fue, fuimos, fuisteis, fueron**
PRES. SUBJUNC. **vaya, vayas, vaya, vayamos, vayáis, vayan**
IMPERF. SUBJ. I **fuera, fueras, fuera, fuéramos, fuerais, fueran**
IMPERF. SUBJ. II **fuese, fueses, fuese, fuésemos, fueseis, fuesen**
IMPERATIVE **ve, vaya, vayamos,** id, **vayan**
GERUND **yendo**

jugar

PRESENT **juego, juegas, juega,** jugamos, jugáis, **juegan**
PRETERITE **jugué,** jugaste, jugó, jugamos, jugasteis, jugaron

PRES . SUBJUNC . **juegue, juegues, juegue, juguemos, juguéis, jueguen**
IMPERATIVE   **juega, juegue, juguemos,** jugad, **jueguen**

leer
PRETERITE   leí, **leíste, leyó, leímos leísteis, leyeron**
IMPERF . SUBJ . I **leyera, leyeras, leyera, leyéramos, leyerais, leyeran**
IMPERF . SUBJ . II **leyese, leyeses, leyese, leyésemos, leyeseis, leyesen**
GERUND   **leyendo**

lucir
PRESENT   **luzco,** luces, luce, lucimos, lucís, lucen
PRES . SUBJUNC . **luzca, luzcas, luzca, luzcamos, luzcáis, luzcan**
IMPERATIVE   luce, **luzca, luzcamos,** lucid, **luzcan**

oír
PRESENT   **oigo, oyes, oye, oímos,** oís, **oyen**
PRETERITE   oí, **oíste, oyó, oímos, oísteis, oyeron**
PRES . SUBJUNC . **oiga, oigas, oiga, oigamos, oigáis, oigan**
IMPERF . SUBJ . I **oyera, oyeras, oyera, oyéramos, oyerais, oyeran**
IMPERF . SUBJ . II **oyese, oyeses, oyese, oyésemos, oyeseis, oyesen**
IMPERATIVE   **oye, oiga, oigamos,** oíd, **oigan**
GERUND   **oyendo**
PARTICIPLE   **oído**

oler
PRESENT   **huelo, hueles, huele,** olemos, oléis, **huelen**
PRES . SUBJUNC . **huela, huelas, huela,** olamos, oláis, **huelan**
IMPERATIVE   **huele, huela,** olamos, oled, **huelan**

pedir
PRESENT   **pido, pides, pide,** pedimos, pedís, **piden**
PRETERITE   pedí, pediste, **pidió,** pedimos, pedisteis, **pidieron**
PRES . SUBJUNC   **pida, pidas, pida, pidamos, pidáis, pidan**
IMPERF . SUBJ . I **pidiera, pidieras, pidiera, pidiéramos, pidierais, pidieran**
IMPERF . SUBJ . II **pidiese, pidieses, pidiese, pidiésemos, pidieseis, pidiesen**
IMPERATIVE   **pide, pida, pidamos,** pedid, **pidan**
GERUND   **pidiendo**

pensar
PRESENT   **pienso, piensas, piensa,** pensamos, pensáis, **piensan**
PRES . SUBJUNC . **piense, pienses, piense,** pensemos, penséis, **piensen**
IMPERATIVE   **piensa, piense,** pensemos, pensad, **piensen**

perder
PRESENT   **pierdo, pierdes, pierde,** perdemos, perdéis, **pierden**
PRES . SUBJUNC . **pierda, pierdas, pierda,** perdamos, perdáis, **pierdan**
IMPERATIVE   **pierde, pierda,** perdamos, perded, **pierdan**

placer
PRESENT   **plazco,** places, place, placemos, placéis, placen
PRETERITE   plací, placiste, plació (or **plugo),** placimos, placisteis, placieron
                 (or **pluguieron)**
PRES . SUBJUNC . **plazca, plazcas, plazca** (or plega/plegue), **plazcamos, plazcáis,**
                 plazcan
IMPERF . SUBJ . I placiera, placieras, placiera (or **pluguiera),** placiéramos, placierais, placieran

IMPERF. SUBJ. II   placiese, placiese, placiese (or **pluguiese**), placiésemos, placieseis, placiesen

poder
PRESENT	**puedo, puedes, puede,** podemos, podéis, **pueden**
PRETERITE	**pude, pudiste, pudo, pudimos, pudisteis, pudieron**
FUTURE	**podré, podrás, podrá, podremos, podréis, podrán**
CONDITIONAL	**podría, podrías, podría, podríamos, podríais, podrían**
PRES. SUBJUNC.	**pueda, puedas, pueda,** podamos, podáis, **puedan**
IMPERF. SUBJ. I	**pudiera, pudieras, pudiera, pudiéramos, pudierais, pudieran**
IMPERF. SUBJ. II	**pudiese, pudieses, pudiese, pudiésemos, pudieseis, pudiesen**
IMPERATIVE	**puede, pueda,** podamos, poded, **puedan**
GERUND	**pudiendo**

poner
PRESENT	**pongo,** pones, pone, ponemos, ponéis, ponen
PRETERITE	**puse, pusiste, puso, pusimos, pusisteis, pusieron**
FUTURE	**pondré, pondrás, pondrá, pondremos, pondréis, pondrán**
CONDITIONAL	**pondría, pondrías, pondría, pondríamos, pondríais, pondrían**
PRES. SUBJUNC.	**ponga, pongas, ponga, pongamos, pongáis, pongan**
IMPERF. SUBJ. I	**pusiera, pusieras, pusiera, pusiéramos, pusierais, pusieran**
IMPERF. SUBJ. II	**pusiese, pusieses, pusiese, pusiésemos, pusieseis, pusiesen**
IMPERATIVE	**pon, ponga, pongamos,** poned, **pongan**
PARTICIPLE	**puesto**

producir
PRESENT	**produzco,** produces, produce, producimos, producís, producen
PRETERITE	**produje, produjiste, produjo, produjimos, produzcáis, produjeron**
PRES. SUBJUNC.	**produzca, produzcas, produzca, produzcamos, produzcáis, produzcan**
IMPERF. SUBJ. I	**produjera, produjeras, produjera, produjéramos, produjerais, produjeran**
IMPERF. SUBJ. II	**produjese, produjeses, produjese, produjésemos, produjeseis, produjesen**
IMPERATIVE	produce, **produzca, produzcamos,** producid, **produzcan**

querer
PRESENT	**quiero, quieres, quiere,** queremos, queréis, **quieren**
PRETERITE	**quise, quisiste, quiso, quisimos, quisisteis, quisieron**
FUTURE	**querré querrás, querrá, querremos, querréis, querrán**
CONDITIONAL	**querría, querrías, querría, querríamos, querríais, querrían**
PRES. SUBJUNC.	**quiera, quieras, quiera,** queramos, queráis, **quieran**
IMPERF. SUBJ. I	**quisiera, quisieras, quisiera, quisiéramos, quisierais, quisieran**
IMPERF. SUBJ. II	**quisiese, quisieses, quisiese, quisiésemos, quisieseis, quisiesen**
IMPERATIVE	**quiere, quiera,** queramos, quered, **quieran**

reír
PRESENT	**río, ríes, ríe, reímos,** reís, **ríen**
PRETERITE	reí, **reíste, rió, reímos, reísteis, rieron**
PRES. SUBJUNC.	**ría, rías, ría, riamos, riáis, rían**
IMPERF. SUBJ. I	**riera, rieras, riera, riéramos, rierais, rieran**
IMPERF. SUBJ. II	**riese, rieses, riese, riésemos, rieseis, riesen**
IMPERATIVE	**ríe, ría, riamos,** reíd, **rían**
GERUND	**riendo**
PARTICIPLE	**reído**

roer

PRESENT	**roo** (or **roigo/royo**), roes, roe, roemos, roéis, roen
PRETERITE	roí, **roíste, royó, roímos, roísteis, royeron**
PRES . SUBJUNC .	**roa** (or **roiga/roya**), **roas, roa, roamos, roáis, roan**
IMPERF . SUBJ . I	**royera, royeras, royera, royéramos, royerais, royeran**
IMPERF . SUBJ . II	**royese, royeses, royese, royésemos, royeseis, royesen**
GERUND	**royendo**
PARTICIPLE	**roído**

saber

PRESENT	**sé**, sabes, sabe, sabemos, sabéis, saben
PRETERITE	**supe, supiste supo, supimos, supisteis, supieron**
FUTURE	**sabré, sabrás, sabrá, sabremos, sabréis, sabrán**
CONDITIONAL	**sabría, sabrías, sabría, sabríamos, sabríais, sabrían**
PRES . SUBJUNC .	**sepa, sepas, sepa, sepamos, sepáis, sepan**
IMPERF . SUBJ . I	**supiera, supieras, supiera, supiéramos, supierais, supieran**
IMPERF . SUBJ . II	**supiese, supieses, supiese, supiésemos, supieseis, supiesen**

salir

PRESENT	**salgo,** sales, sale, salimos, salís, salen
FUTURE	**saldré, saldrás, saldrá, saldremos, saldréis, saldrán**
CONDITIONAL	**saldría, saldrías, saldría, saldríamos, saldríais, saldrían**
PRES . SUBJUNC .	**salga, salgas, salga, salgamos, salgáis, salgan**
IMPERATIVE	**sal, salga, salgamos,** salid, **salgan**

seguir

present	**sigo, sigues, sigue,** seguimos, seguís, **siguen**
PRETERITE	seguí, seguiste, **siguió,** seguimos, seguisteis, **siguieron**
PRES . SUBJUNC .	**siga, sigas, siga, sigamos, sigáis, sigan**
IMPERF . SUBJ . I	**siguiera, siguieras, siguiera, siguiéramos, siguierais, siguieran**
IMPERF . SUBJ . II	**siguiese, siguieses, siguiese, siguiésemos, siguieseis, siguiesen,**
IMPERATIVE	**sigue, siga, sigamos,** seguid, **sigan**
GERUND	**siguiendo**

sentir

PRESENT	**siento, sientes, siente,** sentimos, sentís, **sienten**
PRETERITE	sentí, sentiste, **sintió,** sentimos, sentisteis, **sintieron**
PRES . SUBJUNC .	**sienta, sientas, sienta, sintamos, sintáis, sientan**
IMPERF . SUBJ . I	**sintiera, sintieras, sintiera, sintiéramos, sintierais, sintieran**
IMPERF . SUBJ . II	**sintiese, sintieses, sintiese, sintiésemos, sintieseis, sintiesen**
IMPERATIVE	**siente, sienta, sintamos,** sentid, **sientan**
GERUND	sintiendo

ser

PRESENT	**soy, eres, es, somos, sois, son**
IMPERFECT	**era, eras, era, éramos, crais, eran**
PRETERITE	**fui, fuiste, fue, fuimos, fuisteis, fueron**
PRES . SUBJUNC .	**sea, seas, sea, seamos, seáis, sean**
IMPERF . SUBJ . I	**fuera, fueras, fuera, fuéramos, fuerais, fueran**
IMPERF . SUBJ . II	**fuese, fueses, fuese, fuésemos, fueseis, fuesen**
IMPERATIVE	**sé, sea, seamos,** sed, **sean**

tener

PRESENT	**tengo, tienes, tiene,** tenemos, tenéis, **tienen**
PRETERITE	**tuve, tuviste, tuvo, tuvimos, tuvisteis, tuvieron**
FUTURE	**tendré, tendrás, tendrá,** tendremos, tendréis, tendrán
CONDITIONAL	**tendría, tendrías, tendría, tendríamos, tendríais, tendrían**
PRES . SUBJUNC .	**tenga, tengas, tenga, tengamos, tengáis, tengan**
IMPERF . SUBJ . I	**tuviera, tuvieras, tuviera, tuviéramos, tuvierais, tuvieran**
IMPERF . SUBJ . II	**tuviese, tuvieses, tuviese, tuviésemos, tuvieseis, tuviesen**
IMPERATIVE	**ten, tenga, tengamos,** tened, **tengan**

torcer

PRESENT	**tuerzo, tuerces, fuerce,** torcemos, torcéis, **tuercen**
PRES . SUBJUNC .	**tuerza, tuerzas, tuerza, torzamos, torzáis, tuerzan**
IMPERATIVE	**tuerce, tuerza, torzamos,** torced, **tuerzan**

traer

PRESENT	**traigo,** traes, trae, traemos, traéis, traen
PRETERITE	**traje, trajiste, trajo, trajimos, trajisteis, trajeron**
PRES . SUBJUNC .	**traiga, traigas, traiga, traigamos, traigáis, traigan**
IMPERF . SUBJ . I	**trajera, trajeras, trajera, trajéramos, trajerais, trajeran**
IMPERF . SUBJ . II	**trajese, trajeses, trajese, trajésemos, trajeseis, trajesen**
GERUND	**trayendo**
PARTICIPLE	**traído**

valer

PRESENT	**valgo,** vales, vale, valemos, valéis, valen
FUTURE	**valdré, valdrás, valdrá, valdremos, valdréis, valdrán**
CONDITIONAL	**valdría, valdrías, valdría, valdríamos, valdríais, valdrían**
PRES . SUBJUNC .	**valga, valgas, valga, valgamos, valgáis, valgan**

venir

PRESENT	**vengo, vienes, viene,** venimos, venís, **vienen**
PRETERITE	**vine, viniste, vino, vinimos, vinisteis, vinieron**
FUTURE	**vendré, vendrás, vendrá, vendremos, vendréis, vendrán**
CONDITIONAL	**vendría, vendrías, vendría, vendríamos, vendríais, vendrían**
PRES . SUBJUNC .	**venga, vengas, venga, vengamos, vengáis, vengan**
IMPERF . SUBJ . I	**viniera, vinieras, viniera, viniéramos, vinierais, vinieran**
IMPERF . SUBJ . II	**viniese, vinieses, viniese, viniésemos, vinieseis, viniesen**
IMPERATIVE	**ven, venga, vengamos,** venid, **vengan**
GERUND	**viniendo**

ver

PRESENT	**veo,** ves, ve, vemos, veis, ven
IMPERFECT	**veía, veías, veía, veíamos, veíais, veían**
PRETERITE	**vi,** viste, **vio,** vimos, visteis, vieron
PRES . SUBJUNC .	**vea, veas, vea, veamos, veáis, vean**
PARTICIPLE	**visto**

volver

PRESENT	**vuelvo, vuelves, vuelve,** volvemos, volvéis, **vuelven**
PRES . SUBJUNC .	**vuelva, vuelvas, vuelva,** volvamos, volváis, **vuelvan**
IMPERATIVE	**vuelve, vuelva,** volvamos, volved, **vuelvan**
PARTICIPLE	**vuelto**

Appendix IV

SPANISH VERBS WITH TWO PAST PARTICIPLES

This list contains the infinitive, past participle and the adjectival forms.

INFINITIVE	PARTICIPLE	ADJECTIVE	INFINITIVE	PARTICIPLE	ADJECTIVE
absorber	absorbido	absorto	convertir	convertido	converso
abstraer	abstraído	abstracto	corregir	corregido	correcto
aducir	aducido	aducho*	corromper	corrompido	corrupto
afligir	afligido	aflicto	derrelinquir	derrelinquido	derrelicto
ahitar	ahitado	ahito	desatender	desatendido	desatento
astringir	astringido	astricto	descontentar	descontentado	descontento
atender	atendido	atento	despertar	despertado	despierto
bendecir	bendecido	bendito	desproveer	desproveído	desprovisto
bendicir*	bendicido*	bendito	difunir	difundido	difuso
bienquerer	bienquerido	bienquisto	dividir	dividido	diviso
circuncidar	circuncidado	circunciso	elegir	elegido	electo
cocer	cocido	cocho	enhestar	enhestado	enhiesto
compeler	compelido	compulso	enjugar	enjugado	enjuto
comprender	comprendido	comprenso	excluir	excluido	excluso
comprimir	comprimido	compreso	eximir	eximido	exento
concluir	concluido	concluso	expeler	expelido	expulso
condensar	condensado	condenso	expresar	expresado	expreso
confesar	confesado	confeso	extender	extendido	extenso
confundir	confundido	confuso	extinguir	extinguido	extinto
consumir	consumido	consunto	fijar	fijado	fijo
constituir	constituido	constituto	fingir	fingido	ficto
contundir	contundido	contuso	freír	freído	frito
contentar	contentado	contento	hartar	hartado	harto
contraer	contraído	contracto	imprimir	imprimido	impreso
contundir	contundido	contuso	incluir	incluido	incluso
convencer	convencido	convicto	incurrir	incurrido	incurso

INFINITIVE	PARTICIPLE	ADJECTIVE	INFINITIVE	PARTICIPLE	ADJECTIVE
infundir	infundido	infuso	querer	querido	quisto*
injertar	injertado	injerto	recluir	recluido	recluso
infurtir	infurtido	infurto	reelegir	reelegido	reelecto
insertar	insertado	inserto	refreír	refreído	refrito
invertir	invertido	inverso	reteñir	reteñido	retinto
juntar	juntado	junto	retorcer	retorcido	retuerto
maldecir	maldecido	maldito	romper	rompido*	roto
malquerer	malquerido	malquisto	salpresar	salpresado	salpreso
manifestar	manifestado	manifiesto	salvar	salvado	salvo
manumitir	manumitido	manumiso	sepelir	sepelido	sepulto
nacer	nacido	nato	sofreír	sofreído	sofrito
omitir	omitido	omiso	soltar	soltado	suelto
oprimir	oprimido	opreso	substituir	substituido	substituto
pasar	pasado	paso	subtender	subtendido	subtenso
poseer	poseído	poseso	sujetar	sujetado	sujeto
preelegir	preelegido	preelecto	suprimir	suprimido	supreso
prender	prendido	preso	suspender	suspendido	suspenso
presumir	presumido	presunto	sustituir	sustituido	sustituto
pretender	pretendido	pretenso	teñir	teñido	tinto
proferir	proferido	proferto*	torcer	torcido	tuerto
propender	propendido	propenso	torrefactar	torrefactado	torrefacto
prostituir	prostituido	prostituto	yuntar	yuntado	yunto
proveer	proveído	provisto			

*Old form or archaic.

Reference Bibliography

Alcina Franch, Juan and José Manuel Blecua. 1991. *Gramática española*, 8va ed. Barcelona: Editorial Ariel, S.A.

Alonso, Amado. 1967. *Estudios lingüísticos; temas hispanoamericanos.* 3ra ed. Madrid: Gredos,

American Heritage Larousse Spanish Dictionary, The. 1986. Boston: Houghton Mifflin Co.

Azevedo, Milton M. 1992. *Introducción a la lingüística española.* Englewood Cliffs, NJ: Prentice Hall.

Ballesteros, S. 1978. *Manual práctico de ortografía, redacción y gramática.* México: Editores Mexicanos Unidos.

Bello, Andrés (& Rufino Cuervo). 1958. *Gramática de la lengua castellana.* Buenos Aires: Editorial Sopen Argentina.

Besser, Pam. 1994. *A Basic Handbook of Writing Skills.* Mountain View, CA: Mayfield Publishing Co.

Bull, William E. 1965. *Spanish for Teachers: Applied Linguistics.* New York: Ronald Press.

———. 1968. *Time, Tense, and the Verb.* Berkeley: University of California Press.

———. 1972. *The Visual Grammar of Spanish.* Regents of the University of California and Houghton Mifflin.

Casares, Ángel L. and Marshall Morris, eds. 1986. El tapiz por el revés. San Juan: Academia Puertorriqueña de la Lengua Española.

Collins Spanish Dictionary, 4th ed. 1999. London and Glasglow: Collins.

Cotton, Eleanor Greet, and John M. Sharp. 1988. *Spanish in the Americas.* Washington, D.C.: Georgetown U. Press

Diccionario básico del español de México. 1986. México, D.F.: El Colegio de México.

Diccionario México. Tercera edición, nueva versión. 1994. México D.F.: Herrero Hermanos Sucs. S.A.

Fowler, H. Ramsey, Jane E. Aaron, and Kay Limburg. 1992. *The Little, Brown Handbook.* Fifth Edition. New York: Harper Collins.

Frank, Marcella. 1972. *Modern English.* Englewood Cliffs: Prentice-Hall, Inc.

Fuentes, Juan Luis. 1988. *Ortografía: reglas y ejercicios*. México, D.F.: Ediciones Larousse S.A. de C.V

García-Pelayo Y Gross, Ramón and Micheline Durand. 1982. *Larousse de la conjugación*. México, D.F.: Ediciones Larousse.

Gili Gaya, Samuel. 1980. *Curso superior de sintáxis española*, 13ra edición. Barcelona: Biblograf, S.A.

Hacker, Diana. 1991. *The Bedford Handbook for Writers*. Boston: Bedford Books of St. Martin's Press.

Heffernan, James A. W., and John E. Lincoln. 1994. *Writing: A College Handbook* 4th ed. New York: W. W. Morton & Co.

Hill, Sam. 1985. *Contrastive English-Spanish Grammatical Structures*. Lanham: University Press of America.

Hill, Sam and William Bradford. 1991. *Bilingual Grammar of English-Spanish Syntax: A Manual with Exercises*. Lanham, New York, London: University Press of America.

Hodges, John C., Winifred Bryan Horner, Suzanne Strobeck Webb, and Robert Keith Miller. 1994. *Harbrace College Handbook*. 12th ed. Fort Worth: Harcourt.

Kenyon, John S. and Thomas A. Knott. 1953. *A Pronouncing Dictionary of American English*. Springfield: G & C. Merriam Co.

Klein, Philip W. 1992. *Enfoque lingüístico al idioma español*. Nueva York: Peter Lang.

Lado, Robert. 1957. *Linguistics Across Cultures*. Ann Arbor: The University of Michigan Press.

Leech, Geoffrey and Jan Svartvik. 1975. *A Communicative Grammar of English*. London: Longman Group Limited.

Legget, Glenn, C. David Mead, and Melinda G. Kramer. 1991. *Prentice Hall Handbook for Writers*. 11th ed. Englewood Cliffs: Prentice.

Long, Ralph B. and Dorothy R. Long. 1971. *The System of English Grammar*. Glenview: Scott, Foresman and Company.

Lunsford, Andrea, and Robert Connors. 1995. *The St. Martin's Handbook*. 3rd ed. New York: St. Martin's.

Marius, Richard, and Harvey S. Wiener. 1994. *The McGraw-Hill College Handbook*. 4th ed. New York: McGraw.

McArthur, Tom and Beryl Atkins. 1974. *Dictionary of English Phrasal Verbs and their Idioms*. London and Glasgow: Collins.

Martínez de Sousa, José. *Diccionario de ortografía*. Madrid: Ediciones Generales Anaya, 1985.

———. 1981. *Diccionario general del periodismo*. Madrid: Paraninfo, S.A.

Merriam Webster's Collegiate Dictionary, 10th ed. Springfield, MA: Merriam-Webster, Inc., 1994.

Moliner, María. 1986. *Diccionario de uso del español.* Madrid: Editorial Gredos.

Morales Pettorino, Felix *et al. Diccionario ejemplificado de chilenismos,* vol. I y II. Valparaíso, 1984 y 1985.

Mulderig, Gerald P., and Langdon Elsbree. 1995. *The Heath Handbook of Composition.* 13th ed. Lexington: Heath.

Nash, Rose, ed. 1973. *Readings in Spanish-English Contrastive Linguistics,* Vol. I. San Juan: Inter American University Press.

Nash, Rose and Domitila Belaval, eds. 1980. *Readings in Spanish-English Contrastive Linguistics,* Vol. II. San Juan: Inter American University Press.

———. 1982. *Readings in Spanish-English Contrastive Linguistics,* Vol. III. San Juan: Inter American University Press.

Quilis Morales, Antonio, Manuel Esgueva, María Luz Gutiérrez, and Pilar Ruiz-Va. 1993. *Gramática española,* 2da ed. Madrid: Editorial Centro de Estudios Ramón Areces, S.A.

Quirk, Randolph, Sidney Greenbaum, Geoffrey Leech and Jan Svartvik. 1972. *A Grammar of Contemporary English.* New York: Harcourt Brace Jovanovich, Inc.

Real Academia Española. 1931. *Gramática de la lengua española.* Madrid: Espasa Calpe, S.A.

———. 1979. *Esbozo de una nueva gramática de la lengua española.* Madrid: Espasa Calpe, S.A.

———. 1992. *Diccionario de la lengua española,* 21ra edición. Madrid: Espasa Calpe, S.A.

Rivera Rubero, Pura A. 1998. *La comunicación en el contexto empresarial.* Hato Rey, P.R.: Publicaciones Puertorriqueñas.

Rivers, Wilga M., Milton M. Azevedo, and William H. Heflin, Jr. 1989. *Teaching Spanish: A Practical Guide.* Lincolnwood, IL: National Textbook Co.

Santamaría, Andrés, Augusto Cuartas, Joaquín Mangada y José Martínez de Sousa. 1987. *Diccionario de incorrecciones, particularidades y curiosidades del lenguaje,* quinta edición. Madrid: Paraninfo, S.A.

Santamaría, Francisco J. *Diccionario de mejicanismos.* México: Porrúa, 1978.

Seco, Manuel. *Diccionario de dudas y dificultades de la lengua española,* novena edición renovada. Madrid: Espasa Calpe, 1991.

———. 1986. *Gramática esencial del español.* Madrid: Espasa Calpe.

———. 1982. *Manual de gramática española,* 2 vols. Madrid: Aguilar.

Simon and Schuster's International Dictionary, English/Spanish, Spanish/English. New York: Macmillan.

Solé, Yolanda R. and Carlos A. Solé. 1977. *Modern Spanish Syntax.* Lexington: D.C. Heath.

Stockwell, Robert P., Donald Bowen and John W. Martin. 1965. *The Grammatical Structures of English and Spanish*. Chicago: Univ. of Chicago Press.

Terrell, Tracy and Maruxa Salgués de Cargill. 1979. *Lingüística aplicada a la enseñaza del español a angloparlantes*. New York: John Wiley & Sons.

Teschner, Richard V. 1998. *Cubre: Curso breve de gramática española* 2da edición. New York: McGraw-Hill Companies.

Troyka, Lynn Quitman. 1993. *Simon and Schuster Handbook for Writers*. 3rd. ed. Englewood Cliffs: Prentice.

Watkins, Floyd C., and William B. Dillingham. 1992. *Practical English Handbook*. 9th ed. Boston: Houghton.

Webster's Encyclopedic Unabridged Dictionary of the English Language. New York: Gramercy Books, 1994.

Whitley, M. Stanley. 1986. *Spanish/English Contrasts*. Washington, D.C.: Georgetown University Press.

Zamora Vicente, Alonso. 1979. *Dialectología española*. 2da ed. Madrid: Gredos.

INDEX
ÍNDICE ALFABÉTICO

This index includes lexical items, terminology, and topics featured in this manual. All English and Spanish word items are listed in italics. Topics and terminology are found in regular type. We combine two reference numbering systems in the Index. Numbers with decimal points refer to the unit sections, and numbers in parenthesis refer to the pages of the manual. Example: **abridgement in clauses 32.2–3** is treated in sections 2 and 3 of Unit 32. **Abstract nouns (97)** are found mentioned on page 97.